D1159565

The Prophetic Tradition in American Poetry, 1835–1900

The Prophetic Tradition in American Poetry, 1835–1900

Aaron Kramer

Rutherford • Madison • Teaneck
Fairleigh Dickinson University Press

Library of Congress Catalogue Card Number: 68-11569

Associated University Presses, Inc.
Cranbury, New Jersey 08512

6774
Printed in the United States of America

To my mentor and friend

NELSON F. ADKINS

this work is gratefully dedicated

Contents

Introduction

If the word "Poet" conjures up a unified image to all minds, it is that of a creature mysteriously appointed to be set apart, from whose inspired lips will come strange tidings. On this, even the poets are agreed. "Seer blest," said Wordsworth of the child not yet weaned away from his immortal vision; in similar terms of supernatural assignment many poets have defined their function, since those of Greece first called upon Apollo's daughters for support and thirsted for the divine waters of Castalia. Dante called his work "the sacred poem to which both heaven and earth so have set hand, that it hath made me lean through many a year." "The poet's eye," explained Shakespeare, "in a fine frenzy rolling/Doth glance from heaven to earth, from earth to heaven." To Pushkin came "a six-winged seraph" who "laid his fingers" on the poet's eyes. "True song," Rilke instructed a novice, "demands a different kind of breathing./A calm. A shudder in the god. A gale."

Wordsworth addressed the child—our real poet—as "Thou Eye among the blind." For mankind, in each generation, is discovered to be asleep, benumbed, lethargic—

unable to see, feel, remember, imagine. Only the poet is awake: stalking the unaware city, or—like Rimbaud—engaged in "spiritual combat" through the "arduous night," or leaning from his tower—whether a constructed or an imagined one. At dawn he shall deliver his report. Those "passionately at peace" must have their security vexed by Jeffers' "blasphemies of glowworms," Baudelaire's condemnation: "Horrible life! Horrible city!" Blake's outcry at the weakness, the woe "in every face," Lorca's lamentation: "Agony, agony . . . The dead are rotting under the city clocks." At times, however, even a tower or "a double-turn of the key in the lock" does not suffice; the poet must emphasize his separateness by geographical self-exile, or by soaring in dreams "out of Space, out of Time." But from his "ultimate dim Thule" Poe does not fail to return—even if only to declare that all on earth "Is but a dream within a dream."

The differences in definition begin to emerge as we approach this creature set apart, and try to determine what the tidings are that come from his lips. The vehemence with which Coleridge insists that a poem has "for its *immediate* object pleasure, not truth," and the equal force of Poe's refusal "to reconcile the obstinate oils and waters of Poetry and Truth," merely underscore the almost universal acceptance of the opposing view. Whether "wisdom" is arrived at surreptitiously, *via* pleasure, as Sir Philip Sidney[2] and Robert Frost[3] suggest, or simultaneously with pleasure, as Ben Jonson insists,[4] or not without pleasure, as Wordsworth would have it,[5] or rather than pleasure, as Housman advocates[6]—most poets believe that what their seraph-touched eyes behold *is* the Truth, and that their sacred mission is to transmit the Truth effectively enough for the listener to share.

Up to a point we find agreement as to what this Truth may be: the reality beneath the appearance, the meaning behind the symbol, the generalization beyond the minutiae, the essence within the thing. There is further agreement that the poet must play an active and self-conscious role in the winning of his Truth. Like Sophocles he must "see life steadily and see it whole."[7] Like Blake, rejecting Newton's single sight, he must strive to attain a two- or three- or four-fold vision. Into the woods he must go, with Wordsworth, and by establishing a mood of "wise passiveness" prepare his mind for the moment of transcendental vision. He must follow his "boney nose," with William Carlos Williams, to "taste everything . . . know everything . . . have a part in everything . . ." He must discover, like Mayakovsky, that "Before they can launch a song,/poets must tramp for days with callused feet," that the poem itself is "a journey to the Unknown."

Some poets, like T. S. Eliot and D. H. Lawrence, may challenge the ethical goal and insist that only "the intensity of the artistic process . . . counts,"[8] that nothing should be accomplished "save the journey."[9] Others, like Wallace Stevens, may revere the poetic activity less for the truth than for the godhood it brings them: "Thou art not August unless I make thee so." In the main, however, the enunciation of a truth is treated by the poet as a solemn duty and privilege. For a world in danger, he prophesies. For a world bewildered, he interprets. For a world in darkness, he glows. He claims direct kinship with the inspired singers of all ages, all lands; these are his idols, their flame he holds aloft.

The truth on the prophet's tongue, as we come closer, loses its vagueness and begins to show certain unmistakable characteristics. They are by no means the only characteristics, but their consistent recurrence ultimately gives shape to a solitary seer who defies the tyrant, exposes the hypocrite, rebukes the corrupt, and wakes his epoch from spiritual torpor to reformational zeal. Looming above the frown of Oedipus, the Sophoclean Teiresias cries out: "Safe am I now. The truth in me is strong." To the pious rulers of Sodom, God shouts through the lips of Isaiah: "Your hands are full of blood . . . Cease to do evil; learn to do well." Shakespeare's John of Gaunt gasps, from his death-pillow, into the teeth of his spendthrift nephew: "Methinks I am a prophet new-inspired . . . Landlord of England art thou now, not King . . ."

Almost as consistent as the boldness of prophets is their doom—beyond the bland truism that "no man is a prophet in his own country." Very often the truth-telling profession, especially when those in power feel insecure, has involved a deadly commitment. Jeremiah was persecuted, imprisoned, and nearly killed; Ovid and Juvenal, Li Po and Cavalcanti, Dante and Lope de Vega banished; Seneca and his nephew Lucan commanded to kill themselves; Luis Ponce de Leon dungeoned by the Inquisition; Tasso confined as insane; Giordano Bruno burned at the stake; Kyd and Marlowe haled before the Privy Council; Jonson and Chapman imprisoned; Marston and Milton forced into hiding; Moliere denied burial by the Church; Voltaire beaten, twice imprisoned, exiled; Raleigh and Chenier beheaded.

This ancient relationship of poet versus power has been dramatically reinforced during the twentieth century with such episodes as Miguel de Unamuno's imprisonment, exile, and highly suspicious death. Louis Aragon, Paul Eluard, and Pablo Neruda were forced into hiding for years. Garcia Lorca was shot down outside Granada, Joe Hill and Essenin executed before firing squads. Arturo Giovanitti and Nazim Hikmet were imprisoned; and Ossip Mandelstam died in a Siberian prison camp. Mayakovsky, Toller, and Zweig were driven to suicide; Werfel, Alberti, Jimenez, and Brecht saved themselves through exile. Anna Akhmatova was banned, Langston Hughes summoned before a Congressional committee, Peretz Markish and Itzik Feffer obliterated without trial.

In recent memory, too, numerous American and Soviet poets of stature have cried out against specific acts of their governments or evils in their society. These illustrate the continuity of the prophetic tradition. The arrest of Eugene V. Debs brought forth a fiery volume in 1920, including Carl Sandburg and Charles E. S. Wood. Seven years later a large collection of Sacco-Vanzetti poems appeared, along with indignant sonnets by Edna St. Vincent Millay, Maxwell Anderson's *Winterset,* and William C. Williams' "Impromptu: The Suckers." The 1932 Scottsboro trial produced another flood of verse, including works by Kay Boyle and Muriel Rukeyser. A volume of poems—by Alfred Kreymborg, W. E. B. DuBois, George Abbe, among others—followed the execution of the Rosenbergs. More recently our political climate has been vigorously challenged by Richard Wilbur's "Speech for the Repeal of the McCarran Act," Howard Nemerov's "The Murder of William Remington," and Lawrence Ferlinghetti's "One Thousand Fearful Words for Fidel Castro." In 1965 Robert Lowell refused to attend a White House arts festival, and six Pulitzer-award-winning poets announced their support of Lowell's anti-militarist gesture. Two considerable anthologies, *Poets for Peace* and *Where Is Vietnam? American Poets Respond,* were issued in the spring of 1967.

An electrifying revival of the prophetic role has lately been witnessed in Soviet poetry, with the emergence of Kirsanov, Rozhdestventsky, Voznesensky, and others—apparently uncowed by the fresh example of a Pasternak anathematized and hounded to the grave. Once again the battle lines have been drawn between poet and power. Yevtushenko decries "The blinded judges" and exposes the old commissars, "still ornamented in the idiot glitter," as hypocrites "happy to make outward renunciations/but without inward mutability." His government then forbids a scheduled visit to the United States, excludes his work from the annual Poetry Day anthology, and pressures him to change the sharply critical last lines of "Babi Yar," much as Molière was once pressured to emasculate *Tartuffe*. A gifted young individualist, Josef Brodsky, is sentenced—largely on the basis of his poems—to serve a prison term as a "vagrant." Vladimir Tsibin dares to charge, at Moscow's 1964 Poetry Day festivities, that "Since Pushkin and Lermontov . . . Russian poets have been at the mercy of ruling powers." Several outstanding poets condemn the trial and imprisonment of Sinyavsky and Daniel in 1966. Voznesensky develops strong personal ties with American poets, and is kept from a major New York appearance. And Patricia Blake, in an anthology of new Soviet literature, heralds those who are still "prepared to perform their *historic role of serving as the conscience of Russian society*."[10] (The emphasis is mine.)

This function is what I particularly intend to explore in the following pages: the poet as clear-eyed and full-throated sentry, eternally denouncing Sceptred Evil at the mountain-pass and summoning his people to resist, or on a street-corner in Gomorrah, tearing evil out of his listeners' hearts and holding it before their eyes, contrasting his vision of things as they should be with things as they are.

For this investigation I have chosen a place and a time which, within their limits, provide a rich variety of unmistakable and even sensational possibilities: the United States, from 1835 to 1900. During that period a vast number of American writers took themselves seriously as poets. Not only is their verse readily available; many of them were also tireless correspondents, diarists, and essayists; they wrote to and about one another, producing along the way —with a perhaps exaggerated confidence in their group importance—a bountiful outpouring of biographies and autobiographies. These materials may help us identify their reactions to the major problems of nineteenth-century American life. Some of these problems, and the events that illuminated them, were so extraordinary, so universally publicized, and so significant from an ethical point of view, that they can serve as a fairly solid frame of reference by which to gauge the prophetic impulse of the poets under study. In character these areas parallel much of the social and political iniquity against which the prophets of other times and places have cried out.

An equally important consideration in choosing the poets of nineteenth-century America as the subject of this work is their own consciousness of the prophetic mission with all its implications. We will assuredly not be seeking from them a performance beyond the limits of their awareness. They admired the glowing fury of Isaiah and Jeremiah, Amos and Ezekiel; the savage satire of Aristophanes and Juvenal, Jean de Meun and Francois Villon. Many had studied, in the original, Horace's tribute to Orpheus as the seer who had "weaned savage forest-tribes from murder and foul living," and his reminder that the poets' mission had originally been "to build cities, to check promiscuous lust . . . to engrave laws on wood." They had read Dante's stinging rebuke of his Church, through the lips of St. Benedict: "The Walls which were wont to be a house of prayer, have become dens, and the hoods are sacks full of foul meal." Nor were they unfamiliar with Chaucer's evaluation of his England:

> Trouthe is put down, resoun is holden fable;
> Vertu hath now no dominacioun;
> Pitee exyled, no man is merciable . . .

Sir Philip Sidney had defined the poet's role in terms of Nathan the Prophet, who "made David . . . as in a glass, to see his own filthiness." With equal clarity Ben Jonson had specified that the requirement of the poet was not mere nimbleness of phrase or prosody, "but the exact knowledge of all virtues and their contraries, with ability to render the one loved, the other hated, by his proper embattling them." Few American poets had failed to encounter Milton's ferocious contrasts between the current state of affairs and the betrayed ideal:

> I did but prompt the age to quit their cloggs
> By the known rules of antient libertie . . .
> Licence they mean when they cry libertie . . .
>
> Men whose Life, Learning, Faith and pure intent
> Would have been held in high esteem with *Paul*
> Must now be nam'd and printed Hereticks
> By shallow Edwards . . .
>
> . . . in vain doth Valour bleed
> While Avarice and Rapine shares the Land.

Any well-schooled nineteenth-century poet of America was familiar with much, if not all, of the above—probably before he ever wrote his own first verses. But if one among them had somehow not been properly briefed on those earlier manifestations of the prophetic role, he would still be aware of what his favorite pre-Romantic and Romantic predecessors had written and done. At a time when it was popular to imitate Gray, many knew not only that thrilling curse hurled at King Edward from the rock by the last prophet of Wales, but also Gray's outline for the poem:

> . . . with prophetic spirit [the bard] declares that all . . . [Edward's] cruelty shall never extinguish the noble ardour of poetic genius in this island; and that men shall never be wanting to celebrate true virtue and valour . . . to expose vice and infamous pleasure, and boldly censure tyranny and oppression.

Some of our poets could perhaps recite Goldsmith's admonition to the lords of a decaying England in "The Deserted Village." They probably knew Cowper's far-ranging list of grievances in "The Task," against the British government's abuses at home and adventures abroad. Those who admired Crabbe would remember his description of a land "where guilt and famine reign," where workmen "hoard up aches and anguish for their age."

Even more complete was their acquaintance with the lives and works of Burns, Wordsworth, Coleridge, Byron, and Shelley: the first three—youthful seditionists and adherents of the French Revolution; the last two—exiles at war with all tyranny, all corruption; especially British. The many American poets who expressed affinity with Burns surely knew his attacks on the high-placed hypocrites of his own parish, "wi' screw'd up, grace-proud faces"; his appeal to slumbering Scotland: "Lay the proud usurpers low!"; his incendiary vision of a time when "man to man . . . shall brithers be" and Worth at last be rewarded. Those who idolized Wordsworth could hardly have overlooked his picture of England as "a fen of stagnant waters" in which "Rapine, avarice, expense" are adored, while "plain living and high thinking are no more." Nor could they fail to understand that, in summoning the star-like soul of Milton, Wordsworth was actually invoking the prophetic voice within himself to answer England's need. On their shelves along with "Christabel" were Coleridge's early political verses, including his prophecy to the "Children of Wretchedness":

> . . . The hour is nigh
> And lo! the Great, the Rich, the Mighty Men,
> With all that fixed on high like stars of Heaven
> Shot baleful influence, shall be cast to earth,
> Vile and down-trodden . . .

Coleridge's admirers could not easily have missed Section VIII of his flaming "Ode to the Departing Year" or its equally devastating footnote, Biblical in fervor:

> We have been preserved by our insular situation, from suffering the actual horrors of war ourselves, and we have shown our gratitude to Providence for this immunity by our eagerness to spread those horrors over nations less happily situated. . . . Such wickedness cannot pass unpunished . . . God has prepared the cankerworm, and will smite the gourds of our pride.

Byron and Shelley, America's newest favorites, had recently underscored the prophetic function, as they conceived it to be, by pointing out how Coleridge, Wordsworth, and Laureate Southey had betrayed it. Southey, "my Epic Renegade," formerly praised a regicide, but had since "earn'd his laureate pension." The ex-Pantisocrat "had turn'd his coat—and would have turn'd his skin." So sang Byron, while Shelley delightfully climaxed a list of horrors attributed to various poets (drunkard, flatterer, coward, madman, peculator, and libertine) with the most pejorative title of all: poet laureate! Byron sardonically reminded British readers of a time when Wordsworth, "unexcised, unhired," had "Season'd his pedlar poems with democracy"; he also recalled Coleridge as a young rebel, "long before his flighty pen/Let to the Morning Post its aristocracy . . ." Shelley likewise deplored Wordsworth's desertion of his post "Above the blind and battling multitude . . . " Wordsworth's "honoured poverty" was gone now, along with his "Songs consecrate to truth and liberty . . ."

Byron compared Wordsworth, a prophet turned "poetical charlatan and political parasite," with Milton, the true prophet, who closed his career "the tyrant-hater he begun":

> Think'st thou, could he—the blind Old Man—arise,
> Like Samuel from the grave, to freeze once more
> The blood of monarchs with his prophecies,
> Or be alive again . . . worn—and pale—and poor;
> Would *he* adore a sultan? *he* obey
> The intellectual eunuch Castlereagh?

As if this vivid contrast of prophecy and laureateship were not sufficient, Byron added the stinging footnote: "Would *he* subside into a hackney Laureate—A scribbling, self-sold, soul-hired, scorn'd Iscariot?" Shelley's differentiation was equally clear. He viewed the antagonists, "Poetry, and the principle of Self, of which Money is the visible incarnation," as "the God and Mammon of the world." And in the preface to *Prometheus Unbound* he too singled out for praise "the sacred Milton . . ."

Miltonic are the indignant cadences in which both young poets described George III and his realm. Byron wrote:

> A worse king never left a realm undone!
> He died—but left his subjects still behind,
> One half as mad—and t'other no less blind.

Two years earlier Shelley had censured his king and country in one of the most ferocious sonnets ever written, beginning: "An old, mad, blind, despised, and dying king . . ." Nor did Viscount Castlereagh fare better at their hands; to Byron *"it"* was a "cold-blooded, smooth-faced, placid miscreant . . . Cobbling at manacles for all mankind . . ." Shelley similarly declared that Murder resembled Castlereagh:

> Very smooth he looked, yet grim;
> Seven blood-hounds followed him . . .
> He tossed them human hearts to chew
> Which from his wide cloak he drew.

Not only were American poets acquainted with the inflammatory works of Byron and Shelley, and with the penalties both had paid. Many had read, in translation at least, the seething plays and poems of Schiller, and knew that—after *Die Räuber*—he had fled Stuttgart's tyrant duke. Nor could they have been wholly ignorant of more extreme instances. The greatest of contemporary Dutch poets, Bilderdijk, had been exiled from 1795 to

1806. In 1813 Leigh Hunt had been sentenced to a long prison term after attacking the Prince Regent. Pushkin, Russia's master-poet, had suffered exile in 1820 for his "Ode to Liberty." In 1823 Cuba's Heredia was also exiled after an abortive revolution, and spent the rest of his life in New York and Mexico. In 1837 the great lyric poet Lermontov was banished for a poem protesting Pushkin's violent death. Poland's leading poet, Mickiewicz, after being arrested and permanently deported, electrified all Europe—and some of America's touring writers—with his fiery verses and anti-government activities. Prussia placed a price on the head of Heinrich Heine, whose work was extremely popular in the United States—translated and imitated by Longfellow, James F. Clarke, Howells, John Hay, Leland, and Emma Lazarus. His revolutionary "The Weavers" and his furious satire, "The Slave Ship," were well known, as was his *Deutschland,* with its concluding admonition to the Emperor of Prussia:

> Have you not heard of Dante's Hell,
> The tercets that flamed from his pen?
> He whom the poet imprisons there
> Can never go free again . . .[11]

Other poets abroad, though perhaps not persecuted for their denunciation of domestic iniquity, were widely known as prophetic voices. Leopardi, a liberal and an agnostic when independent thought was dangerous in Italy, expressed contempt in his poetry for the rulers of his country, eventually turning to social and political satire. Thomas Hood's outcry against social injustice, "The Song of the Shirt," swept through the United States in 1843—44, as did Elizabeth Barrett's "The Cry of the Children." The following year came Browning's rebuke to Wordsworth, who had accepted the laureateship, betraying "for a handful of silver" what Browning considered the prophet's basic commitment:

Shakespeare was of us, Milton was for us,
  Burns, Shelley were with us—they watch from their graves!
He alone breaks from the van and the freemen—
  He alone sinks to the rear and the slaves!

Even Tennyson, favorite of the aesthetes, considered renouncing his palace of art in favor of a cottage in the vale. Swept up in the current of reform, he "dipped into the future" and announced his vision of a time when "the war-drum" would throb "no longer, and the battle-flags" be "furled/In the Parliament of man, the Federation of the world."

By 1835 American poets were poring over the work of Keats, encountering not only his fancy and grace, but also that side of his mentality which tended toward the prophetic. They must have found that early sonnet which resembled Wordsworth's "Toussaint L'Ouverture" but was infinitely bolder, since the tyrant Keats addressed was *his own present ruler*:

What though, for showing truth to flatter'd state,
Kind Hunt was shut in prison, yet has he,
In his immortal spirit, been as free
As the sky-searching lark, and as elate.
Minion of grandeur!
                . . . Who shall his fame impair
When thou art dead, and all thy wretched crew?

With a not altogether ingenuous candor young Keats had published his aspiration to be both Tyrtaeus and Jeremiah:

whether by making patriots feel his "stern alarum, and unsheath" their swords, or by thundering out his poems "To startle princes from their easy slumbers." Thus his readers discovered that, instead of ignoring such unpleasant topics as economic oppression, he had in fact seized a far-fetched opportunity to attack those for whom:

> . . . many a weary hand did swelt
> In torchèd mines and noisy factories,
> And many once proud-quiver'd loins did melt
> In blood from stinging whip . . .

It was in "The Fall of Hyperion" that Keats had defined the versifier's choice most clearly. Only those achieve greatness "to whom the miseries of the world/Are misery, and will not let them rest." Those, on the other hand, who "sleep away their days" in a dream-world, are destined to "Rot on the pavement." Here the self-indulgent *fantasy* is contrasted with the *vision* which involves mankind. Any poet who misunderstood that lesson must have been obtuse indeed.

The outpouring of rebellious song throughout Europe in 1848 was sympathetically received here. Some of our poets publicized—by discussing or translating them—the anti-tyrannical verses of Hugo, Lamartine, Freiligrath, Petofi. The American people were deeply moved by the failure of the uprisings and expressed their feelings during Kossuth's visit. His finest young poet, Petofi, was dead. In exile for a decade and more were Hugo, Herwegh, Freiligrath and the Ukraine's great singer Shevchenko. Several poets were among those who fled to America at this time. One can assume that many of our poets knew about Solomos' role in the Greek struggle for liberation. Some were surely familiar with the anti-tyrannical activities of the two great Argentine poets: Echeverria, who in 1851 died an exile in Montevideo, and Mitre, who afterward returned from exile to achieve a brilliant reform record as president of his nation. Later in the century, despite Tennyson's apparent capitulation to aestheticism and laureateship, America's poets continued to be reminded of the prophetic tradition through the eloquence of Swinburne:

> We have done with the kisses that sting,
> The thief's mouth red from the feast,
> The blood on the hands of the king,
> And the lie at the lips of the priest . . .

and Morris:

> It is we must answer and hasten, and open wide the door
> For the rich man's hurrying terror, and the slow-foot hope of the poor.
>
> Yea, the voiceless wrath of the wretched, and their unlearned discontent,
> We must give it voice and wisdom, till the waiting-tide be spent.

It would be misleading, of course, to ignore the fact that powerful counter-currents also appealed to the poets of that time. Definitions of the poet's proper motive, far different from the one on which we are here focusing, were increasingly effective. At this point, however, my purpose is to provide for our nineteenth-century poets a special frame of reference, a fair gauge for their performance as defenders of the betrayed ideal. With this in mind, I have felt it useful to establish first the fact that prophetic commitments had been repeatedly defined and dramatically fulfilled by many of the poets they idolized.

ii

That they were aware of this tradition, and in varying degrees of intensity concerned with it, can be amply demonstrated in their work. Here we find definitions of prophecy in all of its relevant manifestations: visionary, admonitory, denunciatory, inspirational, martial. What is common to all is their urgency. With his special sight, the poet has become aware of ominous signs and symptoms. The moment for utterance has arrived.

The element basic to all prophets is their visionary power. From their vantage point, the eternal and universal are familiar. This may involve no more than a shrinking of the present time and local place within the total perspective. As the seer leans from his tower, the current struttings and wranglings become ant-like. Through his vision the past lives again. He is able to "charm the shadows/From the true life of old."[12] When "life contracts into a vulgar span," the poet is revived by thoughts of Marathon and Thermopylae.[13] And his listener is revived as well, for he sings "as in the centuries olden/Before mankind its earliest fire forgot."[14] In the same way his vision of the future makes him "the lark of the dawn," and his song is "the giving of light."[15]

But the paradox is that, no matter how high and aloof his tower, the "Truest Prophet" is "he who loves his fellows,"[16] who peers more deeply into their memories and dreams than they themselves do. His song, like his tower, is earth-based; his visions of past and future rise from the memories and dreams of the people and are indissolubly linked with the people's present condition. Thus it is for the making of new heroes that Thoreau invokes the ghosts of "great actions";[17] it is "For the lesson . . . they teach" that Longfellow drags "into the light of day/The errors of an age long passed away."[18] As for the future, Lowell declares that the visionary has been commissioned:

> For a bad world's punishment,
> By compelling it to see
> Golden glimpses of To Be . . .[19]

This, the didactic function of visions, is an important concept, and one which is frequently demonstrated; obviously every reminder of what the world *can* be, embarrasses the world that *is*: the more familiar his listeners become with Utopia's "large Loves and heavenly Charities," the "less Utopian" it will seem.[20]

But a more important function is to clarify and verbalize the vague yearnings of the people, and inspire the fulfilling of visions which they have not even dared acknowledge to themselves. It is to the half-prophets, who exclude the essential *present* from their lofty tower-view, that Grace Greenwood addresses herself:

> To thee Humanity, her woes revealing,
> Would all her griefs and ancient wrongs rehearse;
> Would make thy song the voice of her appealing,
> And sob her mighty sorrows through thy verse.[21]

A poet like Jones Very would have accepted those lines as his credo. We often find him wakeful in the night, thinking about those who suffer, wondering "what tongue their want can tell, or pen can trace."[22] Melville expresses the same view in restating Cervantes' principle: "Be the wronged one's knight."[23] And Bryant honors Schiller for his dying wish: "To wander forth wherever lie/The homes and haunts of human kind."[24]

The classic example is Whitman. By taking "the open road," by dreaming in his dream "all the dreams of the other dreamers," he becomes the instrument of "many long dumb voices" and utters *their* "great Idea."[25] At the turn of the century, while Bierce and Sterling are telling each other how much they dislike Whitman, how much better it is to "be the poet of the skies, the prophet of the suns" than to "fiddle-faddle with" earth's "tiresome trivialities,"[26] young Edgar Lee Masters insists on evaluating Whitman as the prophet of heaven *and* earth:

> The eagle eye, which saw
> The spirit's worth, the law
> Of fairer fate
> The Nation's final form
> Through past and future storm.[27]

The test for Masters will come when we look at his own responsiveness to his time. It is enough here to show that he and many other poets of the nineteenth century recognized, comprehended, and endorsed the visionary role of the prophet as being related to his time and place, "Where poetry," in Santayana's words, "rises . . . to the consciousness of its highest function, that of portraying the ideals of experience and destiny."[28]

Not all who prophesy, however, are satisfied merely to record what they see and hear, what they remember and envision; a force within them demands that they confront the evildoer and name every crime to his face. For American poets to pursue such a course would not be to court physical annihilation, as their spiritual forebears courted it; but other forms of retribution were likely to follow. No society, no administration, accepts indictment with a smile, and nineteenth-century America was not notably tolerant. One might suggest that our poets merely gave lip-service when they extolled the great denouncers of the past and declared their loyalty to the Jeremiah or Juvenal tradition. And it is true that their definition sometimes sounds too vague, too rhetorical, to represent a genuine threat. Tyrants, criminals, and fools do not tremble at such words as Tyranny, Crime, and Folly. What matters, however, is that prophecy is persistently related to active denunciation in their verse. Our poets may not be in accord as to when, where, and by whom evil is perpetrated, but they agree that the prophet is he who confronts evil-doers as close to home as he can find them. By this definition America's nineteenth-century poets give us the right to observe their performance in the presence of what they considered evil.

Holmes, rather traditionally, shows "Satire, emptying his corrosive flood/On hissing Folly's gas-exhaling brood . . ."[29] With far greater depth Miss Guiney touches the central nerve of her beloved Juvenal, imagining the agony of his "heart uptorn," and implying that his savage wit had burst from a mind "distraught with love of violated Law."[30] This agony, which once sent John the Baptist crying through the wilderness "to warn and chide," and afterward roused the denunciatory powers of Dante and Gower, draws from Melville "The dire Vox Clamans of our day," a desperate incantation to "make less/The ever-bubbling wickedness."[31] Other poets, however, describe indictment as an act performed less in anguish than with bold joy. Almost playfully, imagining herself a new David facing a new Goliath, Emily Dickinson tells how she took her power in her hand "And went against the world."[32] Bayard Taylor portrays Bryant as an eager champion delivering a "haughty challenge unto Wrong,"[33] and John W. Chadwick—perhaps describing *himself* more accurately than Bryant—claims that his hero was always more powerfully attracted to "the strife with public ill/ Than ever the blue heaven's smile."[34] But the loftiest concept is of the poet as "some human reed" occasionally snatched up by the Truth, through which she blows "her terror-bearing note . . . to scatter her contagion on mankind." It is in the context of this definition that Markham praises William Watson for putting "the wreath of England by/To shake her guilty heart with song sublime."[35] And it is under this compulsion that Mrs. Howe declares: "I cannot choose but stand/Great rights and wrongings to assert."[36]

To denounce one's society is serious and dangerous, but the listener can always allow himself to imagine that his neighbor, not he, is being characterized. Far greater is the risk when the prophet's finger points directly at the one in power. Thus Bryant admiringly quotes a passage of censure from "The Task" and praises Cowper for bearing "witness against the guilt and folly of princes."[37] In the same way Thomas B. Read lauds Byron, Burns, and Körner, whom he envisions leading a host of poets:

> Crying, "Down with the tyrant wherever he be!"
> . . . I read the great words spread like fiery wings
> Where "weighed and found wanting" confronted the kings![38]

Among the most clear and beautiful definitions are those by Longfellow and Whittier, in whose poems the ancient prophets, challengers of king and country alike, serve as examples to inspire the inheritors of their moral passion. Longfellow's heroine reminds her accusers of God's instructions to Elijah:[39]

> Go down to meet the King of Israel
> In Naboth's vineyard, whither he hath gone
> To take possession. Thou shalt speak to him,
> Saying, Thus saith the Lord! What! hast thou killed
> And also taken possession?

Just as Ahab said to Elijah, "Hast thou found me, O mine enemy?" so will it be again for those who "bear false witness" and swear away innocent lives:

> Their enemy will find them out at last,
> The Prophet's voice will thunder, I have found thee!

Similarly, Whittier culminates his survey of current mischief with a ringing appeal for a new Xavier "to rebuke the age's popular crime":

> We need, methinks, the prophet-hero still . . .
> To tread the land, even now . . .
> Proclaiming freedom in the name of God,
> And startling tyrants with the fear of hell![40]

As the century closes, William V. Moody, with equal seriousness, probes the nature of his chosen path. His approach is rather different, yet the definition at which he arrives is identical. Instead of claiming to be divinely-appointed, he sees himself more modestly as the incarnation of his mother's girlhood dream—a brave, remarkable dream of the son she wished to bear:

. . . a sin-defiled,
Earth-encumbered, blood-begotten, passionate man-child,
Who yet should be a trump of mighty call
Blown in the gates of evil kings
To make them fall . . .[41]

It is one thing for the ever-wakeful prophet to hear and express the people's grief and yearning, to recognize and condemn the masked evils of his time; these functions accord with his vow to seek out and publish the truth, let who will listen. It is another matter, however, for the prophet to play a purposely dynamic, shaping role in the events of his age by rousing the bemused multitude and goading it into noble action. With such aims, his urgent need is to discover the most effective means of communication, and his triumph is measurable by the degree of response he wins. Thus Whittier's Xavier treads "the streets of Goa, barefoot, with his bell."[42] We can expect that many of our poets, trained to warble rather than roar, will shun this area as a potential quicksand for their aesthetic standard and a contradiction of their temperament; yet more than a few single out for praise this very act of public prophecy.

Lowell, for instance, admires Lamartine for having "touched the bard's true lyre, a nation's heart," and for "unlocking man to man" with his universally accepted poems of brotherhood.[43] This too is the quality which Dante's great translator, Thomas W. Parsons, particularly reveres in the songs of Burns: "Hearts in every land were stirred/With love, and joy, and scorn of wrong."[44] But the heart is not the prophet's only target: Whitman "walks the States with a barb'd tongue, questioning every one," shaming and shocking those who wish "only to be told what" they "knew before."[45] At century's end, Edwin A. Robinson lauds this disturbing quality in Zola, who "puts the compromising chart/Of hell" before men's eyes, challenging their "shamed indifference" until they scan "The racked and shrieking hideousness of Truth."[46] Emerson also sees the true poets as "liberating gods" who "are free, and . . . make free." His appeal, however, is to the blood —which has forgotten how to race freely. In a time of spiritual lethargy and ethical paralysis, the chords of Merlin's harp "make the wild blood start/In its mystic springs."[47] Just so, after the pogroms of 1881, does a galvanized Emma Lazarus, in her sudden need to accomplish public aims, hear and obey the ancient life-giving command:

> Yea, Prophesy, the Lord hath said. Again
> Say to the wind, Come forth and breathe afresh,
> Even that they may live upon these slain,
> And bone to bone shall leap, and flesh to flesh.
> The Spirit is not dead, proclaim the word . . .

But the Lord has more in mind for His prophet than merely to make people live again. "Where lay dead bones," Emma Lazarus sings, "a host of armed men stand!"[48] Without this ultimate martial power, the prophet is no more than embarrassing and irksome; with it he becomes a formidable adversary, an insurrectionary spearhead. We can well understand why King Edward decreed the annihilation of all Welsh bards. There is nothing far-fetched in Holmes' assessment:

> . . . the throbbing words
> That set the pulses beating,
> Are stronger than the myriad swords
> Of mighty armies meeting.[49]

Some poets go beyond the production of marching songs, the distribution of spears; they actually pull the soldiers into battle. Thus Whitman identifies himself as the one who cries, "Leap from your seats and contend for your lives!"[50] In the same voice Augustine Duganne exhorts his recruits:

> Though fiercely the battle round thee may rage,
> Thou hast cast—take not up, then—thy venturesome gage,
> Till thy chains thou shalt sever!

And Higginson, crying "To Arms! To Arms!" rightly titles his anti-slavery poem "Tyrtaeus."[51]

Not only do we discover that our poets understand the "sword" value of prophetic song, and that some of them accept the clarion-element of prophecy; there are also those who dramatize themselves as warriors against the ugliness around them, warriors on behalf of the ideal. Their battle boasts may strike us as hollow, and we may be somewhat justified in questioning Joaquin Miller's sincerity, for example; what concerns us here, however, is that his boast is also his self-definition:

> I aimed at the heart like a musket ball;
> I struck cursed folly like a cannon shot—
> . . . these did I write for my land.[52]

This note of personal pride is no more strident in Miller than in Thoreau, who exults to see "the routed foemen fly," and whose "bright spears" are fixed.[53] The identical tone is heard in young Garrison, who metaphorically rushes into battle "with spear and shield," despite his literal hatred of carnal weapons.[54] Sixty-five years later it reappears in the equally military lines of the equally pacifistic Ernest H. Crosby.[55]

> I am a soldier too, and I have the battle of battles on my hands . . .
> I have to make war upon all of you combined, and upon the infernal War Spirit which inspires you . . .

Against the iniquity of earth, such prophets constitute God's shock-brigade. Their commission is signed "by a Commander-in-Chief who may wait long for victory, but never waits in vain." It may seem no more than rhetoric when a poet tells Heaven that he "will be her champion new,"[56] but he does indeed represent a two-fold danger: in the first place his rebellious stance offers an incendiary example to those of whom obedience is required; second, he may be in dead earnest about his warrior-role. He may ring the bells of his town hall, publicly tear up the Constitution, organize angry committees, batter down court-house doors, lead an Indian tribe into battle. He may, in other words, turn his figurative spear into a literal one.

We have seen with what clarity and enthusiasm our poets define the elements of prophetic utterance. But this is not all; they also recognize that an alternative—betrayal—is possible. The incisiveness with which they identify such betrayal underscores their awareness of what true prophecy entails. Emerson, for instance, satirizes the poets who "tinkle a guitar" in accordance with the expectations of "pretty people in a nice saloon" and who read them a "pretty tale" instead of forcing the truth upon them.[57] Such a poet is a seller of a commodity—a "grocer green," Melville calls him—who thrives with the "fulsome face/Of a fool serene."[58] Avoiding the unpleasant, he sails "another way" with his reader; and it is this abandonment of the "Present Hour" which Thoreau damns as "a moral death."[59] In the same way the credo of William W. Story forbids pandering to the popular taste, since the poet whose concern is "the success of a day" thereby deserts his holy mission.[60] Thus Mrs. Howe, by praising Dante, whose "hands were pure from gold," implicates those poets whose hands *are* soiled.[61] Once poetry turns into a livelihood, the betrayal can become far more monstrous than merely satisfying "the public's fickle tastes and morbid appetites."[62] In an age when light is needed, the poet may—as Higginson vows not to do—actually veil the "truth by darkening or by hiding" it;[63] he may go further and "mock with lies the longing soul of men"—a crime of which Lowell, in youth, accuses Wordsworth.[64] Ultimately he may find himself reverting to the ancient anti-prophetic seat beside his lord at the mead-hall, warbling—for a ring or a chicken-leg—"The victim's shame, the tyrant's eulogy."[65]

It is both a barometer of the extent to which poetry had in recent years betrayed its ethical purposes, and a sign of a new commitment, that the poets of the 1890's should have given so much attention to the anti-prophetic. Santayana, for example, excoriates the drum-beating minstrels who offer their rhymes on behalf of the dominant mood: "Ignorant of ancient sorrow,/With hot young blood in their veins . . ."[66] Robinson is no less repelled by the "trumpet crash of blood-sick victory."[67] Stephen Crane goes further;[68] to him the war-press is a market "Where wisdom sells its freedom." And Moody charges much the same sell-out:[69] those who have position and eloquence "Fumble and fill their mouths with hollow phrase," intoning "dull commercial liturgies." He himself, Moody confesses, has betrayed his role by striving to evade "That swift and angry stave" his vision demands. In his "Musa Meretrix" Moody's assault on the poet-prostitute is brutal; yet Crane implies no less in portraying the so-called prophet as "a complacent fat man"—laureate of a well-paying society—who intends to see not the truth, but "good white lands/And bad black lands . . ." Some years will pass before Masters' contempt for the poetaster finds its ultimate statement, yet even his earliest work rejects "Petit, the Poet," who wrote:

> Ballades by the score with the same old thought . . .
> While Homer and Whitman roared in the pines![70]

Equally contemptuous, Robinson[71] contrasts the ferocity, the uncompromising honesty of his heroes—Zola, Crabbe, Verlaine—with "these little sonnet-men . . . Who fashion, in a shrewd mechanic way/Songs without souls, that flicker for a day . . ."

That the true men must pay for their truth is terribly clear. It is not easy for a Zola, a Crabbe, a Verlaine, to withstand the vengeful world's "crusade/Against the grim dominion of his art." And America's nineteenth-century poets are under no illusions as to the danger of the mission. To wake and vex a people that prefer lullabies and comfits is not likely to be appreciated—either by the populace or by those who thrive on its slumber. To denounce the character of a society and its rulers; to contrast them with what they once were and should be; to revive the ideal in men's minds and incite them to battle for it—this cannot go unpunished. It is not surprising, when we consider the dramatic nature of the situation, to find that this martyrdom theme is a special favorite among all kinds of poets throughout the period we are studying. Whether or not their lives and productions correspond to the superb note of defiance, it at least establishes a standard by which they give us the right to test them. It also serves as a model for heroic action to readers, and is in that sense a prophetic note.

Whittier, in one of his most impassioned autobiographical poems, traces his own lineage to Ezekiel:

> How mocked the rude, how scoffed the vile . . .
> With bonds, and scorn, and evil will,
> The world requites its prophets still.[72]

This melting of time—place boundaries, this insistence on the continuity of the prophetic agony, is found in poet after poet. They create a single immortal figure which changes in name but not in function, wearing the gloriously fatal robe for which its next appointed wearer is being readied, because "The prophet is a phoenix soul."[73] It is fitting that Bayard Taylor should imagine Whittier as a "martyr, in the arena cast,/Beneath the lion's paw";[74] that John Pierpont (whom Whittier represents as a new Nehemiah) should think of his fellow-abolitionists in terms of Biblical martyrdom:

> The ancient seers . . .
> To God and duty true,
> . . . reviled and put to shame:
> Scorned, hated, hunted . . .[75]

And just as contemporary prophets inspire comparison with ancient "martyrs for the truth," so are Bible champions, entered in the modern arena, once more scheduled for crucifixion:

I wonder not they slew the Christ . . .
And none shall live who tries to balk
The heavy hand of greed . . .[76]

Often the poets choose literary rather than religious heroes as reincarnations of the Doomed Prophet, and here too the boundaries of epoch, of region, disappear. Longfellow is among those haunted by the apparent inevitability of martyrdom:

Such a fate as this was Dante's,
By defeat and exile maddened;
Thus were Milton and Cervantes . . .
By affliction touched and saddened.[77]

In the same way young Albert Pike recalls "Byron and Shelley, Chatterton and Keats . . . and all their co-unfortunates" whose loyalty to their vision won exile, mockery, starvation, and an early death.[78] Even more bitterly Read reminds the world of how it mistreated Robert Burns:

The soul that sings, the heart must bleed . . .
"A living bard! What's he to us?
A bard, to live, must first be dead!"[79]

This theme continues strong. Toward the end of the century Miss Guiney sends messages of love to her special heroes: Lovelace, the imprisoned Cavalier, whose virtue ran "heroic from the heart," and Ovid, whom "wrath and exile" destroyed: ". . . kind head that far in prison/Sunk on a weary arm, feels no god's pity."[80]

From this interweaving of past and present it is an easy step for poets to predict how things are likely to go in the future. Wryly Emily Dickinson warns that only assent is acceptable to the world; those who dare "demur" will be "straightway dangerous/And handled with a chain."[81] Story likewise assures those who remain true to the ideal: "Ye shall be taunted by revilings rude,"[82] a prediction which Ella W. Wilcox echoes half a century later. "If you dare to sail first o'er a new thought tract," she prophesies, the world "will scourge and scorn you."[83] But she, and her fellow-poets, take these penalties in stride—at least, so they tell us; almost all of them couple the expectation of martyrdom with a sense of privilege at being chosen, and confidence in the ultimate triumph of their integrity. Whether the individual prophet "lives to see the day" is unimportant:

> The courage . . . though worlds in rage conspire,
> Conquers, at last, their dull hostility.[84]

Nor is his triumph over his natural enemy merely figurative: a lizard creeps where the tyrant's throne once gleamed—but "the song sings on."[85]

The samplings I have introduced seem to me to demonstrate beyond any doubt that the particular prophetic stance which we shall be seeking in the work of nineteenth-century American poets was known to and admired by them. There now remains the task of selecting several areas of iniquity in society and government from 1835 to 1900—not more than can be adequately explored in a work of this size, yet enough to be fairly representative of the problems which wracked responsible minds. On the basis of these touchstones we shall study the responses of our poets at certain crucial moments which were especially appropriate for the prophetic act.

Our first issue, and our last, will be imperialism, which advanced under the banner of manifest destiny and in the guise of liberation. Our initial focus will be on the wars with Mexico (1836 and 1846). Our final test will include both the Cuban and Philippine phases of the war against Spain with which the century came to a close. From Biblical times, prophets have spoken out boldly against the wars of aggrandizement waged by their rulers. Thus our own military adventures constitute a particularly relevant gauge, as well as an instrument by which the prophetic impulses of 1846 and 1898 can be compared.

Our next touchstone is mobbism. It has been claimed that "life was perfectly safe in the thirties—a trifle dull, perhaps";[86] but the record of riot casualties contradicts such a view. Against abolitionist and reform leaders the mob was notably active from 1835 to 1838; similar outrages were perpetrated in 1844 against religious minorities; and an especially sinister manifestation occurred in "bleeding Kansas" from 1855 to 1858. As the conscience of his generation and the guardian of the democratic ideal, a poet might reasonably be expected to have noted with concern the peculiar fertility of American soil for acts of mass violence. As the fearless foe of injustice, he could find few abuses more vile than the refusal of civil authority, pulpit, and press to intervene other than to sanction and applaud mob action.

Our third area of national shame is the most dramatic and historically significant aspect of the slavery issue: the forced return of fugitives to their ex-masters. The constitutional commitment to slavery by the "founding fathers" raised a difficult tangle of questions, including loyalty to the nation's compact and to the Union itself; yet this was not prophecy's first confrontation with divine versus man-made law. The officially sponsored hunt for fugitive slaves provided a two-fold basis for moral utterance: 1) the prophet has traditionally served as transmitter of God's message to errant rulers; 2) among prophecy's prime targets has always been the enslavement of man by man. The incidence of large-scale slave escape was continual and ever-increasing; it will therefore be necessary to select moments of exceptional agitation such as the 1842 Latimer case, the Webster Compromise of 1850, and the kidnapping of Anthony Burns in 1854.

The next phase of our study will involve the long-continuing American policy of plunder and decimation against its aboriginal population. On a number of grounds this would seem to promise a rich prophetic response. The "noble savage" motif had been running strongly through European romantic literature; some of South America's leading poets had issued massive appeals in their verse, demanding justice for the Indians of their own countries; the "vanishing American" genre was increasingly popular with American readers; finally, prophets of antiquity had often denounced the conquest of the weak by the strong. The period under study includes numerous electrifying and highly publicized episodes which challenged the conscience of the land. Our focus will be first on the forced removal of the Cherokees and Seminoles, then on the shattering finale of Custer's campaign.

Although a number of other areas deserve investigation, and might in the case of certain poets offer greater rewards, these are the touchstones I believe to be most meaningful and promising for our purpose. As symptoms of a national aggressiveness and blindness which devoured a continent in the name of Anglo-Saxon privilege, the events I have chosen dismayed many even outside the circle of prophetic pretension. We shall examine these areas of disgrace, offering in each instance as thorough an historical background as seems necessary; then, sifting the record left by the poets of the time, we shall perhaps be able to gauge the extent to which the prophetic principle, so thoroughly defined in their tributes and credos, was at work in their souls and on their tongues. In some cases I plan to make extensive use of prose and biographical data, since a denunciatory or an incendiary impulse is as likely to be projected in prose or deeds as in verse. Nor shall the silences of these poets be overlooked. When it appears that the silence constitutes a significant ethical failure, we shall try to explain it. But there is a very different kind of silence, akin to the prophetic act, and we shall identify it when it occurs. This is the silence of "rebuke" and "contempt" which Holmes[87] and Whitman[88] permit us to interpret as their vote of "no confidence" in what is going on around them; this is "the absence of our best names in song," which so "mortified" Bayard Taylor, who served by default as America's centennial laureate.[89]

Although my primary concern here is to test the vaunted courage and ethical sensitivity of our poets, I shall by no means ignore the area of aesthetics, and intend to explore the interplay between their artistic and prophetic impulses. The range of illustrations offered in this chapter should make it clear that I intend to take careful notice of those who are now deemed minor figures along with those of acknowledged stature. In such an investigation anyone who considered himself a poet, and was so considered by his generation, seems to me worthy of notice. It is conceivable that the most obscure name may prove valuable for my purposes; nor would it be surprising to discover among them a number of really good poets whose eclipse was the sentence meted out by an anti-prophetic society and its official literary judges.

1

War With Mexico

In studying the genuinely prophetic impulse as it responded to American imperialism, we must first familiarize ourselves with the tunes whistled by the pied pipers of war, often in the guise of prophecy. For these tunes represented the government's rationale and enticement, and provided the inspired opposition with a tangible target for rebuttal, point by point. We shall find this to be as true in 1898 as it was during the Mexican adventure.

i

The Mexican War began with the successful Texas Rebellion of 1835—36. Whatever immediate justification may have been claimed by Ben Milam's men in besieging San Antonio, thus inviting the retaliatory siege of the

Alamo and the Goliad massacre, no motive was stronger than a zest for war. Texas offered the Southern cavalier, who for fifty years had "only half suppressed his military aspirations," a theatre of knightly exploits. It is therefore no accident that war songs were "among the truest . . . Texas poems."[1]

In "The Texas Hunter" William G. Simms registers and encourages this mood, evoking the Arthurian ideal of boldness, but not Arthur's motives of kindness and justice. The speaker invites a "dear maiden" to be his bride "where the sun is setting/But where our sun must rise"—a triple reference to the West, the Mexican symbol, and the rise of a new empire with the fall of the old. He employs the very terminology of the chivalric code: if her love of battle equals his, "As dames in knightly days could share/The rapture of the strife," nothing will keep him from storming the towers of Mexico.[2] This renewal of vainglorious knighthood is personified in Mirabeau Buonaparte Lamar. No sooner does he set his knightly foot on Texan soil than he offers his life and talents to war.[3] His first Texas poem, "The Bride That I Woo is Danger," might have been written in Roland's time:

> Speed, speed the day when to war I hie!
> The fame of the field is inviting.
> Before my soul shall the foeman fly,
> Or fall in the flash of its lightning.

At times, however, his war-lust bursts forth crudely: "I long to thin them, 'two at a blow.' " This is accompanied by a cluster of lofty and far-fetched slogans which represent him as "Insulted Freedom's proud avenger." A second song exhorts the Texans to "Lay low the tyrant hand/Uplifted to enslave" them. His readers may have wondered how "the audacious foe" of the first poem could become "the servile race" in the second; yet they were quick to take up his cry: "Charge, charge my braves on Cos . . ." Lamar had come to the right place at the right time: within two months Mexico's General Cos surrendered! If his poetry did not thereafter improve, his fortunes did; and he rose from cavalry commander to major general, attorney general, secretary of war, vice president, and—by 1838—president of Texas.

With Ben Milam's death in battle, an elegiac note is added to the chivalric, amalgamating many of the catchwords that have served all war-minstrels:

> Thou dauntless leader of the brave,
> Who on the heights of Tyranny
> Won Freedom and a glorious grave . . .
> Enshrined on Honor's deathless scroll . . .[4]

Additional martyrs are provided for the Texan "cause" and for its poets at Goliad and the Alamo. Now blood-vengeance, masked as justice, can be joined to their war-aims. "Remember the Alamo!" is to serve as a rallying cry for the next dozen years. Houston's retribution at San Jacinto introduces into their songs a note of Anglo-Saxon arrogance, which becomes more pronounced when an insurrectionary expedition to Santa Fe is seized and taken to Mexico.[5] Rhymesters egg on their army to "cross the mongrel Spaniard's line," free the prisoners, and guarantee that "For every wound . . . A Mexican shall bite the dust."

When Santa Anna recognized Texas as a republic, its commissioners visited Washington with the strangely contradictory aims of having their independence acknowledged and of being annexed. A clear-sighted and courageous poet might then have voiced suspicion that the old "independence" slogan was false, that the rebellion was in fact a deftly masked method of seizing for the United States the same rich lands which had inspired earlier adventurers. Yet, aside from newspaper versifiers, no voice challenges the dismemberment of a weak young sister republic, even among poets alert to other ethical issues such as free speech and abolition. This may strike us as a prophetic failure, but to them the defeat of Mexico is no cause for tears. For they are convinced that the American eagle carries civilization, and at least a *dream* of liberty, on its powerful wings; and their lines often resound with visionary exuberance.

Bryant's "The Prairies," enthusiastically voicing this "spread-eagle nationalism,"[6] is symptomatic of the Texas mood. Another popular poet, Lydia H. Sigourney, employs the same imperial imagery: she prophesies that both Atlantic and Pacific will battle against her nation's coast, and imagines Congressmen stretching "their line of travel through an empire's length." But her proud eagle is no bird of prey; his wings protect "the exiled, and the crush'd from every clime."[7] Another influential lady of the period, Mrs. Sarah J. Hale of *Godey's*, also celebrates the bird as a symbol of liberation:

> . . . Freedom writes her signature in stars,
> And bids her Eagle bear the blazing scroll
> To usher in the reign of peace and love . . .
> To sweep Earth's thousand tyrannies away . . .[8]

It seems inconceivable to such poets that any nearby region would not desire to achieve sisterhood among the States. Pleading passionately on behalf of the Lone Star for a place "on our banner bright,"[9] these poets unwittingly supply aggrandizement with its most attractive rationale.

Even the poets who oppose annexation are not thereby opposing imperialism: their ethical sensitivity is partisan. Tappan hears "a million voices thunder, NO!"[10] *not* to the idea of manifest destiny, but to the extension of slavery. Whittier, so violently opposed to the use of guns by abolitionists, somehow ignores the guns used on behalf of land-greed.[11] In his hackneyed "Texas," oddly echoing the war-poets, he recalls "the old graves of the land," summons his people to stand "for God and duty" to protect their "homes and altars," and attacks as "traitors false and base" those who disagree; yet only abolition is on his mind. If he has a negative comment to make during the annexation controversy, so far as military aggression is concerned, he presents it obliquely and only once, implying that the mood of London's 1840 anti-slavery convention, unlike America's mood, is "holy" because it includes "No threat of war, no savage call/For vengeance on an erring brother!" Lowell, too, is reticent on this issue. Even at the close of the annexation debate, in "The Present Crisis"—an anti-slavery poem of genuine eloquence—Lowell avoids all reference to imperial conquest. Only once, and indirectly, does he challenge his countrymen's brand of knighthood, by reviving the ancient dream of a Golden Age when:

> . . . conquerors see
> With horror in their hands the accursed spear
> That tore the meek One's side on Calvary,
> And from their trophies shrink with ghastly fear . . .[12]

The reprimand by Longfellow is more effective. Picturing Springfield's arsenal as an organ, he imagines in dread "what a sound will rise . . . When the death-angel touches those swift keys," and closes with an evangelistic vision of the world as it should be.[13] Thus, while songs of manifest destiny flood the land, while Andrew Jackson accuses as "a traitor" any "Senator who votes against . . . ratification,"[14] while William G. Simms warns of "ruin to a race" that "undertakes no march,"[15] Longfellow boldly vexes the national mood. It is in this context that one must study his "Arsenal at Springfield," with its motto from Arnobius urging men to:

> . . . listen awhile unto Christ's wholesome and peaceable decrees, and not, puffed up with arrogance and conceit, rather believe their owne opinions than his admonitions . . .[16]

Garrison astutely links Longfellow's general condemnation of war with the current controversy by reprinting it together with "The Annexation of Texas," an unsigned appeal to the South for a return to the ideals of Washington and Patrick Henry, instead of foisting slavery on other lands:

> Granting they are not strong, but weak,
> Why must they also die?

A reasoning appeal such as this, is not typical. In line with the Garrisonian slogan—NO UNION WITH SLAVEHOLDERS! —the more audacious rhymesters now begin to produce stanzas of a frankly seditious nature:

> Did Freedom's pennon ever flow
> O'er robbers' and invaders' wars?
> Does Liberty descend to guile,
> And shameless fight for sordid spoil!
> Pull down those stripes! pull down those stars![17]

Unaligned poets such as Holmes and Mrs. Sigourney, to

whom preservation of the Union means more than either emancipation or geographical modesty, reproach those whose philippics are becoming too extreme. In a legal sense, anti-government utterance cannot yet be called "treason," since the nation is not at war; but "treachery" is what Holmes calls it.[18] Mrs. Sigourney is no less dismayed by what seems to her an ill-timed display of the apostolic impulse, but she manages to soften her vexation by a coyness of manner:

> Some faults we have . . .
> But other households have the same . . .
> 'Twill do no good to fume and frown,
> And call hard names, you see,
> And what a shame 'twould be to part
> So fine a family![19]

It would be difficult to find a clearer instance of the poet as anti-prophet, demanding that her colleagues accept iniquity in silence, terming slavery, mob intolerance, and military conquest, "a foible here and there . . ." Mrs. Sigourney achieves a remarkable degree of harmony here between the shoddiness of her ethical position and of her versification.

ii

The annexation debate, as we have seen, involved complex differences among American poets: a variety of political and personal interests that often determined what their ethical stand would be. The war with Mexico which followed produced an even greater diversity of response. As expected, Mexico considered the annexation an act of war and assembled an army on the Rio Grande. The United

States sent Zachary Taylor's army of occupation into Texas. The verse that at once began to emerge from this campaign continued the pseudo-Tyrtaean tradition of the war-loving Texas literature. But it was more considerable both in range and significance—not only because the war was larger and the country had been girding for it with great nervous concentration, but also because a cluster of new poets appeared in the 1840's and such established writers as Willis, Mrs. Sigourney, Longfellow, Morris and Poe had been winning a tremendous audience for poetry.

As in the Texas phase, to establish the context of the prophetic challenge we must first examine the productions of the martial group, whose tone and slogans represented what rampant America wished to hear. We see at once that, just as the Democratic, Whig, and Native American parties for the moment joined ranks, their poets also sought to dissolve differences in order to serve the war. This effort, however, was more successful politically than artistically. From all their eager mottoes, charges, and justifications, one can hardly form a single clear notion of what "his country's quarrel"[20] was, which George P. Morris exhorted the soldier to settle.

Certain versifiers feign a moral position, with sometimes amusing results. "Uncle Sam's Song to Miss Texas," for example, portrays Mexico as a tyrant planning to oppose the United States.[21] "Taylor on the Rio Grande" also asserts that "the Mexicans crossed o'er the line . . . brimful of blood and thunder," but playfully revises its charge: "That is—they would have," had General Taylor not been there with his Anglo-Saxons, who never retreat. At times the appeal for expulsion of "the invading band" is coupled with an equally fatuous cry for retribution, to repay unspecified "wrongs too long endur'd . . . countless crimes" which "call aloud for the avenging sword." Can it still be the Alamo? or Goliad? or the unsettled financial claims against the Mexican government? Whatever justice they have in mind, the war poets confidently declare their kinship with "the God who . . . ever guards the just."[22]

Although a candidly predatory note is sometimes struck, as in "The Union's Call," which shows a jaw open for "all Mexico," America's land-greed is usually veiled. More often, these versifiers reveal the almost neurotic concern of a rising young empire "which must be heard" by other lands.[23] There is no timidity in their cry: ". . . down let his flag be hurled,/Shout, as our own from the turret is wide unfurled!"[24] In this connection the Mexican War poems swarm with eagles spreading their wings and banners fluttering high. By using such sacred and imperial symbols, and by summoning the great national ghosts of Bunker Hill and Eutaw, these minstrels simulate the inspirational role of prophecy, invoking the anti-imperial past on behalf of the imperial present.

Their lofty remembrances are accompanied by equally lofty and self-satisfying claims, such as the bringing of civilization and liberty to "savage lands."[25] Lamar has just driven the Cherokees out of East Texas, yet poets ask their countrymen to imagine the descendants of Montezuma raising "the glad cry—'The Saxons are coming, our freedom is nigh.' " Americans are urged to fight "Till all Mexico wears the bright stars of freedom,"[26] and after the Palo Alto victory twenty thousand at a New York war gathering sing Morris' new national anthem: "Arm and strike for Liberty!"[27]

One looks in vain for Liberty, however, as a military aim in Albert Pike's Mexican War poems.[28] As an ex-New Englander whose early poems were strongly Shelleyan and tinged with abolition, he may be more sensitive about the word "liberty" than are other Southern poets, who use it as a synonym for the right to own slaves. Otherwise his rhetoric is typically vague: ". . . for your wives and children, men! . . . Fight for your lives and honors!" Twenty-seven years later the Confederate laureate is to offer the national convention of Mexican War Veterans a long poem filled with the same old zeal and the same old phrases, blandly admitting of the 1846 volunteers: "Little they cared the cause of war to know." But even during the war, despite all pretensions, such an attitude is basic:

> Right be she ever, but though wrong,
> Still bare your breast, each son
> An offering make of patriot blood
> Upon her Altar—Home.[29]

A case might be made for the sincerity of poets who do in fact fear for their country's safety and do believe that she has been wronged. But the tongue is not divinely inspired that denies the significance of the cause or asks that men be willing to die for wrong. Nor is it Tyrtaean of the sedate Park Benjamin to scream:

> Die as your fathers died!
> Go! vindicate your country's fame,
> Avenge your country's wrong![30]

The true prophet of battle refers not to a hazy nationalistic mystique but to a tangible ethical issue; and his call to arms is usually delivered against a formidable adversary on behalf of its weak, encircled victim, and at great personal risk. What might have been splendid if sung by the

Mexican lads guarding Chapultepec is ludicrous on the pages of Benjamin's newspaper: "O! is it not a glorious thing thus on the field to die?"[31] The war-songs of Hosmer are equally laureate-like and no less far-fetched: "Strike for our wives and lady-loves,/Our country and our home!"[32] Even the romantic Southern poet, Richard H. Wilde, embittered and self-muted during the 1840's, bestirs his chivalric breast sufficiently to add his "war-note," as hackneyed and hollow as the rest, calling upon all Americans "In the cause of our country to conquer or die . . ."[33]

Fame, Laurels, Glory are familiar nouns in these poems. Morris assures those who have died for their country that "the garlands of their fame" will remain green. Like his brethren of the South, this New York poet praises "the pride of all our chivalry" who, "like the Christian knights of old," sought their "laurels on the field."[34] In this context O'Hara's "Bivouac of the Dead" becomes a collection of clichés rather than a classic. Summoned to save the flag, his heroes have gladly poured "Their lives for glory," and will be remembered as long as "Fame her record keeps."[35] These poets do not always indicate the nature of Glory, often simply equating it with fortitude in the face of death. Pike's definition, however, is algebraically clear:[36] ". . . honor unto those that stood! Disgrace to those that fled! And everlasting glory unto Buena Vista's dead!"

Obviously the dead do not include Mexicans, for those are not men but "Aztec multitudes," and the real glory is to roll them back "all broken and dismayed." Thus Hosmer gloats to see "The men of Montezuma's land" flying "Like frightened hares before the beagle!"[37] and Alfred B. Street exults:

On! on! we pour our deadly shots: on! on! ha, see! ha, see!
The white flag from San Pablo streams! the foe is on his knee![38]

An equally ferocious note sounds in the stanzas of Thomas D. English. There will be, he declares, no mercy as "we strike our steady blows."[39]

Thus the false and illogical pied piper tune takes shape: Mexico has offended gravely; has invaded or intends to invade; savage lands await civilization and liberty; America craves land and is destined for empire; our flag and our past are matchless; we should support our country whether right or wrong.

The realities of the war apparently have no effect on Pike, as we see in his above-quoted 1874 comments before the veterans' convention. In a number of other cases, however, a significant change comes into their verse as the war's enormities mature them. Hosmer, for example, celebrates not only Captain May, "our Cavalier . . . A knight without . . . fear," but also the vanquished, "Brave Vega," whose "warlike shout" had been heard by "many fields . . ."[40] In the same way, although Street pays tribute to American skill and bravery, it is the agony of the experience, not the glory, that the poet hammers home:

Trumpets and drums were loud in joy, but no joy rose for me ...
Enough of war: it makes God's earth a crimsoned, blackened spoil!

What remains with the reader is a totally unexpected passage in which a wounded Mexican boy, "a father's pride, a loving mother's joy," is murdered while at his prayers by a "cowardly, murderous" dragoon. Later, in a contrasting scene, a wounded American gives the precious water from his canteen to another bleeding Mexican, "he too . . . a slender, delicate boy." The enemies expire clasped as if they were father and son.[41]

Even more impressive is the transformation of English. He wrote "El Molino del Rey"[42] to "impress" on the minds of his readers "a sense of the patriotism and courage" of their forebears; yet the speaker is a Mexican veteran, through whose recollections emerge the heroism and grief of both sides. English's introduction emphasizes the "heroic resistance" of the Mexicans, who "fought fiercely and well . . . displayed daring and steadiness" and, under better officers, "would make as fine soldiers as any in the world." Narrators, to emphasize their hero's splendor, often point out the enemy's skill and ferocity; but English seems less concerned with story-telling strategy than with setting the record straight on Mexico. In an earlier poem he had called upon the God of Justice "to shield the land we love . . ."[43] In *this* ballad, however, the Americans are seen as "foreign invaders" whom Mexican "love of . . . country" and "death-daring spirit" could not halt, since they "were more demon than men." The concluding lines expose, inartistically, but with courage and vigor, a truer motive for the war than the laureates ever admitted:

> And now they come back to invade us,
>   Though not with the bullet and blade;
> They are here with their goods on a railway,
>   To conquer the country by trade.

Among those who, like English, Street, and Hosmer, achieve a moderate position toward the war, Charles F. Hoffman ranks high.[44] Early in the campaign his chivalric verses are reminiscent of Simms' knight: untaught to yield, preferring death in battle as "woman's form . . . marshals him to glory . . ." His hero, "equal . . . to any five," is best defined in "Monterey":

> We were not many . . .
> Yet not a single soldier quailed . . .
> And on, still on, our column kept,
> Through walls of flame, its withering way . . .
> . . . striking where he strongest lay,
> We swooped his flanking batteries past,
> And, braving full their murderous blast,
> Stormed home the towers of Monterey.

It is true that, unlike the other balladeers, even in these early war poems Hoffman refuses to claim superiority over the enemy in terms of race or cause; and he does not gloat over Mexico's defeat. Understating the largeness of his praise, singing softly in the presence of death, he achieves in "Monterey"—despite some battle clichés—a tour de force in the harmony of controlled form and feeling. From "Monterey," however, he advances to an openly pro-Mexican position in "Buena Vista," supposedly written by a Mexican prisoner. For a popular poet to conceive and publish such verses at the height of a war is daring indeed, an invitation to the charge of treason. Instead of stars and stripes, "the sun of Aztec" blazes:

> Upon her banner broad and bright!
> And on—still on, her ensigns wave,
> Flinging abroad each glorious fold . . .

Here the American victory is portrayed as a "carnage" from which Mexico's defenders are forced to "drag" away their "patriot chief," who—although "crushed by famine, steel and fire"—refuses to surrender. Hoffman describes the battle with almost epic objectivity and strength:

Columbia's sons—of different race—
Proud Aztec and bold Alleghan,
Are grappled there in death embrace,
To rend each other, man to man!

An even clearer identification with Mexico, and an equally remarkable war-time gesture, is demonstrated in his sensitive translation of a poem which he entitles "Rio Bravo—A Mexican Lament."

Far and away the most significant and fascinating shift in position occurs in the verse of Simms. That he should write anything at all on the war is surprising. In "History for the Purposes of Art" he calls Bunker Hill and Saratoga poor choices for artistic treatment "because of the proximity of the events and persons to our own time, by which we are made too familiar with all the details in their histories . . ."[45] Yet he writes, from the formation to the homecoming of South Carolina's regiment, some two dozen war songs. These he publishes in Charleston in 1848. Calling them "almost improvvisations" [sic] and confessing that most were "written at the moment" he heard of the "event which they record," he acknowledges that they "may be rude" and that "the lyre of the poet may be wanting." Earnestness of feeling, he stresses, is their saving quality; his intention is to honor the career "of the gallant regiment" in "outpourings of a full heart."[46] If Simms' lifelong ambition, however, was "to receive recognition" from a birthplace which snubbed him, his protestations of strong feeling may be suspect. The production of his *Palmetto* volume may in fact be a shrewd personal maneuver to win Charleston's laureateship while fulfilling an allegedly "imperative duty to his native commonwealth."[47] But of one factor we can be certain: after deploring the so-called spiritual decay of a long peace, he rejoices that there are again heroes to be celebrated.

Hoffman's "Monterey" gave fresh proof that a fine poem *can* emerge immediately after the event it celebrates. One therefore approaches Simms, a writer of far greater talent, with some expectation, only to find that the bulk of his book is, like its motivation, on a level with the shoddiest verses by the most inconsequential minstrels of the war. Most of his battle songs illustrate what Parrington calls the "wasting" of his genius "in trumpery fields that belong to the literary dray horse."[47] The joy in killing is there, combined with the ugliest racism:[48]

> . . . we mow'd the Pinto's [sic] down . . .
> Don Salas did we capture, and we chased Don Torrejon,
> And a host of other Dons did we put in mortal pain . . .
> . . . the combat, hand in hand,
> Never Don or Savage yet with the Saxon could endure!

The noble Anglo-Norman will show "these mongrel Mexicans" that "good blood" has "given two mighty nations/ To sway both hemispheres!" He calls on "the fierce spirit of the land" to take "wild revenge"—for unmentioned offenses. The Mexicans who resist conquest are "foul traitors" to be "mow'd . . . down . . . crush'd, and captured . . ."

Simms' chivalric ideal is defined as he exhorts the sons of Marion and Sumter to speed toward "fields of fame . . . where glory beckons . . ." A soldier entering the fray is described as if he were a reincarnated Arthurian knight:

> His young soul in arms, not a moment delaying,
> To rush to the battlefield seeking a name!

In poem after poem the archetypal hero *almost* emerges. All that is missing is an ethical cause. At times of suffering "no lip complains"; at Chapultepec he "darted among the first" over the walls; when the battle went fiercely, his flag was "among the first to rise."

Invariably introduced at predictable moments and in predictably mystical terms of awe, "the flag of the Eutaw" becomes a cheap strategic device to tamper with the reader's emotional reflexes—in the mask of inspirational prophecy. What it symbolizes basically, however, is the ascendancy of a new empire over the ruins of the old: ". . . their standard down we tore;/Their serpent in the beak of our eagle soaring high . . ." This overturn of dominion finally calls forth a hint of Simms' narrative powers, as a general recalls those who followed him into battle:

> . . . with bended spears
> When Mexico was stooping to her fall;—
> When, at Chapultepec, we crush'd her powers,
> And storm'd through all her gates, our way to Aztec towers.

The dominant tone of the battle songs, however, is bloodthirsty and shrill rather than majestic. Simms appears to beat the drums with special frenzy, so concerned is he lest the peace faction give "the envious foreign foe" cause to rejoice. In his most openly anti-prophetic mood he assaults those voices which ring out against the conquest of Mexico. Unlike others, who pretend that this is a war to end war, Simms belligerently pays tribute not only to the dead, but also to those "who live for other wars . . ."

At this point, as in Hoffman, a profound shift of view becomes evident.[49] Earlier, he eulogized the fallen: "They died!—but how can we deplore them." Toward the end of the campaign, however, the emphasis is reversed. In a series of moving lamentations the glory of heroes is increasingly challenged by the reality of their loss. The speeches, the songs, even "the cry of our eagle upsoaring," cannot "soothe the deep sorrows" felt by a war widow. Nor can "the glowing narration" of his son's death keep an old man—in his nightly dreams—from "calling, 'my Son? O! my Son!' " Of the regiment that went forth proudly, "brave soul'd and eagle eyed," only a few wan "relics" return. Bitterly Simms quotes the song of David:

> How are their mighty fallen,
>   On loftiest places slain . . .
> They won their crown of laurel . . .
>   But paid for it with life!

That Simms' postwar attitude has undergone a still sharper revision[50] is indicated in a major 1850 poem, "The City of the Silent." Not a word is offered on the recent war, but there are long sections about haughty empires that passed "from conquest to decay." Also significant is his total omission of the *Palmetto* poems from his two-volume collected edition of 1853. The only included poem which may have sprung from the Mexican War praises the personal devotion of lovers rather than their patriotic fervor. Love, in fact, triumphs over war. Thus the poet has come full circle from a celebration of battle and a detestation of peace to a sense of the tragic waste in imperial adventure and the evanescence of military triumph.

It is a far cry from the developing humaneness of Hoffman and Simms to the sustained vitriol of Whitman's expansionist 1846 editorials. The irrepressible tread of "Pioneers! O Pioneers!" and "Song of the Broad-Axe" can be distinctly heard in the "narrow jingoism"[51] of these Brooklyn *Eagle* drum-taps, which fulfill completely the Tyrtaean role of prophecy as he is later to define it:

> In war he is the best backer of the war, he fetches artillery as good as the engineer's, he can make every word he speaks draw blood.[52]

This definition, however, ignores the possibility of an unjust war, requires blind nationalism of all poets in wartime, and denies the holy task of castigation assigned to those Bible prophets whose kings waged predatory wars.

If a paraphrase were sought of all the verse produced in support of the Mexican War, it could be most conveniently located in Whitman's prose of 1846—47.[53] Revenge is the keyword of his hodgepodge: Mexico is "an enemy deserving a vigorous 'lesson' . . ." Recalling "the devilish massacres" of American heroes to satisfy the "cowardly appetite of a nation of bravos," the young editor asks for "the vengeance of a retributive God." In the next breath he speaks of teaching the world that "while we are not forward for a quarrel, America knows how to crush . . ." With an imperial hunger he then eyes "the main bulk of" Mexico along with Yucatan, California, and Santa Fe. These rich regions, he declares, must shine as new stars "in our mighty firmament." And it is proper that Mexico should be "a severed and cut up nation," because Mexico's government has been "a libel on liberty." In fact, Whitman assures his readers, her own provinces will rejoice at "the rout of a tyrannical oppressor." The future of the hemisphere is certain. What has a population of "superstitious" Catholics to do, he asks, with the "great mission of peopling the New World with a noble race?"

Taylor's triumphs are thus the fulfillment of the young poet's apocalyptic vision and "clinching proof of the indomitable energy of the Anglo-Saxon character." Lashing out at those who praise Mexico and criticize the invasion, he assaults the *Tribune* as "unworthy the name of American!" Nimbly he minimizes the battle-losses, and lauds this war as "the most bloodless one thus far." While mouthing Isaiah's augury of "that holy era when all swords shall be beat into plough shares," he warns that first a long period of military occupation will be necessary, to turn "an ignorant, prejudiced, and perfectly faithless people" into "a sister Republic." Not a single ingredient is omitted from this pseudo-Tyrtaean goulash. Along with the loftiest-sounding justifications and goals he blends crude racist arrogance and abuse, open avarice, and attacks on those whose expressed ethical standards embarrass his leaders.

By 1848 Whitman has become disillusioned with "Old Zack." Yet there seems to cling to this poet—even after he develops his image as the apostle of universal love—a deep-seated hatred of the Mexican. In "Song of Myself" he alludes to the Alamo with a bitterness that would have been more appropriate in 1836 or 1846, and retells with a fury that belies his aesthetic and philosophic precepts the too-familiar Goliad story, placing the heroism of the American martyrs in sharp contrast with the bestiality of the Mexicans, who "so ruthlessly and needlessly slaughtered . . ." This section is immediately followed by another battle narrative; here the adversary is Anglo-Saxon and praiseworthy. Thus Section 34 provides a jarring, uncalled-for note in an otherwise warm-hearted poem. Whitman has somehow missed the lesson learned by much of the nation and some of its poets since the earlier, more vindictive days.

In general, then, the stuff of 1846–48 martial verse is as I have indicated: exploitation of the flag and eagle motifs, praise of blind loyalty, a plethora of abstract, hackneyed slogans and excuses, an occasional roar of geographic hunger, and an absence of what martial prophecy demands: a genuine ethical cause. In a word, it is laureate-work. Conspicuous in this group, however, are a few, such as Hoffman and Simms, who "rise to the occasion" early in the war, only to discover the weakness of their own and their nation's moral position. By publicly reversing themselves at the height of the war, they graphically illustrate the ethical sensitivity and courage which mark the prophetic spirit.

iii

We turn now to those whose reprimands bear the stamp of prophecy from the outset of the conflict. Although no editor seems to have collected their utterances, those form a far more impressive body of verse than what we have thus far noted—not only in bulk, but also in the stature of the writers. Although the main source of their dismay is the war itself, the altruistic pose of the government and the contradictory claims of its laureates are obviously the irritants that set many poets to mock or chastise.

A Garrison sonnet, for instance, accuses the alleged liberators of actually seeking to enslave. This war, he says, transcends all others "in deep guilt," and whoever lends his support to its success thereby becomes "dear Liberty's worst foe."[54] William W. Story sarcastically echoes and demolishes the excuses offered by the choristers of battle:

Is it to repel invasion?
  Is it then for Freedom's cause,
  . . . To defend our homes and laws?
No, by heaven! a baser motive
  Never prompted man to war . . .

The true motive, these poets charge, is aggrandizement; the true mover—the South! They dispute the expansionist doctrine that America and Liberty are synonymous, and imagine what will happen when Uncle Sam extends "this mighty nation . . . to the farthest creation":

Ah! then will the wilderness bloom in a trice
With cotton plantations, and sugar and rice,
Ethiopia's sons lift their hands up and skip
At the musical crack of each slave-driver's whip . . .

Thomas W. Higginson makes the same point: what good will America's expansion do if "the fatal poison-taint" of slavery is thereby permitted to expand?

For Higginson, however, this seems to be the only reservation. His argument is clearly not anti-imperialist; nor is he the only abolition poet who feels that once God has wiped out "the nation's guilt" it will be appropriate to "swell the Nation's power . . ." Channing openly declares his acquisitive love for "the distant West" and for "each small part/Of this great Continent."[55] Even William B. Tappan, as strong for peace as for abolition, accepts the principle that the United States has "A new world" for its "empire," and that its eagle "should revel with free scope/In the exhaustless West" as soon as the nation repents of slavery.[56] On the other hand there are anti-slavery poets who *do* condemn the imperial nature of the war, thereby challenging the singers of manifest destiny. Alonzo Lewis deplores the growing "lust of fame, of conquest, and of power."[57] In the manner of the ancient seers, Adams warns that the triumph of brute force is of short duration, that in later ages the conqueror's name is loaded "with curses loud and deep."[58]

Some poets make it their special mission to strip war of the glory in which it has been decked by the minstrels of the drum-roll. Horror and grief emerge, as if to challenge Whitman's boast of a "bloodless war." Among the most evangelistic in this group are George Boker[59] and Mrs. Sigourney,[60] whose fiery "Song of the Earth" and deeply felt "The Needle, Pen, and Sword" are unusually close in tone and phrase:

BOKER *(addressing Mars)*	*SIGOURNEY* *(addressing a sword)*
For what horrid uses are the gleaming sabres . . . ? . . . the courteous knight shall howl like a wolf/When he scents the gory steam of battle.	What are thy deeds, thou fearful thing/By the lordly warrior's side? . . . the wolf that laps where the gash is red . . . and the foul hyena know.
The orphan's curse . . . the tears of widowed matrons . . . each cheerless hearthstone . . .	The hearth-stone lone . . . the orphan . . . the pale and widow'd bride . . .
trampled grass . . . wasted and barren fields . . .	the field doth reek . . . the rusted plough . . . the seed unsown . . . the grass that doth rankly grow . . .
thy bloody footprints in their wounds . . . gaunt and leafless trees . . . imprecating arms outspread . . . desolation . . .	the rotting limb, and the blood-pool dark,/Gaunt Famine . . . black-wing'd Pestilence . . . Sad Earth in her pang and throe . . .

See where thy frenzied votaries march! . . . ruin grins . . . Thou hast hurled Man's placid reason . . . and in its place reared savage force . . .

Death with the rush of his harpy-brood . . . Demons that riot in slaughter and crime . . .

I sicken in thy angry glance, and loathe/The dull red glitter of thy bloody spear.

The terrible Sword to its sheath return'd . . . the Pen traced . . . that better time/When the warfare of earth shall cease.

It is remarkable that, precisely when their leaders and countrymen most desire the glorification of war, these poets unmask its ugliness with a passion uncommon in their work. Nevertheless, whether for political or aesthetic reasons, Boker and Mrs. Sigourney fail to identify their target as the Mexican adventure.

Equally ambiguous are the setting and personae in Epes Sargent's "The Conqueror," a deftly constructed ballad of war's tragedy.[61] After a battle the unburied slain surround a wounded soldier whose bloody horse is "his bed." Bitterly he sees at last in their true context all his old "dreams of fame,/Of hosts to conquest led . . ." His sweetheart sinks wounded and dies with him. Unlike others, Sargent's indefiniteness cannot be charged to political discretion. When *he* commands Ambition to "quit the field," there can be no doubt of his meaning. For at this very moment his influential Boston *Transcript* is attacking Polk as "the man who had embroiled the country in a frightful war and stained our Southern frontier with blood and carnage."[62] In addition, he footnotes the ballad by quoting a report from Monterey depicting "a Mexican woman . . . mortally wounded while going to succor a dying soldier."[63] The conclusion, as in Simms' ballad, repeats the old saw that "love is the conqueror," that all must yield "to woman's love." Considering the national mood, even this gentle touch becomes as clear a reproach to the hate-camp as are John Q. Adams' gracious lines "To a Lady":

> . . . nature's plan
> Is ruthless war from man to man.
> But nature . . . gave him woman on the spot . . .
> That if with man war cannot cease,
> With woman reigns eternal peace.[64]

Perhaps Sargent's refusal to be specific in the poem is motivated by the aesthetic principle which Simms enunciates, that the poet does best who:

> . . . shows us his hero but at a single moment,—speaks of him rather than presents him; and, in terms of vague eulogium, clothed in poetic beauty, renders him a graceful abstraction, the ideal of a hero, rather than the hero whom we know.[65]

Not all poets, however, are so fastidious in describing the carnage. Enraged by "the ringing of bells and the firing of cannon in celebration," one poet paints Vera Cruz "in ruins . . . Babes, matrons and maidens" lying "stiff in their gore."[66] In a blistering jeremiad, "Illumination for Victories in Mexico," Grace Greenwood denounces the gay fireworks. She reminds the celebrants that their troops have slaughtered thousands at Buena Vista, that the casualty list at Vera Cruz is swollen high "with maids and wives," that Americans have fought, "madly brave," only to be sharing "a shallow, crowded grave" on foreign soil. At this point she taunts America: "If your hearts with martial pride throb high,/Light up, light up your homes!"[67]

Some poets directly rebuke as pied pipers those who tempt the youth of the land with promises of glory: as brave men fall, thousands more rush to fill the breach "at call of drum"; they expect immortality, only to be forgotten in turn like others whose names have rung aloud for a day.[68] When a singer of Boker's skill takes up this theme, the ring of Old English poetry is heard again: "Hark to the brazen blare of the bugle . . ." Decrying the "witchery that wakes the blood" of the young, he wonders how "this marshalled pageant of shallow glory" will look after the battle begins.[69] True heroism, true glory, the prophetically-motivated poets point out, is quite another matter. Of course, not every 1846—48 poet who contrasts spiritual with physical combat may mean the Mexican War, but their insistence on the ethical basis of glory is significant. Swords and cannon they dismiss as extraneous:

> In Heaven's persuasive manner,
> Our hosts shall take the field;
> Love is our only banner,
> And truth our safest shield![70]

With much the same feeling and didactic impulse, Philip P. Cooke urges man, instead of battling his "fellow-creature," to "strive" for self-perfection through inner conflict:

> . . . in self-war—to smother
> All growth of evil nature.
> Be of the nobler spirits!
> Forgive, forget . . .[71]

By its very title, Henry T. Tuckerman's "Modern Hero" promises to defy the current definition of a much-used word. And, in fact, the poem does deny a "heritage of fame" to imperial troops:

It may no more be won in arms,
And knighthood's loyal toil,
Nor flourish, like Marengo's grain,
Upon a blood-stained soil . . .

Only such fighters deserve the hero's name and fame who remain true to themselves "Amid Opinion's tyrant bands . . ."[72]

In their thorough-going rebuttal of the laureate, the anti-war poets also repudiate his effort to link America's heritage with the conquest of Mexico. Any such comparison must prove an embarrassment to this predatory generation. Only by speaking out against the war, they boldly insist, can America's poets sustain her honor and her laws; for the nation, formerly so high in humanity's hope, now presents a sorry spectacle to the world. True to the prophet's function of setting the reality against the ideal, they contrast the glory of America's past with the iniquity to which she has stooped. James F. Clarke roars at the "degenerate sons" of the Founders:

Yes! they were men of History, and its page
Shall call their epoch our Heroic Age.
But what the Heroism of to-day?
To make a helpless neighboring State our prey![73]

In the same manner John G. Saxe observes in disgust a "degraded Congress! once the honored scene of patriot deeds."[74] But Thomas B. Read goes further. Paraphrasing Shelley's "Mask of Anarchy" he urges Americans to emulate their forefathers in Boston harbor and hurl overboard the errors of their government "like the worthless chest of tea!"[75] By far the most beautiful expression of this theme appears in Margaret Fuller's letters to the *Tribune* from

Italy, written in a rich Biblical prose unmatched either in her own tame verse or in that of most contemporaries:

> O Eagle, whose early flight showed this clear sight of the sun, how often dost thou near the ground, how show the vulture in these later days!

Among the tyrants of the world this nation is now "the darkest offender . . . her eyes fixed not on the stars, but on the possessions of other men." America, "stupid with the lust for gain," has not died:

> . . . but in my time she sleepeth, and the spirit of our fathers flames no more, but lies hid beneath the ashes . . . overgrown with gluttony and falsehood . . .[76]

The doctrine, "our country right or wrong," which the war-poets substitute for a moral base, is also attacked by those with strong ethical concern. A lofty and stinging rebuttal, and at the same time a valuable definition of Tyrtaean standards, comes from the pen of the octogenarian Adams in a group of timely, eloquent stanzas:

> And say not thou, "my country right or wrong,"
> Nor shed thy blood for an unhallowed cause.
> . . . Justice holds no balance for the strong;
> Her sword to sanction wrong she never draws.
> If, then, thy country tramples on the right,
> Furl up her banners, and avert thy sight.[77]

What most infuriates the peace poet is the endorsement, by professed Christians, of what he considers an anti-Christian crusade. Where, he asks, are God's preachers while Polk's cannon roar and their own pious followers assist the bloody work? Why should Christian nations force upon their neighbors "the cup of bitterness . . ."?[78] Channing decries the current "wars of usurpation, by which Christendom on all sides spreads civilized selfishness" while pretending to extend Christ's reign. He deplores the pulpits' "tame . . . cautious, scrupulous" position, when "a firm protest . . . against the Mexican War" is needed.[79] Taking his motto from the Sermon on the Mount, Story denounces the pious hypocrites who bless murder, from whose pulpits rise "Prayers unto the God of battles,/Not unto the God of love." His wrathful questioning recalls the old outcry against the insincere worshipers of Sodom and Gomorrah:

> Is it by a Christian people,
>   Is it in a Christian land,
> That such prayers as these are lifted,
>   Such unholy deeds are planned? . . .
> Our Religion is a pretence—
>   We have only faith in Gold?[80]

To those who encourage America's thirst for empire, the mistakes of the past are used as a warning. Adams, for example, in a particularly effective passage, asks his countrymen:

> Whose triumph waves unfurled?
> Alas! let Cheronea tell;
> Or plains where godlike Brutus fell,
> Or Caesar won the world![81]

Although Frederick G. Tuckerman seldom alludes to specific contemporary struggles, the imagery and thought development of his "Margites" represent, like those of Adams, a counter-attitude to the spread-eagle dream of his generation:

And all by waste or warfare falls,
Has gone to wreck, or crumbling goes,
Since Nero planned his golden walls,
Or the Cham Cublai built his house.[82]

At least three poets—Hoffman, Melville, and Seba Smith—deliver their attacks on expansionism in the form of satirical prose fantasy. The most skillful, extended, and influential—Smith's epistolary *My Thirty Years Out of the Senate*—shows Polk to be rabidly ambitious for re-election, glory, an increase in the power of his party, and the securing of California. A marvelous bit of fancy, with more than a grain of reality in it, is his dream of the United States transformed into a monstrous battleship and setting sail for additional conquests in Asia, Africa, and Europe—"having annexed all North and South America."[83] Hoffman's spoof letters between Taylor and the government show that Washington is determined to "make this war last," for political advantage, and is hopeful of making "a great deal of capital."[84]

Melville also uses letters as the form of his attack. Although Matthiessen finds here "an admiration for General Taylor,"[85] Old Zack is actually presented in a series of the most outlandishly ludicrous positions, such as galloping on a tack, walking "through the flames of a steamboat oven," and responding to a query about his political platform by drawing a picture of the stars and stripes.[86] There is little of literary value here; Smith does better, and Hoffman does no worse. At most it gives evidence of a saucy, but anonymous, disrespect for his nation's most sacred cow while the war rages. It is in *Mardi,* especially in the superb, significantly titled chapter, "A Voice From the Gods," that Melville's antipathy to "the evils of imperialist expansion" finds artistic and prophetic expression: "Be advised; wash your hands . . . And be not too grasping . . . It is not freedom to filch . . . Neighboring nations may be free without coming under your banner."[87] One can understand America's disapproval of this audacious and unsettling work.

Though Bronson Alcott, self-isolated from a society he despises, produces no public denunciations of the war, his influence on Thoreau and Emerson is considerable. Thoreau's inspiration for his act of civil disobedience comes from Alcott's earlier gesture, and it is with Alcott that Thoreau enjoys spiritual solidarity after his night in jail. Alcott's 1846—48 journals are rich in references to the Mexican War, sometimes clothed in language far more lyrical than any verse he ever wrote:

> I cast my silent vote for the emancipation of the human soul, amidst the plants I love . . . the winged freemen of the hives, disturbed now and then by the gunner's crack aiming death to the joyous songsters of the air and groves. They ventured not, these monstrous boys, into my coppice of protecting boughs, nor into my peaceful glebes. Ah me! War rages near me, and the fields . . . are beleaguered round with armed ruffians. Happy for myself if I am as yet a freeman, and a soul at peace . . . in thought if not in deed, independent of the States and times, an honest and upright man in the midst of my age.[88]

We have followed the almost contrapuntal activity of the minor poets: pseudo-Tyrtaean song in the service of the government's imperial aspirations, and a point by point rebuttal which, while seldom rising to the quality of prophetic utterance, does possess the vision and courage of prophecy. In certain cases we discover a rather dramatic shift away from laureateship midway through the war.

Elsewhere we encounter the contradictory ethics of abolitionists who favor expansion—on a free-soil basis. It remains for us to examine within this context the stance of the major figures who in one way or another respond significantly to the Mexican War. These include Bryant, Longfellow, Emerson, Thoreau, Whittier, and Lowell.

iv

Bryant's biographers warn us to seek not among his poems but rather in his editorials for admonitions, scoldings, and exhortations. "When he donned his singing robes and retired from . . . worldly strife," one biographer explains,[89] "he went up into a mountain . . . everything around him seemed eloquent of hope and cheer, of faith and love." Approaching him through his prose, we find that his newspaper "warmly opposed" annexation unless Mexico were consulted, and we mark the negative tone of his 1851 "Reminiscences of the *Evening Post*":

> The eager haste to snatch Texas into the Union brought with it the war in Mexico, the shedding of much blood, large conquests, California and those dreadful quarrels about slavery and its extension which have shaken the Union.[89]

We are therefore puzzled when "Oh Mother of a Mighty Race" is identified as a "militant" call "to the standard . . . for the war with Mexico."[90] There can be no doubt of its militancy; but not a single clue suggests that the poet's target is Mexico. We *do* recognize a theme popular in the war-camp of 1846: defiance of Europe, "the elder dames" who "admire and hate" America's development.

And there *is* the familiar boast that "many a fond and fearless heart" is ready to die in battle for motherland. But the foe is unspecified and, in fact, hypothetical. The current border disputes with Britain may be prompting Bryant to express his nation's resentment at British attacks on American life and letters, the most recent being Dickens' *American Notes* and *Martin Chuzzlewit*. Bryant's personal animus, aired indirectly and with dignity in this poem, can be traced to the superciliousness of British reviewers and slights by British colleagues. That he has Britain and not Mexico in mind is made clear by the lines: "Power, at thy bounds,/Stops and calls back his baffled hounds."[91] These can refer only to the Orostook and Oregon disputes.

A further consideration is the heat with which, during the Texas controversy, the usually dispassionate Bryant depicted wars of conquest. The finest of these passages occur in "To the Appenines" and "A Hymn of the Sea."[92] In the first he exclaims:

How crashed the towers before beleaguering foes,
Sacked cities smoked and realms were rent in twain;
And commonwealths against their rivals rose,
Trode out their lives and earned the curse of Cain!

The second, more obviously contemporary in attitude, contains a violent outburst against the very idea of invasion, and merits full quotation:

O God! thy justice makes the world turn pale,
When on the armèd fleet, that royally
Bears down the surges, carrying war, to smite
Some city, or invade some thoughtless realm,
Descends the fierce tornado . . .

> Downward are slung, into the fathomless gulf,
> Their cruel engines; and their hosts, arrayed
> In trappings of the battle-field, are whelmed
> By whirlpools or dashed dead upon the rocks.
> Then stand the nations still with awe, and pause,
> A moment, from the bloody work of war.

We approach Longfellow with even less hope of discovering a prophetic response to the Mexican War. The poet was, we are told,[93] devoid of "righteous indignation . . . or even the all-inclusive pity that blossoms as gentle humanitarianism. All his emotions were second-hand, bookish." It becomes apparent, however, that those who deny him as a man "the heights and depths of passion" have ignored his notebooks. On the topic we are pursuing here, Longfellow's journal is neither mute nor ambiguous.[94] Deploring the lack of interest felt by his community "in this shabby and to us disgraceful war with Mexico," he lauds an old neighbor for having "expressed his great disgust at our republic's breeding ill-blood between itself and a sister republic." He praises a sermon "against the unrighteous Mexican war," and—along with Channing—argues that more of the same from many pulpits might have stopped the war. Like Grace Greenwood he is dismayed by the ringing of church-bells on the victory of Vera Cruz, and attacks the "intellectual legerdemain" by which "murder becomes glory instead of crime, when the amount is large enough, as in battle . . ."

Although, as is usual with him, he holds back from turning the current unpleasant news into poetry, one lyric suddenly takes shape.[95] The subject is Tegner's death, and the imagery is Norse, but the propelling force is the current war against which he is so enraged. Apocalyptically, in a time of wild hate, he offers his people a vision of peace and love:

> The law of force is dead!
> The law of love prevails!
> Thor, the thunderer,
> Shall rule the earth no more,
> No more, with threats,
> Challenge the meek Christ.

In a time when certain poets are enlisting their craft in the service of a war-machine, he contrasts their glorification of conquest with the function of authentic prophecy:

> Sing no more,
> O ye bards of the North,
> Of Vikings and of Jarls!
> Of the days of Eld
> Preserve the freedom only,
> Not the deeds of blood!

Within the next few years Longfellow produces a number of passages that seem colored by his disgust with the Mexican adventure, but it is not until 1855 that he writes his only poem actually based on an incident of the war. That America's favorite balladeer should choose to commemorate nothing of the great Monterey victory but a bugler's execution for breach of discipline is in itself a commentary on the Mexican War. Closing his song with the bugle's ghostly sound, Longfellow unleashes "the wraith of Victor Galbraith" to haunt the land.[96]

From Emerson we expect perhaps the least in terms of war-verse, since his insistence on the self as "our private theater"[97] dominates his characteristic poetry, and his participation in public affairs is almost always reluctant. Early in his career he had explained the responsibility of a poet: to fetch home from "the god of the wood" the liberating word. War, and the tyrant responsible for it, must eventually succumb to "Merlin's mighty line"; the tempest is to be stilled by songs that "bring in poetic peace."[98] Consistent with this platform is the famous anecdote, probably apocryphal but certainly vivid, of Thoreau's rebuke to his unhappy visitor at Concord jail. To Alcott, Emerson expresses the view that Thoreau's anti-war act is "mean and skulking, and in bad taste."[99] All of this, and the five pages in his journal, devoted to a criticism of his friend's civil disobedience, might lead the reader to suspect a softness of principle: one should, Emerson insists, wait as Socrates and Christ did for a "good case to try the question on"; the Mexican War tax issue is "a tottering cause"; besides, Thoreau's quarrel is really with mankind, not the war government . . .[100] In his only poem with clear reference to the Mexican War, Emerson preaches that excited opposition is unnecessary, since "The over-god . . . Knows to bring honey/Out of the lion."[101] Obviously, the practical effect of such a doctrine at a time of intense political upheaval can be paralyzing; even Alcott, his most loyal friend, decries its implications.[102]

Nevertheless, the indictment of the nation is as scathing in this poem as in anything we have studied:

> Behold the famous States
> Harrying Mexico
> With rifle and with knife! . . .
>
> Virtue palters; Right is hence;
> Freedom praised, but hid;
> Funeral eloquence
> Rattles the coffin-lid.

Equally bitter, bold, and clear-sighted is his journal for 1846. Mocking the flag-wavers who reserve "patriotism for holidays and summer evening, with music and rockets," Emerson attacks the Church for not grappling with the "moral evil" of slavery or war.[103] From the American government "no act of honour or benevolence or justice is to be expected . . . they will be as wicked as they dare."[104] As for the people, they are "no worse since they invaded Mexico than they were before, only they have given their will a deed." In Jeremiah's voice he warns that the "lust of extending their territory" will "poison" the United States, "as the man swallows the arsenic . . ." It will "enlarge the land but dwarf the men." The only cure he offers "the bad world," however, is not to "impeach Polk and Webster," but to "supersede them by the Muse." In other words, Merlin remains his hope:

> The rhyme of the poet
> Modulates the king's affairs . . .[105]

The only poets of 1846—48 to whom such terms of political effectiveness might conceivably apply are Whittier and Lowell. It is doubtful, however, whether theirs is the kind of rhyme or the kind of effectiveness Emerson has in mind. Certainly they would have to respond splendidly indeed to match the prophetic power of Emerson's journal entries. Before turning to their work, however, let us examine the conscience of Emerson's town in its most eloquent manifestation, more eloquent than even "the Sage" could accept.

As with Bryant, we approach not the verse but the prose of Thoreau for any expression of the prophet's denunciatory impulse. And we are not disappointed. Chapter XII of *Walden,* meaningfully titled "Brute Neighbors," contains the one immortal prose satire born of the Mexican War.[106] With Swiftian skill Thoreau reports "a *bellum,* a war between two races of ants" which "never let go, but struggled and wrestled . . ." The black ant, reminiscent of the United States, was "much larger," and there were "frequently two red ones [Mexicans] to one black." The brutality of the current war is evoked as he shows "the legions of these Myrmidons" covering "all the hills and vales" until "the ground was . . . strewn with the dead and dying" of both sides. The "red republicans" and the "black imperialists" battled in "a little sunny valley . . till the sun [Mexico's symbol] went down." The "stronger black one [with modern equipment] had already divested him of several of his members [New Mexico and California]." Their slogan—like Park Benjamin's, for example—was "Conquer or die." In a brilliant thrust at the mistrels of 1846, Thoreau imagines "their respective musical bands . . . playing their national airs . . . to excite the slow and cheer the dying combatants." Diabolically he mimics the pseudo-Tyrtaean songs that have swarmed into being after each victory: ". . . there is not the fight . . . in Concord history . . . that will bear . . . comparison with this . . . for the patriotism and heroism displayed . . ." Taking up "the chip" on which they struggled, he wonders what "the cause of war" might be, and sardonically contrasts the current motives with those of 1775: "I have no doubt that it was a principle they fought for, as much as our ancestors . . ." Lest his intention be unclear, the poet closes by telling us that the battle "took place in the Presidency of Polk." Deftly, right near the end of *Walden,* he plants a final clue on that battle of the "ants," which was fought for a "chip," by using "chip" as a simile for "Empire."

In "Civil Disobedience," illustrating his definition of the

prophet-hero, Thoreau stands before his neighbors at the height of the war and condemns the evils of *his time and place*.[107] Inciting "honest men" to revolt against a nation which "unjustly overruns a whole country," he fairly shouts at his generation: ". . . cease . . . to make war on Mexico . . . " In 1846, he tells them, "the true place for a just man is . . . a prison." Levelling his most profound challenge at the "expediency" of the Northern mind as represented by Webster, Thoreau forces his listeners to set off the reality of the present against the larger truth glimpsed by "those who legislate for all time"—that "the world is not governed by policy and expediency."

The legislators who voted for war, the celebrants of victory, did not heed him. But what we are concerned with is his need to utter the cry of defiance. If any American poet is possessed of prophecy, it is the Thoreau of "Brute Neighbors" and "Civil Disobedience." Yet even those great prose indictments against the ugliness of his time are eclipsed by one simple, deliberate act of July, 1846, that comes flaming down the years.

We have observed Whittier's response to the annexation of Texas: vague on expansionism, violent on the extension of slavery. The coming of the war does not much alter this.[108] He reprimands himself for hating evil-doers: when he hears "the battle's groan of pain" and sees "smooth-faced Mammon/Reaping men like grain," he asks whether his own actions would be better than those of the war-lords, were he in their place. Only brotherly love, he concludes, can silence "the stormy clangor/Of wild war music . . ." When he rouses to action, it is not for peace, but for the familiar "home and freedom . . . God and Massachusetts . . ." True, his leading question is reminiscent of much anti-war verse: "Is the dollar only real? God and truth and right a dream?" But for him slavery remains the exclusive issue: whether or not to "barter men for cotton." When he does finally indicate a position on the war, it is to warn Southern statesmen that the very door through which "slave-cursed Texas entered in" may ironically turn the balance against the slavocracy. Free-soil settlements, he prophesies, may emerge:

> From out the blood and fire, the wrong and sin,
> Of the stormed city and the ghastly plain,
> Beat by hot hail, and wet with bloody rain . . .

In other words, the conquest of Mexico, unpleasant though it may be, will have its compensations when the West joins the North to "heave the engineer of evil with his mine." This is the abolitionist thinking which Emerson satirizes, yet it parallels his own views on evil.

As uncompromising as his heroes, Ezekiel and Xavier, Whittier pictures the "grave men" of the war-time Congress groping in the dust for "largess, base and small," and vilely bartering "Honor's wealth for party's place." True to his mission, he evokes for his countrymen "the old heroic spirit of our earlier, better day," and condemns their "Christless church"; but his target is not the war. He joins battle boldly against the pious hypocrites who seek the Lord's blessing and raise "hands of blood" to heaven. As did the "prophet bards of old," he seeks "Words of power and fear" in order to move "a scornful people, . . . unmask the priestly thieves . . ." But there is still no hint that he has in mind the war raging at this time.

The first significant reference occurs in "Yorktown,"[109] which forcefully develops the theme of national betrayal, comparing America's war of independence with its current predatory adventure:

Where's now the flag of that old war?
Where flows its stripe? Where burns its star?
Bear witness, Palo Alto's day,
Dark Vale of Palms, red Monterey,
Where Mexic Freedom, young and weak,
Fleshes the Northern eagle's beak;
Symbol of terror and despair . . .

Laugh, Russia, from thy Neva's banks!
Brave sport to see the fledgling born
Of Freedom by its parent torn! . . .

Afterward, like Hoffman and English, he produces a ballad in which the speaker is Mexican.[110] Without the rich artistry of *Childe Harold* he conjures up Byronically the atmosphere of war: "Hark! that sudden blast of bugles! . . . friend and foe together fall . . ." The Americans are named "invaders," and the "Northern eagle" is seen as a horrifying emblem, while "the noble Mexic women" are shown pursuing their "holy task" amid the carnage, blessed by the dying invader and cursing those who led him to his doom. As in the ballads of Sargent and Simms, the main point is sentimental: "From its smoking hell of battle, Love and Pity send their prayer."

The most revealing of Whittier's Mexican War poems is "The Crisis." In seventy-two "fourteeners" the poet offers not one syllable of shame or regret, though he writes these lines "on learning the terms of the treaty." How the new lands have been won is evidently of no concern. He suggests that the valley of the Rio Bravo allow its "simple children" to weep. An anti-expansionist poet, however, would direct the *victors* to weep. The coming of "the pale land-seekers" does not bother him; all that matters is whether "the soil of new-gained empire" will be sown by freedom or slavery: ". . . shall the Evil triumph, and robber Wrong prevail?"[111] That he should be asking this *after* Mexico's destruction is ultimate proof of a severe ethical limitation. This, for a poet of such great moral sensitivity as Whittier claims, constitutes an important failure.

Lowell's emphasis, on the other hand, is anti-imperialist, though he is always conscious of slavery as a concomitant issue. Even prior to the war his poems challenge the spread-eagle spirit of the Polk administration.[112] Repeating the imagery of Ozymandias, he tells how the ghosts of ancient empire warn America that the "mighty clamors, wars, and world-noised deeds" of earlier times "Are silent now in dust." Along with this lesson from the past, he once again verbalizes the people's eternal longing for a time when "no war-trump's brawling clangor" will be heard.

In "An Interview With Miles Standish," Lowell taps the rich vein of satire from which he is soon to draw Biglow. Unlike those who have decked "Freedom's coffin" while "all within was rotten," the lively ghost of Standish rises to decry "his country's shame" and to scoff at the "loud ancestral boasts" of after-dinner speakers who made no speeches "when slavery grasped at Texas."[113]

Aside from "The Biglow Papers" Lowell's most noteworthy statement on the Mexican War is an admonitory passage of blank verse, "An Extract." Conquest, the poet warns his arrogant nation, is only geographic. The conquerors lose more than they gain; they become murderers, or are maimed "in the fierce apprenticeship," or die, leaving widows and orphans behind. Though the world pays its respects to "the tyrannous lion" which "preys upon the lamb," it is the respect of fear. A second war poem, "The Falconer," presents America in equally predatory terms:

The herd of patriot wolves, that, stealing,
To gorge on martyred Freedom run,
Fly, howling, when his shadow, wheeling,
Flashes between them and the sun;
Well for them that our once proud eagle
Forgets his empire of the sky,
And, stript of every emblem regal,
Does buzzard's work for slavery.

Only an emasculated remnant of that indictment appears in the collected poems as "The Falcon," without a hint as to its original denunciatory impulse. And "The Extract" is entirely excluded.[114]

Whether these two omissions reflect an ethical or an aesthetic revision is difficult to determine. In the first place, even if Margaret Fuller had not bludgeoned him for being "absolutely wanting in the true spirit and tone of poesy" and for supplying his lack of vitality by means of "his interest in the moral questions of the day,"[115] there is enough of the same sentiment within himself to warrant stern self-censorship. Then, too, by 1859 he can speak in the past tense of his belief that the Mexican adventure was "a war of false pretences" and in the present tense of his belief in "the manifest destiny of the English race to occupy this whole continent . . ."[116] Why, then, does he retain "The Biglow Papers"? Perhaps because they are, after all, the foundation of his fame, and too universally circulated to be dropped into oblivion. Besides, as satire, they have a wider political berth than do such lyrics as "The Falconer" or "An Abstract." We might note in this connection that Story and Read also exclude from their collections the vigorous denunciatory verses of 1846—47. It is, of course, possible that these fledgling poets are being careful not to antagonize reviewers and readers. In the case of

Read, however, a change of heart similar to Lowell's is indicated in later poems such as "The Death of the Veteran," a long nationalistic ballad of the Mexican War, and "The New Pastoral," a pioneer epic which celebrates the westward surge. On another level, Story's increasing immersion in aestheticism parallels Lowell's shift of interest from issues of current concern.

Turning to "The Biglow Papers"[117] we soon discover ourselves on familiar ground. Lowell's arguments against, and illustrations of, American folly are not in any sense original; many of his materials have originated in the daily press, and are being turned into verse and prose by supporters of both camps, such as we have quoted. Why go over the ground again? Because there is no better gauge of Lowell's satiric genius and moral stature than the use to which his contemporaries put the same materials. The poet explains his purpose: "As Truth and Falsehood start from the same point, and sometimes even go along together for a little way," the true satirist's "business is to follow" Falsehood on its diverging path, "and to show her floundering in the bog at the end of it." Thus, every war argument is exposed to his cruel light.

Refuting those minstrels who attempt to mask war in "eppyletts an' feathers," he shows it to be murder, not glory, and taunts the "bold" drumbeaters for not themselves volunteering rather than inspiring others to lose an arm, an eye, or a leg. Reminding Massachusetts of her heritage, he shows what sort of bird is nowadays being hatched in "her grand old eagle-nest," creatures such as Birdofredum Sawin who enlist for no better motive than gold, glory, and fun. More effectively than by a frontal assault, Lowell shatters the myth of liberation through an ingenuous comment by the recruit: "Asshelterin' " the Mexican "under our eagle's pinions," properly translated, means to "walk him . . . right out o' all his homes an' houses." In the same way the poet blasts—through the lips of its adherents—the widely used religious argument of bringing civilization to Mexico and winning its good will:

> I du believe wutever trash
> 'll keep the people in blindness,—
> Thet we the Mexicuns can thrash
> Right inter brotherly kindness,
> Thet bombshells, grap, an' powder 'n' ball
> Air good-will's strongest magnets,
> Thet peace, to make it stick at all,
> Must be druv in with bagnets.

Particularly strong is Lowell's attack on false piety, a theme which arouses several minor poets too, as we have noted. Sardonically he suggests that Satan, not God, is at the head of the Americans who win Sunday victories "with a Protestant fervor"; and he exposes the anti-Papism of the crusade as a cloak for aggrandizement. The beliefs of Catholics, he sneers, "excite our horror in exact proportion to the size and desirableness of their vineyards." Nor does he hesitate to remind his New England neighbors that Northern expansionism is no less rampant than the Southern breed, that "Anglo-Saxon blood" has given the North an equal "hankering after mud . . ." Other poets lament the eagle's changed status from symbol of freedom to bird of prey, as does Lowell himself; but here, in a master stroke, he depicts the expansionists' pique when they hear the reaction of the appalled world to their Mexican operation. They themselves are made to paraphrase the charge:

. . . thet our naytional eagle
Wun't much longer be classed with the birds that air regal,
Coz theirn be hooked beaks, an' shee, arter this slaughter
'll bring back a bill ten times longer 'n she 'd ough' to . . .

Against the more blatant characteristics of the war-camp, Lowell's thrusts are equally severe. Mercilessly he portrays the ugliness of national arrogance. The Anglo-Saxon attitude that Simms and others are at the same moment trying to dignify in their chivalric rhymes is here laid bare in all its grotesque ferocity—not by Lowell, but by Sawin the volunteer! Since "Mexicans worn't human beans," he argues, it wasn't proper for the "ourang outang nation" to "shoot . . . at us . . ." Instead they ought to have stood "right up an' let us pop 'em fairly . . ." The satirist also has something to say about the war-poets who are so eager to impress Europe with America's imperial muscles. God may not find our aggression pleasing, he has an apologist admit, but what matters is that "it makes us thought highly on . . . abroad." Nor does Lowell ignore the mystique of blind loyalty which many laureates substitute for a genuine motive. With imaginative exuberance he traces the origin of the phrase "Our country, right or wrong," to a "speech . . . at a dinner of the Bungtown Fencibles"; then, suddenly shifting to the magnificent seriousness of high prophecy, he declares "our true country" to be "that ideal realm . . . bounded on the north and the south, on the east and the west, by Justice . . ."

Directing his savage laughter to the current deification of military heroes, he blasts them with the vigor we have seen in other poets, along with a controlled diabolism missing in their work. For example, he allows an admiring voter to tell why he advocates the election of "General C.":

He don't vally princerple more 'n an old cud;
Wut did God make us raytional creeturs fer,
But glory an' gunpowder, plunder an' blood?

With more artistry, imaginative wit, and restraint than we find in Melville and the other prose satirists of the war, Lowell punctures General Taylor's vaunted gentleness by having Biglow receive a letter in which a military candidate expresses horror at "abstract war" while endorsing the "powder-cart" upon which "civlyzation *does* git forrid/ Sometimes . . ." The effort then being pushed to make "The Father o' his Country's shoes" fit Taylor's feet, is hilariously ruined, as is the General's pitiful attempt at "definin' his posishin"—which culminates in the discovery that "he aint gut nothin' to define."

Toward the close, perhaps, Lowell's didacticism occasionally shows unpleasantly, but he is at the same time remaining true to his prophetic aims: offering not only admonition and indictment, but also a vision and an alternative. As in "An Abstract," he rejects the hope that victory over Mexico will settle matters: " 't 'll take more fish-skin than folks think to take the rile clean out on 't . . ." He does, however, indicate for the "bad world" a cure which is rather more simple, concrete, and superficial than Emerson's: the coming third-party convention in Buffalo.

That Lowell manages to fuse the entire spectrum of arguments and sentiments regarding the war, along with much on the slavery issue, as well as a great deal of appropriate scholarly background, is a remarkable accomplishment. It is not difficult to understand, but vital for us to note, why Lowell's contemporaries took *Biglow* to their hearts. In the first place the poet is expressing, "in witty and homely phrases," ideas natural to his readers and already "half-consciously formed in many brains."[118] Thus he fulfills his own prophetic definition by taking mankind's distress "to his heart with large embrace"; and, by using their own vigorous, picturesque language, he becomes in fact "the tongue/Of the weak and spirit-wrung . . ."[119] As for his prosody, the imperative nature of the message compels him to find "a catching rhythm and a refrain" that will "sing itself into the memory . . ."[120]

But if this were all, the Biglow poems would have died with the cause. Yet almost sixty years afterward an admiring Brander Matthews must seek some lame excuse for the failure of later satirists to match the triumph of *Biglow* (as if Lowell did not also "shoot his shafts one by one in the papers . . ."[120]) And in 1912 a "devil's advocate" of the Mexican War—or any other war the American government might ever decide to undertake—finds it necessary to challenge Lowell's arguments, one by one, furious that the negative attitude toward our first imperial adventure has "grown venerable with age"[121] thanks to the continuing influence of *Biglow*.

To call Lowell's masterpiece a "black and sticky ball of odium" is to ignore the wild hilarity of his controlled dismay, the uncompromising honesty with which he contrasts the nation's ideal and its reality, the unforgettable personae in which he embodies the American psyche of 1846. Finally, to say that "any stick is good enough to beat a dog with," and to accuse Lowell of laying about him "with a somewhat careless aim,"[121] is to deny the deliberate and masterly way in which Lowell has chosen not only his meters, but also his targets, sparing not a single point raised by our minstrels in their effort to make the Mexican War look right.

We have examined the record of sensitivity to America's first great expansionist action, on the part of her poets. The ledger shows—especially among the major figures—a definite balance on the side of direct, sometimes audacious opposition, to the point of aiding and abetting the enemy during wartime. Among those on the other side are some who admittedly celebrate the invasion on chivalric rather than ethical grounds, thus giving comfort and encouragement to a far from chivalric operation. But it would be unfair to imply that they thereby consciously betray the prophetic tradition, since they are celebrating heroes, exhorting their nation to brave and united deeds, and—especially in the case of Whitman—evoking the great old vision of an eagle bearing liberty and civilization westward. Some poets are obviously ambivalent; at first praising the heroism of American troops, they eventually laud the defeated enemy as well, and lament the agonies of the war without claiming for it any justification. On the other hand, some who become established poets apparently shift in later years from their sharp opposition. There are those, including Emerson, whose philosophic concept of evil may mute their denunciations somewhat, and others, like Whittier, whose abolitionist fervor limits the range of their ethical warfare. Many take no public stand at all; they are silent for a variety of reasons: despairing of an audience; refusing to be drawn away from what they deem a poet's necessary tower; fearing to be identified with a partisan and unpopular segment of the political world; registering their disapproval of the war, as Holmes does,[122] by simply not hailing the victories; or—as is the case with Poe—escaping in total revulsion from the "business" of his countrymen.

Certainly, on this issue at least, American poets deserve to be credited as the conscience of their time. For, while many voices rise indignantly, the American government receives almost no significant poetic support in its conquest of Mexico, and the most considerable body of pro-war verse, Simms' *Lays of the Palmetto,* is to be totally rejected by its author within five years.

2

The Return of Fugitive Slaves to Their Masters

Among the touchstones for a study of this kind, the Fugitive Slave issue would seem to be a natural choice. Ever since the constitutional debate and compromise of 1793 it had served to emphasize the central question: are slaves to be regarded as things or men? The flight of Negroes, increasing steadily after 1800, provided abolition with dramatic, often thrilling proof of slavery's unendurability and of a universal yearning for freedom. After 1840, the choice of sheltering or returning fugitives wracked the nation politically, legally, ethically, and—at last—more than any other factor in the slavery wrangle, brought on the debate of guns.

Even if the rest of the world were not watching carefully, even if Britain had not led the way by emancipating its West Indian slaves, one would expect to find considerable evidence—among those American poets with high moral pretensions at least—of conscience pangs at their inability to reconcile slavery with the Declaration of Independence. Those less concerned with the contrast between America's ideals and realities might still be expected to use fugitive slave material for sentimental or narrative purposes, or at least to record their awareness of a major current issue. It is claimed that passage of the Fugitive Slave Act and "subsequent attempts to enforce it" inspired an extraordinary growth in the anti-slavery movement and most of the anti-slavery literature from 1850 to 1860.[1] If this is so, and if poets do indeed give voice to the ethical unease of their time, our search should yield a harvest of forgotten verse on this theme.

i

Obviously, our highest expectations must lie in the camp of active abolition, which is alert to events and prone to versify them. Although the abolitionist leaders who write verse do not rank high, they do consciously wear the mantle of prophecy and some of them enjoy reputations as poets in ante-bellum America. The top echelon includes Theodore Parker, Maria W. Chapman, and William L. Garrison. What inspires the verse of Parker are such subjects as the martyrdom of slave-rescuers "who toil to save" their brothers, Webster's "stained and dishonored brow" after his Fugitive Slave Law efforts in 1850, and Massachusetts' role as slave-catcher in 1851.[2] It is not easy to equate his ineffectual stanzas with his fiery rescue activities or with his Biblical utterances on this theme. Yet even his sermons indicate that his interest is not in the fugitive, but in challenging the law that seeks to forbid such interest:

> To law framed of such iniquity I owe no allegiance . . . I will shelter, I will help, and I will defend the fugitive with all my humble means and power . . . I will act . . . to nullify and defeat the operation of this law . . .[3]

An identical impression emerges from Mrs. Chapman's few early poems on this issue.[4] Her enthusiasm wakes at any opportunity to challenge the government. Thus, while rebelliousness is almost tangible in her poems, the fugitive is a vague, unreal figure. Using as a title the words of the hated law, "Fugitive slaves shall be returned," she announces total resistance to hunter, lawyer, and writ: "You cross no freeman's door." Elsewhere she weaves into her verses the abolition slogan, "Resistance to tyrants is duty to God!" and encourages her neighbors to shelter the slave—not as an act of kindness but of rebellion! She makes her position clear in essays of 1850 and 1853 deploring the ambitious efforts on behalf of escaped slaves; to set up vigilance committees and underground railroads, she charges, is to "hide from tyranny, instead of defying it." This attitude may explain the relative dearth of poems on the fugitive in her *Songs of the Free* and in *The Liberty Bell,* the annual she edits.

Garrison shares neither Parker's disapproval of slave-rescue by purchase, nor Mrs. Chapman's criticism of the underground railroad. Though his poems[5] are not directly devoted to the plight of the fugitive, his sympathy is revealed in tributes to Lundy and Hopper, the great pioneer slave-rescuers. Like his colleagues he boldly urges Americans to break unjust laws, since the right to freedom is "Heaven's eternal decree." But his commitment goes further than theirs. Not only is he willing to die for all who are enslaved, but also to deprive "the spoiler of his prey." The simple, personal way in which Garrison defends this commitment is moving. Instead of creating, as professional poets do, a hackneyed figure of the panting, bleeding runaway slave who cries out in unbelievably eloquent rhetoric against the slave-society, Garrison imagines, in "Liberty and Slavery," how he might feel if he himself were a slave:

> If my loved wife could from my fond embrace
> Be wrested, flogged, defiled before my face;
> If the dear children, granted me by Heaven,
> Could to the shambles be like cattle driven . . .
> How would my spirit yearn for liberty!
> How would I supplicate to be set free!
> By day, by night, plot how my chains to break,
> And with my wife and children to escape . . .
> And therefore do I cease not to proclaim
> My country's guilt, barbarity and shame.

The difference is clear: while Garrison is infuriated *on behalf* of the fugitive, Parker and Mrs. Chapman *use* the fugitive on behalf of their fury.

Maria W. Lowell, Eliza L. Follen and Lydia M. Child, among the most well-regarded poets in abolition's upper ranks, omit the fugitive slave issue entirely from their published verse, except for several atmospheric songs in an 1858 melodrama by Mrs. Child.[6] Perhaps, with Mrs. Chapman and others, they deplore the emphasis on helping runaways; yet fugitives *are* frequently aided by the Lowells, and Mrs. Child in 1860 issues a spectacular appeal to the conscience of the Massachusetts legislators, a high-water mark in her long public career, and far closer to poetry than are any of her poems:[7]

> Shame on my native State! Everlasting shame! Blot out the escutcheon of the brave old Commonwealth! Instead of the sword uplifted to protect liberty, let the slave-driver's whip be suspended over a bloodhound, and take for your motto, Obedience to tyrants is the highest law.

The fact that neither she nor any other poet of note ever turns an actual slave rescue into narrative verse, though several lesser versifiers do, is made more puzzling by her declaration that "there are no incidents in history, or romance, more thrilling than the sufferings, perils, and hairbreadth escapes of American slaves." Why is she content to predict that "in future ages, popular ballads will be sung to commemorate their heroic achievements," rather than make the effort herself? Her biography of Isaac Hopper swarms with escapes, yet—except for a few simulated Negro songs in a play—not the shadow of a runaway slave crosses the pages of her verse!

There are, however, a few national figures in the anti-slavery movement whose verse does include the fugitive. The songs of Elizur Wright, Benjamin S. Jones, and Charles C. Burleigh, presented in the voice of the Negro himself, repeat the formulae found in dozens of other verses: wife and children beaten, sold, scattered; a feeling of weariness, hunger, and pain; the north wind and north star as companion and guide; and, inevitably, the pursuing pack:

> "The hounds are baying on my track"—(Wright, 1850)[8]
> "The bloodhounds follow on my track"—(Jones, 1852)
> "The dogs are howling on my track"—(Burleigh, 1858)[9]

William Goodell, on the other hand, focuses not on the

fugitive, but on the Christian's duty to disobey the 1850 Law. Taking his title from Isaiah, he assumes—as Isaiah does—the voice of God, and demands that his hearers "Hide the outcasts . . . Scorn the mandates of transgressors . . ."[10]

We find poets among the regionally prominent activists too. One of these, Dr. E. H. Hudson, is imprisoned in Springfield for his role in a slave rescue. Shortly before the Latimer case of 1842, Hudson writes two long poems:[11] one describing a runaway's terror in flight and pledging to guard him from the "hyena-fangs of Law," the other a Negro's song of triumph at having "gained the land of Canada." But Hudson is an exception. For these poets the usual tone is not compassion for the slave but wrath against Webster, Fillmore, and their 1850 Law. When specific cases are mentioned, it is generally to praise the martyred liberator of Negroes rather than the runaways themselves. Thus Sophia L. Little of Pawtucket, in her blank verse drama, *The Branded Hand,* eulogizes the celebrated slave-rescuer, Jonathan Walker.

It is dangerous to assume that one author's predilections and reticences reflect those of another; but we do learn something by seeing an artist at the moment of response. Mrs. Little's preface to her play offers such an insight.[12] She has not dared to represent Walker exactly, because "no imagination can ever reach the real beauty of character of those now immured in Southern dungeons." At the same time she has given to the slaves "that exaltation of character which, though rare, yet is seen among them." The implication is clear: exaltation of character is as rare among slaves as "beauty of character" is typical of their white rescuers. This view of the fugitive as worthy of pity rather than panegyric is consistent with the generally patronizing tone of anti-slavery poets. Almost no references appear in their work to Harriet Tubman, Sojourner Truth, or other Negro underground railroad conductors who toiled harder, better, and longer than either Jonathan Walker or John Brown.

A year after the capture of Thomas Sims, Mrs. Little produces a long, denunciatory outcry, "The Sims Storm." Here again she pays small heed to "poor Sims" while castigating the dying Webster and the opportunistic Fillmore, "sleek puppet of the times." This piece, which often verges on authentic poetry, especially in its storm image, ultimately fails because she descends to shrill namecalling and gleeful predictions of Webster's death.[13] A year later she produces an equally inflammatory novel, *Thrice Through the Furnace,* as a "testimony against the Fugitive Slave Law." The strong impulse for prophecy in all of Sophia Little's work is illustrated in her introductory remarks:

> I wished that my feelings, concerning that law, should reach the ears of the people. I know that we overcome "by the blood of the lamb and the word of our testimony." I considered the mode here adopted, the surest method of access to the people . . .[14]

We cannot leave the work of the abolition camp without noting that host of obscure versifiers who contribute, often anonymously, to the fugitive slave literature. They usually sound like each other, or like Whittier at his most strident and undisciplined moments, or like such overseas idols as Thomas Hood and Charles Mackay. Several, however, write with ardent regularity, and in some cases with popular success; to pass them by would be to ignore the typical—that great flat mass without which the peaks are not peaks.

These writers are as facile as those we have already discussed, and equally ferocious in their assault on the government. They differ markedly, however, in the greater variety of their response, including every aspect of the theme.[15] Also notable is the dating of that response *after* Webster's March 7, 1850, address, in almost all of their many fugitive slave poems. This sharp difference is understandable: in the first place, limited neither by the doctrinal bickerings of abolition's upper echelon, nor by aesthetic restraints and professional fears of nationally respected poets, they can respond wholeheartedly to whatever moves them. Besides, their special anti-slavery world, even more than the workaday world, has been turned upside down by the events beginning with Webster's speech. The times call for great prophetic verse which (with few exceptions) is not forthcoming; great in their sensitivity to the ethical ramifications of those events, and greatly challenged by the vacuum of silence, they raise their little voices as greatly as they can, and thousands who hunger for prophecy applaud.

George W. Putnam is the most gifted of the group, as can be seen in "The Builders" and his fine stanzas marking Commissioner Loring's death. Popular in the anti-slavery ranks because he produces poems at moments of greatest heat and recites them with vigor, Putnam unfortunately often substitutes bombast and length for imagination and grace.

It would be foolish to represent any one of these minstrels of the anti-slavery movement as a serious poet; yet their work provides a framework for what Whittier, Thoreau, and Whitman are doing with the same themes at the same moment, and they do try to carry the flame of prophecy even if they are unable to give it memorable form. At least they are gratefully aware of a truly prophetic manifestation when it occurs. Thus Bungay extols George B. Cheever in 1858 for unlinking a chain with every brave word while "The watchmen upon Zion's walls/Are drugged to dreams and silent sleep."[16] What Frances D. Gage writes in a rather poignant preface to one of her effusions, applies to this entire group:

> If your heart has burned with as deep an indignation as mine has, since the passage of that Fugitive Law, it must be pretty well charred . . . Oh that I had the inspiration of a Shakespeare, a Byron, or even a Hemans or an Osgood . . . Blame me not if my song is tame. My spirit is not.[17]

The verses examined thus far belong to the category of party utterance. This is not to say that they are all artistically feeble, but that the poet's essential concern is not aesthetic. They spring from an indignant soil; their urge is not *to sing,* but *to battle slavery* in song. The writers to be considered next, however, take their art very seriously. They may be no less political and no more lyrical than Garrison and Mrs. Chapman; but—whether or not their work achieves beauty of form—that beauty is consciously sought.

Historians, as we have noted, stress a tremendous increase in anti-slavery literature after the passage of the 1850 Law and the efforts to enforce it. If such an increase includes poets who were hitherto silent on slavery, it will have considerable bearing on our test of the prophetic impulse. If, on the other hand, no such phenomenon occurs, we will have to seek the reasons—remembering, for instance, that there are in 1850 quite a few hopeful young poets with frail reputations at the mercy of publishers and critics. At a time when even established writers are being damaged by daring to take a public stand against slavery, any newcomer mentioning the touchy fugitive issue will be showing a maximum of zeal and a minimum of discretion.

ii

We find that most of the respectable minor poets functioning between 1835 and 1860 publish no verse on this issue. The factors behind their silence are, of course, as diversified as are the poets themselves. Among the older writers, for example, Sarah J. Hale avoids controversy in her poems, but in her novels she battles "the inflammatory influence of 'Uncle Tom's Cabin,' " and in *Godey's* she attacks those "who would have severed the Union rather than see a slave within its borders."[18] James G. Percival, in his idealistic days of youth, sang of New England's sons rising to unlock "Slavery's galling chains." By 1852 he shows that his concern, like Mrs. Hale's, is to keep the "chain of union . . . bright."[19]

John Q. Adams, on the other hand, moves closer to abolition in his final decade. Although his verse omits the fugitive, he does publish inspired anti-slavery sonnets, and in fiery stanzas directed at his colleagues in the House of Representatives he appeals for swift emancipation.[20] Moreover, he undertakes, with brilliant success, the legal defense of the fugitive slave leader, Cinquez.

Much younger than Adams, Nathaniel P. Willis is creatively spent by 1840, at least as a poet. This does not, however, explain *his* avoidance of the fugitive slave theme. Even in his prime, preferring the reputation of a wit, he shunned controversy, and kept out of his collections his sole anti-slavery poem, with its surprisingly strong lines:

"When the fettered slave is loose,/We shall be truly free." Although he never abandons the ethical position stated in that poem, his aesthetic position is even more adamantly maintained. Willis' stubborn rejection of the prophetic role is significantly challenged in a self-revealing comment by Whittier:

> . . . his delicate muse . . . has been too much employed in the weightier matters of rouge and raven tresses. It ill becomes a Poet to tread thus indifferently over the soil of freedom. Liberty . . . has won its holiest triumphs in the region of song. Why does not N. P. Willis dedicate his rich gift in the cause of freedom, and thus acquire a name that would live on the records of humanity in imperishable brightness . . .[21]

We turn next to a group whose creative years are not yet behind them, and whose collected poems appear at the height of the controversy. Without referring to slavery, these Northern poets make clear their position on the Fugitive Slave Law. Typical is George P. Morris,[22] who vows that the compact will be preserved, and calls every disunionist "a traitor." That Morris does not mean the Southern advocates of disunion is plain. His tribute to the cotton society is hearty indeed.

> Old Cotton is King, boys . . .
> And his is the sceptre of right . . .
> Old Cotton will pleasantly reign . . .
> And ever and ever remain
> The mightiest monarch of all . . .

Similarly, William H. C. Hosmer,[23] at the time of the Burns affair in 1854, echoes the charge of treason against anyone "Whose lip ever mutters that foul word—'Disunion!' " His dirge for Webster thrusts directly at the enemies of the Fugitive Slave Law:

> Discordant horn in vain sedition blew,
> While pale with fear the front of Treason grew.
> Unawed by threats he gave the stroke of fate
> To howling Faction, Fraud, and bark of Hate . . .

This may be dull, but its intention is to stir. Our touchstones for prophecy are clearly two-sided. There *are* responsible poets who genuinely support the March 7th speech and the Fugitive Slave Law. Webster and Union are passionately praised—not only by those who have never taken a stand on slavery, but also by some who have hitherto advocated emancipation.

Lydia H. Sigourney's early work, in particular, contains many references to the slave—not sentimentally sympathetic, but outraged and harsh. She blames the Founding Fathers for shackling him, accuses both North and South of continuing his oppression, prophesies divine retribution, and begs God to teach her country the need for emancipation.[24] By 1850, however, her concern has shifted: she now begs her people to "draw the cords of union fast" and obey the laws enacted by "our sages in the Capitol."[25] Apparently deploring not the capture of Sims and Burns but the disuniting efforts to set them free, she oversimplifies the issues between North and South and avoids mention of slavery. Her most ardent elegies of the 1850's are addressed to Henry Clay and Daniel Webster.[26]

Thomas B. Read undergoes a similar change of heart. The incendiary young man of 1847 who bade his countrymen rise against the "empty cant of Freedom," who showed "the eyes of the bondmen . . . lit with their wild desire,"[27] is now the influential editor of *Female Poets of America* and an internationally known poet-painter. He too elegizes Webster, in whose grave lie "a nation's glory and a people's trust." He interrupts his huge, placid epic of 1854, "The New Pastoral," with an inappropriate but unusually vigorous outburst against the Satans and Iscariots of disunion.[28] We cannot expect poems sympathetic to fugitive slaves and their lawbreaking protectors from a writer prepared "to sit in dust and ashes" forever "if the Union breaks."[29] Such poets are not being simply discreet or careerist, although their support of the party in power may appear a betrayal of their role as America's ethical judge. In fact, as Northern fury intensifies during the slave-hunt period, those poets who pay tribute to Webster and plead against disunion may actually think of themselves as voices crying in the wilderness.

The same may apply to a Southern poet such as Alexander B. Meek, whose elegies for Clay and Webster are not likely to please his rabidly secessionist neighbors.[30] In fact, with few exceptions, the poets of the South are silent on the one theme that could earn them a vast and loving audience: the merits of slavery. From time to time, in their prose, Simms and Pike argue the case against emancipation "in keeping with their thinking or with a feeling of necessity."[31] Timrod, too, in 1856, makes "a good speech" before Charleston's riflemen and hears them sing his bellicose "Ode" written for the occasion.[32] But such hints are extremely rare among the respectable poets, entirely absent from Poe, Ticknor, Legare, and others. Nevertheless, it would be wrong to lump all of these poets together and guess at a single factor that might explain their silence. The element of escapism is surely strong in their verse; and this is not entirely unrelated to the prophetic impulse. When, for example, is escape cowardice? When can it be called a rejection of the poet's immediate world? We wonder how much ethical embarrassment kindles behind their neat sidestepping of the here and now: are there other poets who feel, with William Maxwell, that the African is foully treated, but will not risk tar and feathers—as Maxwell does—by publishing their views in a city such as Norfolk? Is it their own region they mean, when they turn their backs, as Daniel Bryan and Richard Wilde do,[33] on

> . . . the darkness and the dearth
> Which sordid passions and untamed desires
> Create about us . . .
> . . . the poor husks and garbage of this world.[34]

Across their pages flit the glamorized ghosts of a better day; if we expect a view of the Dismal Swamp, with hounds pursuing a fugitive, we had better seek elsewhere.

Of all Southern poets, only William J. Grayson acknowledges in his verse that such a phenomenon exists, and his purpose is to warn any slave contemplating escape that runaways are unlucky dupes of abolitionist tempters, that freedom would be his ruination, that slavery is his natural and fortunate condition.[35] Can we call Grayson's "vigorous propaganda" anti-prophetic simply because it nourishes the status quo instead of challenging it? If he, in truth, believes in "the righteousness and humanity of slavery," he has no other choice than to raise his voice in its defense and against its enemies. Is he, on the other hand, the prophet his neighbors no doubt consider him? To measure the genuineness of Grayson's passion is a tricky affair; it is so much easier to identify the apostolic fire when a poet cries out to his neighbors that they, not their enemies, are in the wrong. In any case, one wonders whether this "intelligent and humane writer" cared about "the social ills of the North" only because they provided him with a fine legal argument; whether *The Hireling and the Slave* is, in fact, little more than a brilliantly prepared and delivered brief for the slave power.[36]

Avoidance of the fugitive slave issue is by no means regional. Turning to the young Northern poets whose sentiments remain anti-slavery, we find that many shun this theme or mask their position. Thomas D. English, for example, goes so far as to create a ballad of Negro courage and kindness:

> How thrills my inner soul to know,
> A slave—of all abhorred—
> Though bond in view of all below,
> Is free in CHRIST OUR LORD!

But the poet, perhaps deliberately, safeguards himself by locating the incident on foreign soil, in Guadaloupe.[37] Augustine Duganne also manages to keep his name free of partisan taint. Yet he probably knows that his work is being recited and sung at anti-slavery meetings, and that timely excerpts from his books are being reprinted by the abolition press, as when Sims is captured:

> . . . the Heart of the people first throbbeth indignant,
> When despots would rivet our fetters accurst,
> And fronts with bold bosom the tyrant malignant,
> And swells, till, with glorious burst,
> Out gushes the flame it hath nursed.

In terms of specific events he remains dissociated. Nevertheless, a long attack on Webster, signed "A. D.," is identifiable as Duganne's by its elevated tone, facile prosody, longwindedness, and archaic rhetoric overblown with weak personification and Miltonic inversion. If this is so, Duganne offers here a typical illustration of the serious poet moved to an impetuous outburst which he needs to see published, but cautiously avoids signing (for aesthetic or strategic reasons), and then omits from his collected work.[38]

This is a common device. Edna D. Proctor, for instance, signs several anti-slavery poems "Dean." Perhaps Phoebe Cary and Bayard Taylor, who write for the *Tribune,* Mrs. Oakes-Smith, who contributes to the *Liberator,* and Epes Sargent, editor of the *Transcript,* are responsible for some of the unidentified fugitive slave verses in those and other publications. Lacking evidence, however, and confronted with their authorized volumes, we must assume that none of them refers in his verse to the dramatic issue sundering the nation. Political cowardice cannot be involved. In his editorials Sargent blasts Webster and the 1850 Law; Mrs. Oakes-Smith shares the platform with Garrison, Phillips, and Parker; the Cary sisters are identified with Whittier and sign a number of militant verses in the press; John T. Trowbridge authors a fugitive slave drama including many powerful condemnatory passages.[39] Bayard Taylor contributes an anti-slavery poem to the *Liberty Bell,* works at the *Tribune,* and at one point defies hostile pro-slavery audiences.[40]

A likelier factor in the silence of these poets, as poets, is money. Some, like Phoebe Cary, subsist on verse published by editors to whom the very word *slavery* is anathema. The same is true of Mrs. Oakes-Smith, chief breadwinner in her family. Publishing houses, whose friendliness has to be nurtured with great care, are notoriously hostile; even as entrenched and independent a writer as Longfellow agrees to omit his slavery poems from an 1848 edition. But to suggest that these poets would otherwise produce verse on the fugitive is to charge them, as one abolitionist does, with betraying their sacred vows and selling their souls for bread:

> How many a breather of ecstatic song,
> That might lend voices to correct the wrong,
> Has sold the halo from his poet's crown,
> To gain a dollar, and avert a frown![41]

Though the economic factor cannot be ignored, we must remember that in their verse the same writers shun *all* current issues. Thus Mrs. Oakes-Smith is silent on the subject closest to her heart—women's rights.[42] Taylor, on the other hand, does occasionally succumb to the urgencies of the hour, and at such times he makes sure of being heard;[43] but neither "To Earth" nor "Prayer-Meeting in a Storm" finds its way into his collected poems. That his grounds are aesthetic rather than political is indicated by the exclusion of a third poem, "The American Legend," which is safely on the side of manifest destiny and against disunion. Poetry to him is clearly "something sacred and apart from life."[44] This he emphasizes by repeatedly choosing to praise his heroes—Shakespeare, Dante, Goethe—for their calm aloofness.

Nor is Taylor alone in his devotion to aestheticism and non-involvement. The silence we encounter on the fugitive slave issue must, at least in part, be attributed to what had long since become a pervasive doctrine in American poetry. James F. Clarke's skillfully wrought Phi Beta Kappa poem, for instance, because of its social criticism, is attacked by the press as "inartistic"; [45] Parsons deplores the destructive atmosphere of Manhattan, where "the Present overpowers the Past";[46] Read similarly praises those, in a time of war and trouble, who walk "with prophet eyes uplifted . . . unconscious of the land";[47] Dana, keeping his own verse immaculately free of controversy, urges Bryant to give up the reforming zeal and "Keep eye and heart upon poetry."[48] An especially illuminating instance is Seba Smith, who prefaces his anthology, *Dewdrops of the Nineteenth Century,* thus: "The title indicates its aim in selecting contributions . . . having lightness, purity, and beauty." His *United States Magazine,* on the other hand, is to be "useful, practical, and instructive rather than light, imaginative, or sentimental." Here is a consciously created dichotomy: a removal of the truth-telling function from one's verse, and an insistence upon it in one's prose.[49]

The diligence with which these poets avoided immediacy and anger has not saved their reputations; with few exceptions—such as Poe and Frederick G. Tuckerman—the practitioners of poetic neutrality produced a mass of bland, trite verse and are understandably bypassed today. It is impossible to ascertain what their fate as poets might have been had they allowed themselves to cope with the wickedness of their time and place; yet the question needs to be considered.

Some are temperamentally soft-spoken; although they appreciate the denunciatory voice in others, they cannot successfully echo it and disown their few efforts in that vein. For others a spark of wrath might have the animating effect necessary to make their verses live; thus, ironically, the very element they shun as fatal would save them. Still, we have seen enough work which, for all its fervor, remains wretched in quality. Those who above all guard their artistic integrity and insist on remaining true to their temperament can ill afford to join ranks with the shrill newspaper rhymesters of the day, on the outside chance of rising above the rest and sharing Whittier's questionable laurels.

That their neutral verse achieves high critical honors, both here and in Britain, must justify and encourage their aesthetic program: for they are doing well what their epoch values most. This success helps to explain their rigorous self-censorship, even when their hearts go out to the fugitive and his escape tempts their balladeering urge; even when they burn with dismay at the ethical deterioration of America under the 1850 Law. One can at least send a private note to Wendell Phillips, assuring him that "true hearts afar off and in other circles . . . beat cordially" for him and his "great object."[50] Or one can offer, as John Hay does, an ingenious excuse:

> The harp hangs silent with untrembling chords
> For deeds are now more eloquent than words.[51]

In any case, our study thus far casts serious doubt on the claim that the Fugitive Slave Law inspired a great literary outburst, at least among the respected minor poets. If any shifting of position occurred, it would seem to have been away from abolition and in favor of compromise with the South.

iii

But a considerable group does handle the fugitive slave theme, and it is to their work we turn now. First we will look at the poets who portray the individual slave in flight. Among the earliest and most successful is Elizabeth M. Chandler, who dies just as the abolition movement takes wing. In "The Recaptured Slave"[52] the reader is made to feel what it means to be enslaved. Illogical in meter and weighed down by a ballast of clichés, the soliloquy nevertheless manages to move with stateliness as a slave, having for once tasted freedom, triumphs by suicide over his renewed captivity: "Art thou my master! then come ask the wave,/To give thee back thy slave!" Through an insistence on psychological truth, this poem rises above banality. Mrs. Chandler's slave, for example, unlike those in later poems, admits that he completely forgot wife, children, and friends at the moment of liberation: "I only felt that I was free from thrall." It is disappointing to find, in the tumultuous quarter-century that followed, not a single runaway in American poetry more memorable than hers. Part of the explanation must be that she disciplines her anger by recreating a climactic moment from the slave's point of view —with full, imaginative sympathy, but without foisting upon the reader a set of admonitions and demands.

Twenty-five years later both William D. Howells and Louisa M. Alcott tap this vein—more ambitiously, but less successfully. "The Pilot's Story"[53] flashes its lurid light on the predicament of a white gambler's slave-wife who has been promised her freedom but is lost in a card game and escapes by drowning herself. Howells avoids using his hexameters as a vehicle for moral comment. One might, by a stretch of the imagination, claim that the riverboat passengers symbolize the American people gaping with horror at what can happen when a human being is considered property. And there is, perhaps, an implicit ethical judgment in the depiction of the slave-girl as beautiful, loyal, fearless; her owner, as a vaguely well-intentioned weakling; the winner, as a lascivious brute. But the poet makes no effort to arrive at meaning.

Just as Howells' concern with plot bypasses any possibility of thematic depth, so does Louisa M. Alcott's didacticism utterly overwhelm her story.[54] This artistic failure is peculiar, not only in view of her burgeoning narrative powers, but also because she *does* appreciate the intrinsic greatness of her material. When she hears Wendell Phillips tell an audience how a pair of slave-sweethearts miraculously freed themselves, she feels it to be "a nobler legend" than that of fair Ginevra, and predicts that the young Negro girl of the story will be celebrated by "future poets . . . in brighter tints." Yet, exercising neither story-telling power nor poetic craft, she is satisfied to follow up her lame account with what she hopes will be a rousing appeal:

> Oh men! whose eager hands and lips
> Give to such deeds applause,
> Bestow the tribute of your lives
> To serve a righteous cause . . .

A superb story has thus been reduced to shrill exhortation in the hands of an impassioned but undisciplined young writer, born into Concord's Jeremiah tradition and aspiring to serve as its heir.

A more successful blending of the narrative and prophetic is accomplished by Grace Greenwood in "The Leap From the Long Bridge."[55] Her metrics, at the age of twenty-one, are far from masterly; yet she achieves a sense of flight, pursuit, panic, and ultimate repose, through slightly shifting rhythms, stops and starts, within a serviceable eight-line stanza to which she rigidly adheres. Unlike Miss Alcott, she restrains her emotional response, allowing the story (with a few minor lapses) to make its own impact. The narration is concise; each stanza has its own swift inner motion and moves the story forward as well. The spotlight stays on the fugitive; the poet gives artistic form to her own feelings by presenting rather than discussing the political irony: "From Columbia's glorious Capitol/Columbia's daughter flees . . ." And again, it is through the inflamed imagination of the runaway rather than the poet's angry rhetoric that we hear the jailer's yell sweeping "like a bloodhound's bay/On the low night-wind . . ." Only at the close does she permit her personal bitterness to glow subtly, as she shows the thwarted jailer back in his dungeon while the drowned woman triumphantly "lifts in His light her unmanacled hands . . ."

Although Miss Greenwood is never to renege on her abolitionist position and will occasionally write militant poems, she does not after 1844 publish any verse specifically on the fugitive slave issue. Perhaps there is something attractive to youth in the nature of the subject; for Howells and Miss Alcott, as well as Miss Greenwood, use the theme very early in their careers and never return to it. This is also true of William H. Burleigh. Prior to 1844, in fact, the runaway occupies a major position in his work.[56] This poet boldly rejects the government's demand that, when the fugitive's cries reach his ears, he "strangle pity in its birth." Two of his longest early poems are fugitive soliloquies. In one, Archy Moore—the famous hero of an 1836 novel—looks back over the waves at "the land of the 'charter and chain' " from which he has escaped, and utters "the curse of the fugitive's wrath!" In another, a slave flees North, having avenged himself for a lifetime of agony by destroying his oppressors and burning down their mansion. It is unfortunate that Burleigh's unusual interest in this theme does not result in any work of lasting merit. In each case he keeps the fugitive from taking shape as a real and interesting person by using him merely as a vehicle for his own sentiments. Thus the poet achieves self-satisfying rhetorical release at the cost of the reader's involvement. That Burleigh's fugitives are taken from fiction or hearsay rather than from genuine situations is important, but is not responsible for his failure; were his motive art as well as reform, he might give memorable life to his protagonists. We note that once the newspapers begin to tell of real fugitives, Burleigh drops the theme entirely. This may mean that he has outgrown his youthful interest, or that he has come around to Mrs. Chapman's position against the underground railroad, or that he senses the inadequacy of his art to cope with the electrifying materials of real events. In any case, the alleged flowering of a fugitive slave literature after 1850 is certainly contradicted by such poets as Burleigh and Miss Greenwood.

The general failure to do justice to this potentially great theme is underscored when we discover exciting scenes being ground down by a well-meaning versifier into the drab stanzas typical of him.[57] Niagara had been used before as an exhilarating backdrop for escapes, and William B. Tappan must have felt that exhilaration when he read Harriet Martineau's account of the fugitive's leap to land at Niagara as "the finest sight in the world." But in Tappan's hands that leap involves neither the waterfalls, nor the runaway's heart, nor the reader's. On another occasion he actually shelters a runaway for a night, and records the experience in "A Slave is in My House To-Night":

> I give him food, I give a bed,
> Where his old limbs at ease may be;
> I watch his sleep, but sleep has fled,
> In fear of such as me.

The old Negro's nightmare is compassionately imagined, and the poet's simplicity is moving. But it is the situation, not the verse, that most affects the reader. Tappan's effort at prophecy limps: "Thy master wears a burning stain,/ Repentance can't efface." Only in an unpretentious footnote does he strike home:

> Calling the poor fellow in the morning, I found he had secured his chamber door, on the inside, during the night; such was his fear of his fellow-man!

The poems that focus on dimensional fugitives are rare. Most references are brief, generalized, hypothetical; the runaways who crawl panting and bleeding through mid-century American verse are impossible to visualize; all that emerges is the humaneness of the poet. It is not to a Latimer or Sims, for example, that Sarah H. Whitman responds, but to the sentimental creation of Elizabeth Barrett Browning's mind. In three sonnets she thanks Mrs. Browning for shedding "a wild stormy splendor o'er the story/Of the dark fugitive" who committed suicide off Plymouth Rock.[58] With riper artistry but equal vagueness, Alice Cary refers to the latter-day Hagars peopling America's "wilderness places . . . Where never a taper for guidance was lighted . . ." Again, in the midst of an address to those who hope, she startles us with a beautifully realized but unreal picture of self-liberation:

> Forth from the slaver's deadly crypt
> The Ethiop like an Athlete springs,
> And from her long-worn fetters stript,
> The dark Liberian sings.[59]

Similarly, though his impassioned sonnets defy the law which forbids mercy to fugitives, Jones Very makes no effort to portray fugitives as individuals or to condemn the recapture of any specific slave.[60] Thus we seem to be finding that, even among the few respected minor poets who treat the fugitive slave theme after the passage of the 1850 Law, there is silence on those very cases which rock the land.

It cannot be fear of handling "hot issues" or of being identified with an unpopular cause that holds these poets back. Jones Very, for example, lashes out, right after the capture of Sims, at the cruel enactments against fugitives; in "Philanthropy Before Nationality" he disconcerts Americans by recalling that their nation was built upon the Rights of Man; in a Nebraska Bill poem he raises the Higher Law argument: "Our vow to Afric's sons is writ in heaven"; during the Burns furor, while some poets are forgetting the slave in their concern for Union, Very defines patriotism altogether differently:

> To triumph in the Gospel's might,
> And Christian Patriots be;
> To battle for the Truth and Right,
> And every bondman free.

Finally, when a law threatens penalties to those who assist in slave escapes, it is the Higher Law which Very, in the name of God, invokes once more, with an almost Biblical simplicity and humanity:

> Give all thou canst, food, raiment, from thy store,
> Nor aught thou hast these suffering ones deny;
> Lest they, escaped from slavery's hateful chain,
> Should find but graves in freedom's fair domain.

Also shunning particular cases while decrying slave owners who "fight against the eternal tides," Christopher

P. Cranch takes up Very's theme in a fine sonnet, "The Higher Law,"[61] written shortly after the arrest of Sims. It is interesting to catch a really gifted poet at the moment of impact, after years of Emersonian detachment, rising to enunciate his nation's submerged ideal:

> Man was not made for forms, but forms for man;
> And there are times when Law itself must bend
> To that clear spirit that hath still outran
> The speed of human justice . . .
> Man must be free: if not through law, why then
> Above the law . . .
> When, oh, when!
> Father of light! shall the great reckoning come,
> To lift the weak, and strike the oppressor dumb?

William W. Story's reference to the fugitive slave is likewise indirect. He too prefers to attack the law that denies the runaway his manhood. Unlike Very and Cranch, however, he becomes silent on this issue after 1850. As a matter of fact, even in his 1847 volume he masks his abolition sentiments,[62] praising Mrs. Child (as "L.M.C.") for everything but her anti-slavery stand, and disguising a probable tribute to the deliverer of slaves, Captain Walker, within the protective imagery of the Prometheus legend. "Niagara," coming right after the Latimer case of 1842, may be an imaginative assertion of the Higher Law, but one would have no way of knowing so aside from its historical context:

> . . . . thou unto His eye art nothing more
> Than the frail swallows, that forever soar
> Above thy terrors, by his law made free;
> Flames over thee, and all the fiery sword,—
> Thou servest! Thou art bondsman to the Lord!

From this early volume he omits four glowing sonnets which explicitly affirm God's law over man's.[63] Also missing, on better grounds, is the shrill, long-winded "Plea for Peace," which—despite his own aesthetic standards—was evidently torn from him by the urgency of the moment. In that one instance he allowed himself directly to touch the moral nerve of his time:

> . . . do ye uphold in earnest,
> That the doctrine Christ hath taught,
> Is no weak and empty dogma,
> But a law of life and thought . . .
> Yours to win the words and mercy,
> That shall give the slave release,—
> Yours to help each struggling brother
> In his efforts to be free . . .[64]

It would be unwise to offer Story's ethics, politics, or aesthetics as typical of those who do not respond to the great fugitive slave ferment of the fifties. But he does stand as an illuminating example of the complexities involved. We know, on the one hand, that during Story's expatriation in Europe, Sumner, the abolitionist senator, is his regular correspondent and welcome visitor. Yet, as Henry James has emphasized, this poet suffers a "*malaise* on the Slavery question" typical of the conservative North, which is "rather pitifully ground between the two millstones" of slavery and of the "impatient agitation against it," and which finds both crudities distasteful.[65] This analysis by James, a particularly sensitive student of the mid-century New England mind, helps to explain not only Story's silence but that of other Northern poets.

iv

We have sought in vain thus far among the serious minor poets for a direct response to events; with few exceptions the fugitives running across their pages are imaginary and undimensional; none of the celebrated cases is alluded to, even in passing; and there is no literal, unmistakable assault on either Webster or the law he fathered, though much emphasis is placed on corruption in high office and on duty to God's law. One cluster of minor poets remains to be studied: a group of four preachers and four reformers. All but one are from Massachusetts, yet the range of their vision and the reach of their voices go beyond the regional.

Though Bronson Alcott has sheltered runaway slaves, only once in describing an escaped Negro does he turn to verse, and this not for publication:

> Him pangs of freedom filled with strange surprise,
> And with wild rapture lights his eyes.[66]

Sonnets and Canzonets, coming long after the resolution of the issue, is filled with retrospective tributes to leaders in the fugitive slave struggle, but they are usually unnamed and the meaning of their lives is generalized: "Prophet of God! Messias of the Slave! . . . Freedom's first champion in our fettered land!" A fugitive slave case lawyer is probably the unidentified "People's Attorney, servant of the Right! Pleader for all shades . . ." Clearer is Alcott's reference to the liberational efforts of John Brown, "whose valorous emprise/Orion's blazing belt dimmed in the sky . . ." But such specific allusion is rare and late.[67] Only in his actions does he respond prophetically, thus recalling to us Santayana's high praise for "the visions which the prophets have rendered in action . . . rather than in adequate words . . ." The principals in the great Anthony Burns drama, for example, remember Alcott even fifty years later for the magnificence of an individual act that could easily have meant death, and that had an impact on many thousands of witnesses beyond what he or any other poet could at that moment have accomplished by words![68]

A second Concord poet, William E. Channing, Jr., manages to match word and deed. In marked contrast to Story's direction away from involvement, Channing makes no significant reference to slavery in his verse until Sims' arrest, at which time he immediately sheds his philosophic calm. Not only does he help plot Sims' rescue, but in the wake of that defeat produces several incendiary poems on behalf of fugitives and against the "America enslaved" that is persecuting them. "An Elegy for Freedom" voices New England's dismay and shame, in twenty-three Spenserian stanzas crackling with Old Testament fire. The emphasis, as we have come to expect, is not on Sims, but—more sweepingly—on "The State's harsh writ, the enforcal of the claim/To a poor brother's blood." To vex awake the conscience of his neighbors he mocks the self-deception of a tame population who "sickly dream America is free," pillories their most honored representative, Webster, for betraying his trust, and scores those gold-worshipers who fear commercial losses if the Union is severed. Daring to question the omniscience of the Founding Fathers, he roars in a voice of genuinely prophetic resonance: "Let Union live or die, yet Liberty shall stand." Whether or not his position is strategically wise or historically correct, he is insisting on an ideal which, in his view, has been scuttled by those in power and by their acquiescent public.[69] Later Channing is active in the Burns case, and soon after the Dred Scott decision—in a eulogy to Thoreau—he implies a Higher Law attack on the Supreme Court:

> . . . long shalt thou live,
> Not in this feeble verse, this sleeping age,
> But in the roll of Heaven; and at the bar
> Of that high court, where virtue is in place!
> Then, thou shalt fitly rule, and read the laws
> Of that supremer state . . .[70]

Concord's youngest and most audacious rebel-poet, Franklin B. Sanborn, has less art than Channing; but his literary aspirations are as high. During his great hour of involvement (1859–60) we find him able to direct his entire being first to the slave-rescuing operations of John Brown, then to the battle for clemency, and finally to the transfiguration of his hero. Even an early love song refers to the Burns case in far-off Boston, the city that "sends up to God its shameful cry."[71] In 1858, invited to deliver a poem at Tremont Temple, he forces the once-noble city to wince guiltily over Sims and Burns:

> What late repentance, Boston, can atone
> For rights betrayed and liberties o'erthrown?
> Thy armèd hand, forgetting past renown,
> Struck the poor wretch that sued for freedom down! . . .
> Twice hast thou silently endured the scorn,
> Twice seen the suppliant from thy temple torn . . .

Asked to read the same poem at a Concord meeting held just after "Captain Brown's gallant exploits in Missouri," Sanborn inserts a long passage, perhaps the first verse ever written for John Brown, praising him as the rescuer of slaves:

> The prayers of slaves set free for thee call down
> A potent blessing, brave and noble Brown!
> Then shall our voices join with theirs, to praise
> The manliest action of these wretched days . . .[72]

So important a role does this poet play, that after Harper's Ferry he is obliged temporarily to flee the land. Unfortunately, as we have seen in other cases, the drama of his deeds is seldom evident in his pedestrian verses.

Julia W. Howe hones a far greater gift than Sanborn's, and with far more devoted care. Yet she is not chary of deeds either. Her husband is a key figure in the attempted rescue of both Sims and Burns. Their home is a center of resistance to the 1850 law; it is she who opens the door to John Brown when he visits Boston, and who goes to weep with his wife after the arrest.[73] We are thus not surprised to discover the fugitive in all her early collections. Even in Italy she is haunted by this issue, proving that absence from one's land need not lead to a poetic divorce, though it might appear so from the work of Story and other expatriates. In fact, an enormity too overwhelming for a Lowell or a Longfellow to verbalize in Boston is probably easier to handle from a great distance. Agonized to see "bloodhounds track the inner shrine/Where, sacred once, the outcast slept," Mrs. Howe prophesies to her land that its Judas pieces of Southern silver "will but buy a field of blood."[74] Later she pays tribute to Frederick Douglass,[75] the great fugitive, and praises John Brown because it was "To free the wretched slave/He led a band of chosen men."

During the Civil War she demands, through the lips of a runaway slave, that the days of the hunt be ended once and for all:

> Will you keep me, for my faith,
> From the hound that scents my track . . .
> Are ye come to right a wrong?[76]

The prophet's is a disquieting role, and Mrs. Howe plays it to the hilt, more consistently than the Concord trio—Alcott, Channing, and Sanborn; and, as theirs seldom do, her words match the incandescence of a noble fury.

We consider next four men of the cloth. Abolition poets often attack the clergy for keeping silent on the issue or betraying God's law by supporting the Fugitive Slave Law. Yet they gratefully acknowledge exceptions—priests true to both God and man, from whose lips spring, at the most inhospitable but urgent moment, the word that unblinds and arouses. Such prophet-priests are John Pierpont, whose congregation turns against him; James F. Clarke, whose paper loses many subscribers; Thomas W. Higginson, arrested for treason; and George B. Cheever, maligned as a madman. Each in turn rises majestically in the pulpit to announce God's wrath against the American people and government. At the time of the Latimer case it is Pierpont who challenges the Constitution as a betrayal of God. After the Burns rendition, Higginson incites Worcester and the whole nation to armed resistance. The Dred Scott decision draws from Cheever a savage denunciation of American life and law. And Clarke, during John Brown's trial, is moved to indict the American government for having caused the raid. These outcries, disseminated far beyond the particular churches and cities in which they are preached, bear all the earmarks of prophetic utterance. But our chief concern here must be with the fugitive slave poetry produced by these ministers. Unfortunately, Clarke, whose poems could have filled several volumes, never collected them; Pierpont's last volume appeared in 1843, though he wrote till his death in 1866; Higginson, in old age, collected only what he then considered worth preserving; and Cheever's editor included only the devotional and domestic poems.

A generation older than the rest, Pierpont makes the earliest contribution. His fugitive slave poems enrich the abolitionist anthologies; frequent reprinting and performance attest to their popularity. In one soliloquy a slave tells of his misery, anger, and hope, as he flees to the protection of British law. In another, a slaver curses the north star as "an incendiary," and threatens it with tar and feathers.[77] The Latimer case sharpens Pierpont's focus, drawing from him a series of scornful verses against the judges who return slaves to their masters; "the pliant priest" who kisses "Slavery's foot, in homage"; the Constitution, that ties the North to the slavocracy; and Massachusetts—which has joined the hunt for runaways "Lest her old Virgin sister pout."[78] In 1850 the old fire revives as Pierpont denounces the imprisonment of Chaplin, a slave-rescuer:

> Because God said his heart should melt
> At woe's appeal.
>
> Because, when a poor brother cried,
> He felt the pain;
> And when he saw him bound, he tried
> To break the chain.

After the kidnapping of Sims, he strikes at Webster: "that voice, once heard with awe," which now denies a higher law than man's and leads the hounds to their human quarry. It is easy to see why, at the 1852 commemorative meeting chaired by Higginson, Pierpont's "truly eloquent" reading of this hymn draws repeated bursts of applause, "a *spiritual rapping* which would have done Sims good to hear." Before them a white-haired Ezekiel cries to God: "Exclude us from thy bliss/At us let angels hiss . . ."[79] Lacking that physical presence, however, we find his rhymed outcry weaker than the Latimer sermon of 1842, which dares to label the sacred Constitution "a sinful compromise . . . of moral principle . . . just the compromise that Judas made with the chief priests," and closes mightily: "Which shall we obey—our dead fathers? or our living God?"[80]

Though a respected poet and a fine anthologist, Cheever —even more than Pierpont—seems shackled in his verse.[81] In 1850, warning the Southern senators that their system is doomed, and vowing disobedience to what he characterizes as an anti-Christian law, he then turns upon Webster:

> Ye war not with the powers of men . . .
> But with the living God . . .
> His love, whose Power alone is Might—
> His Law, our only Liberty.

In a second poem he rebukes the defenders of the "impious" Fugitive Slave Act:

> Ye cannot think that we who live
> Some nineteen Christian centuries gone,
> To such a law our heed shall give . . .

Dignity and controlled passion are in these lines, but it is in 1857 that Cheever's language finally takes on the quality of "Old Testament truth" which he himself so cogently characterizes:

> . . . how it cuts, how it probes and pierces, as a discerner and reprover of sin, and how the mighty Hebrew prophets, ever living, ever new, seem to hold a grand inquest over our organic iniquities.[82]

Whittier is not overpraising Cheever's 1857—58 sermons when he defines their inspiration and power:

> So spake Esaias: so, in words of flame,
> Tekoa's prophet-herdsman smote with blame
> The traffickers in men . . .
> Once more the old Hebrew tongue
> Bends with the shafts of God a bow new-strung![83]

Such flame is generally absent from both the verse and prose of Clarke, though his biographer calls him "a poet by necessity" and refers to "his wild and somewhat irregular effusions."[84] The rhymes we have are neither wild nor irregular, but are metrical essays in which a notable man speaks his mind from time to time. Before a Faneuil Hall audience[85] he grows vehement against Webster, and his satiric couplets demolish the Grayson argument that slaves are fortunate:

> Slavery they much enjoy, (though, by the way,
> We want a law to catch the runaway.)
> Be National—the Union we must save—
> The only way is to send back a slave . . .

He forces Boston to recall the time of its moral collapse: its homes were a hunting-ground for the South until the God-touched lyre of Harriet B. Stowe "Shook souls, and turned our cowards into men." Certainly no words of *his* have a similar effect; yet he recognizes and cherishes the prophetic voice even when it appears in the guise of popular fiction.

Clarke's peak of eloquence is the John Brown sermon, torn from him by "too many thoughts to allow" him to remain silent. Here he studies the face of power and announces what he sees:

> When Anthony Burns was taken down State Street, and the people on each side hoarsely roared "kidnappers! kidnappers!" at the soldiers who guarded him—their faces showed that they felt the truth of the charge. We may wear on our hat the cockade of the United States Marshal, or we may be called out as a military company, covered with feathers and gold lace, but that does not vacate the principle. We are kidnappers and man-stealers still.[86]

The youngest of this group, Thomas W. Higginson, publicly criticizes the emphasis on assisting a few runaways instead of helping to free all slaves; yet from time to time he does produce poetry on the theme.[87] Like Alcott, however, it is in his actions that he truly sings. Leading the effort to free Sims, he brings Tremont Temple close to insurrection. Later he smuggles fugitives out of Boston.[88] Finally, at the courthouse inside of which federal guns guard Burns, it is Higginson—supported only by a Negro ally and Alcott—who dares to march up the stairs. Here is a practicing poet who behaves before his people with all the beauty and fire missing in his typical poems:

> Higginson pushed his way through the crowd. There was the beam; there were men to batter it against the door. He . . . seized the front end . . . The door . . . split and swung on a single hinge. They saw . . . the steps that led to Burns' cell . . . Six or eight policemen were awaiting them inside . . . clubs beat on their heads . . . Higginson, in rage and pain, stumbled onto the steps. "Cowards!" he shouted at the crowd. Breathing hard, the blood falling on his coat, he looked back into the lighted hall, and saw . . . pistols pointed toward the door. Where were the reinforcements . . .?

The next day the committee meeting swarms with excuses, but Higginson merely sits "holding his cloak against his wounded face, his hot bright eyes bitter."[89]

It is my belief that his bitterness at the second triumph of the slave power in Boston is transmuted at white heat into "The Eclipse," published a week later under the signature of "H.":

> Thou doest well to hide thy face, oh Sun,
> And darkly veil thy shame-suffusèd brow;
> For never since creation was begun,
> Hadst thou such cause to blush for earth as now.
> It matters not which side thou look'st upon,
> There is no zone where Liberty is safe,
> No hemisphere where justice may be done:
> No isle or continent doth Ocean chafe,
> That Morning finds not in the chains of Wrong,
> Which day doth rivet—Night make doubly strong;
> The lands most blest by thee hath Slavery curst.
> Withhold thy beams! I little reck how long,
> For Right is vanquished, Hell its bounds hath burst,
> And Satan seeks the light, and glories in the worst.
>
> (Salem, May 26, 1854)[90]

This stirring sonnet seems too personal and desperate a sob to have come from anyone else; it is as if Higginson's wound, and not the external one, has found a voice. Besides, the style is not unlike that in other of his poems, and its somber tone leads directly to a great passage of the June 4th sermon, "Massachusetts in Mourning":[91]

> . . . toll the bells in all the churches, and hang the streets in black from end to end. O shall we hold such ceremonies when only some statesman is gone, and omit them over dead Freedom . . .

Mourning, however, is not Higginson's genre. Toward the end of the sermon the old Tyrtaean ferocity is ready to reassert itself. Demanding that his Worcester congregation "no longer conceal Fugitives and help them on, but show them and defend them," he falls into the rhythmic patterns of Isaiah's outburst against Sodom and Gomorrah: "Hear, O Richmond! and give ear, O Carolina! henceforth Worcester is Canada to the Slave!"

Of all the minor poets, these reformers and preachers react most meaningfully and directly to the fugitive slave crisis. In their verse they sing as awakeningly as they can, but (except for Mrs. Howe) it is in their deeds and prose that they best accomplish the prophet's mission.

V

But what of the major poets? Do they respond in a major way, achieving what Santayana calls "the highest poetry . . . that of the prophets"? Do they, more persistently than their lesser colleagues, see the *here* and *now* beside "the ideals of experience and destiny"? Are they complete poets, their "whole experience composed into a single symphony"?[92] How does their aesthetic squeamishness cope with an ethical monstrosity that wracks their souls?

The record of Bryant on the fugitive slave issue provides a classic example of the split personality, the incomplete poet. Though he writes "creatively and searchingly on the issues which his century" brings before him, American slavery is not so much as mentioned in any Bryant poem, even his 1861 battle-hymns! Slave-owners need take no offense at semantic ambiguities *their* poets also use, such as "Freedom" and "Tyranny."[93] In his verse he truly achieves the aim of lifting his speech to a philosophical level, while shunning issues of the day. It is instructive to turn from the innocuousness of his poetry to the extraordinarily concrete thrusts of his prose. In the New York *Post* he delivers telling assaults on every key occasion. With the same moral fury that dictates Whittier's "Ichabod," he denounces Webster's surrender to the South "for a sordid motive." At the recapture of Burns he terms the 1850 Law "the most ruffianly act ever authorized by a deliberative assembly." The Dred Scott decision leads him to cry out: "Wherever our flag floats, it is the flag of slavery . . . it should be dyed black, and its device should be the whip and the fetter."[94] The high point of his eloquence, and his strongest link to denunciatory prophecy, comes in an 1863 address against Lincoln's gradualism:

> Slavery is a foul and monstrous idol . . . . Down with it to the ground. Dash it to fragments; trample it in the dust. Grind it to powder as the prophets of old commanded that

> the graven images of the Hebrew idolaters should be ground . . . scatter it to the four winds and strew it upon the waters, that no human hand shall ever again gather up the accursed atoms and mould them into an image to be worshiped again with human sacrifice.[95]

Would this enflamed utterance demand room in his poetry if he lacked the convenience of editorial page and rostrum? Would he in consequence be a lesser or a greater poet? Is it because he lacks artistic "integrity and self-awareness"[96] that he neatly categorizes his roles, with Jeremiah demoted to the rank of editor?

Holmes' attitude toward the fugitive slave issue, on the other hand, can easily be discovered in his poems.[97] Before May, 1856, he dislikes slavery but not nearly so strongly as he detests "the mad Briareus of disunion." The protector of the fugitive is, to Holmes, an enemy of the sacred 1793 compact and of New England's honor. Even before the American Medical Association he is concerned enough to introduce the disunion issue:

> I give you *Home!* its crossing lines
> United in one golden suture . . .
> A flag . . . with love for centre . . .
> No prowling treason dares to enter!

It is in 1856 that he states the theme most firmly, with birthday tributes to the dead Webster, whom "the envious tongue upbraids" in vain, and to Washington, whose ghost speaks through Holmes as God spoke through the Old Testament seers:

Love your country first of all! . . .
Doubt the patriot whose suggestions
Strive a nation to divide!

After the almost fatal beating of Sumner, however, a change occurs: slight in "Latter-Day Warnings," notable in "Avis," an 1858 tribute to a teacher who has taken a "little refuse child" under her wing:

The primal mark is on her face,—
The chattel-stamp,—the pariah-stain
That follows still her hunted race,—
The curse without the crime of Cain.

Otherwise Holmes avoids the issue. Yet the cause cannot be timidity in his case, for on such touchy matters as religion he deliberately shocks his generation and prides himself on being anathematized. Surely among Boston intellectuals his pro-Compromise position is unpopular, and it may be for this very reason that he airs it so vociferously.

Melville, too, while decrying the "vast enormity" of slavery, pleads (through Babbalanja in *Mardi*) for Northern moderation in order to save the Union. Protectors of fugitives, like others who seek Good, might "nevertheless be productive of evil." How Melville feels about the slave-hunts can only be surmised. We note that in "Benito Cereno" he fails to dramatize the motive behind the mutiny. It seems likely that a story-teller stirred by the Sims and Burns cases would turn the grievances of the Negroes into the crux of the tale, rather than echo his sources in a flat, unimaginative manner.[98] True, a few of his early Civil

War poems touch on slavery. He rebukes America as "the world's fairest hope linked with man's foulest crime."[99] Yet this is not typical. Emancipation seems to move him far less than the agony of the conflict and fear of the aftermath.

As we have seen in the previous chapter, Longfellow—like Bryant—is averse to handling public issues in his art. *Poems on Slavery* thus stand apart from his total work. It has been fashionable to dismiss all eight poems as sentimental, book-born, hackneyed, thin; what is often ignored, however, is the courage involved in publicly taking the unpopular side during the Latimer affair, when "the word *slavery* was never allowed to appear in a Philadelphia periodical, and . . . the publisher objected to have even the name of the book appear in his pages."[100] This courage, and the urgency of his appeal, are characteristic of prophecy. Taking fire from his new friend, the revolutionary poet Freiligrath, and moved by Dickens' "grand chapter on slavery," he meditates his poems aboardship "in the stormy, sleepless nights" and writes them down "with a pencil in the morning." To abandon his high literary nest and cope with an issue of the day, he must have been stirred indeed. Usually gentle, Longfellow here shows an arresting degree of defiance.[101] Under attack he replies: "I am glad of what I have done. My feelings prompted me, and my judgment approved, and still approves." (We note his awareness that these poems constitute a deed *done*.) The sense of compulsion, of being commanded—"despite himself"—to speak, is underscored by his dedication to William E. Channing, Sr., which really constitutes an invocation to himself:

A voice is ever at thy side
  Speaking in tones of might,
Like the prophetic voice, that cried
  To John in Patmos, "Write!"

Write! and tell out this bloody tale . . .

To this high level he returns only in the epilogue, a splendid admonition which compares Samson with America's slaves who may one day "shake the pillars of this Commonweal . . ." Unfortunately, although the versification is deft, his inspired intentions are not fulfilled in "The Slave in the Dismal Swamp," which introduces a fugitive slave imagery common to dozens of newspaper rhymesters. In the same "dark fens" we meet the same "hunted Negro" who hears the same "bloodhound's distant bay" while the same lucky birds fill the air "with songs of Liberty." Typical of the poems on this topic, Longfellow's fugitive slave is pathetic rather than tragic.[102]

He thereafter keeps mum on the slave issue, except for "The Norman Baron," a tribute to a manumitter of serfs, and an uncollected 1845 poem, "The Poet of Miletus," a significant statement against the society that would keep him from giving:

. . . an utterance more complete
To all the voices of humanity,
Even the swart Ethiop's inarticulate woe.
And this is eighteen centuries after Christ![103]

"The Building of the Ship" may lead the reader to conclude that by 1849 Longfellow, like Melville and Holmes, is concerned more with union than with slavery. But his journal records an ever-increasing disgust with the 1850 law, its makers, and its results. No new poems match the fiery jottings in his journal, and his relation to the abolition movement may be "never more than that of a sympathetic bystander," yet he gives great spiritual sustenance to Sumner —his personal knight in the fugitive slave battle; and throughout the Sims and Burns affairs he mentions nothing else in his journal. At least to himself he must cry out: "O city without soul! When and where will this end? Shame, that the great Republic, the 'refuge of the oppressed,' should stoop so low as to become the Hunter of Slaves!" If this angry mumbling gives him little ease, he can at least feel that the voice of his dearest friend, Sumner, raging across the land, is in a sense his own.[104] And in his New England tragedies he manages, in sometimes soaring blank verse, to dramatize the conflict between man's law and God's.

If prophecy includes the urge to transmit distressing truths to hostile ears, Emily Dickinson's work, like Poe's, cannot be a promising field of exploration. Poe rejects truth-telling as the poet's function, and his most significant comment on mid-century America is a persistent effort to escape it; but he, at least, seeks to communicate. With Emily Dickinson the introversion is stronger; she chooses reclusion and—unlike some transcendentalists—engages in her private wars without urging others to do the same. At most we can sense the direction of her sympathies, and surmise that—were she an editor or pastor—we might have before us a file of volcanic prose on the events of the fifties. For we know that, despite her father, she read with enthusiasm the radical works of Parker, Emerson, and Mrs. Child.[105] Here and there in her letters we come across a pertinent clue. Early in 1850, for example, she mocks the South's secession talk:

> Magnum bonum, "harum scarum," zounds et zounds, et war alarum,
> man reformam, life perfectum, mundum changum, all things flarum?

At the time of the slave-hunts in her state she growls: "I don't like this country at all, and I shant stay here any longer! 'Delenda est' America, Massachusetts and all!"[106] More important, the imagery of her poems remains consistently sympathetic to the defeated, the imprisoned, the hunted—especially so in that finest of fugitive stanzas:

> I never hear the word "escape"
> Without a quicker blood,
> A sudden expectation,
> A flying attitude.[107]

We note too her decision to seek out for literary guidance in 1862 the key figure in both Sims and Burns affairs, Thomas W. Higginson, the only leader who stood his ground in 1859, affirming John Brown when all others reneged or ran for cover!

Throughout this chapter we have briefly noted the poets whose crucial utterance on the fugitive slave issue takes other forms than poetry. We shall, however, give Thoreau's prose and actions as close scrutiny as if they were poetry—because to Thoreau they are, and so he tells us; no stanzas have ever been shaped with more passion, imagination, or care:

> My life has been the poem I would have writ,
> But I could not both live and utter it.[108]

Perry Miller speaks of this poet's *mental* development as "a journey toward . . . fanatical devotion to the specific."[109] But his *actions* are equally specific, for he is demonstrating how to be alive rather than "dead,/Only not buried . . ." To his neighbors, rotting in complacency and acquiescence, he becomes a trumpet, proving day by day that to be fully alive means to *act,* and that a life of action can be heroic. Of himself he demands nothing less than a hero's life: this is the obsessive theme of his verse,[110] the strategy of his "little acts" and greatest moments. Repudiating aloofness and escape, he insists that our acts are grand only "within their native clime"; they mean nothing if done "Away from home"; nor does the hero escape battle by staying "In his lonely cell." To seek other than "the Present Time" is equally futile: the ghosts of ancient heroes may, in an unheroic age, inspire a man; yet he must "earn their bread" himself, praying for "earnest work" to make life and death worthwhile:

> . . . great actions piled on high,
> Tasking our utmost strength touching the sky,
> As if we lived in a mountainous country.

In pursuit of some worthy endeavor he must despise the life of comfort that would kill his soul, and must welcome the agony that will "preserve his tenderness." Ever alert, he must leap to the next confrontation: "Give me an angel for a foe,/And straight to meet him I will go." How then shall such a poet, in whose midnight vision "every hero seized his lance," respond to Concord's bells announcing the capture of Anthony Burns? How shall he express his sympathy for "The Afric race brought here to curse its fate . . ."?

At once Thoreau becomes what he has dreamt of becoming: "a hero in coat of mail." Tugging at his belt he marches on his post, and finds in the town hall:

> . . . that what had called my townsmen together was the destiny of Nebraska, and not of Massachusetts . . . though several . . . citizens . . . are now in prison for attempting to rescue a slave from her own clutches, not one of the speakers . . . expressed regret for it, not one even referred to it . . .

To rekindle the flames that once made Concord glorious, he reminds his town of the Buttricks who once held her bridges, and aims his inspired darts at those in Boston Court-House who are "trying a MAN, to find out if he is not really a SLAVE." "Does any one think," he roars, "that justice or God awaits Mr. Loring's decision . . . when this question is already decided from eternity to eternity . . .?"[111] Hitherto Thoreau's scalding verses have accused his anti-slavery neighbors of being slaves, each with a price;[112] now, standing before them, he jeers: "There are perhaps a million slaves in Massachusetts."[113] But he does more than unmask and vex; to save his beloved Union from the dissolving hatred of "Every Congress,"[114] to defend the ideal his hearers have betrayed by their silence, he bids them trample underfoot the 1850 Law:

> It was born and bred, and has its Life, only in the dust and mire . . . and he who walks with freedom . . . will inevitably tread on it . . . and Webster, its maker, with it, like the dirt-bug and its ball . . . The law will never make men free; it is men who have got to make the law free. They are the lovers of law and order who observe the law when the government breaks it.[115]

For Thoreau the test of a man is simple:[116] "There's but the party of the great,/And party of the mean . . ." In John Brown, Thoreau finally sees the knighthood to which he has so long aspired: here is one from whose forge a great sound has "been heard in the gorge," who has shown "strength like the rock/To withstand any shock," who has marched "uncompromised and free." What urgency commands Thoreau in 1859 to peal the town hall bells? Not merely to plead for Brown, though that is bold enough at the time, but most of all to announce with joy that his definition of the hero has finally found its man:[117]

> No man in America has ever stood up so persistently and effectively for the dignity of human nature, knowing himself for a man, and the equal of any and all governments. In that sense he was the most American of us all . . . When a man stands up serenely against the condemnation and vengeance of mankind, rising above them literally *by a whole body* . . . the spectacle is a sublime one . . .

It is with "The Last Days of John Brown," however, that Thoreau and American prose arrive at a splendor rare in the literature of the world:

> John Brown's career . . . was meteor-like, flashing through the darkness in which we live. I know of nothing so miraculous in our history . . . What a transit was that of his horizontal body alone, but just cut down from the gallows-tree! . . . No such freight had the cars borne since they carried him Southward alive. On the day of his translation, I heard, to be sure, that he was *hung,* but I did not know what that meant . . . not for a day or two did I even *hear* that he was *dead,* and not after any number of days shall I believe it. Of all the men who were said to be my contemporaries, it seemed to me that John Brown was the only one who *had*

> *not died* . . . I meet him at every turn. He is more alive than ever he was . . . He is no longer working in secret. He works in public, and in the clearest light that shines on this land.

No matter what they seem to be at a glance, these words are high prophetic poetry—ranking with Whitman's among America's noblest elegies. At the same time, they illuminate Thoreau's own life, which he has made truly "coeval/With his breath" by creating "better deeds than verse"[118]—a life which is becoming a great poem because he deliberately selects as its central imagery the most crucial, pain-promising specifics of his *here* and *now*.

The successful, influential, comfort-loving family man on the other side of the jailhouse door, who can half-mock his young friend's "somewhat military" nature, might not be expected to take as open a stand against the 1850 Law; and, indeed, Emerson admits great reluctance.[119] Public questions he finds "odious and hurtful"; to speak out seems "like meddling or leaving your work." Yet his 1844 "Emancipation in the British West Indies," which his neighbors hear unwillingly, somehow becomes an assault upon the seizure of Massachusetts Negroes; and his "Fugitive Slave Law" address of 1851, which wins hisses and catcalls, violently damns Webster's role. On the fourth anniversary of Webster's speech Emerson not only dares to strengthen his condemnation of the statesman, now dead and deified, but also characterizes, to their faces, the disastrous betrayal by America's intellectual leaders as "the darkest passage in the history" of the land. Their great ethical defection demonstrates, he tells them, "that our prosperity had hurt us, and that we could not be shocked by crime."

Reluctant to leave the realms of contemplation, Emerson nevertheless continues to rebuke his neighbors and their government, fiercely and often, as the decade draws to a close. In 1859, asked merely to appeal for relief on behalf of Brown's family, he chooses instead to show how John Brown's distrust of democratic forms has sprung from the decisions of the Sims and Burns judges, the "court-house full of lawyers so idolatrous of forms as to let go the substance." Such men, after destroying the honor of Massachusetts, "wring their hands, but they had better never have been born." As for Brown's family, the poet goes on discomfitingly, it includes "all whom his fate concerns," and the best way to aid him is not just to raise funds but to set Massachusetts free! Emerson's acts have one important prophetic element lacking in Thoreau. The unattached young man welcomes "a roll of the drum, to call his powers into full exercise"; the graying sage, again and again, is torn unwillingly from his cave of thought, dragged before his guilty people, the voice of wrath forced from his throat.

The power of the fugitive slave issue to draw a response is even more surprising in his usually aloof poetry.[120] A brief but memorable outcry occurs in his great "Ode Inscribed to W. H. Channing." Here he refuses praise to "the freedom-loving mountaineer" so long as the valleys of the North are open to "the jackals of the negro-holder." A later couplet teaches his countrymen what manhood is not:

> Why did all manly gifts in Webster fail?
> He wrote on Nature's grandest brow, *For Sale.*

In "May Day" he imaginatively contrasts the slave-hunting

Congress and its gun-firing supporters in Concord with "Blue Walden"—which "rolls its cannonade" not for evil enactments made by rulers, but for the conquest of winter:

> . . . the bondage-days are told,
> And waters free as winds shall flow.
> Lo! how all the tribes combine
> To rout the flying foe.

With greater directness, but less artistry, he decries an invitation to Congressman Mason of Virginia, a key architect of the Fugitive Slave Law:

> O much-revering Boston town
> Who let the varlet still
> Recite his false, insulting tale
> On haughty Bunker Hill.

Ashamed at the rendition of Burns, he attacks "the unworthy sons" of Boston's great past, calling them "reckless clerks in lust of power" who have forgotten the rights of Man and are selling "the blood of human kind." He mocks the excessively civil gentlemen who revere bad men more than they fear God. A true gentleman, the incendiary poet suggests, will break the 1850 Law "on the earliest occasion; a law which no man can abet or obey without forfeiting the name of a gentleman." Finally, for Concord's July 4th celebration in 1857, he writes the one significant Dred Scott protest in American poetry:

> United States! the ages plead . . .
> Go put your creed into your deed,
> Nor speak with double tongue . . .
> Be just at home; then write your scroll
> Of honor o'er the sea . . .

Facing his auditors with a revulsion reminiscent of the old Hebrew poets, he warns them that God frowns to see "rights for which the one hand fights/By the other cloven down." It is typical of Emerson that he chooses the harmless occasion of a fundraising banquet at the town hall, to disturb once again the conscience of his community.

The legalized slave-hunt is equally repugnant to Whitman; but he lacks a public platform such as Emerson's. Very early in his career, under the name of "Paumonok," he transmits his hatred for Northern compromisers and expresses his support of maligned abolitionists, in a long "Dough-Face Song" remarkable less for its anti-slavery sentiment than for the crudity of stanzas that echo the worst newspaper verse of the time.[121] By 1850 Whitman begins to see himself as prophet; but *his* prophecy will avoid denunciation, stressing instead the interplay of good and evil, the need to encompass a total reality, to be both "the poet of slaves, and of the masters of slaves."[122] Looking out[123] "upon all oppression and shame," he intends to remain silent. Further, in his effort to achieve universality, he "will not sing with reference to a day, but with reference to all days." Forewarned so fairly, the reader can expect no response from Whitman to any specific "meanness and agony" of the 1850's.

Excluded from *Leaves of Grass,* however, are two early free-verse poems on the fugitive slave issue. These are full of fire and foreboding, and their prophetic nature is underscored by Biblical mottoes and titles. The precise springboard for these poems, however, is unclear. If "Blood Money" is "inspired . . . by the Fugitive Slave Law," it must be dated September, 1850, or later; yet it appears as early as March,[124] while Whitman's authorized *Collected*

Prose dates it April, 1843, in the wake of the Latimer case.[125] A second fugitive slave poem, "Wounded in the House of Friends," develops the Judas theme introduced in "Blood Money." Although Holloway implies that it is merely a personal reaction against the poet's political ex-backers in 1849,[126] even the incomplete text he furnishes clearly pertains to the events of 1850, and implicates all in the North who have sold their principle:

> Dough-faces, Crawlers, Lice of Humanity—
> Terrific screamers of Freedom,
> Who roar, and bawl, and get hot in the face . . .
> A dollar, dearer to them than Christ's blessing;
> All loves, all hopes, less than the thought of gain . . .[127]

One uncollected passage resembles Thoreau's blasts at the self-righteous North, advising those who boast of freedom to "Stop this squalling and this scorn/Over the mote there in the distance,"[128] since they themselves are morally enslaved. It is obvious that the denunciatory impulse evinced in these poems must be disowned by Whitman, for it contradicts his credo of inclusiveness and affirmation.

Of less interest to us is his 1856 lecture, "The Eighteenth Presidency,"[129] because it is unuttered utterance, the unvoiced "Voice of Walt Whitman to each Young Man in the Nation . . ." Though he may be antagonistic to the "incendiary" abolitionists,[130] his argument here is as audacious as theirs: a wide-swinging assault on America's leaders as unmanly, treasonous, greedy, prostituted. As for the Fugitive Slave Law:

> insolently put over the people by their Congress and President, it contravenes the whole of the organic compacts, and is all times to be defied in all parts of These States, South or North, by speech, by pen, and, if need be, by the bullet and the sword.

Unaired, this lecture at least provides an outlet for Whitman's fury without upsetting the universal embrace aimed for in his poetry.

The fugitives we meet in *Leaves of Grass* do not disturb that aim, nor is it surprising to find them there. Should he respect one taboo while defying all others? The runaway is little more than a searingly presented item in his catalog, to be listed at appropriate moments: when "the poet sees himself or observes others in activities which isolate the individual," or when an *"evolutionary* interpenetration" occurs.[131] Thus he at first merely entertains the fugitive and washes his wounds (an illegal act publicly confessed by the poet); later, he himself becomes "the hounded slave" at the moment of recapture. Like Emerson, however, Whitman cannot always maintain his philosophic stance. When he sees, during the slave-hunt era, that there are "bats and night-dogs askant in the capitol," masquerading as Presidents, Congresses, and Judges, he cannot refrain from exposing them. In "A Boston Ballad (1854)" he damns the "orderly citizens" of Boston who have permitted the rendition of Burns. Boston's "show"—a nightmarish kidnapping witnessed with horror by agitated "Yankee phantoms" and with joy by the "regal ribs" of an avenged George III, is depicted with a heavy-handed irony and an almost hysterical use of the grotesque, as Whitman tries to awake the memory and conscience of his countrymen.[132]

It is true that this poet's "ripest creations . . . did not spring from desire to reform." And, surely, neither "To the States" nor "A Boston Ballad" compares well with his "impersonal, timeless, universal" songs.[133] The point is that, although he clings to his aesthetic and philosophic tenets as strictly as any of the poets, Whitman is not immune to a tremendous public event and does, on a few notable occasions, break his vow of silence. "Blood Money" and

"House of Friends" indicate a direction that might have arrived at a less sunlit, more troubling kind of beauty than that which he decided to cultivate.

Of those who choose the opposite direction for their poetry, exposing and assaulting what they deem to be evil rather than accepting it, the prime American example is Whittier. In the past half century his reputation has suffered severely at the hands of critics who deplore the denunciatory impulse. It has been fashionable to declare of him that "the death of the reformer marked the birth of the poet," that his poetry ripened when the slavery issue was settled and other than "moral stimuli" could touch him. Even his admirers do not dare to claim more than minor rank for him, while some deny altogether that he was noteworthy as a poet or competent as a craftsman.[134] This judgment coincides with literary histories which portray the involvement by nineteenth-century American poets in contemporary issues as a betrayal of their talent.[135]

Many Whittier poems *do* overflow in ardent clichés; yet to reject him for not being a Whitman or an Emily Dickinson is to miss what he is. If the successful prophet is he who compels the attention, irritates the conscience, restores the vision, and incites the motion of *his own* time and people, then Whitman is—as he knows himself to be—unsuccessful, and Whittier is, for an amazing span of years, brilliantly triumphant. Using this gauge, Markham finds—contrary to current views—that Whittier becomes truly great when protesting "the oppression and plunder of the people." And Stedman, while himself no prophet, recognizes in Whittier "the incarnation of Biblical heroism."[136]

Stubbornly, narrowly, from 1833 on, this poet battles slavery; his work traces fully the rise and culmination of the fugitive slave issue: a proper discussion of his contribution merits a separate study. Throughout the period he leads the way, echoed by many others but seldom surpassed.[137] His "Hunters of Men" is the only fugitive slave poem in Mrs. Chapman's 1836 collection, *Songs of the Free;* and in 1840 he edits *The North Star*, the first fugitive slave anthology. He writes hearty tributes to Torrey, Dillingham, Rantoul, Sumner, and many other defenders of the runaway. The cases of Latimer, John L. Brown, Walker, Sims, Burns, and others draw from him impassioned song. And he mounts an unsparing attack against the 1850 Law: its shapers, apologists, and executors. When Higginson and others are imprisoned for defying the Fugitive Slave Law, he lauds them early in 1855 in one of the decade's great poems, "For Righteousness' Sake," even while gently repudiating their "hot words." In the five years from "Ichabod" to that poem, Whittier's prophetic flame has run high. The mood ranges from pride in those who defy the law, to compassion for the runaway woman "Like a sacred fawn before the hounds"; defiance of Sims' captors whose "harvest, scorn/And hate, is near"; mockery against the pious judge who locks the door of Hope to the Negro and whines "a prayer for help to hide the key"; and horror at Liberty in the person of Burns "Marched handcuffed down that sworded street." No other poet of reputation comes close to matching that record; and along with the emotional comes a heightening of the artistic power. True, the world that emerges from these pages is somewhat lacking in humor, variety, sensuousness; but let us not mistake his spirit as a narrow one merely because the thirty-year grip in which it is held allows time for few extended excursions. With less absorption in the slavery struggle he might produce a body of work thematically richer, artistically subtler; but such a choice would be unthinkable to a man who rejoices that "the burden of a prophet's power" has fallen on him.

The one-tracked passion which utterly masters Whittier, to be felt fully, should be set against that zeal which serves Lowell as a temporary literary fuse. Nowhere is the contrast sharper than in their handling of the fugitive slave theme. Lowell, a dozen years younger, throws down the gage in 1843, though not in response to the Latimer case. His college verse had mocked abolitionist fanaticism;[138] the shift coincides with his courtship of the abolition poet Maria White. Two vigorous songs, "The Fatherland" and "Stanzas on Freedom," avoid specificity, yet the great issue of the day can be traced in lines inciting Americans to break the law by assisting "Where'er a single slave doth pine," and by toiling earnestly "to make others free!" His great anti-annexation outburst of 1844, "The Present Crisis," may spring in part from the recent jailing of Delia Webster and Calvin Fairbank, whose deliverance of slaves illustrated the eternal choice which "parts the goats upon the left hand, and the sheep upon the right." That the subject is entering the marrow of his being can be seen in the imagery of such 1845 poems as "The Contrast" and "The Ghost-Seer."[139]

The capture of some fugitives near Washington finally ignites him, provoking some of his fiercest lines:

> Though we break our fathers' promise, we have nobler duties first;
> The traitor to Humanity is the traitor most accursed;
> Man is more than Constitutions; better rot beneath the sod,
> Than be true to Church and State while we are doubly false to God![140]

His accompanying letter to the editor expresses a compassion for the runaway seldom found in his verse:

> I . . . sympathize deeply with these unhappy beings, who have been thwarted in their endeavor to convert themselves from chattel into men, by the peaceful method of simply changing their geographical position.[141]

For the next few years Lowell sustains his wrathful fervor.[142] "An Interview With Miles Standish" shreds the compromises that have shackled the spirit of 1776 with "slavery's lash upon her back." Torrey's death in a Maryland prison inspires a powerful lament—for the whole land more than for the liberator himself:

> Woe worth the hour when it is crime
> To plead the poor dumb bondman's cause,
> When all that makes the heart sublime,
> The glorious throbs that conquer time,
> Are traitors to our cruel laws!

This theme is not neglected in the *Biglow Papers*. In fact, the first series comes to a rousing finale with Birdofredum's hilarious account of his captivity by the fugitive slave family he had intended to put back on the auction block.

It would seem that Lowell has nothing further to say on this matter after "Anti-Apis," a rebuke to those who uphold "the patched-up broils of Congress" rather than the law of God. Among his disowned pieces, however, are several fugitive slave poems, including two long satires on Webster and a much earlier attack on the law which requires New England to "cheer the hungry blood-hounds on," thus breaking "faith with God to keep the letter of Man's law." For this belligerent appeal he employs a pseudonym, and his reasons for using this tactic provide a valuable insight into his methods as well as his character:

> Had I entirely approved either the spirit or the execution of these verses, I had put my name to them. But they were written in great haste and for a particular object, and I used therefore such arguments as I thought would influence the mass of my readers, viz: a swinging ballad metre, some sectional prejudice and vanity, some denunciation, some scriptural allusions, no cant. I wished *it* to be violent, because I thought the occasion demanded violence, but I had no wish to be violent myself, and therefore, I let it go anonymously. Had I written aught in my own name, it would have been entirely different.[143]

His candor is admirable; but it is inconceivable that a Whittier would have used words in this calculating manner, without integrity and total commitment. Despite his scriptural allusions, Lowell is far from prophecy, which demands not only a concern for the strategy of communication, but also a reverence for its truth.

The vein of insincerity is apparent elsewhere as well: in his resentment of the *"isms"* holding back his Parnassian climb,[144] his complaint at being "beflead with runaway slaves who wish to buy their wives,"[145] his resignation from the *Anti-Slavery Standard* ten days after Webster's speech because "a virtue seems to go out of" him at the touch of politics, his decision to leave America because such monstrosities as the 1850 Law make him "unhappy, and too restless to work well . . ."[146] Lowell's prominence in the anti-slavery movement is said to have lasted only through the years of his wife's influence, "and after her death, he ceased to be interested."[147] This may be somewhat unfair. In private letters he does call the

Burns rendition "nasty" and assures his friends that good must come of evil (re the repeal of the Personal Liberty Bill and the Dred Scott decision). Yet we are faced with his ever-deepening silence, as a poet, on all disturbing issues, culminating on October 29, 1859, in the mumbled reply to Higginson: "Editorially, I am a little afraid of John Brown . . ." Long before Mrs. Lowell's death her Red Cross Knight may have lost the inner battle: "I agonized to write something about the kidnapping of Sims," he explains lamely, "but the affair was so atrocious that I could not do it."[148] It is merely a matter of time before his betrayal is dignified with a public rationale: "Life in its large sense, and not as it is temporarily modified by . . . . politics, is the only subject of the poet." And Dante, Dante of the flaming tercets, is invoked to support his case![149]

We have found among major poets no less diversity of response than among lesser ones. While some successfully resist mention of the fugitive slave issue in their verse, others side with Union and deplore all quarrels tending to divide it. Longfellow, Emerson, and Whitman, on the other hand, are moved sufficiently by the fugitive's cause to break, on a few important occasions, their strict avoidance of current issues. Lowell's denunciatory impulse waxes strong in the late 1840's and wanes at the Sims case, precisely when the national ferment is approaching its height. But the opposite is true of Whittier, whose most vigorous period comes after Webster's 1850 address. All of America's major poets are aroused, to varying degrees, by the question; Bryant, Emerson and Thoreau produce condemnatory prose of high calibre at each key moment, that prose and the circumstances of its deliverance being unquestionably prophetic in the case of Thoreau and Emerson. In terms of ethical sensitivity, this group is as moved by the fugitive slave question as by any matter of current concern, far more so than the lesser poets. That their poetry seldom reflects this excitement proves again how firmly they guard against tendentiousness. That they are occasionally impelled, on the other hand, to bypass their rigid aesthetic rules, illustrates the particular impact of this issue. It must finally be noted that the runaway slaves and their Negro deliverers receive far less attention—from both major and minor poets—than do their white persecutors and protectors. Not one great escape ballad is produced, not one song by a white poet to equal the "poor dumb bondman's" own masterpiece, "Follow the Drinking Gourd."[150]

3

Mobbism Rampant

Mob violence has seldom been more spectacularly manifested than in America during the decades preceding the Civil War. Fundamental rights recently guaranteed by the Constitution were challenged to the point of mass murder and the sacking of towns. The massive anti-Masonic drive of the twenties served as a prelude to the burning of abolition presses, the mobbing of reform speakers, the persecution of religious minorities. For victims there was neither safety nor the hope of redress: clerics, mayors, and editors often inspired the mob—while police, judge, and jury (in whose eyes the victims were guilty) tacitly encouraged the next act of violence. In the rural South, with jails flimsy and far apart, mobs "broke the tedium" with tar, feathers, and rope.[1] Manipulated by men of politics and commerce, these semi-literates and their ruffian cousins in the North became America's defending knights against every new creed; nor were great centers of culture immune to the vigilante fever.

One might expect a poet genuinely reflecting that period to capture the imagery and tone of ruffianism. Besides, if poets *did* (until the twentieth century "flight from ethics") believe it their office "to make men better,"[2] there should have been numerous resonant outcries against what Cranch recalled so vividly in later years:

> The people's mad delusions, cheered and crowned;
> The mob's brute anarchy,—the tiger claws
> That tore to shreds the wise ancestral laws . . .[3]

I have chosen three particularly dramatic and representative displays of the mob spirit, each of which merited powerful rebuke and admonition. Let us see what impact they had on poets who considered themselves the descendants of prophets mobbed in ages past, guardians of the original American ideal, and carriers of light in a dark world.

i

The first phase we shall examine, highlighted by the murder of Elijah P. Lovejoy in 1837, involves the martyrdom of abolition spokesmen. In 1835 and 1836 editors Birney, Whittier, Garrison, and others were mobbed; George Thompson, "that infamous foreign scoundrel," came close to death in Concord, while the gentlemen of Boston announced "a purse of $100 . . . to reward the individual who shall first lay violent hands" on him.[4] The few abolitionist newspaper verses that emerge from these scenes stress the pro-slavery nature of the mobs and the courage of the reform leaders. Lydia M. Child characterizes the anti-Thompson mob feebly, emphasizing instead the superiority of non-violence:

> I've heard thee in the hour of prayer,
> When dangers were around . . .
>
> The evil spirit felt its power,
> And howling turned away . . .[5]

Others, expressing shock not at mobbism, but at its occurrence on Boston streets, conveniently ignore New England's tradition of majority violence against the dissenter. William H. Burleigh, for instance, recalls the ancient multitude's "maniac shout,/'LET HIM BE CRUCIFIED!'" and lectures the South that "tortures and stripes" are powerless against God's warriors; but he neither analyzes the mob as a deeply rooted Northern phenomenon, nor depicts artistically "the wild tumult of the popular rage," preferring to develop it as a partisan didactic theme.[6] Garrison sees the mob as an instrument of his intended martyrdom,[7] and hopes his blood will "find a wound to gush!" On his thirtieth birthday, almost eagerly awaiting the next mob (which in fact comes close to killing him this very year), he writes:

> . . . tis perchance the last
> I shall complete upon this earthly stage;
> For toils increase, and perils thicken fast,
> And mighty is the warfare that I wage . . .

Two years later the murder of Lovejoy and the destruction of his press have the effect "of an earthquake throughout the continent,"[8] calling forth "a burst of indignation which has not had its parallel . . . since the battle of Lexington . . ."[9] Historians have pinpointed this as the turning of the tide toward abolition among many public figures. Why then are there no verses on Lovejoy in anthologies, or at least in studies of his martyrdom—an incident worthy of indignant, defiant song? Here was a man of God, fearless in his insistence on the right to speak, bodily defending the freedom of the press, a man who left behind most of a life-span unlived, a score of poems, a wife and infant, an heroic mother, and brothers ready to fill the breach. Surely partisans, at least, should apotheosize their fallen man! Surely the poets of New England, if no others, can be expected to lament their colleague from Maine. Surely the time has come for the voice of prophecy to cry *Enough!* to mobbism as a way of life . . .

Our expectations are reasonable, but they are not fulfilled. With some responsible Northern newspapers praising the mob, with anti-slavery leaders attacking Lovejoy as a murderer because he fought back, with the pulpit condemning him as "rash and impudent,"[10] and the courts acquitting his killers, it is easier to understand the silence among poets. Some few reputable voices, and a considerable group of newspaper rhymesters, allow themselves to be heard; their rage, however, is against slavery, and only incidentally against mobbism. Slain because he "told a nation of its shame," Lovejoy merits honor.[11] His murderers, the poets declare, have done useful work, since the "dying martyr's groan" will bring emancipation closer. Exhorted to carry on, Lovejoy's co-workers are offered the hope of sharing "a glorious martyr's part,"[12] while his widow is instructed not to "bedew a martyr's crown" with tears, but to rejoice in the cause for which he died and to train his son for martyrdom![13]

Others, however, deplore the note of triumph in these elegies. They stress compassion for Mrs. Lovejoy and grim defiance toward his slayers. A Lovejoy elegy, they insist, should be pure in sorrow, both for him and for the banner whose "folds are stained with gore."[14] Here we see the beginnings of what can be called a denunciation of mobbism itself, rather than slavery, as a national disgrace and as prophecy's eternal foe. Some go even further, echoing Jeremiah's thunder against a particular city: "Alton! thy glory's whelmed in shame!" Once more, they prophesy, a wrathful Jehovah will hurl "hailstones and coals of fire"[15] upon the "Proud City" unless it quickly awakes to punish the murderers. Inspired by the ancient lamentation for Jerusalem, one poet envisions "the bard of the doomed city" wandering amid its ruins, wailing that Alton repented too late.[16] Equating Alton with Golgotha, Lovejoy with Christ, some see the "demoniac" mob of 1837 as a reincarnation of Jerusalem's "hungry tigers," and prophesy that—like the ancient martyrs—Lovejoy will rise again.[17]

Very few call for an end to mob violence;[18] perhaps they feel that it is implicit in their expressions of sorrow and their predictions of divine retribution. Although they recognize mobbism as a national condition, and Lovejoy's death seems a logical occasion for them to deplore publicly an ugly feature of American life, only once does a poet move from the easy condemnation of Alton to a general demand that American freedom "Clothe riots and ruffians with shame,/And to lawless misrule put an end . . ." Elsewhere the mob is shown delighting "in riot and plunder and murder," but it is to Alton, not America, this poet cries "Shame—shame"; it is only from Alton's lawless that he demands the weapons be wrested. As far as mob violence is concerned, he admits to a double standard. Thus, when a wronged population perpetrates an illegal attack, he can "almost, excuse the excitable throng" and cover its offenses with "Charity's veil"; but cursed be the wretches that rise without grievances!

> For your laws promise freedom in word and in thought,
> To all who among you may stay,
> But the first word they utter, and ye like it not,
> Ye mob him and rob him and slay.

Like the above, most newspaper verse on Lovejoy is deficient in quality if not in fervor; yet a pair of unidentified poems are too well-wrought and lofty-spirited to be dismissed. "Sonnet on Lovejoy's Martyrdom" is a dramatic appeal for God to restrain His vengeance:

> . . . Just God! no doubt thy thunder murmureth,
> And soon shall break upon our crimson'd land!
> Yet, spare thine anger, stay thy red right hand! . . .
> Let not thine own hot curse be launched, that long
> Hath waited for its volleyed waking up!
> Spare, spare, good Lord! Avenge not yet the wrong!
> Nor drain, wrath-drugged for *us,* thy terror mingled cup![19]

Though lacking the imagination and skill of this poet, the author of "The Alton Riot" produces, within a framework of controlled grief, a fiery indictment of his land:

> No more be Freedom's name in triumph sung—
> Oh, let the lips be hushed, and stilled the tongue . . .
> To speak in Freedom's name is but to die![20]

Are these two poems the work of established writers who wish to publish their feelings without endangering their reputations? Such reluctance is easy to understand, for at this time not a single respected poet is indiscreet enough to respond openly. They may see the martyrdom as a key episode in the battle for a free press, recognize in Lovejoy the prophet eternally mobbed, and understand mobbism as a dangerous disease in the nation's blood; but to treat the subject in their poems would be interpreted as a declaration of abolition leanings.

What does surprise us, however, is the reticence of the anti-slavery poets, whose reputations are not at stake. Only three of any rank produce Lovejoy poems, and two of these have mixed feelings about the martyr. Maria W. Chapman gently chides him for having carried a gun, and weeps "for the blood of others shed by" him.[21] William H. Burleigh supports a resolution deeply deploring Lovejoy's use of force.[22] Only Alonzo Lewis offers unequivocal praise.[22] The three poets agree, however, that his name shall shine "to remotest time . . ." All see him as the champion "girt to die" for human rights. All laud the "blood poured forth so joyously," because of which the slave shall win deliverance. All evince no concern for the mob that murdered him, except as an indispensable ingredient in the joy of martyrdom.

Neither Mrs. Chapman's sonnet nor Lewis' commonplace, naïve stanzas merit attention as poetry. Lewis is wise to exclude "Lovejoy" from his collected poems. It illustrates the pitiful results when a poet lacks the imagination, spirit, and art needed to serve as a worthy vehicle for his prophetic urge. Burleigh's work is far more ambitious, but the rhetorical wave which carries him along leaves his reader behind. Had he held back, ideas less trite and expressions worthier of his feelings might have had time to gestate. Yet, despite the absence of memorable lines, his seven Lovejoy sonnets are the most considerable prophetic response, in verse, to the martyrdom,[23] and represent that defiance which is, after all, among the glories of the American heritage:

> Who of us, next, on Slavery's bloody altar
> Shall meet his doom? Thou only knowest, God!
> Yet will we tread the path our Brother trod,
> Trusting in Thee! Our spirits shall not falter . . .

The Alton crime at once takes its place high on the catalog of national shame, at least among abolition poets, and is alluded to by many whose angry vision encompasses the whole American scene. These references, brief as they usually are, characterize mobbism as an *intrinsic evil* with far more force and clarity than do the poems dedicated entirely to Lovejoy; this is so because the truth-telling and admonitory aims are not complicated by a need to weep or praise. In "The Tocsin," for instance, John Pierpont cries: "Work a free press!—ye'll see it broken;/Stand to defend it!—ye'll be shot." For these lines he offers lyrical footnotes: "Bear witness, heights of Alton! Bear witness, bones of Lovejoy!"[24] Similarly, in a wide-ranging attack on American iniquity, Arthur C. Coxe sings:

> And Lovejoy's blood is smoking on the ground . . .
> Americans burn men. To faggots bound
> They die for being what our fathers were.[25]

A valuable footnote explains the impact upon him of Lovejoy's *Memoirs,* and rages at his countrymen for damning the martyr while exonerating the mob. The most deliberately Biblical outburst is based on Isaiah's challenge to "hypocritical oppressors" whose fastings conceal a "fist of violence and deceit":

"Cry, cry aloud," cease not, the prophet saith;
Lift, trumpet like, thy voice, nor spare thy breath:
"Shew, shew my people, their transgressors," and
Their sins, which so pollute this guilty land.[26]

This exhortation rightly implies that poets are *not* crying aloud. Some, however, in other media than verse, do achieve notable utterance. John Quincy Adams, for example, who two years earlier mocked the abolitionists as a "small, shallow, and enthusiastic party,"[27] writes a fiery introduction to the Lovejoy *Memoirs* and is henceforth among the outstanding anti-slavery leaders of the land. James F. Clarke, at this time a midwest editor, resoundingly rebukes those who attack Lovejoy's imprudence rather than the murder, and addresses his own peeved subscribers in Alton:

> You have silenced your own press, and you are actually under the rule of a mob. Opinion governs everything, and the opinion of your city is in favor of mob law . . .[28]

Lecturing at Boston's Masonic Temple on heroes of other lands and times, Emerson makes "a cold shudder . . . run through the audience" when he suddenly looks them in the eye and interpolates these words:

> . . . whoso is heroic, will always find crises to try his edge. Human virtue demands her champions and martyrs. . . . It is but the other day, that the brave Lovejoy gave his breast to the bullets of a mob, for the rights of free speech and opinion, and died when it was not better to live.

More important here than the beauty of the prose is the gesture itself, a "calm braving of public opinion," a prophetic acting out of the very words he is speaking.[29]

Nor is Editor Bryant less heroic at the *Post,* under constant attack by those who think Alton's reform editor received his deserts. Bryant's defiant spirit crystallizes in those great final stanzas of "The Battle-Field" soon to be quoted so fittingly on behalf of the fallen Lovejoy: "Truth, crushed to earth, shall rise again . . ."[30] The mobbing of Birney earlier elicited from Bryant a magnificent free-speech editorial, and he warned the land that, "If the stake be set and the faggots ready, there will be candidates for martyrdom." In a blazing editorial following the Alton murder he prophesies despotism or anarchy for a land without free tongue or pen, and eulogizes "The conduct of those who bled in this gallant defense . . . with an obstinacy which yielded only to death."[31]

That Bryant and Emerson keep Lovejoy out of their verse is not surprising: both seek to save their poetry from the day's events. Emerson's admission in "The Humble Bee" is profoundly revealing, despite its playful tone: "Wait, I prithee, till I come . . . All without is martyrdom."[32] The same holds for Longfellow, who tells only his journal of his disgust with "the Little-Peddlington community of Boston" and "the tyranny of public opinion there" which has attempted to block a Lovejoy memorial.[33] For Holmes to rebuke the Alton mob would be even more out of character; at most, the impact of the murder neutralizes him (he dates 1836 as the last year in which he mocked abolition[34]). He probably endorses young Lowell's portrayal:

> Oh abolitionists, both men and maids,
> Who leave your desks, your parlors, and your trades,
> To wander restless through the land and shout,
> But few of you could tell us what about![35]

It would take a somewhat larger spirit than either Holmes or Lowell nurtures at this time to deplore publicly the mobbing of someone he holds in scorn.

The problem is Whittier—like Lovejoy a young New England abolition editor and poet who has tasted mob fury. Whittier has none of Bryant's or Longfellow's reticence about praising an individual martyr or memorializing a specific occasion in rhyme.[36] That he can write with feeling on this issue is evidenced in the 1835 "Stanzas For the Times":

> Shall ruffian threats of cord and steel,
> The dungeon's gloom, the assassin's blow,
> Turn back the spirit roused to save
> The Truth . . .?

Still earlier he proved his ability to celebrate "the glorious martyrdom" awaited by Garrison and "the cruel martyrdom" achieved by Storrs. Yet he keeps silent on Lovejoy. A year's-end editorial poem in Lundy's paper *may* be by Whittier, who is about to assume the editorship. The metrical freedom does recall his poems of general indictment:

> Look to the west. The reeking earth is hot
> With LOVEJOY's blood, shed for the suffering slave;
> Riot stalks unabashed—Justice is not,
> And murdered Freedom sleeps within the grave.
> Such is our country. Rouse ye, ere the wrath
> Of a just God lay desolate her path.[37]

But the likelihood is that these turbulent lines come from another pen. Whittier, the prototype of non-violence, the enemy of guns, cannot be expected to cherish Lovejoy's memory more than do the Grimké sisters or Samuel May. That this is his unshakable attitude is made clear eight months after the slaying, in his editorial footnote to a poem on the martyr. Challenging the rhymester's resolve to follow Lovejoy's path, he comments wryly: "With the exception of using carnal weapons."[38] Nor does his 1840 *North Star* include a single Lovejoy reference. Apparently his quarrel is not primarily with the mob but with its armed victim. Only when a Philadelphia mob in 1838 burns down Pennsylvania Hall—including his own editorial office—does Whittier speak out.[39] Addressing the patrons of the paper he has stubbornly continued to publish, he pictures their noble temple rearing "its black and ruined wall" beneath the sky:

> Telling the story of its doom,
> The fiendish mob, the prostrate law,
> The fiery jet through midnight's gloom . . .

Later, when the impressions of that nightmare have had time to ripen in his imagination, he recalls it vividly, *especially its unarmed heroes*:

> . . . midst the sound of rushing feet
> And curses on the night-air flung,
> That pleading voice rose calm and sweet
> From woman's earnest tongue;
> And Riot turned his scowling glance,
> Awed, from her tranquil countenance!

The razing of Pennsylvania Hall calls forth numerous poems and passages of poems. Partly because this martyr is a building, and partly because ruffianism is now too common and uncontrolled to be overlooked, the praise and grief give way to wrath. Poets at last focus on the faces and actions of the mob, and try to depict the event artistically. The most ambitious and graphic are Sophia L. Little[40] and Charles W. Denison.[41] Both painstakingly narrate the incident, agreeing not only in the details of violence, but also in a final expression of defiance. Mrs. Little's variation of the Spenserian stanza, however, is far superior in poetic finish, with a largeness of vision and exaltation of tone which once again mark her as a poet prophetically motivated, though enfeebled by poeticisms. Like those who sang of Alton, she points out the ineffectiveness of physical annihilation, linking Lovejoy and the razed building with Christ:

> When Virtue's temple falls, or Lovejoy bleeds,
> Then Freedom brightens to her perfect day.
> Have ye not known of old th' Almighty's way?
> Our holy Lord, in dying, conquered death . . .

This is her conclusion, but not her main focus. It is the mob as a phenomenon of American life which interests her, as it does Denison. They see the ruffians as "a rabble-rout" chained by "the fiend," rejoicing in violence for its own sake.

John Pierpont's treatment is less flowery, and more terrifying:

> Go, then, and build yourselves a hall,
> To prove ye are not slaves, but men! . . .
> Within let Freedom's anthem swell;—
> And, while your hearts begin to throb,
> And burn within you—Hark! the yell,—
> The torch,—the torrent of the MOB!

His final stanza illustrates with unintentional force the commitment involved in daring to handle this theme: the mob may silence "pulpit, press, and hall," but the MUSE *will* sing out or leave "a land of slaves."[42]

Attacks on speakers and editors continue in the forties. Abolition poets, still alluding to mob persecution in terms of exhilarated defiance, manifest little concern toward mobbism as an evil. Thus Mrs. Chapman praises Adams for daunting Southerners who "trample our rights with their ruffian tread!"[43] When editor Cassius M. Clay is threatened with death, Mrs. Follen assures him that the one "Who falls in Freedom's noble strife" wins immortality."[44] William W. Story also pledges ultimate triumph to those now being silenced, whose "bitter food" is persecution:

> . . . yet every word
> Hath fiery wings, and shall be clearly heard
> When thy frail lips to silent dust are brought.[45]

It is exceptional to find a sustained emphasis on the evil of the ruffian trend. William H. Burleigh must be singled out for his repeated and impassioned attacks. Nowhere else in his work does he come so close to prophecy as in these execrations, warnings, and battle-cries. Immediately after reading of the 1841 reign of terror in Cincinnati, Burleigh produces two sonnets (distinguished more for rage than art) with which he closes his volume published the same month. Decrying the Cincinnati authorities for having encouraged the mob, he offers the poems as a terrifying illustration of "Our Country" as he envisions her in the body of the book:

Lo! the Arch-Anarch, fierce Mobocracy,
Stalks o'er the land and shouts with demon-glee;
Trampling on law and right and public good,
He bathes his murderous hands in martyr-blood . . .
Foul Treason, Murder, Arson, every crime
That curses earth or blots the page of time,—
These are his pastimes—and his devotees
Must bear the crimson stain of deeds like these![46]

Only Story goes further—and only once—attacking mob-violence on principle, and including his own friends among the culprits:

Truth has stepped down from off her lofty seat,
And her white robes of Justice are defiled,
When she in angry factions sets her feet,
And fires the pyre that Bigotry has piled.
Still let her words be calm, her action high . . .[47]

Such insistence on the neglected ideal is rare. One senses rather, even in Bryant, Emerson, and Longfellow, a tacit acceptance of mobbism as an ugly essential of the American, or the human, landscape. To single out the mob for analysis, or to depict it in a specific action, would be to violate their rules, as well as their sensibilities. Just as Bryant is benumbed by anything that localizes or temporizes his theme,[48] so is it difficult for Emerson to focus on a particular evil while preaching that Evil and Good are one. And Longfellow is not likely to upset the tranquility of his verse with ruffian allusions. One might say that tranquility itself, intruded upon a violent epoch, represents a prophetic comment. But Longfellow makes such an interpretation untenable in his case by his defense of America as the land of "fair play." Since she is working out one of the highest problems in the "celestial mechanics" of man, he argues, "we must not be too impatient nor chide too harshly if in doing this she sometimes assumes an ungainly attitude . . ."[49]

Under Maria White's influence Lowell turns from ridicule to glorification of the anti-slavery martyrs.[50] His hero, or knight, or prophet, defies the physical threats of a blind majority, almost requiring a mob in order to test his stature. There is a "need of martyrs and apostles"; even language, to achieve greatness, needs "lips purified/With martyr-fire." This emphasis on the joy of martyrdom is illustrated in many of his poems, but nowhere so beautifully as in "Prometheus," perhaps the finest poetic response to the mob atrocities of Lowell's time:

> . . . This heart,
> Unscarred by the grim vulture, as the truth
> Grows but more lovely 'neath the beaks and claws
> Of Harpies blind that fain would soil it, shall
> In all the throbbing exultations share
> That wait on freedom's triumphs, and in all
> The glorious agonies of martyr-spirits . . .
> This is a thought, that, like the fabled laurel,
> Makes my faith thunder-proof; and thy dread bolts
> Fall on me like the silent flakes of snow
> On the hoar brows of aged Caucasus:
> But, oh, thought far more blissful, they can rend
> This cloud of flesh, and make my soul a star!

Whitman's only mob-poem[51] comes before he has worked out his aesthetic and philosophic program. Like other poets of the day, he handles the current fever through a delocalizing device—turning Alton, Philadelphia, and Cincinnati into Golgotha:

Thou art reviled, scourged, put into prison,
Hunted from the arrogant equality of the rest:
With staves and swords throng the willing servants of
authority,
Again they surround thee, mad with devilish spite;
Toward thee stretch the hands of a multitude, like
vulture's talons,
The meanest spit in thy face, they smite thee with their
palms;
Bruised, bloody, and pinion'd is thy body . . .

Whitman focuses pessimistically and almost entirely on the face of the mob rather than on the martyr, and finally rejects his own delocalizing device by bringing the incident forebodingly into the present: "And still Iscariot plies his trade." Thus "Blood Money" runs counter to Whitman's optimism and counter to his contemporaries' treatment of mobbism. For, although the murder of Lovejoy and other atrocities do bring "important recruits to the anti-slavery cause,"[52] the verse of the day is poor in attempts to depict or analyze the mob as a thing in itself, organically rooted in the American past, ominously symptomatic of America's current disease, and liable eventually to wreck the national life.

ii

We turn next to the persecution of "outside" religions and nationalities. Our moment of focus is May—July, 1844, for it was then that the anti-foreign drive of the Native American Party (the Whigs' extreme radical wing) reached a peak of destructive fervor. This violently oriented group, under the pretense of exceptional loyalty to the American ideal, had for several years been raging across the country, directing hatred against the newly arriving "hordes" of Irish and others who swamped the labor market. But the anti-Catholic drive of the thirties had more than economic roots. Idealistic preachers such as Lovejoy and Lyman Beecher militantly agitated against what they termed a proselytizing growth swarming cross-continent with papal plots. As the Catholic population rose from one per cent (75,000) in 1810 to ten per cent (3,-000,000) in 1860, its leaders and institutions greatly increased in power. Whether the Catholic "was hated because he was a foreigner or because he was a Catholic,"[53] the fact remains that his vote could and often did affect elections. Thus the nativists called for exclusion from public office of all immigrants, and a twenty-one-year residence requirement before voting. By 1844 the issue had been fatally joined; in many cities the Whig and Native American press incited their readers to the very acts of violence they would afterward blame on the Irish or on "old convicts . . . a motley and depraved crowd . . ."[54]

That there *were* in every city "depraved" persons eager for destructive action can be seen in such contemporary songs as "The Boys in the Bowery Pit" and "One of the Boys," which exult in rowdyism; "Toss the Turk," in which a gang is walloped; "Since Terrence Joined the Gang," a father's lament on the ruffianism of his son; and "There's a Good Time Coming, Boys!"—an expression of longing for a time when reason, not force, will rule the land.[55]

No doubt sheer wildness was a factor in the events of mid-1844. Thus, after the first series of atrocities ended, a Philadelphian rationalized by pointing to Natchez, where "they try to burn down newspaper offices . . . as we do churches in this city, by way of satisfaction."[56] Editors were misled into accepting Native American accounts of their own orderliness and of Irish violence, blaming the anti-Irish terror on men "belonging to no party . . . and rioting for the love of riot."[57] Even if this were so, however, the devastation in Philadelphia, and the efforts to initiate similar attacks elsewhere, might be expected to have elicited a response from America's poets. At the least, they could restate the minimal democratic ideal: that an Irishman is no worse than his fellow man, that a Catholic church has as sacred a right to stand as has any other place of worship. As the appeal to the people's lowest passions became increasingly successful, including the election of a nativist mayor in New York, one might expect poets to have sounded a vigorous ethical alarm.

If any one of our touchstones has revealed a prophetic failure, it is this. Just as the death of Lovejoy called forth no direct verses outside of abolitionist ranks, and little of real literary merit within those ranks, so does the anti-Irish rampage in Philadelphia remain unsung outside of Catholic circles, and feebly sung even by Catholic rhymesters:[58]

> Aye, down with the Cross, let no emblem of love
> Be seen the red City of Riot above.
> Give to Bigots your cheers, and Religion a grave
> In this land of the free and this home of the brave.

When an anonymous versifier, bewailing St. Augustine's Church, describes the "disgraceful, damning deeds" and the "smouldering ruins, black and murk," we are reminded of the Pennsylvania Hall poems, not only because location and victim are similar, but because the same defiance is heard. Despite the storm, their Father is at the helm; He will give them strength to rebuild "His holy fanes destroy'd/By bold and wicked men . . ." These poets, like Whittier in 1837, reject physical vengeance, begging God to forgive their enemies. Considering themselves "God's people" oppressed by "dire and cruel wrong," as the abolitionists did, they too lash out not at mobbism itself, but at the nature of their particular adversary: the slavocracy in 1837, anti-Christ in 1844. The poets of both groups are also alike in that they stress the martyr's role and ultimate victory.

Yet any thought that abolitionist poets, as fellow-victims of mob action, might express compassion, if nothing more, is dispelled by the *Liberator's* anti-Irish outburst following the July 4th riots. Garrison grants that ruffianism is a national danger and that "there will be no safety, no repose, no end to mobocratic excesses" until the Native American party is wiped out; but he gloats that the Irish are now rewarded for turning their backs on the anti-slavery movement, and that Philadelphia has its reward for being the worst anti-Negro, anti-abolition riot city in the land:

> Behold how awful, how just, and how swift has been the retribution of Heaven! 'Alleluia! for the Lord God reigneth!' Truly, they who sow the wind, shall reap the whirlwind . . .[59]

Only one poet, Thomas G. Spear, comes forward to declare the meaning of the 1844 events in larger than parochial terms:

> Forbear! Columbia cries,
> This thirst for wild affray;
> Back, freemen! and despise
> The passions that betray.
> Is this a land of laws,
> To peace and order given?
> Then let the banded pause—
> The recreant hence be driven.[60]

Many of the minor figures have partisan reasons for remaining silent. Epes Sargent, for one, does not conceal his anti-Irish streak and his "leaning . . . toward the Native American or Know-Nothing Party."[61] Seba Smith is in 1844 the editor of New York's Native American paper. William B. Tappan has recently authored a series of virulently anti-Catholic poems, of which the sixth is typical:

> Why not upon the Plymouth Rock
> Erect the bloody "church of God,"
> Whose lordly dome may swell, and mock
> The humble sires below the sod?[62]

In "The Clearing" Frederick G. Tuckerman similarly diminishes himself by delivering a snide thrust against the encroaching Irish—inconsistent with his usual theme and tone, unnecessary to the success of the poem into which he intrudes it, and certain to encourage the basest emotions of his readers:

> Then let us hold what's gone,
> And hug each greener minute,
> Though shanties smoke in every cove,
> And Paddies rule the senate.[63]

Although there is no such allusion in the verse of Charles F. Hoffman, he is clearly not free of this feeling. Following the May riots, a playful letter to his Philadelphia friend Griswold describes an imaginary attack by "our generous but somewhat excitable adopted citizens" upon the anthologist's home, Griswold having "lately abandoned all his other literary labors to devote himself to an anti-Catholic Review."[64]

On the other hand, occasional references by certain minor poets seem to repudiate bigotry. Although one cannot call "Erin's Daughter" Mrs. Sigourney's answer to the Philadelphia riots, it is significant that she conceives and publishes at this time a sympathetic portrait of a homesick, courageous girl willing to do menial work in America in order to "lift the load/Of poverty" from her far-off parents.[65] For a clearly denunciatory statement, however, we must turn elsewhere. In "Schism Among the Methodists," a violent satire, John Burke unmasks the hypocrisy of ruffian zealots:

> Thousands on thousands of those knaves
> Who most abuse their wretched slaves . . .
> Are found the loudest freedom boasters
> In all those anti-Popery musters![66]

If anti-Mormonism was more localized than "those anti-Popery musters," it was because the Mormon Church represented no national threat. Only in a few regions had Joseph Smith's followers established their obnoxious prosperity, and it was the local violence of their neighbors that drove them from each new settlement. The strange, communistic theocracy, guilty of extreme land-greed, had been scourged out of Missouri after broadcasting its leader's promise "that the whole state . . . would ultimately belong to them." Smith had proselytized the Indians and incited the Negroes, had engaged in wildcat banking and left a trail of vengeful apostates behind him. Persecution-oriented, he had announced "a war of extermination" to any mob that might disturb his sect, and had in fact raided the property of some Missourians.[67] In Illinois, although Douglas and Lincoln courted their vote and both parties stumbled over each other to approve their city charter, the Mormons angered their neighbors by introducing polygamy, voting as a block, demanding a separate territory for Nauvoo, and allowing their city to become "a happy hunting ground for fugitives from justice." The burning down of an opposition newspaper in June, 1844, and the hasty trial of its editors, became the "final straw." Upon the governor's guarantee of protection, Joseph and Hyrum Smith surrendered and were swiftly martyred in Carthage jail. A gigantic ruffian assemblage from the whole Mississippi valley prepared to annihilate the stunned Mormon capital on the pretext that the Saints were planning revenge.[68]

Thus, like the Irish, these victims of mobbism were far from blameless themselves; what seems to be overlooked, however, is the link between the nativism of Philadelphia and of the Mississippi valley, where thousands of British immigrants streamed through a resentful St. Louis on their way to flourishing Nauvoo (population 9,000 in 1841; 16,000 in 1845). Furthermore, Joseph Smith's nomination for the Presidency, two weeks before his death, disappointed Whig hopes for the Mormon vote, and was accompanied by an ultra-radical platform advocating that slaves be freed, army deserters go unpunished, and congressmen receive only two dollars a day.

Within Mormon ranks, the verse inspired by their persecution has the same parochial tone and trite phrases as the abolition and Catholic rhymesters. We are told how Smith "bared his breast before . . . these lawless ruffians" and declared, "Death has to me no terrors." The shrill description of his captors as "hungry beasts of prey" is devoid of all depth. Individual hostile congressmen are likewise attacked for "wild barbarity." Although the poet cries "shame" to Illinois and Missouri, there is no indication that mobbism in general is evil, and that it is a national condition.[69]

Outside the ranks, despite the more unsavory features of the Mormon story, it would not be far-fetched to expect that at least one reputable American poet, with eyes sharper than most, might recognize in the mob's fury against Smith and his "new Jerusalem" a re-enactment of the eternal crucifixion; for—charlatan or no—he was the spiritual leader of a new creed, and America's vaunted freedom of worship was once more being seriously tested. There is, however, dead silence. When a Garrison does speak, it is to disregard the governor's duplicity, the lynch-cry raised by the suppressed paper, the years-long hounding by mobs, the generally peaceful nature of the Mormons; instead he reviles Smith as an "infatuated leader" at last fallen a victim of lawless violence after having "sanctioned a mobocratic assault" on an anti-Smith paper. " 'They that take the sword,' etc."[70] One senses here the Puritan's disgust with Mormon practice, the abolitionist's hope that Smith's elimination as a candidate may gain some votes for Birney.

I have found no 1844 poem which directly deplores the murder of Hyrum and Joseph Smith. Perhaps W.W. Lord has Carthage in mind when he speaks in 1844 of having often "mourned silently . . . for violated law."[71] Mrs. Sigourney, too, may mean these slayings when she asks Americans to repress "Each ruder breath that stirs to wrathful deeds."[72] But several years are to pass before the first, and only, cry of condemnation is heard. In 1848 a Western tourist interrupts his verse travelog with a seventy-five line narration of the Mormon agony. No admirer of Joseph Smith, "Who claims to be commissioned from above," this obscure poet nevertheless feels impelled to shatter the nation's shameless silence:

In this good land where every mind is free
To worship God as well beseemeth him . . .
Who thus could sport with law . . .
And suffer lawless miscreants to usurp
The laws of State, and take into their hands
The sword of justice, to avenge on men
Their hate, and seize their substance for themselves.
A poor man for his vineyard Ahab slew,
And met dire punishment, although a king.[73]

Both in its length and attitude, this passage stands as a remarkable exception, underscoring the general prophetic failure on this issue.

Otherwise, the few direct allusions to Mormonism among America's minor poets include not a wisp of compassion or apology mixed with their hard contempt and ridicule.[74] As the lynch-frenzy builds up in the West, a Boston rhymester depicts a conglomerate performance by exotic thinkers at Faneuil Hall:

Alike, may jibber, fume, and squeak,
All equal, Mormon, Jew, and Greek.

Three years later, cataloguing those of whom "New England does not boast," Abby Allin laughingly includes "Smith of Mormon glory" along with the millenium-prophet Miller. In a more somber vein, E. R. Place is moved not to deplore the murders, but to brand the "wily Mormon" who, spouting Biblical names and toting the Holy Book, takes advantage of Americans' reverence for Hebraic "myths . . . and Mosaic law." The chief poetic response to Mormon martyrdom comes from Frederick G. Tuckerman, whose contempt is not for the mob but for its victim's persistence:

> The end of things he prophesies and paints,
> And of the rest remaining for God's saints;
> To one conclusion all his reasons run,
> And this he sees, taking his hearers on
> From point to point; though still discursively
> The addle-eggs about his temples fly . . .
> And, in the middle of the jeering press,
> He, smeared with mud and yellow yolks is,
> Giving the law, like Zeno or Zamolxis.[75]

It is extraordinary that this usually hermetic mind, avoiding mean temporal matters and insisting on personal freedom, is disturbed to the point of versifying—not by the tribulations of the Irish or the Mormons, but by their presence!

A poet such as Tuckerman, who reflects and encourages the bigotries of his generation instead of deploring them, thereby weakens his prophetic position no matter what his technical excellence may be. It does not follow, however, that a rejection of bigotry guarantees greatness or even competence, but that it increases the potential scope of vision, making the poet's world larger and fuller. We are therefore justified in expecting of major figures a reverberating condemnation of bias; in other words, their inclusiveness ought to recognize anti-Irish or anti-Mormon exclusiveness as its enemy. Further, as conscious guardians of the American ideal, they should identify the intolerant mob as a threat to the nation's essence, even if its victim is of a race or creed they personally do not like. What, then, is there for us to examine in their work?

According to Canby, Thoreau is unfriendly toward the Irish; yet his 1843 correspondence with Emerson shows that both poets admire the hardihood and pity the poverty of this maligned minority. Only a few months before the great 1844 outbreaks Thoreau waxes lyrical over this group.

> The sturdy Irish arms that do the work are of more worth than oak or maple. Methinks I could look with equanimity upon a long street of Irish cabins and pigs and children revelling in the general Concord dirt, and I should still find my Walden wood and Fair Haven in their tanned and happy faces . . .

Nor is there a hint of unfriendliness in his verse. He celebrates, for example, "The Old Marlborough Road," which "only the guests of the Irishman Quin" enter—Thoreau apparently included. As for his ballad, "I am the Little Irish Boy," it may indeed represent, as Bode points out, "Thoreau's only sinking into the bravely pathetic"; but it is even more remarkable, in the context of this discussion, as a tribute to the Irish spirit which cannot be crushed by extreme hunger and cold. We meet a child who "sometimes" has "some bread" for supper, who "if it's cold" goes "right to bed" and lies "on some straw" under his "fathers [sic] coat." Despite the bitterness of their existence, this boy declares proudly, almost cheerily:

> My mother does not cry
> And my father does not scold . . .
> Every day I go to school . . .
> And if my feet ache
> I do not mind the cold
> For I am a little Irish boy
> & I'm four years old.

With an irony reminiscent of Blake's chimney-sweep song, Thoreau depicts the naïveté of the lad's values:

> I shall grow up
> And be a great man
> And shovel all day
> As hard as I can.

Thoreau's usual definition of "a great man" is, as he knows we know, rather different; yet he would be among the first to acknowledge whatever greatness did exist:

> Down in the deep cut
> Where the men lived
> Who made the Rail road.[76]

It may seem odd that a poet so sympathetic to the underdog, so ready to challenge his nation's dominant mood, has nothing to say about the riots of May and July, 1844, or about mob intolerance in any form. Yet his recurrent emphasis on individualism can be said to strike at the very roots of the mob mentality per se, even when the people are buying Kossuth hats in unison rather than burning down St. Augustine's Church.

If Thoreau and Poe see eye to eye on anything, it is on this issue. Hatred for the mob is intrinsic to the temperament of both poets, implicit in the texture of their lives and works. It would almost seem extraneous of them to bother dealing with a local display of that American characteristic they obviously fear and despise most. Yet we do find, in the prose of Poe,[77] what appears to be a response to the 1844 violence. Although he left Philadelphia a month before the actual rioting began, Griswold and other colleagues remained, and Mrs. Clemm was still there in May. Thus he surely received first-hand accounts. In "Mellonta Tauta" Poe compels his smug generation to see itself through the more enlightened eyes of creatures a thousand years hence. By this means he gives warning that "the 'Republic' (So the absurd thing was called)" shall eventually succumb to "a fellow by the name of *Mob,*" who is going to take "everything into his own hands and set up a despotism":

> This Mob (a foreigner, by-the-by), is said to have been the most odious of all men that ever encumbered the earth. He was a giant in stature—insolent, rapacious, filthy; had the gall of a bullock with the heart of a hyena and the brain of a peacock.

Poe's bias seems to be anti-Irish; his tone matches perfectly the mockery in Hoffman's above-cited letter to Griswold. But Poe, unlike his colleague, has all mankind in view. The implications are as clear here as they are later to be in Melville's bitter poems on mobocracy: man cannot rule himself without becoming a mob; "democracy is a very admirable form of government—for dogs." An 1845 satire, "Dr. Tarr and Professor Fether," may well be considered in the same context. One can understand how this poet's native disgust would be nourished by the ugly demonstrations of 1844; what arrests us is the courage involved in Poe's expressing that cynicism to a public which has use only for affirmation. Poverty has not brought him to heel.

Poe's impulse to respond to iniquity cannot, by his own strict aesthetic rules, use poetry as a vehicle. In the verse of Holmes, however, the bigotry of 1844 seems to come under direct attack. He excoriates the anti-Catholic majority for its abuse of "Poor Nora, exile from Killarney's side!"

> Must thou be raking in the crumbled past
> For racks and fagots in her teeth to cast? . . .
> Thy sneering voice may call them "Popish tricks,"
> Her Latin prayers, her dangling crucifix,
> But *De Profundis* blessed her father's grave,
> That "idol" cross her dying mother gave![78]

Despite his lifelong attempt to maintain the position of "gentle poet" as contrasted with "the acrid pulpit and the corrosive newspaper," Holmes cannot help "pitching into giant vices."[79] On this issue, lifting the ethical standard as high as do any of his more pretentious contemporaries, he demands that his countrymen "blush for the wrongs that stain" their epoch and omit wrath in future dealings with those of other faiths.

Whitman, on the other hand,[80] has "no toleration for the Mormons," because free love, or anything like it, is "utterly repugnant to his mind." Perhaps for this reason he excludes them from his long catalogues, despite their monumental resilience and their leaders' martyrdom. As for the Irish, he asks editorially in 1844: "Has it come to be, that the American people cannot gather together . . . without being broken in upon by a gang of foreign outcasts and bullies . . .?" Nevertheless, Whitman deplores mob intolerance and decries it in the *Times, Eagle,* and *Star*. If specific ruffian acts are not depicted in his literary work, he is "not alone," as Allen rightly points out, ". . . in ignoring these ugly facts." What matters here is that he keeps his limitations out of his prophecies.[81] This, of course, he must do—not only because his aesthetic resolve is to "add, fuse, complete . . . celebrate the immortal and the good," but also because an admission of bigotry would destroy his basic assertion: "I am in love with . . . all my fellows upon the earth." Whitman, one might suggest, faces the task of establishing his image as universal prophet, "embracing man, embracing all." Yet this very act of publicly surpassing himself, of repeatedly discarding the local dross within him for the sake of an inspired cosmic message, is a perfect instance of prophecy achieved. When the poet, dressed as a man of the people, employing their language, stands before them to announce: "I respect Assyria, China, Teutonia, and the Hebrews,/I adopt each theory, myth, god, and demi-god," is he not thereby decrying the mobbist spirit in American life, offering his "I" as a symbol of the better direction to be taken?

Just so, we can see almost all the major figures, in their public commitment as God-touched voices, rising past the meanness they share with their time. Although on the one hand we might decide that their vast body of *generally* tolerant poetry emphasizes a prophetic failure in the *specific* test of 1844, on the other hand we can point to that very body of work as an indirect but valid utterance aimed at the bigot-mobs of their time and the exclusionist mood which allowed such mobs to fester.

We may, for instance, assume that Lowell's failure to condemn the Carthage murders and the near-massacre of Nauvoo's population is related to his sarcastic treatment of Joseph and Hyrum Smith in "A Fable for Critics," "The Unhappy Lot of Mr. Knott," and the *Biglow Papers*. Nor can we ignore his occasional anti-Irish or anti-Semitic hints.[82] But these are insignificant within the context of his total humanist output. Our attention turns to his powerful and timely assault on anti-Papism during the Mexican War, the portrayal of a mob action (more full, vivid, and artistically sound, perhaps, than any other in American poetry) with which Biglow's second series opens, and his vision of the America that is to be when "Thor's hammer" succumbs to the "Weaponless . . . Christ":

> Here shall a realm rise
> Mighty in manhood;
> Justice and Mercy
> Here set a stronghold
> Safe without spear.[83]

With Bryant, too, an extremely rare lapse—such as his allusion to "the dark,/False Malay"[84]—merely serves to underscore the soaring universality of his dominant spirit, as illustrated in impassioned hymns to the Greeks, Spaniards, Italians, and Swiss. In 1844 he runs true to form, responding not in verse but in the perceptive and powerful prose of editorials that sound like lamentations. Arriving at his office in the morning, he picks up with repugnance the news accounts from Philadelphia and Carthage:[85]

> This repugnance arises from an apprehension, excited by our recent experience, that a large number of these papers will contain records of the perpetration of brutal and disgraceful acts of violence in some part or other of the United States. The spirit of wrong-doing seems to possess so many of our citizens, that the only impression left upon our minds . . . is one of exceeding painfulness and sorrow.

It is surely from this kind of sorrow that Byrant continually escapes into the world of nature. There is, however, no escape on his editorial page. Here he places the blame squarely, calls the death of the Smiths "as cowardly and atrocious a murder as was ever committed," and identifies the disease infesting the land. Although his denunciation of the 1844 mobs and the society which engendered them takes editorial rather than poetic form, he also makes it clear in a resonant verse passage that he abhors mob action of any kind, even when the grievances of the rioters are justified:

> Let him not rise, like these mad winds of air,
> To waste the loveliness that time could spare,
> To fill the earth with woe, and blot her fair
> Unconscious breast with blood from human veins.[86]

From Whittier, who is responsive to current evils and has made the persecution of minority creeds a major theme in his ballads, one expects a word of rebuke for the anti-Mormon and anti-Catholic mobs. Yet he keeps his silence, as he did at Lovejoy's murder. Is he temperamentally incapable of expressing indignation at outrages when the victims resist? Is he so anti-Mormon that he cannot deplore Mormon martyrdom, so stirred against the Catholic as persecutor in Europe that he cannot pity the Catholic persecuted in America? This may be; yet he does, along with occasional anti-Catholic references, produce "Kathleen," an 1849 ballad sympathetic to the Irish;[87] and the purpose of his many narrative poems based on America's past is clearly didactic. In this light we can profitably examine the portrayals of religious persecution in such Whittier poems of the forties as "St. John" (Catholics vs. Huguenots), "The Exiles" (Puritans vs. Quakers), "The Knight of St. John" (Mohammedans vs. Catholics), "Cassandra Southwick" (Puritans vs. Quakers), and "Barclay of Ury" (Scottish Presbyterians vs. Quakers).[88]

This pattern is worked out most strikingly in Longfellow, who, through his art, manages to overcome the anti-Semitic bent he exposed while in Europe, among friends.[89] First in "The Jewish Cemetery at Newport," again in the *Tales of a Wayside Inn,* and finally in *Judas Maccabeus,* he condemns the mass persecution of Jews. From his early *Outre-Mer* to the last period, we are repeatedly impressed by a universal love less stridently announced than Whitman's, but equally genuine and far more affecting. We may be disappointed by the apparent silence of a poet who "disliked intolerance in every area,"[89] and several of whose works "radiate the spirit and atmosphere of the Catholic faith."[90] But to expect a poem directly connected with the 1844 riots would be to ignore Longfellow's way of working. Such a poem would be slow in taking form. Usually he "had an idea . . . for a long time, without finding any expression for it . . ." before it suddenly crystallized.[91] Thus, if we seek his response to the burning of churches, the killing of Irish and Mormons, or the expulsion of Smith's followers from Illinois, we must give him months, even years, before his heartache softens, generalizes, turns into song that offers inspiration rather than cynicism or despair.

From this point of view Longfellow offers richer rewards on the mass bigotry theme than do his contemporaries. The vast number of admiring references to Catholic ritual, thought, and tradition, which Gavigan sees as an infatuation, is more than merely "unusual in a New England Protestant,"[92] although it surely is that. At the peak of anti-Papist fervor, which captures many of the poet's readers, he is positively defiant in offering a sympathetic and sensitive depiction of Catholicism, both before the Philadelphia riots (in *The Spanish Student,* for example), and afterward, notably in *The Belfry of Bruges, Evangeline,* and *The Golden Legend*. This last Mrs. Longfellow describes as "almost too Catholic, and rather dangerous to publish in these excited times!"[93] One recognizes here the same prophetic valor manifested in the *Poems on Slavery*. Not aesthetically, but ethically, his works challenge his time.

If any one poem can be pinpointed as the closest Longfellow comes to commenting on the 1844 outrages, it must be *Evangeline*—begun in 1845.[94] In Part One the poet finds occasion to exclaim that "Daily injustice is done, and might is the right of the strongest!" Although he warns the persecuted against using mob-vengeance "with violent deeds and hearts overflowing with hatred," and shows the Jansenites finally praying, "O Father, forgive them!" precisely as the victims in Nauvoo and Philadelphia had prayed, he leaves with us a horrifying picture of the sacked village, the flame "like the quivering hands of a martyr," the parishioners crying "aloud in their anguish,/'We shall behold no more our homes . . .' " The tale ends, significantly, in Philadelphia. Although the poet does not directly refer to the recent demonstrations of unfriendliness in its streets, he does wryly comment on its veneer of friendliness, "the Thee and Thou of the Quakers," as opposed to old Acadia, where in truth "all were brothers and sisters." Suddenly, in a tone that recalls the telling of Egypt's ancient plagues, Longfellow introduces a striking detail: "Then it came to pass that pestilence fell on the city . . ." This is not at all essential to the plot, since Gabriel might have "crept away to die in the alms-house," pestilence or no. It seems almost as if the poet were employing against Philadelphia here the same high admonition which God commanded Jonah to utter in Nineveh:

So death flooded life . . .
Wealth had no power to bribe, nor beauty to charm, the
oppressor;
But all perished alike beneath the scourge of his anger . . .

Wherever possible in the years that follow, Longfellow reiterates his plea for universal inclusiveness and an end to violence. That he is harrowed by such nightmares as those of 1844, and that he refuses to let America forget its ruffian character, is amply documented. His rebuke leaps up at the reader from such unlikely pages as *The Song of Hiawatha* ("Wash the blood-stains from your fingers,/ Bury your war-clubs and your weapons"). It appears in "The Saga of King Olaf" ("Love against hatred,/Peace-cry for war-cry!"); and, most strikingly, in the *John Endicott* prologue. When the dramatist is asked why the errors of the past should be dragged "into the light of day," he answers:

. . . 'For the lesson that they teach:
The tolerance of opinion and of speech . . . '
Let us remember, if these words be true,
That unto all men Charity is due;
Give what we ask; and pity, while we blame,
Lest we become copartners in the shame,
Lest we condemn, and yet ourselves partake . . .[95]

Longfellow's parables are no less pertinent to the ethical failures of his place and time, and sometimes more effectively communicated, than are the brilliant philosophic thrusts of Emerson, who ignores the specific events in Philadelphia and Carthage while applying his compensation theory to the mob phenomenon:

> The fact of two poles . . . is universal, and each force by its own activity develops the other. Wild liberty develops iron conscience. Want of liberty . . . stupefies conscience . . . A mob cannot be permanency; everybody's interest requires that it should not exist, and only justice satisfies all . . .[96]

Emerson's poetry is not without pertinent lessons for his bigoted readers. Rather pointedly, his squirrel-minority reminds the mountain-majority that both "must be taken in together," and his countrymen are forced to hear the Earth laughing at all nativists everywhere: "How am I theirs,/If they cannot hold me,/But I hold them?"[97] When an Emerson or a Longfellow hurls such truth into the mob's teeth, he is beautifully performing the prophet's office to "make men better."

It is clear that mob intolerance is publicly deplored by America's chief mid-century poets despite their personal limitations, unlike the lesser poets, whose limitations tend to overcome their ethical standards. It is equally clear that to the particular instances of mob outrage in 1844, sensational and meaningful as they are, most minor poets play deaf, blind, and dumb, while only Holmes among the major poets responds directly in his verse, and only Bryant —in his editorials—raises his voice aloud in rebuke and warning.

iii

The final phase of mobbism which we will consider overlaps somewhat the earlier attacks on abolitionists. The language of abuse, the threats, the defiance, and the crimes were similar. Many of the older participants, on both sides, had probably played some part in the violence of other years. We know, for instance, that John Brown's presence in Kansas stemmed from his public vow of 1837 henceforth to serve Lovejoy's cause. But the action was no longer merely that of huge, frenzied throngs against a tiny number trapped in their midst; gradually it became a matter of force against force, functioning as military units using surprise tactics over a huge battle-area, the very center of the continent, itself to be the prize of war. Their primary motive was no longer hate, or a need for excitement, or a desire to defend a point of view, but a geographic line to be held at all costs. Government was no longer simply unable or unwilling to protect those threatened, and to punish those who assaulted them; by 1855 it actively sided with the marauder when he was pro-slavery, and joined in the hounding of his victim. Thus the free-soilers could either return east, as many did; settle in ever-greater numbers, wielding spiritual weapons only; or arm themselves and test the courage of ruffians who had never met their match before.

For poets there is also a choice. They can ignore Kansas, side with one or another of the antagonists, or lament this latest manifestation of mob violence as more dangerous to the existence of the country than any before. We will again focus on a particularly dramatic and pivotal moment which can perhaps serve as a test for the ethical sensitivity of poets: the third week of May, 1856, beginning with Sumner's great address on Kansas atrocities, followed by his near-fatal beating on the Senate floor, then the sacking of Lawrence, Kansas, and John Brown's retaliation at Pottawatomie.

Prior to that colossal week, the struggle for Kansas is ignored by poets outside anti-slavery ranks; but the work produced within those ranks helps us to know the period. The sunlit recruiting songs of early spring, 1855,[98] suddenly give way to stanzas of rage and defiance as news arrives of many ruffian outrages against free-soil settlers. We discover a far more self-confident and belligerent response now than in the thirties.[99] The new battle-songs urge resistance to "the black banner of blood-stained Oppression" raised on "the green sunny plains of ill-fated Kansas." One poet reminds his readers of their heroic heritage, exhorting them to defy the "ruffian crowds assailing" them, as Alfred the Great dared to stand alone when surrounded. Free-soil can win, another tells the South, without resorting to *"your* favorites, *mob* and *lynch."* A call for armed recruits, early in 1856, is at once taken up by the poets, who now sound like trumpeters rather than mourners for unavenged victims. "Avaunt, ye tyrannizing mobs!" they cry, exhorting free-soilers to make Kansas their Thermopylae. These songs typify the martial mood, long simmering beneath the old vow of non-violence, now finally bursting into the open. The poets of abolition paint Kansas as bloodily as they can, holding up the Border Ruffians as "armed invaders, burning with desire/To blast with Slavery's curse this paradise"; and they damn the pro-ruffian Chief Executive for polluting "the place once filled by WASHINGTON." But there is much more than a listing of grievances. In the rousing peals of Tyrtaean prophecy Ohio and her sister-states are asked to "join the teeming East in marshalling . . . hosts of freemen" on the plains of Kansas. God is begged not for some vague retribution, as in Lovejoy's time, but for military assistance, and the sons of the Pilgrims are reminded of their military heritage:

God keep our wanderers well! let them not yield
Their rifles in their hands; in Freedom's name,
Cromwell remembering, and old Naseby's field,
Keep bright the Puritan fame!

It would be wrong to suggest that abolition became martial only in reply to Southern atrocities in Kansas. It is even further from the truth to ignore the ruffian murders, election outrages, and destruction of Lawrence, to make light of the assault on Sumner, and pretend that John Brown's retaliatory attack was the cruelest occurrence in Kansas.[100] The fact is that free-soil met violence with violence, and that among the advocates of gunfire were certain traditionally militant figures, such as Higginson, who hated slavery, not mobbism. In fact, he had himself turned the Anthony Burns audience into a mob that "hearkens to a fiery harangue, surges down the street, pounds on a prison door, defies the policeman, and displays the ordinary symptoms of the mob spirit."[101] Returning from abroad in May, 1856, Higginson at once committed himself entirely to the Kansas struggle, and set out to play a dangerous role there. At burned-out Lawrence he preached from the text: "Be not ye afraid of them; remember the Lord, which is great and terrible, and fight for your brethren."[102]

It is at this time that the Concord poet, Franklin B. Sanborn, defiantly associates himself with John Brown. The taste of violence does not appall him; it is Brown's retaliatory vigor that appeals to him most:

Twice thy bold counsels and thy ready hand
Conquered for freedom Kansas' bloody land;
A third time in the field, thy heaviest blow
Falls like swift lightning on the sleeping foe![103]

Other young poets actually accompany Brown on his scourging missions. The best of them, Richard Realf, stays on in Kansas for a while and produces admirable poems from within the eye of that hurricane; these we will examine later. What concerns us here is the mood which catapults Realf and others out of their safety in the East. It is partly, of course, the demand of young energy for a playground. But something else is involved, for those who are more than adventurers. By juxtaposing the jaundiced view of Realf with Whittier's rosy prophesies, we see that the one is as ready for war as the other shuns it:[104]

> Out upon the craven worship
> Of the grandeur of our time!
> Out upon our little greatness
> And the Age's mock sublime!
> Out upon the brainless braggarts
>   Who are boasting evermore
> Of the world's emancipation
>   From the thralling gloom of yore!

In June, 1856, Realf bursts into Kansas with a shriek of "Anathema Maranatha" at Sumner's attackers and a prophecy that "the tyrant falls/When stricken Sampson [sic] grasps his pillared halls."

The Kansas warriors are attacked from several sides.[105] Non-violent abolitionists, clinging to their idealistic position, continue to plead, even after the assault on Sumner, against carnal weapons. Whether or not they are justified by history, we cannot overlook the integrity of their rebuke to the large militant faction surrounding them:

Though others murder, steal and swear,
Is it for *us* to follow them?
For *Christ* shall we the dagger bare?
A *devil* turn to evil stem?

Cleanse thine own soul, thou man of sin,
Ere thou the ruffian hordes condemn;
Look! find the same base heart within,
Which thou canst plainly see in them . . .

Then, too, there are the pro-Southern versifiers, quick to satirize abolitionist females who donate toward the purchase of guns:

Quick march upon the foes!
(A Bible in your pocket,)
Hold up your head! turn out your toes!
Present your rifle—cock it!

Motivated by party interest, such anti-prophetic rhymesters "respectfully" dedicate their vituperative attack "to the Fusio-Republican-Abolitio-Free-Soil-o-Disunionists." Conveniently they ignore the crux of the mob-movement, which their Senator has nearly been killed for documenting, and instead accuse the anti-slavery ministers of advocating "bowie-knife and arson!"

Simultaneously from the South—spawning-ground of most mob-actions in the fifties—comes William J. Grayson's assertion that "Violence and outrage are increasing yearly at the North," where:

Seditious schemes in bloody tumults end,
Parsons incite, and senators defend . . .[106]

His indignation, though one-sided and perhaps insincere, bases itself with some justice on prison and courthouse scenes in the North. And W. W. Lord, a Vicksburg parson since 1854, clearly has cause to chide after the Pottawatomie massacre. The vivid, Elijah-like imagery in his 1856 drama *André* is remarkable for its resemblance to the Kansas nightmare:[107]

> Cities and villages shall burn by daylight
> Around their silent bells; and fire shall hiss
> Along their streets against the stream of slaughter.

Benedict Arnold's concluding prophecy seems to verbalize the mood of the South as it begins to lose ground in Kansas:

> The hour is theirs—they have a moment's triumph:
> But in achieving it they have begun—
> Where tragedies end—a drama whose first act
> Is murder—but whose last shall be as pale
> With retribution. They shall have no cause,
> Like common murderers, to start at spectres.
> Shapes of substantial evil, real horrors,
> Shall be the conscience of their homicide.

The most interesting aspect of Southern anger is its similarity to the tone and language of Free Soil: neither side deplores or even acknowledges its own ruffianism, nor do the 1856 poets—with but a few exceptions—make clear that they hate mass violence no matter what the target. What they do, unknowingly, record is a steadily increasing mob-momentum. Is there a poet who sees, as prophets see, better than his countrymen—who feels, as prophets feel, constrained to warn of the larger violence toward which America is moving?

There are hints of this in several poets. Josiah G. Holland, for example, in late 1855 appeals for men with

"Strong minds, great hearts, true faith, and ready hands" at "a time like this," when "Freedom weeps,/Wrong rules the land, and waiting Justice sleeps!"[108] Looking homeward from Italy, Thomas B. Read grieves to see "The temples by our young hearts reared," battered down by "ruffian malice."[109] Similarly Mrs. Sigourney seems to depict the Kansas mobs, though she uses the Danites as her "lawless multitude, intent on spoil,/Marauding o'er the country . . ." We can be certain that this is a genuine rebuke of her generation, for she openly declares her legend to be a warning example:

> . . . Ill fares it with a land
> Where . . . wayward passions fill
> The place of righteous law.
> May our own realm,
> By Heaven's blest page instructed, give its aid
> To order, and authority, and peace . . .[110]

The indirectness of these poets may reflect a general reluctance, before 1856, to mention Kansas specifically. Then came one of the most electrifying series of events in the nation's history, which should—hypothetically—have served as a catalyst to anyone claiming ethical concern for his country. Almost fifty years later Henry James recalled vividly the news that Sumner, after a monumental address against Kansas ruffianism, was mobbed within an inch of his life on the floor of the Senate, while several rather pleased colleagues looked on:

> To very young minds, inflamed by the comparatively recent perusal of 'Uncle Tom's Cabin,' it was as if war had quite grandly begun, for what was war but fighting, and what but fighting had for its sign great men lying prone in their blood.[111]

The Senate's refusal to take action against the culprits, the lukewarm censure in the House, the vindicating kisses of Southern ladies, the almost unanimous re-election of the defiant assaulters, the Boston *Courier's* attack on Sumner and defense of his near-murderers, the midnight destruction of Lawrence, Kansas, the endorsement of a Ruffian platform and candidate by the National Democratic Convention—all of this might be expected to have activated at last the vocal strings of those who referred to themselves as Jeremiah's inheritors. For the nation they loved was coming apart at the seams—schoolboys could see it—and at this moment if ever in the history of America a word of admonition or sorrow, if not wrath, should have forced its way through their jaws somehow, despite aesthetic reticence. How then did they respond?

The minor abolition poets, of course, produce as loud a storm as they can, probably unheard outside their circle, but invigorating to those within. Sumner and Lawrence are henceforth linked in their undaunted songs.[112] Like Lovejoy's death, the new outrages are welcomed by some as "milestones" that "mark our way." Sumner's wounds have given that "harlot, SLAVERY" its death-wound, and the "smoking homes" of Lawrence have served to enrage the land. Not all, however, are able to sustain that note of defiance while government-led atrocities multiply. "Let us," they suggest grimly, "march in sad procession to old Bunker's heights of fame." Others ease their rage by satirizing the "chivalry" which canes a man pinned helplessly in his desk-chair: "How is it, knight, you strike before you warn?"

These poets may be no more than competent—and some barely that—but they provide a useful barometer of the great shift in Northern sentiment.[113] Daniel S. Whitney, for example, still clings in June to non-violence:

> True, we have strength to "wipe them out,"
> Draw the last drop of ruffian blood,
> But 'tis not meet for *us*: without
> A stain we would approach our God.

Instead, he would transform Northern wrath into disunion:

> Shall we still praise the Union's claims,
> While Lawrence burns and SUMNER bleeds? . . .

Equally bitter, William W. Hebbard laments the "fresh martyr-blood . . . flowing free," and excoriates his country:

> . . . he who dares indulge the dream
> That this 's a land of liberty,
> Is weltering senseless in the gore
> That calls to thee, O Brandywine,
> To wash it from the Senate's floor . . .

But Fremont's campaign and strength at the polls, plus the turning of the tide in Kansas itself, transforms them. Thus Whitney's Hiawatha-metered "Wail for Massachusetts" culminates, after a detailing of Missourian crimes, with an exhortation to "manly effort" unlike his earlier non-violence plea:

> This foul monster must be slaughtered . . .
> Everywhere its reign be ended,
> Or these outrages in Kansas
> Will be found in every free State . . .

Similarly, although Hebbard continues[114] to paint, in nightmare colors, "The border-ruffians striking Freedom's knell," he is now confident that Freedom will trample them underfoot and rear "a Bunker-hill on Kansas plains!" He prophesies a volcanic eruption: "Mount Etna's soon to burst in flame," and warns the South to retreat before vengeance issues "from its crater-mouth."

The shift is even more pronounced in the verse of those who commit their lives along with their rhymes to the anti-Missourian campaign. Perhaps for psychological reasons these poets play down the current horrors and stress the coming triumph.[115] Richard J. Hinton, first to cross the border in the June, 1856, crusade, rallies his fellow-emigrants to rescue the territory "Crush'd now by tyrant hand." He exults at the capture of a Southern flag that has flown above Lawrence's destroyed newspaper office:

> Trail in the dust the bloody flag—
> On the ground let it lie;
> Never again that flaunting rag
> Above our homes shall fly.

A Boston poet, urging the settlers not to flee, refers to the mob actions as "a passing scowl." From Kansas, John E. Cook (later to be executed with John Brown) replies: "We'll Not Go Back!" Another versifier, rejoicing when Lawrence hurls back the Missourians, mocks the predatory attacks as "Edicts from the Right of Might." By the following August the pro-slavery tide has receded. The famed correspondent James Redpath can write cheerfully from Lawrence of the ruffians and their free-soil conquerors as a thief "suddenly . . . seized behind" by a "faithful Growler" when he "climbed over a garden wall

. . . to gather up all/The flowers and the fruit he could find." In general, the surviving verse by Kansans makes their "bloody" territory appear not half so bloody as from afar.

That a cluster of young poets plunges bodily into Kansas after the week of Sumner and Lawrence is a significant fact in itself, and—in a sense—a lyrical act, far more effective than their songs. Among them, however, is one authentic poet, Richard Realf, who combines rifle and pen outstandingly. Arriving in Kansas at twenty-one, he soon finds his place beside John Brown. A violent activist, he cannot be expected to express shock at ruffianism: Missourian outrage goes almost without saying. The targets of his wrath are free-soil cowardice and government hypocrisy; his usual form of prophecy is exhortation. Dated after the tide has begun to turn, his productions represent a new phase in the Kansas battle.[116]

"The Defense of Lawrence" celebrates the heroism of the town he reached a month after its victory. Narrative power and exalted feeling combine to achieve an inspiring effect. In other poems he extols the heroes and martyrs who have dealt a blow in the face "Of the robber and spoiler," who have "kissed the Truth and died,/As grandly as a bridegroom goes/Unto his waiting bride." He reminds backsliders that they "held no parley" with proslavery men when the "ruffian's torch" blazed along their thrifty valleys. Realf is at his best when retorting to Douglas' "We will subdue you," or Stanton's warning of "war to the hilt":

> We fear no doom that thou canst give,
> Thou canst not either curse or bless.
> It is alike to die or live,
> To those who work in righteousness.

Nowhere, outside of Brown's own words, is the crescendo of impatience more eloquently recorded, the determination to take Justice into one's own hands. At Buchanan's inauguration Realf recalls the unavenged "smoke of burning hamlets." Where is Justice, he rages, "that she comes not fronting the accursed wrong?" And he sneers at those who "like the feet of Power,/Because its hands are red and strong." By October, 1857, Kansas oppresses him with its ugly peace. At the graves of the martyrs he writes a vexing, inflammatory sonnet:

> . . . O, the dead,
> How they do shame the living! How they warn
> Our little lives that chaffer for the bread
> Of peace . . .

A week later, having found "No grand resolves for Sacrifice" there, the poet of heroic action turns his back on Kansas.

Other poets, though deeply involved, remain in the East.[117] James F. Clarke's congregation sends rifles to Kansas. After the burning of Lawrence, Edward E. Hale makes his first Faneuil Hall speech. Frederick H. Hedge relinquishes his transcendental calm long enough to rally New England for the 1856 Kansas crusade.

> Tyranny threatens, and foemen invade . . .
> Bid thy brave children make haste, and deliver
> Soil yet unsullied by Slavery's chain!

Franklin B. Sanborn, one of John Brown's most vital Eastern links, finds time to write a skit in which Manifest Destiny tells Slavery:

> Let Kansas go—her blood-besprinkled plains
> Shall ne'er be added to your wide domains . . .

Unafraid to announce his vision of the coming death-struggle, John Pierpont, over seventy, rushes into the field with a lusty prophecy:

> Ay! let WAR come, for come it must . . .
> Far better make those plains our graves,
> Than leave them to be filled by slaves!

In Pierpont's "Ruffian Rally," an outstanding mob-poem—in length, detail, and satiric drive, if not in profundity—the beautiful but unworkable form of non-violence is indirectly exposed:

> Puritanic Yankee fools—
>   A psalm-singing, canting squad—
> Meeting-houses build, and schools,
>   Trust in Christ, and pray to God.
> Let 'em see, while at their altars,
>   Ruffian rifles—hangmen's halters!

Unlike Pierpont, who apparently requires a sensational event to set him in motion, Jones Very is blessed (or cursed) with overdeveloped nerve-ends which find causes enough for genuine prophetic passion.[118] Even before the caning of Sumner he feels impelled, in "On the Late Disgraceful Scene in Congress," to censure his nation's leaders "for brawling and for strife." Even before Lawrence he condemns "The Destruction of Public Property by Mobs," expressing a lofty and impartial abhorrence at those who destroy. " 'Tis their own work their maddened hands pull down!" he grieves. The third week of May, 1856, however, draws from Very one of his most exalting sonnets, "Be of Good Courage":

Ye who against the evils of our lot,
  Alone and single-handed do contend,
Faint not; though you to greatest straits are brought,
  And earthly succor fail, and earthly friend.
Near you in sympathy the angels stand . . .
And near you, though invisible, are those,
  The good and just of every age and clime,
Who, while on earth, have fought the self-same foes . . .

Higginson, Clarke, Hale, Hedge, and Pierpont are ministers, and the pulpit is their basic vehicle for arousing the conscience of the land. Since, however, by far the richest poetic response to Kansas comes from a woman, we are grateful that Julia Ward Howe cannot dissipate her urgent vision before Sunday morning congregations. In *Words For the Hour* a prophet rises to the events of May, 1856.[119] This we sense even in the shorter poems. It was Sumner's eloquence, she declares, which caused "The evil thing he smote at . . . To hurl its vileness at that Master brain." The ruffian philosophy, "The strong shall rule," had been proclaimed in Congress undefied until "God's candidate," Charles Sumner, rose "with soul indignant stirred." When he returns to his seat, with "mournful pity to the wretch/Whose weapon gave the bloody accolade," he will offer a Christ-like contrast to Southern "chivalry."

Turning to her most ambitious and memorable work, "The Sermon of Spring," we find ourselves suddenly in the thick of Jeremiah country. For Mrs. Howe here troubles her land with a series of terrifying revelations. First Kansas, "like a guilty ghost at a banquet," intrudes her anguish at a "brilliant assemblage" in the White House. "Me dost thou murder," she charges, seizing the President's hair:

> Scarcely I hold from my heart the death wound of thy Bravos . . .
> The heart of the Nations shall loathe ere it gladly forget thee . . .

When God tells her, however, that His thunder falls on "the crime, not the paltry offender," we are lifted beyond the shrill tones of typical partisan verse. We then see Sumner leaping to defend not only Kansas but the eternally challenged *ideal,* which must eternally be restated: "Doctrine of Right . . . of Freedom . . . of Justice . . . Known to the Ancients, known to the Gods and their poets." In a *real* world of selfishness, fright, and inaction, the prophetess hails Sumner as the *ideal* man, "a champion" ready to stand "a mark for the thief and assassin to aim at."

At the sight of Lawrence in ruins, Mrs. Howe begs God to "sweep from the outraged earth the vile chief and his legions," crying: "Our friends and our brothers are murdered!" Her rhetoric rises to a thunderous pitch as she demands the impeachment of the "smug President" who "subscribes their death warrant":

> Man! walk not forth, lest the beast of the meadow upbraid thee—
> True to their office, fulfilling the task God appointed . . .
> Yea! let the meanest thing that is faithful deride him;
> Let stocks and stones thank God that they cannot do treason.

For the blood Pierce has counseled, the poet foretells grimly, he shall have blood "poured to God with a holy intention."

She then holds before us, in contrast to the visible average priest, an ideal priest who is *not* for sale, who stamps his congregation "as melted wax, with high feeling and purpose." As she praises his apostolic act, we realize that she is defining her own motive—to cause unrest, embarrassment, reform:

> 'Tis but a spark—let it kindle the wide congregation
> With that clear redness of shame which hath grace before
> Heaven,
> With that good tingling that rouses men's slumbering
> virtue;
> Each confessing to each, we were careless and brutish;
> Sat unawakened by, while they hewed down our
> brethren . . .

Washington now appears, spokesman for a nobler past, appalled that those who praise him reject his maxims, that the city which bears his name "is meanness . . . Filth of the market defiling the innermost temple." With a prophecy of civil war her great sermon draws to a close. Yet she prays:

> Heaven enlighten their hearts, ere we close for the
> death-tug,
> Flinging them far from our bounds with their wrath
> and their rapine.

It is not enough to excoriate her people for their wickedness; she must voice their deepest yearning as well:

> Give us, great God, beyond these anarchic convulsions,
> The high, synthetic repose of thy progress and order.

This poem embodies almost the entire range of prophecy. In its sustained and reverberating ecstasy of vision it is unparalleled not only in Mrs. Howe's work, but perhaps in the entire body of American political poetry. It offers a tangible reference by which to gauge other verse of this genre. Modestly she digresses, begging the Muses not to be angry "If, in my hotness and haste, I have jarred your sweet fetters." But she is, in fact, so much the master of her medium, that her very "hotness and haste" become the life-giving ingredient for the "sweet fetters" without either jarring or melting them; we simply do not stop to admire their competence.

No major poet matches Mrs. Howe on Kansas. That Bryant, Longfellow, Holmes, and Emerson address public meetings of protest after the May, 1856, outrage testifies to its impact—at least on the North.[120] Longfellow has hitherto shunned political oratory; Holmes, *a month before,* publicly rebuked New England as "the hot-bed of abolitionism," terming anti-constitution sentiment "treason," and insisting that the North has no right to "abuse" slavery, its contracted "partner."[121] As poets, however, most of the major figures maintain a silence consistent with their tendency to transcend or transform current issues, preferring to "Read not the Times" but "the "Eternities."[122] Thus, while Bryant responds to Kansas by helping to organize the Republican Party and heading its militant anti-slavery wing in New York, his poems are frankly escapist, as though he needs, for survival, to glide away—with the river—"from those abodes, that bring/Pollution" to its channel. "A Rain-Dream" candidly admits the need of escape:

> These strifes, these tumults of the noisy world,
> Where Fraud, the coward, tracks his prey by stealth,
> And Strength, the ruffian, glories in his guilt,
> Oppress the heart with sadness.[123]

As for Emily Dickinson, we must seek among her private papers for direct comment and decipher her poems for clues.[124] Early in 1856, for instance, her complaints about moving show (however playfully) full empathy with the free-soilers moving west:

> It is a kind of gone-to-Kansas feeling, and if I sat in a long wagon, with my family tied behind, I should suppose without doubt I was a party of emigrants!

At Sumner's death her appreciation of his role overflows superbly:

> I am picking you a flower for remembering Sumner—He was his Country's—She—is—Time's—
>
> When Continents expire
> The Giants they discarded—are
> Promoted to Endure—

Such a poem as "The Mob Within the Heart," although it is undated and employs mob-imagery for a subjective purpose, supports the view that she is aware "of the subversive events of her America," and that "her lack of particular allusion is deceptive."[125] In only thirty-four words she constructs a complete mob narrative from its slow subterranean development "in a congenial ground" to its unpredictable time and place of explosion, which "Police cannot suppress."

For months after the attack on Sumner, Longfellow's papers are filled with grief and rage. "What infamy to the country! What a wound to Liberty!" he cries, seeing, as does Mrs. Howe, that "At length Freedom and Slavery stand face to face in the field as never before."[126] More important, the mood and imagery of *John Endicott,* a verse-drama he begins in 1856,[127] recall Kansas in much the same fashion as Lord's *André,* though from the opposite point of view. A speaker named simply "The Voice" is in fact the harrowing voice of prophecy:

> O foolish people, ye that think to burn
> And to consume the truth of God, I tell you
> That every flame is a loud tongue of fire
> To publish it abroad to all the world . . .

Equally scorching are John Endicott's words:

> When bloody tragedies like this are acted,
> The pulses of a nation should stand still;
> The town should be in mourning, and the people
> Speak only in low whispers to each other.

As Thoreau failed to take note of the 1844 outrages, so he seems to ignore Kansas. But we know his strong sympathy for the manly violence with which John Brown answers Southern violence. Less surprising is Lowell's failure to acknowledge the events of May, 1856; for he abdicated the role of gadfly even before his wife's death and his assumption of high-salaried dignities. Two years before the sacking of Lawrence he speaks boldly—in a letter—of Northern retaliation "if things go on and the old Puritan spirit once get up again."[128] Again, in an uncollected 1856 poem, he sings boldly: "Let Kansas answer from her reddened fields"; but the line soon becomes: "Make this proud answer, from thy reddened fields."[129] Is it the *specific,* or the *controversial,* that he shuns in removing the word "Kansas"?

Lowell's desertion of the prophetic role at just this moment is underscored by the opposite motion of Holmes,[130] whose silence Lowell once scolded. A few months after denouncing "the discord-note of shame," Holmes adds his own discord-note against legislators who fail to "keep the law," preachers and "party leaders" who fail to "tell us all they think." In some of his most haunting lines, he seems to commemorate the bloody fields of Kansas:

> Alas! each hour of daylight tells
> A tale of shame so crushing,
> That some [flowers] turn white as sea-bleached shells,
> And some are always blushing.
>
> But when the patient stars look down
> On all their light discovers,
> The traitor's smile, the murderer's frown . . .
>
> They try to shut their saddening eyes . . .

Emerson's[131] 1856 poetry gives no hint of his *feelings;* "Brahma" merely restates his *philosophy*. But on May 26th, Concord town hall rings with a sorrowful, manly prose:

> The very conditions of the game must always be,—the worst life staked against the best. It is the best whom they desire to kill. It is only when they cannot answer your reasons, that they wish to knock you down . . . The Murderer's brand shall stamp their foreheads wherever they may wander in the earth . . .

It is at Cambridge, in September, that he once again soars into greatness, turning an appeal for Kansas relief into a tremendous attack on the President and the nation, as if God's thunder has made his mouth its vehicle, calling for the extirpation of a ruffian-led government, demanding disunion and a new revolution:

> Send home every one who is abroad, lest they should find no country to return to. Come home and stay at home, while there is a country to save. When it is lost it will be time enough then for any who are luckless enough to remain alive to gather up their clothes and depart to some land where freedom exists.

Of this extraordinary address, Bancroft wrote, "It would . . . be . . . perhaps impossible to find any speech made in the same year that is marked with so much courage and foresight as this." In the beauty of its language it is approached only by Mrs. Howe's unjustly neglected "Sermon of Spring."

For Whitman to respond inadequately to the 1856 violence is not surprising. Even after the 1863 New York draft riots, which Melville depicts with horror and candor, the poet of democracy refuses "to abuse the poor people, or call for a rope or bullets for them." Arvin argues that an "Amos or Juvenal . . . would not have written Drum Taps";[132] just so, a prophet of wrath would not write the exuberant songs of 1856.

Yet a denunciatory impulse does stir within him,[133] and he satisfies it in an undelivered lecture, describing the Southern mob as:

> . . . altogether the most impudent persons that have yet appeared in the history of lands, and with the most incredible successes, having pistol'd, bludgeoned, yelled and threatened America, the past twenty years into one long train of cowardly concessions, and still not through but rather at the commencement . . .

His rejected "Poem of Remembrance for a Girl or a Boy of These States" represents another 1856 effort to attack "the angers, bickerings, delusions . . . of the idea of caste . . . the bloody cruelties and crime." Without naming Kansas, he asks his country to "remember the pledge of the Old Thirteen . . . to the rights, life, liberty, equality of man." Like Mrs. Howe, he recalls the ideal of Washington; unlike her, however, he is satisfied to affirm the *dream,* "two hundred millions, of equal freemen and freewomen amicably joined," while ignoring the *reality* without which the dream has no meaning and the poem no dramatic life. To mutter parenthetically, "Cursed be nation, woman, man, without hospitality!" is fine, but would the free-soilers driven from their homesteads know what he means? He does not here match, in his vision of America, the harsh details which give solidity to his vision of Europe in 1850. To gloss over the unpleasant, to declare, "I am myself just as much evil as good, and my nation is—and I say there is in fact no evil,"[134] is to rob his social verse of tangibility, contrast, and point. His failure is thus aesthetic as well as prophetic, and he is wise not to include this poem in *Leaves of Grass.*

Among the major poets, Whittier alone gives serious attention in verse to the Kansas violence.[135] As usual, his ethical code dominates the choice and treatment of material. In 1854, he sings: "We go to rear a wall of men/On Freedom's southern line," naïvely dreaming that there will be no bloody consequences: the Border Ruffians will "shake off the dust of Kansas" at sight of "The Yankee abolitionists . . . coming . . . like a flood—grim, stalwart men." With the "Burial of Barber" his playful handling of vigilantism yields to solemnity, but his platform of nonviolence so overwhelms the occasion that he cannot face the crime squarely. Instead, he uses Barber's murder to cry "Patience, friends!" Fearing the mood of vengeance, he addresses young hot-heads such as Realf:

> Not to him who rashly dares,
> But to him who nobly bears,
> Is the victor's garland sure.

Early in 1856 appears Whittier's largest political poem, "The Panorama," born—according to its author—of "a voice and vision . . . Such as might Milton's jarring trump require." The role of poet as truth's unwilling instrument, is new for Whittier:

> Oh, not of choice, for themes of public wrong
> I leave the green and pleasant paths of song . . .
> Forget the poet, but his warning heed,
> And shame his poor word with your nobler deed.

Obviously he feels compelled to show his people what they do not see—both their present condition and the choice of good or evil which "the dread angel of the future" holds out to them. He begs the North not to strike "The braggart Southron, open in his aim," or those in Kansas who shift "Their drunken franchise . . . from scene to scene," but to turn their fire upon Northerners who betray their principles while prating "Of constitution, union, and the laws." Violence remains his major target, and he urges the militants not to let "Passion wrest from Reason's hand/The guiding rein . . ."

The impact of May, 1856, upon Whittier is great. For a time he actually withholds "the honest doubt" he had so long raised toward violence as a "means." He tells Pennsylvania to heed the cry of her "children's blood," and—if need be—to strike, like Brutus, "For Fatherland and Freedom . . . As Justice gives the sign." A year later he goes further, accepting "thunder and the whirlwind's roar," since it is God's will that Good and Evil, in a final confrontation, "Close dim and vast on Armageddon's plain." By 1858, however, he has returned to his fundamental position, praising martyrs for their acquiescence, urging that "tears quench the curses," and prophesying a non-violent victory. Thus he draws back from the edge of martial prophecy. That he can more or less sustain an unpopular position against increasingly violence-oriented readers shows stamina, even if it lacks the historical acuteness of Emerson, Mrs. Howe, and John Brown. Certainly it is a genuine inner force that commands him to express his "scruples and . . . fears," proferring to the zeal of his auditors "A well-meant drag upon its hurrying wheel." In this respect few poets can be classed with him. Violence in any form is so detestable that, like Thoreau, he does not bother with its most obvious manifestations. It is rather of Lovejoy in 1837, of the Lawrence free-soilers in 1856, that he demands ideal behavior. Their armed defense mutes him—nor do the armed Irish and Mormons of 1844 win his tears or tributes. Thus Whittier's great message to his raging generation, second in urgency only to his cry for emancipation, is that noble ends do not justify base means; and his silence says the same.

Clearly, nowhere is the gulf wider between the blood-curdling mid-century news items and "the graceful but pallid derivations of a Longfellow or a Lowell"[136] than on the subject of specific mob acts; yet those two are less "pallid" than most. With few exceptions, America's poets do not directly acknowledge, let alone deplore, this sensational feature of the national experience, thus doubly betraying the prophet's duties of keen sight and ethical utterance. It is as if the poems and the newspapers are produced on different continents, in different centuries. The few minor poets who respond do so, with notable exceptions, because of partisan rather than ethical concern, and show no interest in mobbings outside their circle. Some of the major figures, on the other hand, make their anti-mobbist position brilliantly, consistently clear—in prose, in the total impact of their poetry, and in parables of other days. Yet Emerson as philosopher, Lowell as Red Cross knight, and many minor poets as abolitionists, imply a certain hospitality toward the Mob as a valuable and inevitable proving-ground for heroes.

Failure to react prophetically against the specific mob actions of 1837, 1844, and 1856, involves several factors. Some poets are muted by personal bias against Catholics, immigrants, abolitionists, Mormons, or guns;[137] others shun widely publicized events which show the more sordid and frenzied side of the mankind they idealize, the land they glorify. Many feel the poet's task to be inspirational, entertaining, or pacifying; depicting horrors would invite fury or despair. A few are unable to do artistic justice to a theme that moves them too deeply. Others quietly accept the mob as an eternal phenomenon of the human race—like sin, which they also exclude from their poems. To the Jeffersonian, the mob in its less violent forms and when its grievance is worthy might well be wholesome as the town hall of the streets. In any case, here is one notorious aspect of American life especially in need of analysis, rebuke, and admonition, to which the discreet, fastidious, and sometimes mean-spirited poets—overlooking a great prophetic occasion—fail to address themselves. Ironically, if they think their poetry likelier to live without such impure elements, their calculations have misfired; for a world of sunlight without shadow is aesthetically dull, ethically meaningless, and historically false.

4

Mistreatment of the Indian

The racists of the 1830's, rampaging against Mexicans, immigrants, and abolitionists, were not likely to ignore the remnant of the white man's first victims, especially where desirable lands were at stake. At the same moment that its forces were expelling Mexico from Texas and harrowing vocal critics by mob and by law, aggressive "Americanism" won its most sensational victories against the red man. Its basic principle was Manifest Destiny; its basic policy was to ruin tribes, scuttle treaties, and offer the choice of removal or extermination. To object profoundly was to challenge the unchallengeable: one's forefathers, the original Indian-fighters. With President Jackson adamant, with a land-hungry population ready to give the presidency to another hunter of Indians, it was no easy matter for an ethical outcry to be heard. This John Howard Payne learned in 1835 when he visited the Cherokees and barely escaped with his life—after vigilantes imprisoned him and finally warned him never to enter Georgia again![1] Forty years later, as a proud and powerful America celebrated its centenary, it would be equally difficult to clamor against the mistreatment of Cheyenne and Sioux, with President Grant adamant, with a land-hungry population ready to embrace a victorious Indian-fighter.

I have chosen two anchor-points: the death of Osceola in 1838, and that of Custer in 1876. These were not only among the most widely publicized and affecting incidents in the Indian wars, but they may prove useful here for other reasons as well. First, they test an ancient prophetic function: praise of the hero who welcomes death for an ideal. Second, they allow us to examine the ethical sensitivity of post-bellum poets whose motives were connected neither with the nativism and abolitionism of the 1830's, nor with the Indian as a literary fad. Next, they provide a sunset look at poets who had been young enthusiasts in 1838. Further, this forty-year span may illustrate or contradict an alleged post-war devitalization among poets. Then, too, despite continuing attention to the Custer episode among historians, almost no notice has been taken of the verse it evoked; as for Osceola, a considerable group of poems has been overlooked. Finally, some of the Indian poetry that emerged in the forties may be more than the continuation of a popular genre; their composition may have been affected if not motivated by the Seminole and Cherokee tragedies, just as some Indian literature of the 1880's and later may be rooted in the Custer period. Thus, what is supposedly nostalgia may be—at least in part—a prophetic response to recent affairs.

The dispossession of the Cherokee is too long and familiar a story to warrant retelling here. There is "no record so black" in "our Government's dealings with the Indian tribes . . . as the record of its perfidy to this nation,"[2] a remarkable people driven from their ancestral home not because they could not be civilized, but "because a pseudo set of civilized beings, who are too strong for them, want their possessions!"[3] The seven-year Seminole War is also too well known and complex for extended narration here. Unlike the prosperous Cherokees, who had embraced Christianity and slavery, the poor Seminoles had maintained their ways and sheltered fugitives. Destined to be overwhelmed by the invader, they nevertheless preferred to "be killed by a white man in Florida than die in Arkansas." The government, heeding only the demands of frontiersmen and land seekers, offered death to both tribes as an alternative to surrender, for Jacksonian thinking placed "property rights of voters ahead of treaty rights of American Indians."[4] Those voters included not only land-seekers, but slave-owners eager to penalize the Seminole for sheltering runaway slaves. "You may rest assured," declared General Jessup, "this . . . is a negro, not an Indian war . . ."[5] As for the slave-holding Cherokees, they could be wildly linked not only with abolition, but also with the Mexicans; this was, in fact, Mirabeau Lamar's pretext for expelling them from Texas.[6]

i

If we expect America's poets to execrate these outrages, we are asking for the pure sight and fearless voice of prophecy. In light of their performance on other issues, our hopes cannot be high. We shall, first of all, discover expressions of hostility toward the victimized Indians on the part of poets whose sincere concern is for the white settlements threatened by attack. That their position coincides with the government's plans does not necessarily make them puppets of power. Their ethical impulse may be limited, but within those limits it is strong. Thus the poet William H. Timrod, father of Henry Timrod, marches at the head of Charleston's Volunteers to save St. Augustine, "which otherwise would have afforded an easy prey to the savage foe."[7] A Carolina poetess, moved in 1836 by "a voice . . . of ruin and carnage" from the villages of Florida, is true to her prophetic impulse when she celebrates "the light of true courage" on the brows of Charleston's knights; nor can we question the motive of another, who laments the slain volunteers mouldering away "In the land of the savage."[8]

It is necessary to differentiate between such responses and other contemporary verse which presents the Indian in an unpleasant light. Poets who elsewhere show sympathy for the Indian cause unwittingly support the most unscrupulous and lawless elements in American life, who need to have the Indian portrayed as a cowardly assassin striking from behind and gloating as the lifeblood pours from the crushed bodies of his victims. The reader is made to feel himself scalped along with a sentry taken by surprise:

> A fierce red eye met mine, and gnashing teeth
> Whence the hot breath came hissing . . .
> The sharp, cold knife swift glided round my brows,
> My hair was clutched, and then with keenest pangs
> The scalp was wrenched away . . .[9]

Chilling the American imagination with fiendish shouts and gestures, such poets undoubtedly aim to evoke the past or satisfy a taste for horror stories; but their timing harmonizes with the false and vitriolic political songs that help bring victory to Harrison in 1840, songs about "the red Locos" whose tomahawk and warwhoop prepared graves for all Americans "on that perilous night" of Tippecanoe.[10]

Just so, many poets, in their apocalyptic vision of America's future, unintentionally lend strength to the anti-Indian cause. Nor could they easily do otherwise. To ignore the great Westward Trek would be to rob their work of its most thrilling indigenous motif, and deny the concept of human progress for the sentimental sake of a lost cause. The poets who during this period laud the courage and hope of the future frontiersmen, cannot realize how basically they are endorsing current aggressions against the Indian remnant. Thus Chivers in 1836 evangelistically celebrates America's westward flight as "A scourge to Darkness which flies on before,"[11] though he has recently been a sympathetic guest of the Cherokee nation. Another defender of the Indian, George P. Morris, voices the same mood of aggrandizement that anonymous song-makers reveal more crassly in their "get going" verses against the Cherokee. The "Westward Ho!" approach, soon to find its greatest visionary spokesman in Whitman, is seen in the lines of Morris:

> We have our rifles ready, boys! . . .
> When we've wood and prairie-land,
> Won by our toil,
> We'll reign like kings in fairy-land,
> Lords of the soil!
> Then westward, ho! in legions, boys!
> Fair freedom's star
> Points to her sunset regions, boys . . .[12]

With equal exuberance, many poets celebrate the epic transformation of the continent in the two centuries past. Thus, while they sigh for the annihilated aborigine, they encourage the current anti-Indian drive by extolling the results of his annihilation. How could Jessup's campaign in the Everglades not take heart when James G. Percival[13] sings love-songs to a virgin land "Just rescued from the wilderness" and flourishing in "the blessed gift/Of liberty and law . . ."? For "the fair-haired Saxon . . . Rich with the spoils of time,"[14] has turned a wild land into "fruits and golden grain,/And clustering domes and temples . . ." On this point, if on any, poets of North and South stand united: holier motives than gold brought the first colonists from England. In Freedom's name the mighty empire they founded now "lights the gloom of guilty earth."[15] Even abolitionists draw the line at where their ethics must end and their ancestral pride begin. More rigidly principled than most, Garrison writes "No" under a contributor's lines: "It was a holy fight your fathers fought . . . When by your homes the dark-browed savage stood."[16] But more typical than that fiery editor is Channing, proud to "be a Son of those stern men,/Who took this Indian land" in order to live as freemen:

> Noble adventurers! godlike Puritans!
> Poets in deed! who came and saw and braved
> The accumulated Wilderness, and read therein
> The fatal policy of Indian guile.[17]

Obviously, such views of America's future and past, while strengthening the government's moral position, are not so intended. On the other hand, it would be a mistake to assume that the great body of pro-Indian verse emerging at this time necessarily implies a denunciation of the government's "infamous" Cherokee and Seminole programs. Giving "rein to their imagination," many poets sentimentally depict the "poetical life, and picturesque eloquence, of the Indians,"[18] without indirectly censuring the removal of the tribes. Some seek to create works that "breathe a national spirit" independent of British critics and standards; others are advised to use the Indian as a perfect theme for an American epic.[19] That such works are enthusiastically received by the public must be a factor for poets whose livelihood depends on sales. Yet, coming at this moment, a sympathetic portrayal of the Indian's character and a publication of his grievances *do* refute the pretexts of the Indian-fighters and undermine their aggressive aims. The nostalgic poems of Hoffman, Simms, and Mrs. Sigourney, whatever their primary purpose, *do* generate pro-Indian sentiment and contribute to a nationwide revulsion against the Seminole War.

But certain retrospective verses seem too pointedly appropriate to be dismissed as mere literary coincidences. By means of a past artistically safer and more palatable, some poets appear to be deploring the ethical disgrace of their own time. "My forest home is taken,/And the stranger bids me flee," laments Chivers' heroine.[20] To this poet the Indian is obviously not the midnight prowler, as Charleston wishes him to be imagined, but the unflinching victim of pale-face treachery. Alonzo Lewis, also assuming the voice of the red man, accuses the Anglo-Saxon of having "taken the realm our ancestors gave." Even the right to flee is denied: the Christian bullet is "aimed by too fatal a hand!"[21]

As the Florida war continues into the forties, melancholy poems multiply, evoking sympathy for betrayed tribes of the past and admiration for their fighting chiefs. Among the most ambitious is Seba Smith's clumsy *Powhatan,* written "at intervals for several years" but "more than half of it" during 1840—in the midst of the Seminole War. Although Poe found the proem of this work "unintelligible," it is in fact not only intelligible but urgent in its mournful prediction:

> They are scatter'd like leaves by the tempest blast . . .
> And time o'er the straggling remnants bends,
> And sweeps them away with a hurried pace,
> Still sounding the knell of the warrior race . . .[22]

Like Seba Smith Mrs. Sigourney had for years considered writing a long Indian poem. Her *Pocahontas,* appearing soon after his *Powhatan,* illustrates her prophetic vigor on this issue. Adams, Jefferson, and Marshall had rebuffed her earlier assaults on the land-greed of her countrymen and the betrayal of the tribes; they had termed the efforts of her group "an interference with government policy."[23] Now her sympathy follows the exiled natives westward, and she again presses Congress for justice. In *Pocahontas* she is not satisfied (as are Mrs. Sarah J. Hale and George P. Morris) merely to depict the princess placing her head beside the doomed Captain Smith. Digressing from her narrative, she decries rampant Anglo-Saxonism:

> I would ye were not, from your father's soil,
> Track'd like the dun wolf, ever in your breast
> The coal of vengeance and the curse of toil;

More than a tribute to Powhatan's daughter, her poem is an apology and a memorial to these "scorn'd and perish'd people . . ."[24]

Alfred B. Street does more and better work in this vein. While describing Indian cruelty and glorifying the pioneer who personifies "The Spirit of our land," he also creates a group of remarkable narratives justifying Indian revenge and spotlighting Indian nobility.[25] This duality evidently does not disturb the poet, for he again combines the contradictory strands in his huge Iroquois epic, *Frontenac.* Throughout his work the dominant slant is pro-Indian, but the negative element saves him from sentimentality. Street insists on reminding his countrymen that the Indian's savagery is an *effect;* that the white man is guilty of the cause. Only after the whites, "like vultures for their prey," have stalked and destroyed his people, does a maddened chief swear everlasting hate. Dying in captivity, a great sachem recalls his family—wiped out "by white man's ruthless hands." The nobility of the chief is itself a refutation of the current stereotype:

> Up from his couch the dying sachem sprung,—
> Up from his couch, and with one warrior look
> In his clinched grasp his knife he feebly shook,
> From his weak tongue one faltering war-whoop passed,
> Then down the chieftain sank—death, death had come
> at last.

Similarly, in "The Last of His Tribe," Epes Sargent effectively refutes the Indian-fighter's libel of his disadvantaged prey. In this unusually concise unrhymed lyric, Sargent extols the red man's spiritual invincibility in the face of a physical hopelessness such as the Seminole's. His concluding lines define heroism much as do *Beowulf* and "The Battle of Maldon":

Though his little band
Fall in heaps around him,
Yet he does not quail.[26]

Even when the Indian is presented wistfully, there is often an undertone of dismay at American iniquity. Hoffman's fine sonnet, "The Last of the Race," shows the same ripening of emotion we have noted in his Mexican War poems. In this "terminal" scene a tribeless chieftain sees, unlike Moses, no Promised Land from the Pacific mountain-top to which he has dragged himself:

. . . no Blessed Islands of Delight,
Believed in fondly, greet thine aching sight—
No spirit-voices from the waters sweep
To tell where rest thy race, and where thou too mayst sleep.[27]

"Mark Atherton," the most ambitious of Frederick G. Tuckerman's poems, is also saturated with this sense of a gigantic disgrace. The red man's vigor in King Philip's time is poignantly contrasted with his current deterioration. Tuckerman's vocabulary is not picturesque but sharply accusing; with rich irony he uses the very terminology we would expect to find in a description of Indian cruelty:

. . . now . . . the tribes
Shot, scalped, and scattered, flee on every side;
Their bark-boats staved and sunk, their lodges burned,
And plantings, and even the lands that grew them, seized,
They scarce can draw to head . . .[28]

There is no Mason-Dixon line in this area of charged nostalgia. Southern poets too can deplore Anglo-Saxon aggression without directly opposing the South's current program of removal or extermination. Thus, while one poet sighs, "How many of the banished race,/Those old red warriors of the bow,/Have slumbered in this shadowy place,"[29] another narrates with restraint and force the murder of a Shawnee chief by a white mob . . . in 1777!

> Awful and stern outbrake the cry,
> "The Indians in the fort must die . . ."
> And he stood in his robes with a stately grace,
> And spoke with an air of majesty—
> "My son," he said, "fear not to die . . ."[30]

Such poems form the largest body of pro-Indian responses during the Seminole War. As we have seen in earlier chapters, it is common for poets to condemn the evils of their own world in terms of other epochs and regions. Often the reason is aesthetic: they hope the perspective of time may give their work the scope, balance, and durability lacking in newspaper verse. Still, their gesture can be considered prophetic; although the death of Cornstalk took place sixty years before Osceola's, the ruffianism of the Indian-haters and the stoic beauty of the chief, as the poet portrays them, provide a clear parallel—perhaps more effective than a *direct* denunciation of the Osceola outrage would be, could the poet's sensibilities permit such an attack. Even the most fragile lament at the passing of the red man can be interpreted as an expression of shame. For no matter how hackneyed the theme or their treatment of that theme, these poets have chosen to register their compassion for the Indian at the very moment when their government would most appreciate anthems favoring its campaign of extirpation.

ii

To side with the dispossessed Indians in the 1830's and 1840's requires an aroused conscience, but little courage. Editors who ignore works on slavery and shun the word in their columns often praise pro-Indian books and condemn government actions.[31] Thus, on the day of Osceola's capture, Willis' innocuous *Mirror* publishes a stinging note on the "policy of embroiling the Indians with each other" by pitting Sioux against Seminole. A few months later the equally uninvolved *North American Review* explodes:

> . . . our regard to the faith of treaties is so delicate, that we persist in driving away, at the point of the bayonet, the plundered inheritors of the soil, careless of all the ties we break, all the lives we shorten, all the scenes of woe we cause.

Since such sentiments are expressed in leading literary journals of the day, it is not too much for us to expect an outpouring of verse in which the poet clearly repudiates his government's duplicity and his neighbors' acquiescence. It is to such work we now turn.

Among the most furious outbursts are those sparked by Christian hypocrisy. The great folklorist, Henry R. Schoolcraft, for example,[32] himself favors conquest by conversion, and in one poem rejoices that the Christianized Iroquois has discarded drum and rattle. But in a second poem, the family of a converted chief is wiped out by the guns of the pious white man; the Indian then digs up his hatchet to avenge himself against these hypocrites "engender'd beyond the big seas." Similarly, in a blistering reproach to his countrymen, Alonzo Lewis scoffs at a

Christian nation that proclaims the merit of grace "By dealing to the Indian race/The friendly sword's salvation."[33] Thus the contrast between what their nation preaches and practises is mercilessly exposed to shame the conscience of the land. Only occasionally, however, is the religious theme directly related to the specific outrage unfolding at this time. The Seminoles, one poet charges, are being punished because they practice Christ's teaching:

> . . . the fugitive from wrong and toil
> Sought an asylum on their Indian soil,
> Weary, a stranger, and they took him in,
> And now they expiate their heathen sin![34]

A second general target of prophetic fury is the character of Anglo-Saxon avarice. In *Black Hawk* Elbert H. Smith spells out most clearly the central historic fact that the Indian was a kind *host,* the white man a greedy and bloody *guest*. He traces the entire infamy, impudently characterizing his ancestors as "th' aggressors" who lied, plundered, enslaved, and butchered. Nor does he absolve Congress, which has been allowing its good laws on behalf of the red man to be violated with impunity through the years by "outlaw frontier men,/Land speculators, traders . . ." to whom we owe "Indian barbarities, and border wars." This poet hurls into the teeth of his people a great catalogue of their atrocities, adding that if he were to tell more, it would be "a scandal on our nation;/ Humanity would shudder at the tale."[35]

Smith is by no means the first to attack manifest destiny as it has affected the Indians. But at this time few go so far, outside of anti-slavery circles; and when abolition poets seize upon the theme, they sometimes seem happy to add another grievance against the government and society with which they are at war. But this is not the case with Jones Very. In his simple ballad of indictment, "The Indian's Retort," he sings with as warm a fervor as is found in his sonnets:

> The white man's soul, it thirsts for gain,
> He makes himself the slave of gold!
> The Indian's free and boundless lands,
> Once all his own, are bought and sold . . .
>
> "The white man came! he stole the woods,
> The hills, the streams, the fields, the game;
> The Indian never was a thief!
> The white man steals, his is the name!"

Very's Indian poems often assault the American conscience. Only once, however, and indirectly, does he seem to respond to the Osceola tragedy, demonstrating in "King Philip" the prophetic use of historical parallel:

> . . . Ye urge me still in deadly chase,
> Betrayed, abandoned, and alone.
>
> I scorn your power; could arm avail
> To drive you from my native soil,
> I should not feel my spirit fail,
> This arm would still be nerved for toil.[36]

Such a declaration, by an avowed pacifist, is especially strong.

Prior to Osceola's captivity, few poets directly condemn the expulsion of the living tribes, though Very and others appear to defend the rights of the red man in terms of earlier struggles. Here and there we come across a line or two, such as W. W. Lord's confession that his soul has often "mourned silently . . . for the dark tribes" expelled from "their old graves and shattered forests."[37] More arresting are the digressions in George H. Colton's *Tecumseh.*[38] Against the exile of the gentle Cherokees he cries:

> These *were* their homes—but now no more! . . .
> They rest, as witheringly they die,
> Not where their kindred's ashes lie!

He counters the charge of the war-camp that the Indian is guilty of "all the blood his hand hath spilt." Any visitor to the natives' friendly homes, he declares, would know how long they patiently "bore aggressive wrong." Even more that pertains to Florida appears in Mrs. Sigourney's 1841 volume.[39] Powhatan's prophet, for example, exhorts his people against the invader: "Ye once were brave;/Will ye resign the world that the Great Spirit gave?" And, as Jones Very uses King Philip, so does Mrs. Sigourney parallel Osceola's death with that of the last Seneca chief, displaying not only his courage and nobility, but a hatred of Christian hypocrisy which is doubly impressive in light of this poet's missionary zeal:

> Hear my last bidding, friends! Lay not my bones
> Near any white man's bones. Let not his hand
> Touch my clay pillow, nor his hateful voice
> Sing burial hymns for me. Rather than dwell
> In Paradise with him, my soul would choose
> Eternal darkness and the undying worm.

Here her references are still indirect, but in the concluding stanzas of "Pocahontas" there is no mistaking the allusion to the current use of bloodhounds by the Everglades troops:

I would we had not . . . on ye turn'd
The blood-tooth'd ban-dog, foaming, as he burn'd
To tear your flesh . . .

Colton and Mrs. Sigourney are exceptions. Most anti-removal verse comes from abolitionists.[40] They lash out at a government of broken treaties, whose bayonets gleam "above the Seminole," whose troops trample on the Cherokee, driving him forth "far from his native wilds" because *citizens* want the land and have the power; now he seeks another home, "Where (vain the hope) the white man will not come." The essence of prophecy is here, though unfelicitously transmitted; for these poets see the Indian removal as a manifestation of a general ethical disease, and their vision encompasses a huge landscape of agony. "My country, oh! my country!" they weep; "Go, spread the sackcloth o'er thee,/And scatter ashes round." Human rights, as well as Indian tribes, are being ravished, and the soul of acquiescent America is debased. Thus, before slavery has elbowed all other iniquities aside in his thinking, William L. Garrison responds gratefully to Frelinghuysen's famed senatorial address against the Cherokee removal:

If Honor, Justice, Truth, had not forsaken
The place long hallowed as their bright abode,
The faith of treaties never had been shaken,
Our country would have kept the trust she owed . . .
Fruitless thy mighty efforts—vain appealing
To grasping Avarice, that ne'er relents . . .
The red man's woes shall swell the damning story . . .[41]

A few abolitionist poets produce verses from the Cherokee point of view. Along with expressions of despair we hear accusations against the "cruel" invaders from overseas who "Despoiled us of our land." In general, however, they speak in their own generous but ineffectual voices, commiserating with the poor native whose harvest shall once again be reaped by the white man:

> As on, his waves of population roll:
> Dominion still his thirst—unhallowed gain his goal.

Most of these verses are doom-ridden and lugubrious, but there is an occasional spark of ironic comment on the "treaty" disavowed by most Cherokees:

> . . . the treaty is *finis,* ('let those laugh who win,')
> We, agreeably to scripture, the stranger *take in!*
> And, of course, there cannot be a shadow of doubt,
> That 'tis equally proper to take strangers *out!*
> And if they perversely refuse to comply;
> Why, they know the decision—*surrender or die!*[42]

This is obviously newspaper work and of more historic than literary interest. That a poem of occasion *can,* however, have merit is once more proven by the productions of two New England women. In one of her rare outbursts, inspired by the visit of several chiefs to Boston, Margaret Fuller assaults the Bay State:[43]

> From the far border to which they are driven,
> They might look up in trust to the clear heaven;
> But here—what tales doth every object tell
> Where Massasoit sleeps—where Philip fell!

Grieving that the stately form of the red man is on the verge of vanishing from his ancestors' eastern coast, she foretells angrily:

Beneath the sun, to us so kind, they melt—
More heavily each day our rule is felt:
The tale is old—we do as mortals must;
Might makes right here, but God and Time are just . . .

Two years later an exasperated government decides to track down the Seminole remnant with the help of bloodhounds. At once, hoping to shame her nation into a sense of decency, Sophia L. Little echoes Margaret Fuller's warning in stanzas that resound with Biblical passion:

What! call for bloodhounds to thy feasts . . .
Are these thy deeds! my country, thine! . . .

Yet once, the warning voice aspires;
Ye southern forests, trembling hear—
Jehovah's sin-avenging fires
Soon will your lofty branches sear . . .[44]

iii

Such outcries are rare, even within anti-slavery ranks. Outside the circle of abolition poets, however, an almost complete prophetic failure seems to prevail—until Osceola emerges as a great national figure with his spurning of the removal treaty. At this point, from a variety of sources, interesting poems are to be found.[45] The first, by an army lieutenant, portrays the chief as one who loves to hear his enemy's dying moan; yet the poet cannot help admiring and empathizing with the man he has been commanded to capture or kill, for Osceola stands as a warrior should:

I scorn your proffer'd treaty,
The pale face I defy . . .
And I'll taunt ye with my latest breath,
And fight ye till I die.

Another poem, allegedly the work of a Miami tribesman, is in fact a typical example of contemporary newspaper verse so far as its texture is concerned:

> We own not your laws nor your treaties: This soil
> Shall be ours till your armies have made it your spoil,
> For 'twas ours by the gift, by the charter of God . . .

This writing is familiar in phrase and meter; yet the sentiment is true to Osceola: "To die in our own native shade" is better than to live beyond the Mississippi!

By far the most striking narrative of the young chief's defiance is Mary E. Hewitt's "Osceola Signing the Treaty." Warning his brothers that the white man is "Hungry and crafty as a kite," and accusing his hosts of having bought the Indian lands "with little gold and many a wound," he gives them the Seminole's answer:

> The red man is a foe to fear—
> He will not sign your faithless scroll,
> Nor yield to you the lands you prize . . .

Eyes aflame, he drives his glaive through parchment and board, declaring: "*Thus* Osceola signs your claim!"[46]

After the capture of Osceola, along with his war chiefs and eighty of his finest warriors, the anti-removal poetry intensifies in wrath. The brave, lofty-spirited Seminoles are contrasted with the villainous whites whose acts of "noonday murder and deep treachery" are called *victory* by self-styled Christians. Florida Territory and the neighboring states are execrated as *"The darkest spots beneath the eye of heaven!"*[47] The popular lyricist, George P. Morris, a sure barometer of public feeling, issues one of his few really impassioned poems, written from the Seminole point of view.[48] The invader is shown surrounding the forest with his boats and blood-hounds:

> Right he forgets while strength he feels;
> Our life he drains, our land he steals;
> And when the vanquished Indian kneels,
> He spurns him from his sight.

After superb resistance, the decimated tribesmen prepare to leave their untenable home—not for the West, but for that better world "beyond the borders of the west." It is a stirring death-song, out of character for Morris, and significant in its appearance soon after the seizure of Osceola.

One historically valuable verse record emerges from the warrior's captivity. Though less vivid and finished than Catlin's famous portrait, "Osceola at the Charleston Theatre" deserves better than the vicious review it received in Willis' *Mirror* and its subsequent oblivion. Written by a Charleston eyewitness three weeks before Osceola's death, and considered by many who had been present "a just and striking description of the scene," Ransom's verses (despite what the *Mirror* terms "his offences against . . . the 'Queen's English' ") shine with genuine sympathy and imaginative perception:

> I . . . watch'd his listless mien and careless bow,
> As though he saw the play, but heard it not.
> And then his lips would breathe some secret vow
> To strike for injuries ne'er to be forgot . . .
>
> Yes, there he sat, subdued, but still enraged;
> Like [sic] the fierce tiger, when he's caught and caged,
> Will lie composed; yet, when you pass him by,
> You'll see a demon spirit in his eye . . .

For his wild thoughts, like some unfetter'd bird,
Flew swift as lightning, to that home too dear,
Where his undaunted host still long'd to go,
To raise the savage yell, and fight the foe.

Charleston, hating the tribe that sheltered fugitives, was the very core of anti-Seminole feeling and action. To write and publish this poem in Charleston took some courage. It is not surprising that the sympathetic biography, of which this poem is the postscript, appeared in New York rather than Charleston, nor is it surprising that the author withheld his name.[49]

In Lucy Hooper's more facile but less rewarding verses, we see the Osceola facts beginning to take legendary form even while he is alive. Although inspired by a picture of him in captivity, this poem makes only passing reference to his "glance of scorn . . . folded arms and aspect stern," while it rides along on a rhetorical tide of grief for his "high but hopeless struggle," and shame for the stain on our country's banner. Ignoring his chiefs and warriors, the poetess insists that Osceola came to his fatal rendezvous "a noble offering—and alone!" and that he is a solitary prisoner. Malaria is translated by Miss Hooper's imagination, so that he "dieth of the fevered heart!"[50]

Cleveland Coxe's response to the Catlin portrait parallels the poem by Lucy Hooper. Barely noting the chieftain's aspect, Coxe emphasizes the deceit of Jessup, that flower of chivalry, and the moral corruption of supposed Christians who applaud "a slight ruse that well may do/In savage warfare." Like Miss Hooper he laments the brave and noble savage, and prophesies darkly:

Weep oh, my country, not for him but ay
　　For thy sad self; lest a just God should wield
Some stronger sword against thee. Thou should'st fear![51]

The poets who deplore the incident as part of a larger bankruptcy come closest to prophecy. Coxe, for instance, includes the Lovejoy murder and other recent atrocities, along with Osceola's death, in a general indictment of his land. John Pierpont goes further, charging that it is at Slavery's beck America sends its sons "To hunt down Indian wives and maids," break a truce, and seize Indian lands.[52] Hoffman, on the other hand, not only ignores the matter of slavery, but praises General Scott's firmness toward the Cherokee. Jessup, who merely carried out the government's orders, serves as a convenient scapegoat at whom the poet rages for "the base treachery which wrought the confinement and consequent death of Osceola."[53].

On the wave of universal indignation that follows this episode, there emerge several long poems in praise of earlier Indian heroes. Most of these are kept at a safe aesthetic distance from the latest news reports; but in Colton's *Tecumseh* Osceola is directly identified as the most recent embodiment of Tecumseh's fury:

> Though then the fiery oath went round,
> The fruits in later days are found,
> In Os-ce-o-la's liquid name,
> Enrolled on mournful lists of fame
> By struggles long and treacherous death,
> Whose soul brooked not the dungeon's breath . . .

When this epic appears, the war in the Everglades against the "pale insatiate strangers" has not yet ended. Interrupting his narrative, Colton prophetically shames the land in which "Os-ce-o-la, a pure and nobleminded savage," was led to his confinement and death by the decoy of a truce-flag.[54]

The best Osceola poem, by Alfred B. Street, differs from the rest not only in form and tone, but also in the essence of its statement.[55] The poet presents two high points of Osceola's career: his ambush of a white regiment, and his death. The contrast is not only historically true, but dramatically stunning; and the hero's death is doubly poignant, following without transition his moment of greatest vigor. What gives the poem its binding strength is the replay of Osceola's opening triumph in his final feverish dream: on the flood of battle his eagle-soul passes away! In Part One, with a minimum of rhetoric, Street depicts a superlative leader in action; we participate in his controlled excitement as the moment approaches for his followers to electrify "the soft and sleeping air" with their warwhoops. It is a sneak attack, the kind by which Indian Agent Thompson had been murdered, the kind that Osceola's captors gave as their excuse for perpetrating a truce-ambush against *him*. Although Street admires Osceola's regal face and bearing, his first view is unsympathetic. Like a butcher in the most lurid Indian tales, the chief "shrieks as he bathes in the crimson rain," waking the hamlet and the nation with his tomahawk's lightning. In Part Two the poet tries to eclipse the horror he has just depicted, by showing the young warrior quivering and gasping for breath "in a dark and dungeon room." But to mention in passing that he had fought well "For his own green forest home" scarcely offsets the cruelties that have just overwhelmed us. And the initial horror is reinforced as the dying man ecstatically relives, in dreams, the scene of battle—thus indicating that the core of his life has been not the defense of his people but a joy in slaughter. A complex and disturbing clash of feeling emerges: although we admire the soul that fell "at the touch of a fetter" after breasting a nation's arms, we are likewise relieved that divine justice is still operating, that "The conqueror, death," has taken the measure of:

> . . . the proud, victorious chief
> Who smiled mid the pale-face slain . . .
> And bathed in the crimson rain.

This poem is a far cry from the shrillness and sentimentality of most Osceola verse, in which captor and nation are denounced, victim extolled and bewailed, but neither the chief nor his career is made real. Street may forgo the role of prophet by stressing the wrong link in the chain of cause and effect, but he has remained true to his vision and his art: *an* Osceola, if not *the* Osceola, lives in his stanzas.

That such a large group of minor poets should pay tribute to a contemporary Indian hostile is unusual. Some are simply anti-government. Others find the situation picturesque. The contrast between Jessup's perfidy and Osceola's loftiness enthralls them. Once again the ancient hero-definition applies:

> Warriors, I know that I shall fall.
> What then? It is my country's call.
> It is not death revenged to die:
> Death is to live in infamy![56]

That a Lovejoy's stance might be equally lofty does not matter; America is not yet ripe for a "fanatic" hero. No Street, no Catlin is about to rush Altonward, with pen or brush, to immortalize an abolition editor defending his press.

Between the end of the Seminole War in 1842 and the Sioux' "last stand" in 1876, incursion, betrayal, bloodshed, removal, and decimation involved every tribe in the path of westward expansion. As their tide receded, more urgent matters—disunion, emancipation, reconstruction—demanded the attention of ethically alert poets. The Indian receives some notice, but it is usually the notice of curiosity and a backward sigh. Those poets like Longfellow and Thoreau, who embark on monumental projects, assume that they are preserving relics of a vanishing race. Northern and Southern poets remain indistinguishable in this area. Thomas B. Read is the one poet of stature in whose work the nostalgia is persistently charged with bitterness.[57] Thomas B. Aldrich is more typical, treating the theme only once, in an Indian story which stands among many equally well-wrought, detached, exotic pieces. What is noteworthy in "Miantowona" is Aldrich's demand that America "revere these wildwood legends." How ravenously the possessive pronoun is used by a poet who nowhere indicates a sense of guilt toward the aborigine!

> Richest of heirlooms . . .
> They are ours only,
> Like our grand rivers,
> Like our vast prairies,
> Like our dead heroes.[58]

William G. Simms uses the same tradition, in poems pervaded by gentle sadness; nor is he grudging in his praise of Indian heroism. But the foe is invariably Choctaw, Spaniard, or Pawnee—not the pale face![59] Simms' fellow-Carolinian, William J. Grayson, is also able to sympathize with the Indians,[60] particularly as their "defeated assailants were not our own people or kindred," but Spaniards. One would be hard put to find a more open confession of parochial ethics; yet we have seen the same double standard in many New England poets. If there is any real difference between Grayson's nostalgia and that of Northerners, it is not in his sad vision of the natives as a cowering remnant, whom the westward surge will sweep "headlong from their transient home," but in his brand of anthropology:

> . . . a barbarous people perishes always, if placed in contact with a stronger civilized race, except when they occupy to each other the relation of master and slave.

Yet even on this point many a Northern poet, while angrily disputing the slavery slant, would agree with Grayson that the red man is doomed.

iv

In the seventies the government's monstrosities against the dwindling western tribes stirred outbursts of embarrassment, rage, and warning among those whose conscience was at work; but if we seek a denunciatory response from American poets at this time, there are several factors we must consider prior to such an investigation. In the first place they have before them the warning example of Joaquin Miller, who cannot find an American publisher for a book sympathetic to a harassed tribe. Second, the dominant genteel poets are hostile toward the treatment of any current happenings, at least in verse. This applies particularly to occurrences that show the more uncouth side of the American character. That Bayard Taylor, for instance, would have nothing to do with such events as the

Custer battle, is illustrated by a hilarious parody published in *Scribner's* a few months after the Little Big Horn tragedy. *"It is not difficult* to tell," says the editor, "whom Bayard Taylor 'echoes' in the following galloping lines":

> Far on the hot Apache plain
> I sinched the girth and I buckled the rein . . .
> I crashed through the flame, I dashed o'er the sand,
> Bearing my songs in my red right hand . . .
> Take them and read them, and yield me the crown
> Which the old Sierras on me cast down . . .[61]

The derision, encompassing Joaquin Miller's landscape and subject matter along with his prosody and stance, is overt evidence of a revulsion against wild-west Americana implicit in the dignified stanzas of Taylor, Stoddard, and their circle. If, as Parrington claims, the poets under Boston's sway "missed . . . everything vital and significant in American life" by barricading themselves "against the intrusion of the unpleasant,"[62] we will find little response to such catastrophes of the seventies as the torment of the Plains tribes and their terrible moment of retribution.

A third obstacle to prophetic utterance on behalf of the Indians is the great eagerness among poets to help heal the wounds of the Civil War and reunite the nation. Thus Aldrich reminds the South that the "hallowed dust" of New Englanders in its keeping "should knit us closer yet."[63] Another poet, describing as a *fact* the harmony he yearns for, adds censoriously that "No home-born hates" had better intrude.[64] Richard H. Stoddard, in his pretentious, long-winded centenary ode, goes so far as to credit God with having reunited the states for mankind's sake; he warns America not to permit any of her children to "rend asunder" what God has joined.[65] It is inconceivable that poets so ardently concerned with national unity should look with favor on bands of recalcitrant Indians defying the American government to the point of military rebellion.

Next we must consider the self-imposed tyranny of exuberance as an impediment to prophecy. One cannot recognize the "dreadful decade" in these insistently affirmative poems. The editor of *Scribner's,* "keenly ashamed and . . . deeply discouraged at the condition of public affairs," proclaims that there is "No room for self-glorification here"; but his poetry department has room for nothing else.[66] This dichotomy demonstrates an ethical deterioration of the poet's role from prophecy to laureateship, curiously matching that of America's idol, Tennyson. In stately pseudo-prophetic strophes, Bayard Taylor's "National Ode" repeats the arrogant platitudes America wishes to hear:

> She won the inviolate soil
> By . . . faith in the royal right of Toil! . . .
> Nor paused till her uttermost home was built . . .
> The race, in conquering,
> Some fierce, Titanic joy of conquest knows.[67]

Clearly, such emotion cannot enlist itself on the side of the vexatiously uncooperative tribes who dare to hinder the glorious conquest. Like Taylor's, the 1876 verses of George Woodberry, under their veneer of apocalyptic inspiration, are in fact a call to empire and a blatant whitewash of the seventies:

> O throned Freedom, unto thee is brought
> Empire; nor falsehood nor blood-payment asked . . .
> . . . common are thy fields; common the toil;
> Common the charter of prosperity,
> That gives to each that all may blessed be.[68]

It would, of course, be unrealistic to expect that Woodberry, while generously distributing the land of the Indian, would identify him as its owner and, in fiery stanzas, resist its plunder by the Anglo-Saxon. He makes clear enough his belief that this change of ownership is the noblest triumph in human history. An almost identical position is taken by others, including Cleveland Coxe, whose 1838 fury at the treatment of the Seminole bears no resemblance to the song he sings in 1876:

> Undaunted they came, every peril to dare—
> Of tribes fiercer far than the wolf in his lair;
> Of the wild irksome woods, where in ambush they lay;
> Of their terror by night and their arrow by day . . .
> The wilds they have conquer'd, of mountain, and plain—
> Those Pilgrims have made them fair Freedom's domain.[69]

Representative as such verses may be of an ethical lapse among poets, the Indian policy they endorse is usually of the past. No such remoteness, however, veils the centennial prose of William D. Howells, who publicly advocates "The extermination of the red savages"—allegedly to save the Pueblos of New Mexico "whom they have harassed for hundreds of years." Even Custer could not have equalled the murderous *Atlantic Monthly* barrage written in May, 1876, by the gentle Howells:

> The red man . . . is a hideous demon, whose malign traits can hardly inspire any emotion softer than abhorrence. In blaming our Indian agents for malfeasance in office, perhaps we do not sufficiently account for the demoralizing influence of merely beholding those false and pitiless savage faces; moldy flour and corrupt beef must seem altogether too good for them.[70]

Were the general's strategy to succeed, there would be no tears for the Sioux from Howells' camp, for Custer on that westward march is the incarnation of their own hope.

Bearing in mind all of the above reservations, we can begin to examine the response of poets to the Indian affairs of the late-nineteenth century, focusing first of all on the Custer battle, which—hypothetically, at least—would seem to warrant a rich harvest of elegiac, narrative, and denunciatory verse.

V

News of the disaster struck like a thunderbolt. Across the sky loomed the image of a death-defying hero bearing his nation's tattered flag: as perfect a fireworks display as '76 could have wished for. At once the vengeance-cry arose. Volunteers rushed west for the kill.[71] We comb the great literary journals for a poetic response—whether it support or challenge the nation's emotional surge. What we find in those periodicals is silence: not a line of verse on Custer, his motives, his folly, his tragedy, his glory; not a couplet on the Sioux—their grievances, their terrible triumph, their future. Months, years go by, yet not a single poet is heard in *Scribner's, Lippincott's, Harper's, The Living Age, The Atlantic Monthly*. We turn to the new volumes of verse with little more success. It would seem, from this silence, that Whicher is altogether right in characterizing America's poets as a Brahmin-dominated chorus standing "aloof from the sordid spectacle" and offering "a thin, incongruous obbligato to the bustle of life."[72] It would seem that Pattee is equally wrong to consider the 1868—78 decade "in every respect the most vital and significant one in the history of America."[73]

Here and there, however, a poem does emerge. Wittingly or not, the creators of these half-score productions offer an interesting blend of ethical, political, and professional motives that help to delineate the state of prophecy in America as she strides into her second century as a nation. Bryant's New York *Post,* for instance, publishes "Custer's Immortality," by Laura S. Webb, first in its pages, then as a slight memorial volume.[74] A hodgepodge of undigested viewpoints and trite expressions, this poem is often clumsy and never felicitous. Typical of pseudo-prophecy, Mrs. Webb's ethical straining is far-fetched and confused. She repeatedly mentions "the vengeful hate,/Of the revengeful Sioux," without telling what they intend to avenge. She stresses the fact that the Black Hills, with their "fearful curse of GOLD," have incited unspecified parties "to Crime and Death!" But, instead of relating Custer's war to the rush of rails and prospectors, she offers the theory that he and his men gave their lives to purchase their "Country's fame and good" when its hour of need came. What the *good* or the *need* was, she fails to spell out, unless it was "to conquer the revengeful Sioux." If Custer indeed fell a selfless sacrifice, as she claims, her praise is appropriate enough, and no more hyperbolic than what can be found in elegies by genuinely prophetic poets. His was, she declares, "the noblest act of daring/That History ever gave," and she confidently prophesies that the future will consider the battle "upon our distant Western wilds . . . A new Thermopylae!"

But her enflamed imagination turns the sun-dance which Custer interrupted into "the war-dance of the savage/As he glided 'round the stake"; and she invents a baseless myth that Custer endured "the torture of the barbarous foe . . ." We might ask how such a portrayal of the Indian can assist her prayer for "a *lasting* Peace" between "the Red Man and the White." As we read further, however, it becomes clear that the lasting peace she really seeks is between South and North, and that this political motive is the true impulse of her poem. A Confederate widow is using the death of a Union hero as a welcome opportunity to *achieve,* by a graphic personal gesture of salute, the reunion of Blue and Gray for which other poets rhetorically *yearn.* Shrewdly she assures the North that during the Civil War Southern troops had admired Custer's "daring, dashing fearlessness . . . That pink of Chivalry!" Former enemies, she observes merrily, are now united against the Indian war whoop which so shockingly broke in upon "the glad, sweet hymn of Love" sung by "United millions" during the centennial celebration.

No other Custer poem is quite so politically motivated, but in "Miles Keogh's Horse"[75] John Hay has more in mind than simply to memorialize "the only living thing" of Custer's regiment that survived the battle. Resenting the fame of his "racy" 1871 Pike County ballads, hoping those six "diversions" would be forgotten, and intent on "becoming an orthodox lyric poet," Hay may have seized upon the poignant figure of the horse to prove that he could write a western ballad without "any suggestions of vulgarity."[76] Thus a personal aesthetic motive may accompany the more obvious one of celebrating heroes who fought bravely within Sitting Bull's "fiery scorpion ring." What gives the ballad its point, however, is a third motive, the poet's rancor, directed *not* against the Sioux, but against "the will of Congress"—which he blames for the disparity in numbers at the battle. This accounts for his description of the dead staring up at heaven "With wide, accusing eyes." Even greater is his protective rage against those outsiders who criticize the army, rending "its honest fame" like beasts. While Hay thanks the army for honoring the fallen regiment through its sole surviving creature, he is in fact damning the rest of America as "a callous people" who have forgotten "the sense of a soldier's worth . . . the love of comrades, the honor of arms . . ."

Elsewhere among the Custer poems we find hints of what is to become a major controversy. When a versifier[77] snidely suggests that at the graves of the regiment should be placed "the cannon which spoke not/In dreadful tones of vengeance deep," he is probably referring to Major Reno's failure to attempt a suicidal flanking operation in support of Custer. Stedman[78] may also have Reno in mind when he writes:

> . . . when some craven heart
> From honor dares to part,
> Then, then, the groan, the blanching cheek,
> And men in whispers speak,
> Nor kith nor country dare declaim
> From the black depths his name.

As the "most popular American Poet of Occasion, the Universal Official Poet," Stedman is relied upon by his generation "for an illuminating, artistic, sympathetic, even prophetic, expression of the dominant spirit or ideal."[79] He had sung memorably in 1859, at John Brown's hanging; here once again he celebrates a fallen hero, not in his own voice, but as the mouthpiece of many. The difference, however, is clear: to praise John Brown in 1859 is less than popular; to call Custer "a new star" in the heavens, is to crystallize the national pride and grief of 1876. Stedman in 1859 had defended the slave against his oppressor; now he lauds the "gallant charge" against red men fighting for their ancestral home, and regrets that Custer shall be seen in no more attacks on Indian villages. Through this event Mrs. Webb of the South and Stedman of the North have reached a profound agreement: both appreciate "pink chivalry," applaud the "brave darling of the soldiers' choice," denounce the Sioux as a "wolfish foe," and deplore the unfortunate timing of the fiasco: "all our birthday song is hushed indeed!" But, while Mrs. Webb at least gives lip service to the hope of peace between the races, Stedman openly raises the cry for blood, cheering on the soldiers who vengefully seek the trail where Custer's "red doomsmen be."

There are those poets, however, who wish simply to record an act of heroism and to predict immortality for "That wild, mad dash to the river side,/Where the glorious Custer, fearless, died."[80] The grievances of the Indians, the brilliance of their leaders, and the ultimate hopelessness of *their* position, are nowhere indicated. Frederick Whittaker, along with the rest, depicts them[81] as a savage enemy whose roar of attack is a "chorus from hell" and whose knife leaves mangled limbs behind. Unblenching before "those torturing fiends" who circle him, Custer inevitably cries out: "We can but die once, boys,—we'll sell our lives dear!"

A surprising response comes from Joaquin Miller, advocate-extraordinary of the Indian cause. In a brief lyric—ignoring the issues involved in the battle, failing to identify the foe—he praises the way Custer died:

> On glory's front, with trumpet's blare,
> And battle's shout blent wild about—

The sense of sacrifice, the roar
Of war!

That Miller should praise an exterminator of Indians is less puzzling, however, when we consider that this poet, a lover of bold action, is generous enough to admire his adversary as a "brave, white soul"—overlooking the *motive* in appreciation of the *ideal stance*.[82] Of the poems produced at this time that catch Miller's martial note without specifically referring to Custer, A. R. Grote's "A Last Word" is particularly apt:

Hold thy heart within thy hand
Where the fools around thee stand,
So that when they torture thee
Thou canst crush it and be free;

They will show their brutal strength,
They will have their way at length;
This at least they shall not say,
They have touched thy heart today.[83]

It is not until some years later that Ernest McGaffey and Ella W. Wilcox turn their reactions into verse. In McGaffey's case the delay is all to the good, since he could probably not—at fifteen—have achieved the impartiality that gives a tragic impact to his stanzas and makes the narrative ring true. The closest he comes to Anglo-Saxonism is in contrasting the "wild, painted faces" of the squaws with the laughter of Custer's "reckless blue-coats." But there is none of the blatantly racist language or slant we have noted in most earlier Custer poems. Aggressor and defender are clearly identified:

. . . fierce on the wigwams
The soldiers descended,

And madly were blended
The red man and white
In a hand-to-hand fight
With the Indian village assailed and defended.[84]

Mrs. Wilcox's mammoth poem, however, does not benefit from its twenty-year perspective.[85] Closing the century with a superficial acknowledgment of the factors behind the Sioux' fury, this work proves that America has retreated not one jot from the racial arrogance of its founders. In Book Two the poet whitewashes her hero's midnight attacks on Indian villages, obviously availing herself of Mrs. Custer's rather than Mrs. Jackson's facts, and thereby compromising her pretensions to the truth-seeking and truth-telling of prophecy. A twentieth-anniversary poet could do nothing more endearing than describe the valiant troops of brave Custer on their way "To rescue fair white captives from the hands/Of brutal Cheyenne . . ." Book Three is ferociously anti-Indian; seldom in peacetime has an American poet so candidly published so rabid a viewpoint:

. . . if the last lone remnant of that race
Were by the white man swept from off the earth's fair face,

Were every red man slaughtered in a day,
Still would that sacrifice but poorly pay
For one insulted woman captive's woes.

In a sense, we are fortunate that Mrs. Wilcox lets her feelings overflow with more facility than sophistication; seeing eye to eye with a vast American public, she needs but put their sentiments into meter and rhyme, and success is assured. What we have is essentially anti-prophetic: a glorification of the reality, even its ugliest details, and an absence of the ethical vision by which that reality can be judged. As art, Mrs. Wilcox's *Custer* is a huge failure; as history it is false; as a psycho-sociological specimen of America flexing its muscles two years before the Philippine adventure, it is a prize. Some of the earlier Custer poems had revived that "rally 'round the flag" mood upset by the Civil War but absolutely essential to the official literature of a dynamic empire. With Mrs. Wilcox, whose hero arises "in his strength . . ./More daring, more intrepid than before," whose Indians are exactly Theodore Roosevelt's in *Winning the West,* the Rough Riders are ready to move.

vi

This, then, is our Custer harvest—somewhat meager when one considers the scores of minor poets producing well-regarded work, and striking in the absence of a single poem sympathetic to the Sioux. Quinn, specifically thinking of the Custer battle, suggests that "the shrinking from the primitive . . . was entirely natural" while America "was busy acting out the raw materials for a still-unwritten epic."[86] This shrinking, along with Boston's desire to impress Europe with its gentility, is obvious. Yet to accept such a state of affairs as universal is to charge a total hiatus of the prophetic impulse in American poetry while almost every significant nineteenth-century poet is still active. That so many poets express "their dissatisfaction at the weakness of contemporary verse" is itself proof of a certain strength.[87] These are the years when Lanier, Gilder, and even Taylor hurl some inspired epithets at the rulers of the land,[88] when Miller denounces the nation itself:

O, these money-getting times!
What's a heart for? What's a hand,
But to seize and shake the land,
Till it tremble for its crimes?[89]

Obviously, the American conscience *is* "alive and kicking" at this time. Perhaps it is the overwhelming brutality of the Sioux retribution that awes friendly poets into silence; perhaps they are temporarily cowed by the nation-wide cry for vengeance—though in retrospect we can see how urgent a moment that was for the prophetic voice to be raised. But on other occasions they *do* speak, sometimes resoundingly, giving the lie to those historians who depict them as bloodless.

Even Lanier, although he omits the Indians from his verse and celebrates the westward-driving spirit that is crushing them, has this to say about seventy-three tribesmen imprisoned at Fort Marion:

> . . . what might have become of these people if so be that gentle contact with their white neighbors might have been substituted in place of the unspeakable maddening wrongs which have finally left them but a little corner of their continent.[90]

And Bret Harte, although he is said to keep the Indian "conspicuously absent from his crowded stage,"[91] does show in some of his stories that the Western tribes "were not justly treated by the immigrating race."[92] More important for us, however, is his "Truthful James to the Editor. In the Modoc War. 1873." In this poem Harte skillfully unfolds, through the unwitting lips of a hostile white, the Modocs' grievances against a frontiersman who kidnapped a squaw and later wrought havoc in a Modoc village, burning a tribesman's rancheria and family. Here Harte exposes the ugliest feature of the frontier mind egging itself on to a massacre of natives:

> Is this Nation a White Man's . . .?
> . . . folks of that stamp
> Hez no rights in the Law,
> But is treacherous, sinful, and slimy . . .[93]

Soon after the Custer tragedy Miller resumes his role as whiplash of the white man's conscience, in a series of frontal assaults on the national ethic, notably "The Heroes of Oregon" and "The Sea of Fire."[94] The first may well refer to the Black Hills:

> . . . that which men call good I find not good.
> The lands the savage held, shall hold again,
> The gold the savage spurn'd in proud disdain,
> For centuries; go, take them all; build high
> Your gilded temples; strive and strike and strain
> And crowd and controvert and curse and lie
> In church and State, in town and citadel, and . . . die.

"The Sea of Fire," originally published in 1877, concerns the fate of a tribe which had destroyed the Spanish plunderers of their gold, their land, and their daughters. With furious irony, Miller suddenly turns the mirror upon his readers' faces:

> The Christian found the land, and came
> To take possession in Christ's name.
> For every white man that had died
> I think a thousand red men fell,—
> A Christian custom; and the land
> Lay lifeless as some burned-out brand.

The same bitterness wells up in other late-nineteenth-century poets, though seldom with such sustained force as we find in Miller. Touring the West, for instance, Richard Burton is struck by a painful irony:[95]

> . . . dominant Saxons from the hurtling trains
> Smile at the aliens, Mexic, Indian,
> Who offer wares, keen-colored, like their past . . .

He wishes his smug countrymen to hear the sound that haunts him:

> . . . a shuddering ethnic moan, the saddest of all sad sounds;
> The cry of an outraged race that is driven otherwhere,
> The Indian's heart-wrung wail for his hapless Hunting grounds.

The variety and sharpness of such rebukes belie somewhat those literary historians who characterize the period as effete. Among the most powerful outcries on behalf of the mistreated race is *The Song of the Ancient People.* As *Hiawatha* emerged seventeen years after Osceola, so does Edna D. Proctor,[96] seventeen years after Custer, publish her ambitious work, lovingly researched and long ripening into inspired utterance. Proudly her Pueblo hurls back the white man's contempt:

> Alas for us who once were lords
> Of stream and peak and plain!—
> By ages done, by Star and Sun,
> We will not brook disdain!
> No! though your strength were thousandfold
> From farthest main to main;
> For we are the Ancient People,
> Born with the wind and rain!

Miss Proctor writes other sympathetic poems as well, ranging from the Mexican border to the Columbia, the Grand Canyon to Pennsylvania. She retells a legend of Lake Mohonk, and celebrates the Indian girl who guided Lewis and Clark. In the 1880's, demanding citizenship for the native, she addresses the guilty memory of her neighbors:

> The Red Man was the primal lord
> Of our magnificent domain,
> And craft, and crime, and wasting sword
> Oft gained us mount and stream and plain.

Like Mrs. Sigourney fifty years earlier, she urges America to cease adding "wrong to wrong." In her ideal republic the tribes now violently excluded would be welcomed:

> Then will the 'reservation' be
> Columbia's breadth from sea to sea,
> And Sioux, Apache, and Cheyenne
> Merge proudly in American!

Other poets, such as John B. O'Reilly[97] and Hezekiah Butterworth,[98] show their sympathy in narratives that illustrate the red man's superiority to the race allegedly destined as his successor. In "A Savage," for example, O'Reilly ironically depicts a sentenced Indian's voluntary return to his amazed executioners. In the beautifully controlled hexameters of "A Song for the Soldiers," he celebrates the epic valor of forty braves against a cavalry regiment in 1880:

> "On to the rocks!" and the soldiers have done with their feelings of mercy . . .
> Awed stood the troopers who followed, and lowered their swords with their leader . . .

There at their feet lay the foemen—every man dead on
his rifle—
The two who had charged the troops were the last alive
of the Cheyennes!

Butterworth, on the other hand, prefers to recall remote instances of white injustice and Indian nobility. He dramatizes Spanish treachery in Ponce de Leon's Florida:

The crowns Castilian could not bring the withered stalk
a leaf,
But came a sabre flash that morn, and fell the Indian chief.

Elsewhere an old Chicago pioneer sadly recalls the Illini removal:

On, on to the West, to the Great River's tide,
On, on, 'neath the white stranger's ban,
And never the chief or the maid turned aside
To look back on the blue Michigan . . .

In another poem he returns to the time of Roger Williams' exile from Salem, when "the red hand supplied what a white hand denied him." Harmless as such allusions seem, their persistent recurrence in the work of a gentle writer such as Butterworth must have troubled the souls of his readers.

To accomplish the same prophetic goal, Eugene Field chooses humor as his strategy.[99] He paraphrases with mock horror the typical raid and captivity legends that had sobered naughty children since 1620. It may be a kite that "The skulking Injun crew" hustle away, or the heartless chiefs may have seized a "beauteous maid/And rent her doll in twain." This child's-play makes Indian-fighting grotesque, but there is a carefully planted familiarity in his exhortation to rescuers: "Ready with gun and sword/Your valorous work to do," or:

> Spare neither Injun buck nor squaw,
> But smite them hide and hair!
> Spare neither sex nor age nor size,
> And no condition spare!

Deftly—"out of the mouths of babes"—Field has exposed the end-product of a master race's record. Elsewhere this not altogether innocuous poet satirizes the scare campaigns by which tribes were decimated. In Yellowstone Park "a sharp, startling sound" is taken for "the savage war-whoop" of the "skulking red beast." A group of campers, "rendered fierce by fear," soon find their kill, "in bullet-torn coats," to be "the earthly remains/Of a pair of coyotes." Field's sophisticated impudence seems intent on parodying the hackneyed racism of anti-Indian balladeers such as James Whitcomb Riley and Rose Terry Cooke.[100]

Hamlin Garland's approach is neither didactic, narrative, nor humorous, but purely lyrical. In *Prairie Songs* the young poet (who was sixteen at the time of the Sioux battle) sets out to sing of his childhood memories.[101] He laments the "files of Indian armies," and their buffaloes which survived "centuries of struggle—/In swarming millions—till the white man came." Indignantly he recalls the continent's purer past:

> . . . those sun-lit prairie lands,
> Unstained of blood, possessed of peace and plenty
> Untouched by greed's all desolating hands.

His most richly imaginative and moving poem on this theme is "Rushing Eagle," focusing (as in his later prose portrayal of Sitting Bull) on a noble leader who epitomizes the great, tragic story of his race:

> What tragedy compares with this—
> A racial death! Here and there
> A chieftain understands. Guiltless as the panther
> Wild as the soul of every wronged
> And cheated man, he leaps upon
> The wall of circling flame, and falls and dies
> Like a trapped wolf . . .
>
> Blessed be his faith in happy hunting-grounds,
> For nothing here is left but beggary
> And melancholy change.

This sorrowful, accusing poem, published in 1893, may well have been inspired by the murder of Sitting Bull three years earlier.

The most unquestionably prophetic voice among all minor American poets who consider the Indian question—prophetic in motive, tone, and impact—is Helen Hunt Jackson's. Awakened in 1879 by the government's cruelty toward the Poncas, she at once thrusts backward in time, uncovering an ethical enormity of long duration, wide acceptance, and profound ramifications. Her essence and her talent, in the tradition of the greatest evangelists, become instruments of a passion greater than herself. Of *A Century of Dishonor* she writes: "All the heart and soul I possess have gone into it."[102] And of her novel she says: "I did not write Ramona. It was written through me. My life-blood went into it."[103] Even her choice of forms is prophetic. In *A Century of Dishonor* she "tried to tackle the conscience directly," documenting—tribe by tribe—the abuse of the Indians by their conquerors. Three years later, convinced that her efforts have failed, she sugars her "pill"[104] by returning to fiction to show what the older Californians "suffered from the predacious vanguard of the Anglo-Saxon conquest."[105] That she discards poetry to reach a great audience is evidence of the diminished arena for serious poets in late-nineteenth-century America; but more important here, it demonstrates Mrs. Jackson's willingness to sacrifice the form that pleases her most. The irony is that her permanence is based entirely on these two books after a career in poetry which her contemporaries considered distinguished, but which is now dismissed as "a prolific career of romantic hack writing."[106] Dying, she terms her Indian work "the only things I have done for which I am glad now. The rest is of no moment. They will live on and they will bear fruit."[107]

Mrs. Jackson's example might lead to the assumption that aesthetic triumph depends on prophetic motive. The simultaneous rebirth of Emma Lazarus as prophetess, followed by five years of similarly passionate devotion which consumed her body yet resulted in her only permanent work, dramatically supports such a view. That this conclusion is unwarranted, however, has been proven over and over by the success of many poets whose concern is not ethical, and by the failure of many others, including some we have considered, whose intentions are as elevated, whose souls are as fervent, as are Mrs. Jackson's. An artistically ambitious but feeble-hearted work is as grotesque as a great-hearted work whose vehicle is feeble. Sometimes, however, the prophetic spirit finds its appropriate form; when this occurs we are on high ground. I do not claim the highest ground for Mrs. Jackson's two volumes; their weaknesses are serious. Had she been given more time, she might have produced soaring poems and more polished prose on this theme. Yet it must be granted that, after a century of rather pitiful poetic responses, America's conscience finds "tardy but memorable expression" in her work as in her life.[108] If Richard W. Gilder remains silent on the Indian agony, he can at least pay tribute to a spirit which "smote with its own sword":

> Herself has lit the fire whose blood-red flame
> Shall not be quenched—this is her living fame . . .
> None who e'er knew her can believe her dead . . .
> Ah, where that bright soul is cannot be night.[109]

And if Thomas W. Higginson's life is now so filled with family and work that Mrs. Jackson is unable to "fan the spark of an old enthusiasm," he can at least define her superb transformation:

> O soul of fire within a woman's clay!
> Lifting with slender hands a race's wrong,
> Whose mute appeal hushed all thine early song,
> And taught thy passionate heart the loftier way . . .[110]

vii

The work of no major figure compares in significance, on this theme, with that of Mrs. Jackson. All indicate some ethical concern for the red man, but this is true of the lesser poets as well. As in other areas of iniquity, some of our largest and most prophetically motivated figures often reflect the moral weakness of their time rather than contrasting it with an ideal. Thus, although his melancholy Indian songs imply sympathy, Bryant[111] seldom—and only in his early verse—speaks of "The pale race, who waste" the native. His last poems reinforce the spread-eagle Americanism of his youth. That sigh for the passing Indian has after all been little more than part of a general sigh for the transitoriness of life. Never does it have the ring of truth with which he celebrates "the white woodman" who doomed the Indian by opening "these fields to sunshine," turning the soil, and strewing the wheat. It is true that in his gracious letter to Mrs. Webb[112] he expresses only sorrow at Custer's death, omitting any praise of the General's motives; it is also true that in the supplement accompanying her poem, which he may have written or supervised, the moral position of the Sioux is sympathetically voiced. Yet he does allow the poetess to use his letter as a public endorsement of her rabidly anti-Indian verses, and he greets those verses as "a favorable sign of returning friendship between the North and the South."

Holmes is even more representative of the "official" position.[113] Echoing the very words with which his ancestors embarked on their crusade from Leyden, he honors the Pilgrims who went "to bear the saving word" to the Indians. He has no doubt that the invaders were indeed "chosen" to flourish "while feebler races melt away." Only once in his poetry does Holmes admit that "the page is red with the record of shame" in the white man's dealings with "the tribe of the Sachem." Only once does he hint that "the skulking foe" aimed his arrow in defense of "his last cornfield." The typical Indians in his poetry are "those scalping . . . devils" who killed great-grandfather; and this poet never stops believing that great-grandfather "held from God the charter of the soil."

In 1830, as a fledgling editor, Whittier had damned

"The unjust ejectment of the Indians" as "a crime which man may never forget, nor eternal justice forgive."[114] Soon after, utterly concerned with the North—South wrangle over the newly acquired lands, he ceases to fret about the tribes from whom those lands were torn, acknowledging them only in nostalgic ballads and in prayers for their conversion.[115] His horror-scenes of Indian raids on early settlements develop from "Pentucket" in 1838 to their most lurid flowering in his 1890 "Haverhill," unrelieved by any hint of the red man's grievances. Like Riley and other racist minstrels he evokes the time when forests hid wild beasts "And human shapes as fierce as they"; these could not—he adds proudly—thwart "The Saxon energy of will." Ecstatically his gaze follows "westward, wave on wave, the living flood . . ." And he placates the American conscience most ingeniously: since neither "home nor rest" matters to "the lank nomads of the wandering West," they don't mind the white man's invasion! His hope for the native is conversion. Thus, when Rain-in-the-Face enrolls at Hampton College ten years after the Little Big Horn tragedy, Whittier finally feels moved to sing of the Custer battle. He envisions the golden day when "The pale and the red shall be brothers." Fleetingly, as his ideal recalls Isaiah, the old fire of 1830 seems to stir within his bones, and he delivers a surprising rebuke, placing the blame for Custer's death squarely on America's shoulders: "Enough of the lying words/And shame of a broken faith!"

Longfellow, who in each of our tests has shown himself to be among the most ethically alive, does not at any point censure the aggrandizing spirit of the white man. In "To the Driving Cloud" he warns the Omaha chief that "the big thunder-canoe" breasting the Missouri, and "the breath of these Saxons" in their westward caravans, will doom his race; but the poet remains impartial:[116] Europe's starving millions have also "been created heirs of the earth, and claim its division!" Like Whittier, his major hope for Indian survival is conversion. Thus he honors John Eliot, the Puritans' apostle to the Indians, and in "Evangeline" he introduces a Shawnee woman who achieves a sisterhood of grief with the heroine and leads her to the Mission. In *Tales of a Wayside Inn* an Indian princess becomes a baroness, "Transfigured and transfused." And Hiawatha solemnly commands his people, after the priest's sermon:

> Listen to the truth they tell you,
> For the Master of Life has sent them
> From the land of light and morning!

Although curious and compassionate, Longfellow has clearly not been among the crusaders for Indian rights. But nothing in his work prepares us for his reaction to the Custer tragedy. With a promptness most unusual for him, he turns the first bloody reports into a ballad the basic "fact" of which later proves untrue: Rain-in-the-Face did *not* cut out Custer's heart. With grating partiality, at the very moment of national hysteria, he paints the would-be exterminators of the Sioux as "that gallant band," while the "Savage, unmerciful" natives seek death for "all the race/Of the White Chief." The Custer battle has apparently moved him to an immediate, unripe response in which—momentarily—an anti-Indian sediment rises to the surface. Yet his prophetic impulse is not entirely overwhelmed, and he concludes by reminding the American people as they clamor for vengeance: ". . . our broken faith/Wrought all this ruin . . ."

More candid and less sentimental than Longfellow, Lowell[117] early confesses an ethnic hostility; even in old age, Indian place-names sound "uncouth" to him, and the "highest art" of the primitive is "scratching on a bone,/ Or chipping toilsome arrowheads." By 1876 the concept of manifest destiny, which had been his prime target in *Biglow,* has become his credo; like his brother-laureates he envisions "a thousand miles of neighbors" who hold their land "by toil-worn titles fresh from God." This frank arrogance is accompanied by an openly anti-prophetic position. Instead of loving his nation with open eyes, alert to any swerving from the ideals that make her worth loving, he proudly restricts his sight and demands that others do the same. "The love is all that I can see," he declares; only thanks "unstinted . . . and not a doubt behind!" should be offered to one's land. To experience the completeness of his transformation one need only turn back to his 1838 class poem, a tremendous condemnation of his land's behavior toward the red man. Inspired by the prophetic example of Emerson, whose great plea against the Cherokee removal had just been published, he sang:

> One heart hath plead against a nation's sin;
> Where Liberty's first blood was dearly sold,
> One voice hath risen o'er the work-day din,
> And told far better than my heavy song
> Our Country's baseness and the Indian's wrong.

Although, unlike Lowell, Whitman includes the aborigine as an essential strand of his indigenous fabric, he too does not permit ethical considerations to slow down destiny's pioneers.[118] For this poet, beyond all others, is the prophet of a "new empire grander than any before," and inspiritor of the "resistless, restless race" shaping it.

How can he doubt the ethics of his vision, since Democracy is the "new rule" by which "the English brood . . . must rule the earth"? At the very moment of the centenary, when Lowell is publicly announcing the self-limiting of his vision, Whitman likewise declares what to him is apparently a visual triumph, although others may deem it a prophetic betrayal: "I only saw, at last, the beauty of the ship." How else but with mutilated eyes could he possibly see that wherever the red man goes "men and women accept and desire him,/They desire he should like them, touch them, speak to them, stay with them"? It is euphoria, charmingly documented by the marriage of a trapper to "a red girl" and a squaw's loving treatment by the poet's mother long ago.

Among the major poets, only Whitman pays swift and direct tribute to Custer. This is to be expected, since he is the poet of heroes "cut off before their time,/Possess'd by some strange spirit of fire." Frankly he admits on a personal level what is true of the whole nation in 1876, that "in dark days" one needs "the old, old legend of our race" to be re-enacted by a Custer. It is not for a poet—as Whitman defines him—either to explain or condemn "The Indian ambuscade, the craft"; nor does he consider what Custer's aims were against the race "men and women accept . . ." That the soldier ended "well in death the splendid fever of his deeds," is cause enough for celebration.

Fourteen years go by before Whitman attempts to correct once and for all his double standard as the poet of only certain heroes and as chronicler of the not-so-total American experience. In his room is Catlin's picture of the dying Osceola. He recalls what a Fort Moultrie marine told him fifty-two years earlier, in 1838. Still refusing to acknowledge even the slightest hint of guilt toward the

Indians, he makes a gesture in remembrance of Osceola's "name and death," in ten rather picturesque, sympathetic lines—and, in a prose note, half explains why the "young, brave" chief died "tightly grasping the tomahawk handle."

That Emily Dickinson differs from the poets we have already discussed can only be surmised,[119] since the sole Indian references in her poetry are embedded in her imagery—an occasional pipe, mocassin, or arrow. But her devotion to the crusading Mrs. Jackson is an important clue. We can also guess at her opinion of the exuberant and conscienceless westward thrust, for the following verses she writes in 1876 smack of a saucy anti-centennialism:

> The Heart and the Mind together make
> A single Continent—
>
> One—is the Population—
> Numerous enough—
> This ecstatic Nation
> Seek—it is Yourself.

In a sense, Thoreau turns his life into a poem dedicated to the aborigine. With typical independence, when discussing the red man, he takes particular delight in shattering his neighbors' idols.[120] Thus he unglamorizes their sanctified ancestors. "The white man comes," says the poet:

> He buys the Indian's mocassins and baskets, then buys his hunting-grounds, and at length forgets where he is buried and ploughs up his bones . . . town records . . . contain the Indian sachem's mark perchance . . . and the few fatal words by which he deeded his hunting-grounds away.

Of all the nineteenth-century poets, only Thoreau dares to suggest that Christianity may not offer the Indians a better spiritual life than the one they previously enjoyed. Gazing at a corrupted Indian island in Maine, he remarks sardonically: "a row of wigwams, with a dance of powwows, and a prisoner tortured at the stake, would be more respectable than this." What makes it possible for him to maintain the highest level of prophecy, unmasking the cruelty and hypocrisy which most poets would not or could not see, is his insistence on subjecting America to the ethical standards she claims to follow. Thus, while others adore America as a religion and resent any questioning of her character, he asks the central question: "What is your whole republic worth?"[121]

He goes much further than simply objecting to the treatment of the tribes; it is the original act of settlement which he rejects as predatory. In his destroyed early verse he may have expressed himself strongly; in the later lines, scarcely hinting at the "master passion"[122] which left 2800 manuscript pages on the Indian, he sounds like many others who "See the red race with sullen step retreat,/ Emptying its graves, striking the wigwam tent."[123] How the poet—whose "last distinct utterance . . . was the word 'Indians' "[124]—must have felt about the plundering of their *continent,* is indicated in his treatment of a rude *fireplace*:

> . . . he carefully covered up his find and replaced the turf, —not wishing to have the domestic altar of the aborigines profaned by mere curiosity.[125]

This extreme sensitivity would have been chuckled over as sentimental by his friend Emerson, who made public on a number of occasions his own level-headedness on the matter of the Indian. "The cultural flowering" which would follow the inevitable conquest of the continent, would—he states with cold emphasis—"be an ample compensation for any Indians . . . who were incidentally exterminated . . ."[126] Such a conclusion, brutal though it may sound, follows logically from Emerson's philosophy. In the same tone he criticizes Longfellow for "tenderness" in *Hiawatha,* for not dealing "very roundly" with the Indians—who are "really savage, have poor, small, sterile heads,—no thoughts . . ."[127] This view, which he persists in advancing, finds its most ruthlessly clear exposition in "The Adirondacks":

> It is not Iroquois or cannibals,
> But ever the free race with front sublime . . .
> Who do the feat, and lift humanity . . .
> We praise the guide, we praise the forest life:
> But will we sacrifice our dear-bought lore
> Of books and arts and trained experiment,
> Or count the Sioux a match for Agassiz?
> O no, not we![128]

How extraordinary, then, bearing these sentiments in mind, to see how Emerson performs when the specific ethical challenge comes! In his early sermons[129] we find him deploring the treatment of the Indians, announcing "The cause of the Indian is mine," crying out against their threatened banishment "from the remnant of their territory to barren wilds without water and grass." Later,[130] given the opportunity to flatter his neighbors' pride in their heritage, he blasts the Concord bicentennial proceedings by forcing the celebrants to consider their ancestors' infamy: ". . . no man spoke for the Indians . . . Concord . . . permitted a disgraceful outrage . . . For them the heart of charity, of humanity, was stone." In 1838, against all his inclinations and "for the sad reason that no other mortal will move, and if I do not—why it is left undone," he delivers a magnificent public appeal to the President:

> . . . a crime is projected that confounds our understandings by its magnitude—a crime that really deprives us as well as the Cherokees . . . for how could we call this conspiracy that should crush these poor Indians our government, or the land that was cursed by their parting and dying imprecations our country, any more? . . . the name of this nation, hitherto the sweet omen of religion and liberty, will stink to the world . . .

Soon after the Custer battle and amid the cries for Indian blood, Wendell Phillips and Emerson are in correspondence about "these friendless victims" and about the generals' unfulfilled boast that they would exterminate the red man.[131] Surely, on this issue, Emerson beautifully demonstrates authentic prophecy: the individual instrument shedding personal reluctance or antipathy when a truth greater than himself must be uttered.

Melville, too, fulfills nobly his own definition of the prophetic role.[132] With a courage matched only by Thoreau he places religious and racial arrogance at the root of the white man's difficulties "in Pequod wilds" long ago: "Hittites—foes pestilent to God/His fathers old those Indians deemed . . ." To the Anglo-Saxons of 1876, still pushing on "in the name of Christ," he says that their conversion dream is doomed, for they lack the grace "To win the love of any race." As the most keen-eyed and bold-tongued American incarnation of the Bible seers, he renounces, precisely at the centennial moment, his "birthright . . . in hope," his "sanguine country's wonted claim." Only Melville, at the time of Custer's fall, dares or cares to identify the sickness at the root of the American psyche:

> . . . Anglo-Saxons. What are they? . . .
> Hated by myriads dispossessed
> Of rights—the Indians East and West.
> These pirates of the sphere! grave looters—
> Grave, canting, Mammonite freebooters . . .
> Deflower the world's last sylvan glade!

Later, with unslackened wrath, he refers to the forcibly removed remnant of a tribe "all but exterminated in their recent and final war with regular white troops, a war waged by the Red Men for their native soil and natural rights . . ." Compared with the lustiness of this alienated poet, how sickly appears the morality of those locked in embrace with their nation!

We have arrived at answers to some of the questions opened by our choice of this touchstone. First, it is clear that few nineteenth-century American poets leapt to fulfill the role of panegyrist. For neither Osceola nor Custer was there a really significant outpouring of song, a redefinition of heroism. Several minor poets used the chieftain's death to denounce government policy, but the only poem in which he seems real depicts him as the cause of his own downfall. The Custer tragedy, however, was acknowledged by several major poets and some of their notable younger contemporaries. We are able to catch them at the moment of exhilaration, when their thirst for bravura has been satisfied. The praise of Custer is hyperbolic and vague: what he was doing at the Little Big Horn, although a pertinent question, was not asked.

We have found that some post-bellum poets were indeed sensitive to the mistreatment of the red man. The liveliness and variety of their response challenges the legend of post-war devitalization. That others remained aloof, adhering to the rules of the genteel tradition, underscores the strength of the prophetic impulse in Helen Hunt Jackson, Edna Dean Proctor, Hamlin Garland, and Joaquin Miller, to name a few. Of the two 1838 enthusiasts for the Indian, Lowell swiftly reneged and Emerson in 1876 was too tired to duplicate his splendid appeal to Van Buren; the others of the "old guard," still entranced by Manifest Destiny, cared little about its victim.

After both Osceola and Custer, much poetry sympathetic to the native emerged. This work often challenged the government's Indian program and the frontiersman's cruelty; but there is one level of prophecy which only Thoreau and Melville dared to reach, striking directly at the root-evil itself: the ethical monstrosity of setting foot on occupied soil with the assurance of proprietorship.

5

War With Spain

The war with Spain, half a century later, differed from the Mexican adventure in that the adversary was not a weak young republic but an ancient tyranny. The lands involved were not part of the enemy's mainland, but a group of mistreated colonies yearning for liberation. The United States were not divided on the question of free-soil, but were united under an ambitious military organization which, having recently served industry in a union-wrecking program at home, would not be coy about undertaking an overseas mission. Finally, a group of unscrupulous, circulation-hungry newspaper publishers were by now able and eager to electrify the national imagination and sweep aside all ethical questions. In other ways, however, the second war paralleled the first closely. The shame at playing an imperial role was drowned out by the dynamic concept of manifest destiny, by the theory of America's civilizing function, by the pride in heroic actions and dazzling victories. In each case a sensational catastrophe was turned into an effective slogan for revenge: the *Maine* merely replaced the Alamo. An aggressive mentality, permeated by Anglo-Saxonism, sneered at the native to be "saved." Liberation led to independence, then annexation, then annihilation of resistance.

The verse of 1898 underscores all these differences and similarities. One additional factor, a crucial complication, bears directly on the theme of this study. Literary historians assert, and our Indian study partly confirms, that post-bellum poetry was devitalized by the genteel tradition, that the "angry young" pre-Civil War poets were dying, dead, or mellowed. As for the 1890's, impatient comments by Moody, Gilder, Santayana, and Robinson indicate a decade of hot-house verse. If this is so, we can expect in 1898 little of the denunciatory spirit that raged in 1846. We shall nevertheless search for prophetic tendencies, in whatever forms they may appear. First, however, we must thoroughly familiarize ourselves with the pseudo- and the anti-prophetic verse of 1898, since it documents every phase of the conflict, provides the government with a glamorous moral position, and—as in the Mexican War—serves as a direct contrast and target for the voices of genuine prophecy.

i

American poets had decried Spanish tyranny in Cuba[1] as far back as 1822, when James G. Percival vowed to the "island of plunder and slaves" that America would free it from Spain. Fifty years later Clarence E. Stedman pictured the island as "our desolate sister . . . a virgin" led to the slaughter while those who love her sleep. He prodded the conscience of his country: "Must ye see them trample her, and be calm? Speak out at last to the treacherous spoiler!" Soon after, when Spain paid an indemnity for capturing an American vessel and executing its men, James J. Roche raged against a financial deal which permitted the murder of free men and Cuba's continued woe. "Our flag may droop in foul disgrace," he sneered provokingly, "But 'Peace' be still our cry . . ." These poets sound sincerely fervent; and it may be that they were unaware of the lustful spark which Cuba had long aroused in expansionist eyes. Perhaps they did not know how welcome their stanzas were to the administration they seemed to be assaulting. Not all poets, however, were so naïve. Whittier, for instance, satirically proposed in 1854 that the slavers turn from Kansas to Cuba, "That golden orange," to keep "pace with Providence, or, as we say,/Manifest destiny."[2] Similarly, Franklin B. Sanborn in 1858 imagined Manifest Destiny telling Slavery to help "gain fair Cuba" whether "by purchase or war."[3] And, as usual, one rhymester less subtle than his fellow-minstrels can be depended upon to "let the cat out of the bag." This happens in 1875, when an American threat of intervention forces Spain to grant reforms. Emboldened by his country's diplomatic victory, Harvey Rice reverts to the most strident tune of the 1846 trumpeters:

God meant thee to be free,
And wills thee to be ours! . . .
From towers and mountain crest,
Our flag shall be unfurled!

In truth, it is but just,
That Freedom's hand should hold,

Confided to her trust,
The key to lands of gold![4]

We are not to encounter this degree of candor again for many years.

In 1895 new abuses led to new revolts, and American poets joined the battle with ever-increasing passion. Coincidentally, expanding American industry desperately needed expanding markets, and a large segment of public opinion had become empire-minded. It is impossible, however, to detect any self-interest beneath lines that blaze with Arthurian idealism. Having itself known oppression, the poets argue, and been succored by "a sister's aid," the United States should now pay the debt by sending a Lafayette "out of the starry Western land."[5] The same "robbers" who are now at Cuba's throat, once inquisitioned Jews, exterminated Indians, "bound Columbus, foot and hand." Revolution-born America, Joaquin Miller insists, should hear Cuba's cries, "bid her smite . . . espouse her glory."[6] One poet, attempting to drown out the voice of Isaiah, roars that Right—to vanquish Wrong—"must oft beat pruning hooks to spears."[7]

There are, it is true, a few contrary voices. Robert U. Johnson,[8] for one, calls on the English to help curb the war-minded in both nations who, "like rash children, tamper with" the sword. Months before San Juan Hill he admonishes his belligerent countrymen by ironically describing war-games in a nursery-room, where brave troops fell on the fleeing foe "And sacked their camp, and took their town." Another warns the *Maine,* before it sails, not to be too proud of its power, and to "seek no end beyond the avowed end" of protecting American life and property in Havana.[9]

The explosion, of course, explodes the tinderbox of American emotion. "Remember the *Maine!*" at once becomes a rallying-cry, intensifying a war-spirit already enflamed and self-justified by exaggerated atrocity stories. This would be the logical moment for voices of sobriety and warning to be raised; yet very few poets support McKinley's peace stance pending the results of an investigation. The most responsible figures in American poetry are mute, and even among the lesser versifiers known to be critical of administration policy, not one challenges the presence of the ship in Havana or suggests that the explosion might have been engineered to bring on the war. Here and there a note of caution is timidly raised.[10] "The verdict wait; your wrath restrain," advises one. Another begs the God of Battle: "Subdue thy people's fiery will." A third tells Patience to keep its hand on the hilt. But even these very voices imply an itch for battle. Prayer is apparently to be no more than a conscience-cleansing ritual "before we bathe our hands in blood." As soon as Justice has weighed all in the balance, Patience may "loose the appointed sword."

Other poets, who have their verdict ready at once, memorialize the dead with ominous solemnity.[11] Rupert Hughes objects to Spain's burying them like "alien mendicants." Another shrieks: "Iberian! By thine hands . . . they were slain!" There is only one way for Spain to avert war, they say: by freeing Cuba. For these eager spirits the investigation takes too long: "Peace if it may be; red war, if it must! For we love peace—but we love honor more."[12] Henceforth the *Maine* is their goad and their program. Ballads of that ship sweep the land, become anthems. The war-spirit has been released "like an eagle" from its cage,[13] and at the thought of the *Maine*—sing the poets—"We are ready to storm gates of Hell."[14] They have good reason to adopt the national "we," for they are voicing the dominant national mood. This public identification seems to give their work the ring of prophecy; but one must remember the difference between poets who express the buried fears or yearnings of their neighbors, and those who air the very sentiments which the regime most wishes to encourage. The "we" of false prophecy is always easy to market, never more so than during a war-frenzy such as 1898. One can readily recognize it by its dependence on catch-words and its ethical confusion.[15] Thus one rhymester boasts that, unassisted, we can "free the sons of Cuba/ And take vengeance for the Maine." Another doesn't think much of Cuba and suggests that she "fight it out with Spain"; his concern is only for those "murdered when/The Spaniards sank the Maine." In the next breath this ingenuous warbler asks: "Did the Spaniards sink the Maine?"—No matter!

> It is now too late to explain;
> Hurrah for our country, right or wrong,
> And the heroes of the Maine.

This familiar salute returns us to the high seas of imperial adventure.

ii

Once the war begins in earnest, the more sophisticated laureates dignify it with a variety of high aims and inspiring symbols—reminiscent of the Mexican War, yet with some new ingredients. Our first task is to identify this attractive rationale. Training their sights on Spanish tyranny and greed, many poets show Cuba, blighted by a savage reign, awaiting redemption from what John T. Trowbridge calls "four centuries of wrong!"[16] With the help of America's heroes, Cuban patriots will plant "their own loved banner on the ramparts of their foe."[17] In the Pacific, Dewey will also crush the oppressors. Not only freedom, but civilization as well, will be the happy fate of the islanders, east and west; cleansed of mire and swamp, they will "hear the glad laughter of children."[18]

But the minstrels of 1898 are not satisfied with such modest aims. The gigantic rape of old Spain demands gigantic justification, and the war-poets prove worthy of their task. Spain must be portrayed as an ancient dragon whose "coils of blood and darkness" have been curled "all too long . . . about the new-born world."[19] As the scourge of Man, the poets bid their nation strike. Even the dead are at last to be avenged: it is for the Inquisition's martyrs, for Montezuma, the murdered Inca, the harmless Carib tribes, that Spain, "Ishmael of nations, false and foul from foot to crown," must die.[20] All lands will rejoice to see her overtaken by Justice. Thus altruistic America strikes "for a Continent;—nay, for the World!"[21]

But even this is not enough. America is also to be the scourge of God. It is not the State Department but the Lord's Inquisition that condemns Spain. As the apostles once paraphrased God's messages to their people, so does Madison Cawein report a new writing in the sky. With the scales that "once weighed Babylon," God now judges Spain:

> One scale holds thy pride and power and empire, begotten of sin,
> Heavy with woe and torture, the crimes of a thousand years . . .

In the other, for justice and mercy, a blade with never
a stain,
Is laid the Sword of Liberty, and the balance dips,
O Spain![22]

How can America hold back when the voice of Michael is heard above the Cuban's cry? Out, then, come the avenging ships-of-war. Not arrogantly, but obediently, America hales Spain up to God's judgment place and smashes her "by God's decree."[23]

In that time of lyrical exuberance, however, a curious shift in rhetoric occurs. As "their country's God" becomes "God's Nation,"[24] the flag of God's nation begins to exert a militant religious power similar to that of the cross during earlier crusades. "Old Glory" flies high, pure, and sanctified by heroes' blood. There is "A hush among the kingdoms" when, like a rocket, she rifts the night and blossoms into stars.[25] From hundreds of 1898 poems the flag leaps out at the reader, a flag that has never lowered to any foe.

Such a banner itself becomes a cause. Men are summoned to defend its glory. The war, for them, is a chivalric test. To fail, Ina Coolbrith warns them, would be to disprove "their fathers' worth" and challenge their own love for America.[26] But they cannot and do not fail. The Rough Riders die happy because the flag flies before them; and at home a poetess exults: "Ah, what glorious lives we fling/To the flag!"[27] Cuba means nothing; what matters is that their invincible flag rides more gloriously than ever, and they have proven themselves proper heirs of Old Glory.

We are told that the "ringing ballads" in praise of his vainglorious knights please Roosevelt, a sometime connoisseur of poetry and an advocate of heroics for their own sake. Like their robust admirer, these verses do not quite compensate in energy, directness, and narrative excitement for what they lack in sensitivity, vision, and depth. To the imagination of the public, however, the Rough Riders "became synonymous with Romance."[28] It might be argued that the balladeer, expressing his country's pride in grand deeds, performs one of the prophet's ancient functions, as Deborah did after Sisera's fall. One need merely compare Deborah's song of deliverance with the best American song of conquest to see what is missing in 1898: a noble cause nobly uttered. These ballads ring, but—lacking a cause—they ring false, or thin. What remains is heroism for its own sake, and the great names of other wars are invoked for their courage alone; the cause for which Decatur, Nelson and Farragut fought is extraneous—they are asked to "move over" on their pedestals, because Dewey's "doughty deed" takes precedence.[29] Obviously, in the half century since the Mexican War the qualifications of the "true-blue" hero have undergone no change. He remains the one who laughs at odds, makes his cruise "When death lurked everywhere . . ."[30] Taking his cue from the famed Crimean regiment, the American soldier likes "only . . . to do as he was bid," and the American laureates take their cue from Tennyson:

> Who is there willing to offer his life? . . .
> Cannon for drum and torpedo for fife?
>   Eight men! . . .
> Was there a man who in fear held his breath?[31]

Here are fighters who never submit, but fix their flags amid the cartridges of the enemy.

This sounds much like the Mexican War. There are,

however, some marked differences between the pseudo-prophetic songs of 1846 and 1898. Foremost among them is the development of a new mystique. Repeatedly in these poems the brotherhood of the heroes is stressed. Clearly the war is welcomed as a long-sought occasion to re-unite North and South, so that a monolithic voice can address the new century. Southern poets are particularly responsive, as was Mrs. Webb at Custer's fall. They know neither "North nor South . . . Each loves her own but loves the Union best."[32] On the old Chickamauga battleground now trains a single army of patriots—a fusion of blue and gray, facing a common foe. It does not matter that their fathers were adversaries; those years are "blotted from their memory." The sons stand together now:

And the fierce old fight
Slips out of sight
  In the clasp of a brother's hand.

For the old blood left a stain
  That the new has washed away . . .[33]

News that the old Confederate soldier, "Fighting Joe" Wheeler, has enlisted creates an electrifying effect. The nation imagines him "with flashing eyes and gleaming sword, and hair and beard of snow," as he leads his brigade at Santiago.[34] Perhaps it was not the cause of Cuban freedom, but rather the call of gunfire that roused his cavalier spirit. Perhaps it is incongruous that, in liberating an enslaved people, "the North and South, with a Southron chief," should keep time "to the tune of 'Dixie.' "[35]—No matter! By swearing allegiance, Wheeler has done the work of sixty years, swearing away "mistrust and hate and tears!" When a warship is christened "Dixie," a Southern poet dreams of cheering on deck. This christening, he explains happily, "means we're all united . . . An' 'Way Down South in Dixie' is national today!"[36] One Atlanta poet, however, forgets himself in the general festivities, and viciously satirizes the Negro troops:

> Dere ain't no yella fever—no,
> Nor small-pox comin' nigh
> Me, long as I gits reg'lar grub
> An' sweats fomaldeehigh! . . .
> An' ef de wah las' long enuff
> An' camp crap I kin hit,
> Dere ain't no swearin' but I'll be
> A Majah Jin'ral yit![37]

When Edward E. Hale praises the armed forces of 1898 as "the liberators of to-day," does he have in mind the troops and the victory-crowds who appreciate such verse?[38] It is, perhaps, a minor consideration—if limited to Atlanta. On the other hand, if "Way Down South in Dixie" has truly become "national," then the Blue-Gray nuptials may take on new meaning, the Jefferson-Lincoln principles may have been betrayed, and the ruffianism which was officially tolerated in 1856 may be in 1898 the official policy of the American government.

A second element strong in the war with Spain but absent in 1846 is the idea of an Anglo-American alliance. To court Britain would then have seemed inconceivable. But the need of the hour is greater than concern for the past. Thus John Hay, the poet-statesman, works for an alliance "rooted in the ideals of a common race" as the only bulwark against Pan-Germanism. Had his feverish efforts failed, an admirer writes, "we should have been forced to call off the war with Spain, a humiliation for which modern history has no parallel."(!!) This alliance needs an aura similar to that of the Blue and the Gray; "material interest . . . mere trade . . ." will not suffice![39] At once a host of rhymesters leap forward to create the new mystique. The British, they argue nimbly, have fought us as kin, but the Spaniards are a lowborn race of strangers. Thomas N. Page reminds his readers that Raleigh once drove "the Spanish wolves with noble rage" and Drake was "A scourge with flaming breath" wherever Spain sent its ships.[40] Now, together with America, the motherland can again lead the way, for God's glory and man's. Mary Baker Eddy ecstatically suggests that "Brave Britain, blest America" consummate "a bridal betokened from above."[41]

Few singers of Anglo-Saxonism, however, seem suitable for the alliance of "high minded men" sought by Hay. More often the exalted pose deteriorates as the enemy troops are termed "those bloody Dagoes . . . the Spanish curs . . . dem yaller Spaniards . . ."[42] Their ships invariably "skulk" or "lurch." They fire once and run for cover. Nor is this appeal to man's basest qualities limited to hot-blooded newspaper rhymesters. Edward E. Hale, one of America's most distinguished humanitarians, an outstanding peace advocate and future Senate chaplain, writes at this moment:

> Charles Francis Adams . . . said, 'Do not expect anything of Spain, Mr. Hale. *The truth is not in them.*' In this . . . is the secret of all the difficulties between England and Spain in Drake's time, between this country and Spain in Jefferson's day, and in each of the crises . . . since. Spain and her statesmen really think that a lie well stuck to is as good as the truth. Our representatives do not think so.[43]

It is in this context that Richard Le Gallienne chants wildly: "Strike for the Anglo-Saxon . . . sweep the Beast away," and ends with a loud blood-cry: "Let no feeble pity your sacred arms restrain . . ."[44] Here is the very tone of the 1844 mob, uniformed at last, the 1856 ruffian reincarnated in those well-named Rough Riders storming San Juan Hill.

The cruelty, the joy in killing, which only a few ingenuous versifiers admitted during the Mexican War, has in 1898 become the trait to be cultivated and admired. Unlike the knights of old, these rough-mannered boys are all muscle. Their nation, too, is in a rough mood, much as in the days of bloody Kansas:

> . . . we laid our loyal clutches on the gentleman from Spain,
> An' we run him to a jack-oak in the rear o' Murphy's store,
> An' the Spanish-Yankee question interested him no more.[45]

False prophets if ever poets were, these minstrels revive the nation's lust for violence. Proudly they describe the men who fight with joy and who thirst for the death of Spaniards. Nothing will do but to "scatter 'em, an' spatter 'em permisc'ous roun' de place," after which the troops will yell victory-shouts.[46] For they are in Cuba—all this liberation talk aside—to kill or be killed. Roosevelt's joy, sing the balladeers, exceeds that of his men, for hunting is his sport. Any game he follows is doomed; thus he is sure to "put the Spaniard in a bag." We see him, rifle cocked, assassinating enemy lads "all around the place."[47]

On its more dignified level, this body of militant verse recalls the yearning of certain Southern poets for the Mexican War to begin.[48] "The jarring roll of hostile arms" is described as America's paean and psalm by poets who advertise the delights of war and sneer at the time of peace, when cowards "winnow" their "meagre souls." Only when we trust to swordplay, Arthur Guiterman suggests, do heroes emerge.

Just as these laureates of 1898 unwittingly present blood-lust without the usual mask of heroic glory, so do a few let down their guard long enough to show precisely how altruistic, under the veneer of liberation and justice, their nation really is. No sooner has The Scourge of Man and God swept Spain from its islands than one poet greedily dreams of "Santiago and Manila like new stars" on the American banner.[49] Another sees the war as simply a conflict of future versus past. To the Philippines, which have served as "a dump-ground for the . . . old miasmal rubbish heaps of Spain," America brings rebirth *along with* "the new flag."[50] But it is Maurice Thompson who records with the most open pleasure the imperial significance of this upheaval:

> Now the old may dote on the past, and the weak may pule and cry,
> And shrink from the change that comes;
> But the young and the strong, with their hearts beating high,
> Have the pulse of the trumpets and drums.
> Their guns have spoken the word, and their trumpets have borne it far
> In triumph from shore to shore;
> Our flag on the isles where our heroes are
> Shall be held there for evermore.[51]

Thus, even more obviously than in the Mexican War

verse, the slogans of 1898 are assorted, contradictory, and vague. These heroes battle "for the Right," wrestle "with wrong." The reader cannot determine whether it is the voice of patriotism they heed, or the hope of humanity they lift; whether their motive is to end "Spain's misrule," or gather fame and glory "in great gobs!"[52] If it is fame and glory they crave, the war poets certainly bequeathe both in great gobs indeed; nor do they neglect humanity's hope—whatever *that* is!

When Hezekiah Butterworth writes, "False is the war no poet sings,"[53] he implies, first, that what the Russians call "the tradition of silence" is in fact a kind of prophecy, and, second, that morality is an essential factor in true song. What Butterworth means specifically, however, is that the 1898 war, waged under false pretenses, has won no support among poets. This is disproved by our quotations from such respected writers as Rupert Hughes, Richard Le Gallienne, Madison Cawein, Thomas N. Page, Arthur Guiterman, Robert U. Johnson, Ina Coolbrith, John T. Trowbridge, Joaquin Miller, Maurice Thompson, and many others. Do their poems, along with thousands more, make the 1898 war a true one? Or are they fooled by pretenses, as the keen-eyed seer is not? Do they demand enthusiasm of themselves as an act of loyalty? Or do they deliberately betray their solemn prophetic mission in order to please the popular mood? Of one thing we can be sure: the drive to annex Spain's colonies will serve as a "rude awakening," affecting some of our poets rather dramatically.

iii

Several outstandingly popular poets of 1898, though

varying in artistic aims and powers, are united in seeing themselves as poets of the people. These work diligently to speak *for,* rather than *to* or *against,* the millions. Unlike others, as we shall find, these writers turn out to be truly official—for they go right on celebrating the war no matter what happens to their government's moral position. Of the lot, Richard Hovey wears the prophetic mask most impressively.[54] As God's representative to errant man, he blames America for the *Maine's* destruction:

> Because ye have fawned and bowed down
> Lest the spoiler frown,
> And the wrongs that the spoiled have borne
> Ye have held in scorn,
>
> Therefore with rending and flame
> I have marred and smitten you . . .

In a word: Spain should long ago have been attacked. But what sounds like an Old Testament reproval, is actually sweet music to the ears of his government and countrymen. Unlike the true prophet, he places on God's lips the very word America most wishes to hear. Elsewhere Hovey demonstrates the magnitude of John Hay's diplomatic success in London, as the Anglo-American alliance bares its imperial teeth in his lines:

> The children of the sea queen's brood
> Will not give up the main;
> We hold the sea against the world
> As we held it against Spain . . .
>
> Take warning by Manila . . .
> For England and America
> Will keep and hold the sea!

More than once Hovey's adulation of Kipling is revealed as he catches the very essence of the Queen's balladeer:

> And who shall say nay to our navies—the ships of us, sons of the Sea?
> And who shall say nay to our Empires, to the Law that we set for the free?
> But the best is the bond that's between us, the bond of the brothers in blood . . .

Dying in 1900, Hovey leaves a confident augury of America's yet-to-be manifested destiny: "It shall be high . . . it shall be great." That he gives utterance to a vision there can be no doubt. The moral quality of that vision is another matter. One might say that he turns into enticing meter the blueprints of his nation's magnates and their dynamic State Department.

With Will Carleton and James W. Riley we are on equally familiar ground. Though their poems swarm with ethical arguments, they never examine their government's actions or their people's values. With far less finesse than Hovey, but with even greater zeal, Carleton registers the transformation of America from liberator to conqueror.[55] At first he transmits Columbia's warning to proud Spain that from the wreckage of the *Maine* liberty may soon "grasp another jewel" as our fleets save the crushed people of Cuba. But the tone soon changes; he supplies his huge audience with the martial clichés they want. Having "right . . . backed with might" and Anglo-Saxon courage, nothing can stop "the greatest land that ever the world has known!" His heroes are battling for "God and the right." But what is "right"? Not Cuba's freedom, but "their native land!" For this preposterous slogan the poet actually invents an invasion-threat by Spain's armed forces. After victory, however, he becomes precise and honest. Nothing less than dominion over the hemisphere is America's war-prize: "We ruled the main, and lashed foul Spain/From our Western world forever!" In an extraordinarily candid turnabout, six years after his pledge to free Cuba, he composes a sequel in which Columbia puts the island in its place, demanding gratitude, patience, loyalty to its rescuer, and annexation: "Climb to OUR constellation . . . And—nation within a nation—/Gleam bright for a thousand years!" In exchange for obedience Columbia offers what the Viking pirates once offered: protection. The alternative is ominous: ". . . we are dwelling side by side,/Ready for clasp or thrust." The liberator has turned marauder.

Riley, America's best-loved public poet, celebrates the Philippine conquest heartily, though the motives he advances are unclear.[56] The soldier's veins may be drained "at Freedom's holy shrine," or he may smite "For God and man and space to kneel and pray." The few Filipino references lack ethical concern. When the gun of a resisting native stops our soldier, the glory goes not to the foeman, who fought at home, but to the American, who "for love of home . . . proudly died." Why Americans are in those wild places, finding "A grave all nameless in a clime unknown," is not to be questioned. What matters is to fall into line with Old Glory waving us on "Where our glorified, sanctified betters have gone." Nor does Riley see any difference in the merits of wars. By 1898 the mystique of the banner is beyond logical or moral probing:

> There's a shout in the throat and a blur in the eye
> And an aching to live for you always—or die,
> If, dying, we still keep you waving on high.

Soldierly valor is Clinton Scollard's inspiration.[57] He sees the poet as balladeer "for the men of to-day," who have proved themselves the equals of history's heroes. These are the men who leap ahead while "the black mouths belch and thunder, and the shrapnel shrieks and flies." Oblivious of any ethical differences in America's wars, he links the 1898 heroes to "the blood of the boys of Anthony Wayne!"—undisturbed that Wayne's boys were rebels, while *his* heroes drive "The stinging rebels out of their hive." The logic is simple: because the Tagals oppose Old Glory they must perish. What they fight for is of no import; their angry guns must be silenced and they must learn to respect attacking Americans as "an avenging destiny." What there is to avenge is not specified; but by 1898 the word "destiny" surely needs no further explanation.

It might be charged of Scollard that he is "cashing in" on the war by producing marketable poems, abdicating what he knows to be the prophet's ethical role. Obviously he does well by the war, as his magazine work and collections of battle-ballads testify. Yet his praise of bravery seems genuine, and unpolluted by the usual assortment of contradictory "causes." His theme is *manhood* (Anglo-Saxon) proving itself through terrible trials. This he makes clear in assessing the Civil War too. It does not matter now whether a soldier wore the blue or gray. Let all be laurelled, since "each fought for what he thought was true." As for the current war:

> . . . laurel every dauntless one
> Who marched on death with level eyes
> Beneath the scorching Cuban sun,—
> The Philippines' unpitying skies!

Were Scollard equipped with a prophet's eyes or heart, his

manly fighters might include at least *one* Spaniard or Tagal, and his facile verses might merit attention for historic truth and tragic depth.

The most respected poet of this group, and the one least likely to be motivated by popular passions or financial need, is George E. Woodberry. Yet his war verse carries no distinguishing mark, either in rhetoric, prosody, or thought.[58] His initial slogans too are vengeance for the *Maine* and liberation for Cuba. Since God has called America "to do justice," her troops follow in the path of duty. Duty to Freedom? God? No—their concern is to "serve the Country wherever fly her Stars," no matter what the cause. After the war his poems hint at a change. Exeter's graduates shall not be the servants "of brutal wars/ That only leave a nation's scars," but healers who prefer persuasion to force. May our youth, he prays, "be simple, kind, and brave,/And bring the reign of peace!" Yet the same poems call for another good fight if "our foes increase." With martial intent he echoes the melody of "Crossing the Bar":

> And may some cause to die for lead them forth
>   When they go out to war!
> And may they nobly do and greatly dare,
>   And true be every son,
> While o'er her children breathes the Nation's prayer,
>   "Thy Will be done."

That "Will" is easy to predict, since America is the chosen land whose spires and hills are touched by "God's hand." Apparently without wishing it, America has been found by its destiny. Much in the brash manner of pre-

Isaiah victory hymns, Woodberry sings with equanimity and resonance:

> God is shaping the great future of the Islands of the Sea . . .
> He has given a haughty nation to the cannon and the sword . . .
> Rejoice, O mighty Mother, that God hath chosen Thee
> To be the western warder of the Islands of the Sea;
> He lifteth up, He casteth down . . .

Who would dare challenge a blueprint so divinely covenanted?

iv

As liberation ends, however, and annexation begins, the challenges do come. Even more poets shift their position in 1898 than did during the Mexican War. It is to a few of them we turn, for they bear graphic witness to the ethical sensitivity among poets. Thomas B. Aldrich, for instance, "repented of voting for McKinley when he saw the enslavement of the Philippines," and wrote: "I am not proud of my country."[59] Before seeing action, Sandburg and his brother:

> . . . go downstairs with a big blur of guns, men, and hills in their heads. They . . . tell the family war is a wonder and soldiers are a wonder.

> One breaks out with a cry at supper: I wish we had a war now and I could be a soldier.

War service convinces Sandburg that he has been tricked into "a dirty and lousy affair"; his letters to the Galesburg press are bitter.[60]

Soon enough Edith Thomas repents of her role as "A pure-browed maiden urging men to war!"[61] Her bellicose early stanzas[62] reverberated with vengeance-cries for the *Maine*. In those days she presumed to say, on behalf of the dead, that they had no regrets and were still dreaming of Cuba's "One Star . . . Saluting with joy the Many-in-One." She prophesied that the Anglo-Saxon Union of eagle and lion would overcome Evil, conquer the World and cede it to Peace!—Then comes the change.[63] In a moving personal plea against war she asks that her sisters, who "know not the words they utter," be forgiven for sending men to die. Could they see the horrors of battle, "their lips would be holden of speech." In another poem a woman finds a wounded foeman on the battlefield; while tending him, she is touched by Love: "Thou art my country's foe —not mine!" At the moment of America's victory, Miss Thomas stresses the superiority of spiritual triumph:

> What if the rubric of the sword have sealed
> A more imperial harvest to yon plain?
> Each soul hath, also, some such battle-field—
> It hath the vintage, too, of Thrasymene!

The shift in George Sterling's position is less dramatic, though real enough.[64] First he claims for America the destined role of liberator in Caribbean waters, where "Awful and dumb, the cannon lift." America, "The Mother," answering the God of Liberty, girds herself gladly for the carnage, and Cuba will soon be free. Soon, however, Sterling pooh-poohs the significance of the war; the thunders of battle are unheard by dead soldiers, though above them "cumbrous nations prove their might." The motherland for which they died is revealed to be "in vassalage to monstrous lords." She has decayed from her original merit; lusting for power, she has forgotten how other empire-minded peoples, "faithless to their trust," crumbled to dust at the avenging hour of Time. In a sonnet reminiscent of "Ozymandias," he warns empire-dreamers that their expectation of immortal fame is folly, that empires vanish "like the music of forgotten dreams!" And in a second, especially poignant sonnet, turning outward from himself to verbalize the aspirations and disappointments of mankind, he grieves that the new century comes —not peacefully, as the people hoped, but "with a sword in his uplifted hands,/Crying the red evangel of old War."

Even in Wallace Rice's most affirmative ballads of heroism and victory we can see the seeds of disaffection. Increasingly during the Cuban phase he praises the enemy's heroism and regrets the ruin of Spain. With many other poets who celebrated Cuba's "liberation" sincerely, he is significantly silent on American action in the Philippines. Instead[65] he writes about a life-saving fireman, and ranks him higher, for "his duty simply done," than a "warrior red with the blood he has shed." Outraged by the prevalent war-spirit, Rice sees April's promise of joy shattered by the "crash of drums," love and beauty succumbing to hate. His last poem on the war, "A Vision of Peace," while acknowledging the heroism of soldiers, berates the lie, the bribe, and the theft poisoning American life. Sick of the Philippine conquest, Rice is for once seized by the ancient Biblical ardor. This is an impulse he has not learned to handle as artistically as he handles narrative, but his ethical strength is impressive:

> Never success worth the having gained through another
> soul's fear.
> Smiles mark the highway to triumph when a man's title
> is clear . . .

—Greed stands the root of all ill.
No end can justify evil: Piety, Culture, and State
Stand as accursed forever, else on Jehovah must wait:
Think you for "civilization" God will His Justice abate?

Concluding audaciously that Freedom is dearer to him than Nation, and Truth "dearest of all," he prays that Verity, Liberty, and Country will some day be united. The voice is cool, but the dismay profound. By holding before his people a vision of the ideal nation, he undermines their pride in the America of 1898, and goads them to bring the ideal closer.

The most stunning transformation, however, occurs in Richard Le Gallienne.[66] It is impossible to detect in his post-Cuba writings the same mind that a few months earlier produced two of the most bloodthirsty Anglo-Saxon battlecries. He now denounces the glamor of parades which make men forget their abhorrence of war. No infamy of disguise can match the "embannered lies," the tunes of glory masking death. In "The Cry of the Little Peoples," those now threatened by power recall their own "hollow pursuit of fame." Today they seek neither "coaling stations, nor ports," but leave the "shopman conquests" to the "big child-nations." They wish only "to sow and sing and reap" in their little corner of the earth, but the iron world goes crashing on, controlled by "the cruel sons of Cain," and the weak are sure to be broken by the strong. The mood of despair that these stanzas provoke may not be in accordance with the evangelistic tradition of guidance and inspiration, but it does powerfully refute the self-satisfaction with which America and Britain contemplate their imperial future. At the same time it gives voice to the yearnings of the "Little Peoples."

Le Gallienne's book on Kipling, written in the spring of 1899, reveals a swiftly maturing hatred of imperialism and its pseudo-prophets.[67] "Recessional" and "The White Man's Burden" are "not poetry at all," he charges, but "political catch-words imbedded in rather spirited hymns." Expansionism with "the inflammatory jingle" is his characterization of Kipling's "later Methodistical-Jingoistic manner." British-born, addressing a British audience, Le Gallienne boldly condemns Britain's greed masked by Christian pretense. Of his new homeland, America, though she *may* have some right "to talk of taking up the white man's burden," he wryly augurs that she will "hanker after more such burdens" when she sees "how small is the cost . . . compared with the subsequent profit . . ."

These poets and others reflect an upheaval in the conscience of intellectual America following the "liberation" of Cuba, and help to point up the difference between those who championed the Cuban cause honestly, and those whose aim was imperial. Aside from the numerous minor poets who shift to open hostility, there are those who have sung the loudest early in the war but turn silent when their government begins killing Filipinos. In other cases the shift, while noteworthy, is somewhat hazy in outline. Especially hazy is the position of Joaquin Miller, who has undeservedly been listed[68] among the four "responsible for the most notable anti-imperialist poetry produced" at that time. True, his anti-British *Chants for the Boers* might also apply to "the imperialists of Washington," but *he* does not so apply them, and Miller is seldom coy. A true prophet would excoriate his own nation *first*. On the contrary, he follows his war chant—"Cuba Libre!"—with a flag-waving, destiny-claiming, sire-invoking piece called "The Fourth in Hawaiian Waters." All of his possibly negative comments on the war are presented in a metaphoric manner alien to him and smacking of an unwillingness to tread on the toes of his marching countrymen.[69] The closest he comes to prophetic response is a comparison of scenes before and after combat. Setting forth, man is godlike, dying "for the right," and God is "manlike . . . to revenge the wrong!" But leaving the field, alas, "is another thing!" This is a well-wrought but hackneyed lyric. It could scarcely have disturbed Ambassador Hay, whose only 1898 poem shows a similar midnight tendency to sigh against War while by day he takes pride in the "splendid little war."[70]

V

Butterworth's claim is obviously unfounded: some poets of stature *do* celebrate the war he calls "false," even after the motives have become clear. To assert, on the other hand, that "Norton . . . almost alone among our . . . men of letters . . . took fearless issue with the national administration at the time of the war with Spain," is preposterous.[71] It is closer to the facts to suggest, as Gibson does, that "With . . . few exceptions American poets . . . sided with the anti-imperialists."[72] By 1899 this was certainly the case. For Harrington in 1937 to dismiss their verse as unimpressive requires a stronger argument than that "only 'An Ode in Time of Hesitation' has stood the test of time." Other factors besides "real merit" are involved in a forty-year test, especially at a time of complete revolution in aesthetic taste, when most of the pertinent poems are nowhere mentioned and difficult to find. The present investigation, while merely a beginning, challenges

Harrington's verdict that no "sustained or finished efforts" came from the anti-expansionist movement.[73]

As in the Mexican War, every enticement and justification offered by the laureates is shattered by their prophetically-motivated adversaries, who insist on exposing the realities beneath the pretexts. Thus we find poets in whose agonized landscapes the glory of battle is exploded. Some of their verses are personal in address yet belligerently political in tone. More muted and poignant is a moving dialogue of two soldiers who had killed each other, and must now:

> . . . pray at the Lord Christ's knee
> That never on earth again
> The breath of the hot brute guns shall cloud
> The sight in the eyes of men![74]

The horror of battle is implied through an ironically presented victory scene: banners flaunt triumph, troops toss their caps, the General proudly gallops down the line and shouts thanks. Nearby the dead, neither blind nor deaf, know "how brief a thing this triumph of a day." The real victory is theirs, and they laugh to one another: "We are at rest, where foemen cannot reach,/And better this than fighting in the sun."[75] A soldier, challenging the glamorous myth of war, prays for death "in the white coil" of his beloved's arms, rather than:

> . . . on the field of conquest red
> Where the crimsoned victors lay,—
> Not there with my laurels round my head,
> Not there in my glory find me dead . . .[76]

With equal effectiveness, praise and tears for the loser

challenge the Anglo-Saxon mystique so tenderly nurtured by the minstrels of war, and embarrass the more blatant rhymesters of race-hate. Poets pay generous tribute to the gallant enemy for sailing out to greet a fate which he already knew. They see the foe as proudly bold, "Which was ever the Spaniard's way," and cheer "the dauntless boat that charged our fleet/And sank in the iron hail."[77] With a vivid sense of the tragic, Wallace Rice[78] depicts the annihilation of a great fleet:

> There in the shallows 'mid the white surges
> Her guns, deserted, moan out their dirges;
> Swelling and knelling . . .
>
> Spain weeps her wounded, wails a lost navy;
> Fails them, bewails them,
> Says them an *Ave*.

Imagining the domestic impact of a defeat such as America has not yet endured, Rice sings with a large-hearted compassion and respect, for which his gloating countrymen could have had little patience:

> In old Madrid sad eyes are hid for an empire sore bestead . . .
> As the great bells toll each gallant soul Castile shall see no more.

A genuinely prophetic assault upon the advocates of manifest destiny had been mounted in 1846. Now the young son of Ambrose Bierce, in a lament for Spain, takes up the ancient admonitory mission and smites the imperial lust enflaming his land:

> The vict'ries of man are but fleeting,
> His empires crumble and fall;

Eternity laughs at the conqueror
And levels the dust over all.[79]

The grim fate of empire unfolds far more searingly in several of Lloyd Mifflin's sonnets.[80] The picture he presents of a conqueror does not flatter America:

Behind him, burning cities, and the roar
Of cannon in the night. The road he fled
Lined on each side with stiffening corpses dread.
His ruthless steps reek with the sickening gore . . .

Eventually, the poet warns, the gate of hell closes upon all who conquer. In another sonnet he tells his exuberant countrymen that although Man is now an "Imperious master with high front unbowed," famine shall one day crumble his "trillions of increase." Arthur Upson's vision of New York Harbor in 2900 is equally grim. Addressing those, like Hovey, who foresee only greatness for the imperial Republic, this poet forces upon them his nightmare: serfs, under a tyrant's command, are seen drawing from "a swampy bed of ancient mould/A shattered torch held in a mighty hand."[81]

Among the purest lyrical voices of his time, Trumbull Stickney avoids direct topical references, yet his poems are also saturated with images of doomed empire.[82] In "Oneiropolos" he tells of:

. . . a thirsty multitude in riot,
With women, gold, flocks, armour, camels, coins;
Maddened with hunger for another world . . .
They sacked the land, then weary sat them down . . .

After a hundred years visitors gape at the scourged and

dying city in which nothing remains of the beauty, prosperity, and power, but "void shadow, blown by wind . . ." Elsewhere Stickney evokes a ruined greatness, mourned by one illuminated mind in a dark world. "Across the country I remember," reports the poet in an Eliot-like dirge, "It's lonely . . . It's dark . . . It rains." Human life, he reminds his materialistic neighbors in an imaginative sonnet on their predatory hero, Columbus, has other use than aggrandizement.

Once again we face the uncertain task of deciphering the metaphors used by poets who are constitutionally loath to handle public themes. Stickney cannot be proved to have the current war in mind. But he does, precisely at this time, write precisely such poems, forming a consistent pattern that challenges the dominant note of conquest. There is, he declares in a superb sonnet, a more meaningful war, a more genuine triumph than storming a hill:

> Not all is night in failure, and the shield
> Sometimes well grasped, tho' shattered in the strife.
> And here while all the lowering heaven is ringed
> With our loud death-shouts echoed, on the field
> Stands forth our Nike, proud, tho' broken-winged.

Nor is his the only voice that indirectly shrivels the paeans of military victory by comparing it with spiritual combat. Right, sings Theodore Dreiser, is a unique warrior-queen who turns the lowly into giants when they take up her cause. Only on *her* behalf should one fight:

> Mercy speaks in her command . . .
> She is tender, without error,
> And her dead wake to her hand . . .[83]

At times the horror of war, the emptiness of victory, seep through the defenses of a personal poet and enter the marrow of his verse. Perhaps it is unrelated to the war then going on, that C. H. Towne hears "the armies of the sky . . . coming down amid the gale"; that at dawn, after the cannonade of thunder, he sees Autumn among her "dead crimson leaves," like a war-robbed mother grieving "for all that she has lost."[84] Perhaps another poet is posing when he declares that he would rather be relaxing under a tree:

> With a song or a handful of daisies,
> Than the darling of victory
> 'Mid the bray of the rabble's praises.[85]

But such comment, belittling military triumph, defies the national jubilation with which it coincides. One poet goes so far as to hold even a scrub-woman's courage in higher esteem than battle-valor, since cheers and brassbands can help a soldier "forget the bite of bullets . . . ."[86] Ella W. Wilcox agrees. She allows that the Navy has crushed Spain brilliantly; but more deserving of glory are "the heroes of peace and the martyrs of wrong" who wage war in mine and shop and die silently at their posts. Playing with the words *fame, heroes,* and *glory* as if mimicking the laureates of war, she dares to call the battle a petty merry-go-round compared with the life that has no future "but ill-paid labor and beds of pain."[87]

The joy in killing, so openly asserted by the balladeers of San Juan Hill, is a favorite target of prophecy in its ancient, Juvenalian form. None of these satirical poets manages to deliver his thrusts with the graceful ferocity of a Pope or a Byron; none even approaches the effectiveness or scope of Lowell's *Biglow Papers;* but their intentions are genuine: to correct iniquity by exposing it to ridicule. Thus Miss Wilcox,[88] in an outwardly playful nursery rhyme, shows a little boy—with a Puritan cap—bloodthirstily avenging, "every hour, the martyrs of the Maine." Greedily he plants his flag on the shore of every island, joyfully hastens to shed Spanish blood, and overwhelms the Philippines so often, that "There's very little left of them . . . at this hour." By locating America's vaunted victories in a child's room, the poet effectively dwarfs them, at the same time rebuking the national mood that turns even children toward plunder and murder. With less subtlety Henry B. Fuller shows the new type of knight, represented by Roosevelt, to be far removed from those golden names of the past which the war-choristers invoke:

> I'm a cut and thrusting bronco-busting
> Megaphone of Mars,
> And it's fire I breathe and I cut my teeth
> On nails and wrought-iron bars.[89]

Other poets, however, spoil their satiric tone by allowing the intensity of their fury to spill over.[90] Thus one sneers while the Tagals are being slaughtered: "God is with us, and our guns./Pile up his bleeding flesh in tons!" Another imagines the soul of a slain native appealing to the white men's God for justice: "Thy love their cannon roar . . . And for light to read Christ's word aright, our pagan roof-trees flame."

It is the minstrel-song of America as the bearer of civilization and religion, that especially warps under the furious laughter of some of these poets. The hymns of Kipling and his American imitators are repeatedly paraphrased: "Am I my brother's keeper—/Or keeper of his land?"[91] With a clever triple-pun on the notorious word "burden," one poet explains that the white man's Burden is guilt for patriots slain, and that the Burden of his false song dies on his lips as ships bring home his Burden—loot! Another warns that the stars and stripes are winning hatred, since "stripes alone" are reserved for the "poor yellow-skins."[92] Delightfully reversing the position of conqueror and native, William DeForest debunks the civilizing crusade of those whose real concern is markets.[93] What makes "Atlantis the Holy" a particularly vulnerable land is the smug and false religiosity of "lamblike and lowly" burghers who fast while they sleep, gorge while awake, and walk "in the narrow way slowly,/Much cumbered with Beelzebub's wares." The skill of DeForest's versification and the sardonic drive of his imagination are admirable, but he finally becomes editorially grim:

> The Cannibals came out the winners . . .
> The hungriest, greediest pack
> Of robbers and pickers and skinners
> That ever sent region to rack.
> Henceforth they were chiefs of the nation
> And lived by relief legislation . . .
> Their appetites daily increased;
> A lunch was a patent, at least,
> While railroads and steam-navigation
> Scarce furnished the joints for a feast.

More ferocious but less deft is the verse-satire of Fuller, like DeForest a distinguished novelist. He depicts Benevolent Assimilation and Holy Christian Civilization as overworked horses drawing through the Philippines "a load of dripping corses" on behalf of Imperial America. Rather zestfully he piles horror on horror, till the reader is too benumbed to respond:

Impaled on rows of sharpened sticks,
(One of the old Imperial tricks),
The Filipino babes and wives
Yield up in agony their lives,
Smeared and alight with burning tar . . .[94]

More controlled, and more telling, is the satire of Edmund Vance Cooke. He introduces a predatory ape which claims title to a tree:

All monkeys climbing on this tree
Must bring their gathered nuts to me,
Cracking the same on equal shares:
The meats are mine, the shells are theirs.

Like the Filipinos, the monkeys rebel—but more successfully: apes, the poet points out, must still climb for their food, and the ill-advised monkeys "Still eat their nuts, uncivilized."[95]

Satire, which serves these poets so well in exposing the slogans of Christianity and Civilization, fails them on the issue of Liberty. What rouses them to a particularly high pitch of fury is their sense that America's old ideals have been egregiously betrayed, and that the rebels being shot down are the true inheritors of 1775. But the indignation of these minor poets is too great on this point to accept the discipline of satiric art. Cooke, for instance, descends to sarcasm when he argues that the Filipino is "a rascal and a thief" for stealing America's early beliefs: having filched Patrick Henry's "Liberty or Death!" he should be granted the second choice—Death![96] Fuller, on the other hand, comes much closer to inspired song when for once he gives up satire, elegizing a Filipino warrior who proudly bared his breast "To the ribald Yankee rifles' aim." Freedom disowns its old favorite, America, and guards the Tagalog's corpse; the spiritual victory is his:

> We win but the husk, and slam the door
> In the face of God. Thou, thou art free,
> And we thy enslavers, the slaves to a mortal dross.[97]

This is Fuller at his atypical best; but Mifflin's expression of dismay is much finer. He recalls the promise of his country's first years: "That earliest quest of immaterial things,—/High principle, religion, honor, truth." In its place he finds a cruel and accursed lust for wealth. Decrying America's vaunted Progress, which cloaks banal greed, he demands a better time: "What shall relume our spiritual night?"[98] There is no such loftiness in the attacks directed at a President who symbolizes America's betrayal of its heritage.[99] We are shown McKinley's blood-stained hands tainting his bread; we hear the "sad ghosts of . . . victims" who keep vigil by his bed. While the martial singers call America the instrument of God's justice, Fuller turns the tables on them—angrily prophesying that God will punish "the base Predestinators," especially the President, "That slavering Anti-Christ obscene,/The gray Imperial Libertine . . ."

Is such indignation prophetic? Surely it shows courage and strong ethical concern. But it bears no other resemblance to the Bible prophets, who—even at their angriest—abide by aesthetic rules. Those ancient challengers of iniquity are never overwhelmed by their fury; their cumulative effect is large and positive; the alternative of a better way is implicit even in their harshest outcries, and those attacks are never petty. Too often a Fuller becomes personally vindictive; instead of singing, he shrieks; with apparent relish he weaves phrases of abusive ugliness, thus casting doubt on the quality of his impulse. For the truly prophetic voices we shall have to turn elsewhere.

vi

Six poets, while not of major rank, deserve individual study here because their response to the war is distinctive, considerable, and unswervingly critical. They divide into two contrasting groups. While Richard Burton, Edwin Markham, and Louise I. Guiney are devoted wholeheartedly to the creation and propagation of poetry, William L. Garrison, Jr. and Ernest H. Crosby produce verse as a facet of their crusading activities, and Bertrand Shadwell has only one book—a political thunderbolt—to his credit. The poems of Burton, Markham, and Miss Guiney are subtle, lyrical, soft-spoken, metaphoric; those of Garrison, Shadwell, and Crosby are direct, didactic, loud, and stark.

Burton's war-songs[100] encompass the civilian experience: leave-taking, battle "extras," meditation on the dead, homecoming, and decoration day. The undertone throughout is ironic. A peaceful day of crocuses is blasted by war news. Victory? defeat? the flowers remain calm. Pre-battle glamor is followed by the homecoming of wise, maimed veterans, just as the "cry of welcome" for those returning is opposed by the silence of mothers, wives, and children whose loved ones far off "lie all uncaressed." As he recalls the fate of empires, Burton approaches prophecy, despite the modesty of his canvas and the quietness of his melody. He shows how war intoxicates "the conquering strong"; soon their cities "lie deep in their slime." Although his location is the Orient, the parallel is clear. In the old days, he sarcastically begins, "when to battle was good and to kill was held no crime," the peaceful dwellers in Laish were annihilated by the manifestly destined Danites. With fine irony he pretends not to dispute a ravishment which, "since so it is written," must be proper; yet he admits "a feeling of pity and pain" for the vanquished, and in the imagery of Isaiah he expresses mankind's eternal longing for peace:

> Will some day that is hope of the dreamer, some place never chanted in song,
> Show peace in its borders unbroken, where men are both gentle and strong?
> Shall the lamb then be couched with the lion?

Markham's war poems are also somewhat oblique. His attitude must at times be ferreted out, but it finally is unmistakable:[101] the people are "flung as a meat to the cannons that hunger in battle." Liberation is the false excuse of armies that fling "their foolish glory on the air." The true liberator does not use "bugle-cry nor roll of doubling drums." As for the prizes and the conquests, only the flowers in the fields are "pillage worth a war." Discomfitingly Markham compels America to hear the imperial bugles breaking Babylon's nights and "crying through Nineveh." But that realm is dead; only the ghost of Semiramis sits "rocking on an ancient road of Hell." The dust of Tyre and Baalbec speaks forebodingly to the new empire raising its "pillars upon Self-Desire":

> There was no substance in their soaring hopes:
> The voice of Thebes is now a desert cry;
> A spider bars the road with filmy ropes,
> Where once the feet of Carthage thundered by.

A high-born poet, as Markham defines him, has only one military mission: to "Take down the horn wherein the thunders sleep" and blow battles into men—battles against "blind oppression . . . gray injustice." When his nation wages predatory war, the prophet must tell his boastful countrymen who "fling forth the triple-colored flag" that there are higher adventures than war, spiritual jousts without which the nation cannot remain whole. True to his definition, Markham demands a return to America's original vision:

> The fine audacities of honest deed;
> The homely old integrities of soul;
> The swift temerities that take the part
> Of outcast right . . .

Not all poets, however, are temperamentally suited to turn themselves into a bugle-cry. Louise I. Guiney's silence in 1898–99 recalls the frustration of Longfellow's prophetic impulse during the Mexican War. Like Longfellow, she comments indirectly in her verse, and her letters are rich in references. In three splendid poems[102] she pits spiritual against imperial combat. Only God's banner, "The stick and rag of Honour," is worth carrying into battle, nor are any other than spiritual wounds worth celebrating. A knight, who is yet to find a war worthy of his sword, observes the far-off cavalry-charge:

> I have seen higher, holier things than these,
> And therefore must to these refuse my heart . . .
> Though all your flags sweep stormily in air,
> And thousand hoofs are whirling fiery seed . . .

Like that knight, the poet forthrightly rejects the war, for she dwells "high above hate." Loudly at her sill play the "daggered thunders," yet to her they sound smaller "Than a young fay's footfall" and are "winnowed into silence" on the wind that bears off "wars like a dust." Elsewhere[103] she allegorically condemns the betrayal of America's past: a precious, protecting, century-old oak is cut down by evil men who reward such fatherhood by turning its "murmuring immortality" into "a cargo and a trade." This protest matches her letters of June and July, 1898:

> It's a weary business; and orations about "imperial America," and the new policy, which must keep the respected spirit of George Washington in a scowl, are not calculated to make it less so, to some of us . . . I hated the war, until we got into it; and I thought it avoidable then, and think it ominous now. It means a new and non-American general policy.

Like Thoreau, however, her most important response to what she deems a national disgrace is not in words, but action. "Outdoor Litany," her only poem in eleven months of meaningful silence, and her 1899—1900 letters, contradict the implication that she is to leave America in 1901 as an anglophile who lives "in a dream of the seventeenth century."[104] So painfully is she awake to her own time and nation that she must pray for fortitude to "endure the Pit . . ."[105] Soon after, while discussing "the whole Imperial-America business," which seems to her "the wickedest thing" she knows, Miss Guiney expresses a yearning "to see Lunnon, and never, never go away no more." The reason is only too clear: her "Americanism is in a bad way, since this abominable bettering of the Brown Man began."[106] Is her public indirectness and eventual self-exile a betrayal of the prophet's role her beloved Juvenal, Ovid, and Lovelace had so gallantly played

—or a fulfillment of that role? We know only that her vision is keen, her ethical revulsion complete, and that she expresses her disaffection in terms appropriate to her aesthetic and personal standards. From that point of view she addresses us with haunting eloquence.

We turn now to three openly political poets whose lines need no interpretive skill. Like his father's workmanlike verse, the urgent messages of William L. Garrison, Jr., have courage and dignity, but lack imagination and word-magic.[107] He sees "as in a fearful nightmare" the butcheries committed by a "nation lost in darkness, reason fled." Since poets more gifted than he are silent, through blindness or fear, Garrison begs America to hear "his warning cry for life." He condemns the "mellifluous siren song" of false prophecy that seeks to justify the slaughter of Filipinos, Lexington's true sons. America, he charges, is "falsely clad/In altruistic garb"; the church defends murder and pillage; under the deceitful banners of Duty and Destiny the ship of state rides "in pirate hand," bent on grasping whatever it covets, driven by a crusading ruffianism:

> Our savior is an admiral upon the quarter-deck . . .
> And Bibles take a place behind the bullets and the beers! . . .
> Then onward, Christian soldier! through fields of crimson gore . . .
> The profits on our ledgers outweigh the heathen loss;
> Set though the glorious stars and stripes above the ancient cross!

There is more significance in the work of Bertrand Shadwell—whoever he may be.[108] It is not that greatness can be claimed for a particular poem in *America,* but that the volume comes so promptly, contains so strong a denunciatory impulse, develops so many pertinent themes in so many competently handled forms, and sounds so much like early Edgar L. Masters, whose books were also published in Chicago displaying the same fury in the same verse-forms and under a number of pseudonyms.

The betrayal theme is introduced on the title page. Once a refuge of peace and justice, America has become a conquering power, "Crushing a weaker people to her will." Holding the mirror up to his neighbors' exultant faces, he assures them that when the "fierce ecstatic thrill" of war is over they will meditate on their "heroic homicide" until the face of Cain looks back at them. There is much pity in Shadwell's lines—for the victims of the *Maine* who shall never "feel the morn's sweet breath," the mothers who dream of "their slaughtered children," the conquerors who "took the sword, and perish with the sword," and the conquered whose name and empire were once great. Saluting Spain's flag and heroes, he laments the decay of her nobility and prophesies her phoenix-like resurgence. He celebrates Aguinaldo too, and damns that patriot's hunters: "What devil tempts thee to descend/To conquest, robbery and crime?" By giving thankful prayers to God, he jeers, America makes Him "the accomplice of the crime." Shadwell, on the contrary, dares to pray for defeat, if "our quarrel be unjust." He alone among American poets challenges the *Maine* slogan which the minstrels of war exploit for a "doctrine of unreasoning hate"; that explosion, the poet suggests, may have been engineered by Cuban insurgents. Attacking the Kipling rationale, he scoffs: "It's to civilize their race/That we butcher them by scores." Finally he charges that although soldiers are applauded as heroes, their true function is to "satisfy the trader's greed." The completeness and force of this volume reveal a spirit of tremendous ethical life, a prophetic fervor urgently seeking its form and its audience.

Ignoring Shadwell's massive assault, Harrington[109] calls Ernest H. Crosby "the leading anti-imperialist poet" in quantity, and declares that Crosby is forgotten "chiefly . . . because he thought less of his art than of his arguments." This is unprovable; but, even were it the case, oblivion is not therefore justified. Such an attitude toward their art is common among those whose sense of urgency is strong. Yet, as in the case of Emerson, their very roughness of form can add to the grand effect. True, Crosby "used writing not to win fame, but to further causes." Yet how many, among the *great* poets, did use writing "to win fame"? And how many of Crosby's most gifted contemporaries, who avoided writing "to further causes," *are* remembered today? Crosby's 1898 poems are less than memorable because they lack poetic imagination and inspired use of language. An angry heart and an independent mind are not enough. His predictable arguments, clothed in commonplace rhetoric, often seem to have no higher motive than rebuttal.[110] Thus the parading troops are splendid, but so are those they will gleefully slay, "Against whom they have no grievance." The victory is great, but another capital is "cast down with mourning and humiliation just in proportion as ours is raised up, and that is the very spice of our triumph." McKinley leads a victory-prayer "to the tribal god," but his Christian capital is "an outpost of hell . . ." America dreams "the old, old dream of empire," but men have always relied "In vain on such a course." Decked in murder-medals, the hero is "vain of his manliness in the field," but indulges in "effeminate quarreling over the honors." He obeys orders blindly, but hurries home "to advertise himself in the magazines at a hundred dollars a page."

There is, the poet reminds his bellicose brethren, a better war: "righteousness and integrity" are its battleships; brotherhood and forgiveness, self-respect and a quiet conscience, are its equipment. Only when he delivers his universal message on a personal, Whitmanesque note, does Crosby fuse enflamed rhetoric with imaginative vitality to produce emotionally convincing utterance:

> You little warriors who, while fighting each other, are yet at heart agreed, and see the same false life with the same distorted eyes,
> I have to make war upon all of you combined . . .
> I set my courage against your courage.
> It is fine not to flinch under fire.
> It is also fine to tell an unwelcome truth to a mob . . .

To this definition of the prophet's role Crosby and the others in this group are true. Whether metaphoric or direct, murmurous or thunderous, these six do unmask the "false life" which their neighbors prefer to see with "distorted eyes"; and by the personal courage with which they face the "mob," they illustrate what a true war and a true hero can be.

vii

We turn finally to examine the impact of the war upon seven figures of the first rank: William D. Howells, Ambrose Bierce, George Santayana, William V. Moody, Edwin A. Robinson, Stephen Crane, and Edgar L. Masters. To what extent does their response match the ethical involvement of their lesser colleagues? In what ways do they outstrip the others and rise to inspired speech?

Since the later poems of Howells remain uncollected, we do not know whether he wrote any verse on the war; but we do know that he was vice-president of the New York Anti-Imperialist League. It has been said that Howells produced no "articles" or "quotable phrases that could have helped the cause,"[111] but this is not the case. He was in fact neither "restrained by consideration for his wife, a lady who had persuaded herself to approve of imperialism," nor frightened—as Gibson[112] makes clear—by the "risk of aiding an unpopular cause." Publicly, privately, and by deeds, he attacks the war. An article in *Harper's,* urging sympathy for the Spanish prisoners, censures the American government and press for causing the war. Elsewhere he condemns Kipling's chauvinism and praises John Davidson's poetic outcry against "the inalienable criminality of aggressive war . . . the hardy insolence of money-might." A third essay denounces the peace treaty whereby "a barbarous aspiration for freedom in the Far East" has been crushed. He then mocks the inkwell barrage of "infuriate non-combatants" which "began long before the first shot was fired." In a satirical piece on Roosevelt, Howells expresses his sorrow at our having "gone back to the old musket-worship." And a year later he again vexes the American conscience by contrasting the expansionist present with the idealistic past:

> It is . . . very sad, to reflect that . . . once in our national consciousness . . . we stood for something different from anything a people had stood for before. Call it universal liberty or instinctive justice, or even by the tedious name of

humanity, it was something novel and brave and generous, and it differenced us from all the monarchies limited and unlimited, the conquerors, the oppressors . . .

Like that of Howells, the jaundiced eye of Bierce saw through the national optimism long before 1898. Though "chained to the oar of yellow journalism," he maintained an independent, often insurgent, position. Surely the "decent restraint" he praises in Sterling as compared with poets who would have "ranted and chewed soap,"[113] is not always evident in his savagely satiric *Devil's Dictionary*.[114] ABORIGINES "soon cease to cumber" desirable soil: "they fertilize." ABRUPT is "like the arrival of a cannon-shot and the departure of the soldier." DESTINY is "a tyrant's authority for crime." FLAG is "a colored rag borne above troops and hoisted on forts and ships." MINE belongs "to me if I can hold or seize it." PATRIOTISM is "combustible rubbish ready to the torch of any one ambitious to illuminate his name." RIGHT includes "the right to do one's neighbor." TAKE is "to acquire, frequently by force but preferably by stealth." His verse-definitions are equally sardonic. In "Corporal" he mocks hero-worship:

> Fiercely the battle raged, and, sad to tell,
> Our corporal heroically fell!
> Fame from her height looked down upon the brawl
> And said: "He hadn't very far to fall."

"Disobey" not only grants another's right to govern *him*, but insists on *his* "duty manifest to disobey." Thus Bierce employs revered terms to undermine the principle of blind loyalty. In "Tortoise" he challenges the present by envisioning a better age:

> A President not strenuously bent
> On punishment of audible dissent—
>
> Who never shot (it were a vain attack)
> An armed or unarmed tortoise in the back;
>
> Subjects and citizens that feel no need
> To make the March of Mind a wild stampede . . .

"Vanity" exposes the glamor of war-parades: the drum-major is a "gorgeous creature" in "blazing breeches and high-towering cap—/Imperiously pompous, grandly bold," whose only virtue is that he won't fight. Finally, America's dreams of empire are scoffed at in the Rubaiyat-quatrain of "Worms'-Meat":

> Build deep, build high, build massive as you can,
> The wanton grass-roots will defeat the plan
> By shouldering asunder all the stones
> In what to you would be a moment's span.

The *Fantastic Fables* of 1899 are even more significant as a response to the war, and deserve notice here even though they seem to be told in prose. Glowing in phrase and fancy, they are essentially poems. More than thirty anecdotes satirize imperial America.[115] Here moral principle succumbs to material interest; intervenor turns into annexor; white Christians scourge heathens for fiercely defending themselves; a President goes marketing for the whole planet; huge aggressors accuse tiny victims of aggression, and punish defiance; a statesman saves his country in order to get it; a hunter tells his quarry that shooting is "fair game," not "cruel sport"; two dead soldiers argue about the values of victory, life, and plaudits; a President denies that his war threat is a war threat; a great country in defeat is stripped of colonies, liberty, credit, and self-respect; a President holds on to his foolish Secretary of War, being himself a fool; Aguinaldo has no trouble with the American volunteers in Luzon, but their Commander does; in battle a soldier learns that Expansionism is a Vulture.

Despite its high pitch of fury, the force of its stanzas, and the charm of its characterizations, *Biglow* is not far superior to the *Dictionary* and *Fables*. Using the common materials of the daily press, Bierce—like Lowell in 1846—lifts them into lasting art by the scope of his vision and the brilliance of his wit. The America he forces his countrymen to see cannot have made them feel intelligent, humane, honest, or true to their forefathers' ideals.

Lowell is again recalled in the sparkling satiric verses of Santayana, "Young Sammy's First Wild Oats."[116] Born a full generation after Howells and Bierce, the young Harvard professor is in 1898 very much concerned with the prophetic function and with its denial by the dominant voices of his time. By choosing rhymed wit and everyday language to express his disgust with things as they are, he emphasizes his desire to move the widest possible audience. The framework he builds is fresh, and the expression felicitous, but many of the arguments are familiar: what "should have been a Zion" has become a Babylon; led by the ancient imperial thirst, America has betrayed its past. Posing as a liberator, the new regime first kissed Cuba "Like a brother"—

> But with that poor Filipina,
>   When she shrank from his caress,
> His contemptible demeanor
>   Isn't easy to express.

First he bought her, then he kicked her;
But the truth is, he was drunk,
For that day had crowned him victor,
And a Spanish fleet was sunk.

Unlike Uncle Sam, his "prim, pompous, pious" father, the young Rough Rider is "Lavish, clever, loud, and pushing." More than other poets, Santayana probes for the root of this transformation and finds that, instead of nurturing his soul, Cousin Sammy was taught "To scorn all he couldn't buy." The one hope for him now is to behold the fate of earlier empires and humbly declare his "dependence on the world."

In "Spain in America"[117] Santayana skillfully uses the Spenserian stanza to trace, step by step, Spain's rise, dominion, and fall, and to question the very nature of expansionism. "Sloth . . . lust . . . mindlessness and pelf" have brought ruin to Spain; but she gave glory to the world, and merits pity. Let America, the poet warns, "beware of peaks" in her "southward flight," lest she too fall to earth. Let her earn the love of weaker lands, and neither thrust her "unctuous sophists" on them nor expect them to admire her "sorry riches." Let her modernizing zeal not sweep aside the spiritual values bequeathed by Spain . . . If Santayana was "the withdrawn, contemplative man who takes no part in the every-day work . . . of the world," the urgency of 1898 must have been great indeed to have drawn from him two major political poems condemning his nation's iniquity and pleading for a return to its early principles.

With others who have cheered the wresting of Cuba from Spain, Moody resents the violently achieved annexation of the Philippines. Influenced in Chicago by

Fuller and Garland, then swept up in Boston's anti-imperialist mood, he voices his feelings in "An Ode in Time of Hesitation."[118] Invigorated by a statue of Shaw's Civil War regiment, the poet wishes to sing proudly of his land; but sounds from the Pacific, which others ignore, disturb him: "sounds of ignoble battle." The ghosts of American glory demand that *he* sing a song of shame, since Whittier and Whitman are silent and the "fluent men" of today speak hollowly, stopping debate with "their dull commercial liturgies." Finally, on behalf of America's heroes, including those who fell "on the awful slope at San Juan," he speaks out: is our eagle to be exchanged for "the talons and the maw" of a vulture? No! America's leaders must not further outrage the heritage of their land! Unless they "let the island men go free," warns the incendiary poet, vengeance will crash on their guilty heads:

> The cup of trembling shall be drainèd quite,
> Eaten the sour bread of astonishment,
> With ashes of the hearth shall be made white
> Our hair, and wailing shall be in the tent . . .
> We shall discern the right
> And do it, tardily,—O ye who lead,
> Take heed!
> Blindness we may forgive, but baseness we will smite.

These arguments are used by a score of poets; what makes Moody succeed is not so much the slow majesty with which his thoughts unfold, or his felicity of language, or the appropriateness and unity of his symbolism, as the personality of the speaker. It is as if the conscience of the land had concentrated itself within one person and dramatically wrestled him into speech. Once more, as in the case of Emerson, a larger than human voice emerges from unwilling human lips, and we are in the presence of high prophecy.

Although he never equals this performance, he does continue to exercise his evangelistic impulse.[119] "On a Soldier Fallen in the Philippines" is a minor triumph. Bitterly Moody commands "the grists of trade" to wait while the soldier is carried home. "He did what he was bade to do," and should not now discover that his bullet struck "Home to the heart of his darling land where she stumbled and sinned in the dark." In "The Quarry" Moody comments allegorically on American intervention in China, which several (other?) predators are about to dismember. With dismay, as in the ode, the poet asks his eagle-nation: "Alas! What dost thou here? What dost *thou* here?" To prove "how completely Moody was dominated by his emotions," one blundering critic manages to find in this ambiguous, aloof, probably sarcastic comment an "ecstasy," an "unreasoning and over-enthusiastic laudation of the 'Open Door' policy."[120] Perhaps the poet himself is not entirely certain of America's role at this time, since he tells us that he cannot understand the eagle's answer to his question. But that he feels deeply troubled and insists on sharing that feeling with his country, is clear.

Edwin A. Robinson thinks Moody's ode "big," and singles out as "prodigious" the denunciatory ending of the Philippine elegy.[121] But he also condemns the latter poem of his friend as close to "popular rot," and strictly avoids any such public utterance in his own work. Instead, like Miss Guiney, he dreams of getting "out of this region" in order "to keep the machine going."[122] His few war references are oblique.[123] "Cortege," perhaps inspired by the *Maine* disaster, laments a multiple burial at "four o'clock this afternoon" fifteen hundred miles away, and hints at the future horrors which the dead have avoided. "Twilight Song" sounds like the chant of a defeated army whose empire was long ago doomed by a "new sun":

> We have earned the day's rest . . .
> We have fought, we have died,
> And we've burned the King's bones.

"The Field of Glory," written somewhat later, exposes the uselessness and bestiality of war: "The sound of man destroying man"; its heroes: "Rough, bloody, ribald, hungry, lame"; and its temptations: "Arms, and fiery deeds."

His most questioning, unsettling war poem is "Captain Craig," written in 1899.[124] By calling Craig a "captain," Robinson emphasizes spiritual warfare as his theme. The indiscreetly blared funeral music celebrating the old man's victory over a harsh life contrasts with the brass band for a soldier "who fought one fight and in that fight fell dead." Turning his back on the Rough Rider, Robinson lets him "go roaring his own way." It is the thought of "men on stretchers . . . things without shapes or names," that maddens him, and he imagines:

> . . . some poor devil on a battle-field
> Left undiscovered and without the strength
> To drag a maggot from his clotted mouth . . .

Not until "Cassandra," his 1914 admonition to a blindly arrogant young empire, does Robinson drop his reticence;

but the seeds are in "Captain Craig." For in this poem he forces his country to hear its own voice: "Implacable, renascent, farcical,/Triumphant, and American." At the close of every hill-storming day, says the poet, "squandered men" march down the street dragging "ruins of half-warriors to the grave . . ." But the true hero, the spiritual champion, mounts "from these low roads of measured shame" and treads—with Captain Craig—"the leagueless highway." No wonder the war-minstrel Scollard frowns upon this "disturbing volume," and that other laureate of battle, Bliss Carman, judges it "a mistake"![125]

Stephen Crane's first response to the war is not as a poet, but as a journalist obligated to both editor and reader.[126] His personal motives are various: to "regain his balance," earn money, "experience war . . . and challenge the possibility of death." At first his own and his readers' anti-Spanish bias leads him to imagine the foe as bravos "gathered around some cognac bottles," thinking they've beaten Dewey in the East and expecting to thrash America's Atlantic fleet. Soon, however, the horror seeps in, even while he cheers hero and flag. A boat overturns; Negro troops are senselessly drowned. Soldiers poise for "the ambush of death," and Crane wonders what "scene of somebody's last gasp" waits beyond the hills. A wounded private's look is "of a man weary, weary, weary." There is the "grim and frightful field sport" of shooting down trapped Spaniards—murder "arranged on a system." The poet has recorded much, digested little. After "liberation" he still snaps at the Cubans for cowardice, lying, theft, ingratitude, immaturity. They will "be given their independence . . . but . . . not until they have grown to manhood." In a tone reminiscent of Whitman's Mexican War editorials, he predicts harshly that "this natural mother-country will heat the little Cuba to its proper temperature." As for the Filipinos, if they don't believe America's words of comfort, "there will be fighting on some . . . islands." Much in Hovey's vein he warns the world: "America challenges whomsoever she challenges, and whomsoever comes may find her weak, but . . . never . . . unwilling . . . We can be military if we choose."

Few writers maintain so rabid a position so candidly; few reverse themselves so swiftly and profoundly. Disturbed and dying, Crane manages to absorb his war experiences by the close of 1899 and to give them artistic form. "War-Memories," a series of prose-poems, is dominated by a deep sense of agony.[127] At a victory-parade, the troops willingly leave "the clacking" about heroism "to all those natural-born major-generals who after the war talked enough to make a great fall in the price of that commodity all over the world." What the poet hears is "the sound of women weeping"; what he remembers is the impact of an unexpected encounter:

> . . . the schoolmate, lying there in the mud, with a hole through his lung, awed me into stutterings, set me trembling with a sense of terrible intimacy with this war which theretofore I could have believed was a dream—almost . . . A number of people got killed very courteously, tacitly absolving the rest of us from any care in the matter. A man fell; he turned blue . . .

In the context of his prose and the work of his contemporaries, Crane's war poems become clear.[128] Thus a drowned Negro soldier turns into:

The puff of a coat imprisoning air:
A face kissing the water-depth
A weary slow sway of a lost hand
And the sea, the moving sea, the sea.
God is cold.

Coldly this God appears to lead the new forever against the archaic; His wisdom is "the clang of swords"; behind His standard march blind crusaders, "tools of nature's impulse," who swing "a creed like a censer." *Does* God lead these blue battalions far and high, or does He coldly allow the use of His name? A man raises a "warrior's shout" to the "deaf spheres" until the sky is "filled with armies"; has God responded to His chosen, or is it that war-mongers inevitably get their wish?

Elsewhere Crane is more explicit, exposing the lust for battle and its horror. A knight rides fast, "ever waving an eager sword." Booming drums represent the "little souls who thirst for fight." Coldly the Battle-God rules "a field where a thousand corpses lie." At the foot of the stormed castle-wall the knight's horse lies dead. Alone in the woods that impassively beheld "the threshing of his limbs," the hunter lies—never again to hear his beloved's call. And in the far-off cities the glamorized report of war lures the reader with "eternal stupidities," while the truth of war, learned by the poet, remains unprinted: that there are not "good white lands/And bad black lands,/But the scene is gray." He has learned, too, what the hill-stormer, stripped of glamor, really is:

The successful man . . .
Slimed with victories over the lesser
. . . buys silken banners
. . . limned with his triumphant face . . .

Complacent, smiling,
He stands heavily on the dead.
Erect on a pillar of skulls
He declaims his trampling of babes.

This may be a composite of all "natural-born major-generals," or a portrait of Roosevelt alone; but, unlike those by Fuller, it is artistically controlled, visionary in concept, and devoid of petty namecalling. Crane's voice has the ancient, inspired resonance; it is tragic indeed that he was silenced before fully crystallizing his 1898 experience.

Two of the most extraordinary responses to the war are by Edgar L. Masters. *The New Star Chamber,* a collection of political essays, exposes in solid prose a conquest resulting from "a compact among the trusts to get trade."[129] The difference between the newly apotheosized McKinley and his successor, Roosevelt—according to the impudent young poet—is that one was a crafty, plausible dissembler, while the other, a man of "inordinate egotism and prostituted principles . . . obtrudes his imperial plans" and "appeals to the brutal tendencies in man." Having taken "the plunge into national animalism," America is bowed under an awful guilt, conscious of "duty forsaken and ideals discarded and shattered." The fiction of manifest destiny carries away the masses on "gusts of false sentiment" while "empire builders laugh in their sleeves." The war has been neatly turned into "a question of honor," and one does not besmirch the nation's honor! In such a climate, Masters explains, discussion is taboo and "the constitution is made a huge joke." Settling down after duly ravishing its past, America enjoys the "reports of pillage, murder and rapine . . . in the great work of destroying an Asiatic republic." Such is his vision of the America that is. Not satisfied to excoriate his nation for its self-betrayal, however, the poet proclaims what is to be: ". . . the passion for glory and power destroyed the governments of the past and is hastening the destruction of those of the present."

To say that little in this volume or in *The Blood of the Prophets* indicates "the vigor and driving honesty which propelled" *Spoon River,* is utter nonsense.[130] Both books are indeed characterized by those very qualities. The power and truth of Masters' prose are ably transformed into the furious verses of his 1905 collection[131]—from the huge opening "Ballad of Jesus of Nazareth," probably inspired by Wilde's "Reading Gaol," whose stanza he borrows, to the slashing sonnet, "America in 1904," reminiscent of Shelley's "England, 1819." The historical parallels are trenchantly drawn:

> When Caesar back to Rome returned
> With all the world subdued,
> The soldiers and the priests did shout,
> And cried the multitude;
> For he had slain his country's foes,
> And drenched their land with blood.

He lists leaders and nations that had opposed tyranny until "The Dragon of Greed destroyed them." Why, asks the poet, does America repeat the past, "Dreaming of splendors of battle . . . When the Caesars pillaged for lust of gold and hunger of power." Somberly he remarks that the old ideals of "Wisdom and peace and fair intent" have become tedious, that gold is now the national dream. At the graves of pioneers he imagines their sunken eyes from which "the light of life" has fled, as the glory has fled from their land. For an imperial army has galloped over them, and America's "blinding sword" has brought woe to Manila. How dare that flag, so glorious at Valley Forge, be raised against the Filipinos, the new sons of Liberty? "False to thy fathers and time," he cries out, "thou wert not born for wrong . . ." And he begs his countrymen to abandon conquest, "the path of the beasts . . . the deserts of death." Jeering at those who link God's name with "the bloody rag they call the flag," he exposes "greed, the python," curled around the banner of the cross. Finally he compares Jefferson, "a man whose soul gave light/Intolerable to kings," with Roosevelt, "Usurper, hoodlum, wed to his desire," whose lust for glory and war gives victory to old Europe.

As Roosevelt changes, so does Masters' attitude toward him; but he never revises his assessment of the war. In a much later poem he recalls a chat with the President. Roosevelt asks how one whose Spoon River celebrates "The pioneers, the soldiers of the past," can "flout our Philippine adventure." To this, Masters replies: "No difference, Colonel, in the stock; the difference/Lies in the causes."[132] Of course, this rejoinder beautifully illustrates the unbending integrity of Masters as a man, and the purity of his ethical perspective as a poet. But it also crystallizes the theme of this chapter as a whole, and the chapter on the Mexican War. It helps us to differentiate between those poets who celebrate *any* war waged by their country because it is their country, and those who prophesy against any *unjust* war waged by their country—because it is their country. What makes 1898 particularly valuable in such an investigation is that for the average reader the *justice* of this war could be determined only as it progressed. Thus we are apt to gauge the sincerity of those whose slogan had been "Cuba Libre!" by the position they took when liberation turned into annexation, when the deliverer of the Filipino became his plunderer and butcher. Some, we find, matched in their verses the increasing harshness of their government; others went on celebrating victories and heroic deeds as if nothing had changed; still others became conspicuously silent. Of special interest, however, is the large number who swiftly registered the shift in their nation's ethical position by publicly declaring their revulsion, thus joining the small nucleus of astute and courageous poets who had recognized from the beginning the falseness of their government's altruism.

Injustice has been done the poets of this period by scholars who portray them as hot-house creatures. Even of Stedman, Gilder, and Aldrich—who were silent on the war—this is not necessarily true; for their silence may be interpreted as a form of disaffection, a refusal to sing the hymn expected of them. It is equally unjust to claim that Moody alone produced memorable work against the war. There were, as we have found, other voices which blended the resonance of inspired truth and a craftsmanship worthy of that truth. Many poets, then respected, now forgotten, were alive to the iniquity of their age and sometimes achieved noble utterance. If anything, the prophetic response in 1898 was fuller and deeper than that of 1846—especially among the younger poets. This phenomenon parallels Britain's return to immediacy and disconcerting truth in Housman and Hardy, after reaching the dead end of late Victorian verse.

Conclusion

i

I undertook this study first of all to test the validity of the traditional view that the poet as prophet represents the conscience of his age in its most sensitive and eloquent form. The United States, between 1835 and 1900, seemed a fair and useful choice as my "theatre of operations," since American poets of that period often defined poetry in terms of the prophetic impulse and committed themselves to the prophet's ancient mission of alarming the dormant, vexing the complacent, unmasking the iniquitous, challenging the powerful, and comparing the real with the ideal—no matter at what personal cost. Furthermore, America's poets were confronted during this time with numerous dramatic opportunities to display the ethical awareness and personal courage of which they boasted. I restricted my test to several areas in which the immorality of an imperial-minded population and its government exposed itself in particularly predatory and cruel forms. My hope has been to discover how such episodes affected poets—whether they endorsed the dominant mood, were silent, indirectly deplored the iniquity, or were magnificently indiscreet.

The response of the minor poets proves to have been clearly inconsistent with regard to the issues that challenged them. For example, during the conflicts with Mexico and Spain, large numbers spoke with courage and passion, often approaching Biblical expression in their dismay at America's imperial role, at the horror of the war itself, and at the embarrassing spectacle of a false altruism. Besides, as America's true aims became clear, a considerable group of previously loud balladeers turned silent, and an impressive number publicly reversed themselves, giving strong evidence that—during those wars at least—the American poet *was* to a large degree the conscience of his land, and did indeed fulfill his commitment to the prophetic tradition.

The same, however, was not nearly so true in other areas of this study. The anti-Indian campaigns of the thirties and seventies aroused little direct condemnatory response in verse. Osceola's capture and death caused a slight furore, as much for the picturesqueness of the episode as for its ethical significance. Outside of abolition circles, which would have fought the government on *any* available issue, very few poets of 1838 challenged the justice of Anglo-Saxonism's westward drive. The forties and the eighties, however, brought a considerable delayed response in the form of ambitious narrative poems, which portrayed the heroism and tragedy of the red man, along with two extraordinary prose indictments by Helen Hunt Jackson.

Our other touchstones, the legalized slave hunt and mob intolerance, drew almost no acknowledgment from minor poets. Even in abolitionist ranks there were notable silences, and those who spoke often achieved their most inspired utterance in the form of prose. The fugitive himself was seldom presented dimensionally, and we find—contrary to the general pattern of anti-slavery literature in the fifties—that the response in verse diminished as the issue grew in urgency. As for the mob, it too was seldom scrutinized as a dimensional thing. Few poets outside the victim's party acknowledged that an outrage had occurred; and even within the ranks there was a tendency to welcome martyrdom as a sign of hope rather than to deplore the attack as a sign of national sickness.

Another aim of this study was to explore, at least tentatively, a problem in aesthetics which is no closer to resolution in our day than it was in 1835. There were then, as there are now, critics and readers who believed that without great ethical fervor a poem cannot be great. Margaret Fuller, for instance, publicly accused Lowell of operating under this illusion. Other critics and readers were certain that an involvement in current issues, no matter how great, destroys the possible greatness of a poem. Emerson, in a journal entry, expressed just this belief: no muse would assist him if he tried to turn the slavery issue into poetry.[1] From time to time in this investigation, when confronted by a particularly fiery outburst or a particularly strategic reticence on a current issue, I have considered this problem.

Both views regarding the relationship of prophecy and art have proven fallacious. Some of the poets whose work I have been reading seem in constant search of great issues to set them lyrically ablaze, no doubt in the hope of achieving greatness. Edna D. Proctor, along with many others, was a perpetual champion of causes, proud "that the subjects for her poems were chosen somewhat sternly."[2] From all those raging throats few great, or even memorable, works emerged. Other poets sought greatness by avoiding great issues; they relied instead on technical prowess. From all those subtle tongues few great, or even memorable, poems emerged. The excellence of a poem, as demonstrated by the large group examined here, depends on a combination of factors, a harmony of image, music, architecture, and word. All of these factors being present, the addition of moral fervor, based on a critical response to reality, may turn poetry into prophecy and raise it to sublimity. Such instances have, of course, been rare in this exploration, as in the literature of any country. On the other hand, as we have painfully discovered hundreds of times, without the qualities necessary for artistic excellence, all the moral fervor in the world cannot save a poem from mediocrity or worse: for in such a case the verses become pretentious, shrill, and strikingly lame.

Finally it was my purpose to test several current notions concerning the status of ethics in American poetry during the nineteenth century. Garrod, for example, though he may not have this country or period specifically in mind, declares that "the anti-ethical fashion" is of recent date, and that up to now the purpose of poetry has been to reform mankind.[3] This view is supported by literary historians who say that during Whittier's fifty-year creative span "almost all the leading American poets" became, at times, propagandists.[4] A more prevalent belief is that, prior to the Civil War, poets displayed great moral vigor in their criticism of society and government, but that post-bellum poetry was emasculated by the genteel tradition. A third, entirely contradictory view is presented by Edward E. Hale, who wistfully recalls, late in the century, that "Now the fashion of Cambridge runs to social problems, but then we were interested in literature."[5] Hale's recollection of the thirties is verified by those who indicate how slowly the ante-bellum poets turned their attention to the unpleasant realities in American life. I have hoped that this investigation, which embraces a span of three generations, including the full range of work produced by the major poets of the century, might make it possible to determine which of these views is closest to the truth.

My findings indicate that all three views are to some degree defensible. Garrod's theory of a twentieth-century anti-ethical trend is confirmed, for instance, by the prevalence of the attitude that Whittier was born as a poet only when he died as a reformer, and that Emerson's literary powers "were slowly undermined by . . . reluctant participation in public and national affairs."[6] The oblivion that has overtaken some of the fine reform poets encountered in this study is further evidence of an anti-ethical triumph in our day. Garrod's view of nineteenth-century poetry as morally motivated is also partly corroborated by this investigation. For, from first to last, even during the "deep-freeze" period of Brahmin rule, some poets *did* utter loud warnings and execrations, in prose if not in verse, making themselves obnoxious to their neighbors and their government far more often than poets have done in recent years; and by the time of the Spanish-American War a tremendous outpouring of admonitory and denunciatory verse reverberated across the land with greater authority than had been manifested during the Mexican War.

On the other hand, we find that the anti-moralist camp was astir and indeed triumphant long before the turn of the century. Those who refer to the post-bellum years as a low point in the ethical vigor of American poetry need merely quote as proof the long euphoric odes and the Tennysonian lullabies with which our formerly prophetic voices and their disciples tried to drown out the dreadfulness of the centennial decade.

However, those like Hale, who fondly recall the aestheticism of the thirties, are closest to the truth; and they tend to disprove not only Garrod's vision of pre-twentieth-century verse, but also the legend that pre-Civil War poetry was full of blood and thunder against public evil while the sterile aestheticism of the genteel tradition was a post-war phenomenon. For such a powerful periodical as Willis' *Home Journal* was loved precisely "for its avoidance of politics and its careful shunning of all 'strong' subjects,"[7] and throughout the forties the North considered it "bad form" for poets to mention slavery.[8] It was, after all, an 1838 address that kept Emerson from being invited to speak at Harvard again for nearly thirty years. And Mrs. Oakes-Smith later recalled how plainly the influential poets in her immediate circle had shown their disapproval of her reformist views in 1851. Throughout the ante-bellum years, in every phase of this study, the tyranny of the genteel makes its presence felt, so that one is aware of a certain daring when a poet bursts through the gentlemanly silence expected of him.

ii

It is obvious that, in the areas of public immorality I chose as my touchstones, a partial failure of the prophetic impulse occurred. This phenomenon is strange on several grounds. In the first place, the United States, recently and loudly embarked under the loftiest standards yet lifted by man, desperately needed to be reminded of those standards. Then too, such revered forebears as Isaiah, Dante, Chaucer, Milton, and Burns stood as inspiring examples of how to chide and warn. Furthermore, the enormities challenging attention were dangerous and clear. Finally, American poets had far less cause to fear retribution for exposing corruption in high places than did those in rigidly controlled nations.

Some factors involved in this non-fulfillment of the prophetic function are primarily philosophic, and can be readily discovered in the poets' self-definitions, or in declarations by cultural leaders whose attitude toward the artist's role was symptomatic—if not regulative. Rich documentation is supplied by the writers themselves, especially in their poems about art and artists.

Many were convinced that it is thematically inappropriate, aesthetically dangerous, and spiritually debasing to deal with specific, recent, controversial events rather than with lofty, universal, eternal truths. The transcendental revolt against the practical and commonplace was the most significant philosophic justification of this attitude, but it can be found in many other forms throughout the sixty-five-year span of this study. Henry Tuckerman's declaration of self-exile is characteristic:

> . . . to be free from passion's bitter strife;
> Free of the world, a self-dependent soul,
> Nourished by lofty aims and genial truth . . .[9]

Half a century later Markham goes still further, announcing that "The world is a vapor, and only the Vision is real."[10]

There was also a fear among poets that the habit of yielding to moral stimuli might cripple their response to sensuous and imaginative stimuli. Thus Thomas B. Aldrich laments the flight of the muse from America's "polemic . . . air . . ."[11] Frederick G. Tuckerman likewise implies that were he to concern himself with "change and fray" he would lose his ability to watch "the clouds at morning driven,/The still declension of the day . . ."[12]

Another factor is the widely shared view of Poe that the poet should not teach, but create beauty. This anti-didactic approach took some courage at a time when Mrs. Sigourney's formula for popular success was her moral tone, when the annuals and anthologies were aimed at moral improvement, and when no less a journal than the *North American Review* decreed "the true and only object of literary effort" to be purification of heart and enlargement of mind.[13] Against this demand of critics and public there were poets who made Art for Art's Sake a militant credo, and many more who quietly followed that credo without announcing it. To shape and celebrate loveliness, they believed, were the poet's sole and sacred functions. With Keats' lines echoing in his mind, no doubt, John W. Chadwick asked:

> . . . Who would not gladly freeze and die,
> If something lovely from his moulding hand
> Might him survive and be a thing of joy
> Forever in a dull and weary land?[14]

It was also a popular principle among nineteenth-century authors that—in their poetry at least—they should understand and accept reality rather than judge it; by their wholesome tone and positive examples they should engender patience and discourage factional anger. This was the quality which William W. Story, Bayard Taylor, and the other aestheticists particularly admired in the masters of the past, who "Stand so serene above life's fierce array,"[15] and who serve mankind as "A steadfast anchor . . . Mid passions that exhaust, and times that wear . . ."[16] Believing themselves to be in the great tradition, they reasoned that Evil need not be shouted down; it would eventually serve Good. This Goethean concept, transmitted through Margaret Fuller and other transcendentalists, ultimately nestled among Lanier's marshes of Glynn:

> Ye spread and span like the catholic man who hath
>   mightily won
> God out of knowledge and good out of infinite pain
> And sight out of blindness and purity out of a stain.[17]

Finally, there were those who endorsed the doctrine that the only reality is within the individual soul, particularly the poet's, and that his chief concern should be to win his private spiritual battles. Louise Imogen Guiney, at the close of the century, charted the poet's course splendidly in accordance with this belief:

> Schools shall be as they are:
> Be thou truer, and stray
> Alone, intent, and away,
> In a savage wild to obey
> A dim primordial star.[18]

It is important to this study that we note the character of the poets quoted above. They were, in the main, among the century's voices of reform. We are here confronting the crucial dichotomy which flawed the aims of our major poets as well: an everlasting combat of the epideictic versus the contemplative. If any poet exposed that war of motives, it was Christopher P. Cranch. His companion-pieces, "Inworld" and "Outworld," dramatically portray the poet's inner debate; for the spirit that visits him by day announces that Time and Space must rule over him forever, while his nocturnal visitor declares that only within the poet himself is there reality.[19]

What we have noted thus far helps to explain in terms of principle the reticence of America's nineteenth-century poets. But other, more personal, factors were also involved in their failure to respond to specific outrages of the day. These factors are sometimes difficult to substantiate, since they depend on biographical hints, psychological insights, and parallel situations; therefore, in the case of specific poets, they should be given consideration as possibilities only.

One rather obvious possibility involves poets who in youth responded with alacrity to any manifestation of evil in their world, but who afterward either avoided mention of evil or actually reversed their position. This might be laid to the mellowing influence of time, which—as in the case of the transcendentalists—led many "iconoclastic reformers" to exchange their youthful enthusiasm "for the tolerance and conservatism of middle-age."[20] Here we think of Thomas B. Read, who in an 1847 poem lauded Bryant and the "iron-handed Whittier" but in an 1865 revision excluded these stanzas from the poem.[21] Bret Harte comes to mind as well; in 1860 he was driven out of his California town by infuriated vigilantes because he had denounced a massacre of Indians; soon after, he wrote militant Civil War poems. By the mid-seventies, however, he was expressing contempt for both Indians and Negroes.[22] In the same way Joaquin Miller, whose pacifist newspaper was shut down by the government in 1862, sang proudly of Custer in 1876 and of America's victories in 1898.

Of course, Time was not operating alone on the ethical nerve of these poets; there was also the matter of their increasing public fame and financial success. Some of them attained high government office; and it would be unlikely to expect indignant stanzas from John Hay, Secretary of State, or George H. Boker, Minister to Russia, or Edward E. Hale, Senate Chaplain. For those with lesser berths in government service it would be both unseemly and suicidal to bite the proverbial hand. This may help to explain why Boner, proof-reader at the Government Printing Office, and John Vance Cheney, head of a major library, almost never struck a jarring note in their verse. Yet it should not be assumed that they otherwise *would* have carped. Surely their choice of the "thirty bob a week!"[23] was as much an open-eyed commitment as had been their earlier decision to be poets. In other words, it is foolish to lay the blame for Lamar's racist songs on his position as President of Texas, or to say that Albert Pike wrote "Dixie" because he was Judge of the Supreme Court of Arkansas, or that W. W. Lord's poetry failed to condemn slavery because he was an intimate friend of Jefferson Davis and a chaplain in the Confederate Army. Obviously, in such cases the poems came first, perhaps symptomatic of the positions that followed. And if the ethical standards of Halleck, Dana, Stedman, and Stoddard were somewhat shaped by their roles as millionaire's assistant, clergyman, stock broker, and customs official, these poets deliberately chose the direction in which they moved. Their source of income cannot be held responsible for the prophetic failure of such poets; it is, rather, one element in that failure. Yet we cannot overlook the desperate efforts of a Lanier to find a means of support for his family: that is, his glowingly nationalistic verse of 1876 may be connected with his eagerness to win a government post at that time, just as his great need for money the previous year had turned him into what he himself called "Poet-in-Ordinary to a long line of Railroad Corporations," abusing in his published prose the very Indian chiefs he was simultaneously admiring in personal letters.[24]

A second major impediment to prophecy, and one which has seldom been so strong a force in the poetry of other countries, was the profound personal commitment to Americanism as a new and world-saving idea surrounded by mocking enemies. Thus a poet-painter such as Washington Allston, while aware of his nation's faults, would not wish to give ammunition to foreigners; their abuse of America made his "blood boil."[25] Half a century later, Thomas N. Page—having "journeyed the spacious world over"—reaffirmed this position. No matter "How crude . . . and rude" his nation's struggles for greatness may be, America is paradise compared with the lands ruled by tyranny. For poets like Page it is but one easy step further to grant America a worldwide license to overthrow "The Shackles, the Yoke, and the Rod";[26] one can hardly expect such poets to deplore expansionism, or to countenance the criticism voiced by other poets who would cheat America of its "mighty heirdom" and "leave behind a clipped and shrunken realm."[27] Grace Greenwood may be playful when she confesses a reluctance to chastise her land, but the grim fact is that those who chastised *were* called fanatics, battling "Against the mighty Union, and the almighty laws."[28] They were also accused of treason—not only by the partisan public, but by gentle poets like George P. Morris, whose friendship they sought and whose influence they needed. Thus the patriotic threat to the integrity of American poets was two-pronged: to report that one's homeland was "happy, united and free,"[29] was to earn the gratitude of one's nationalistic and comfort-craving generation; to report public wickedness, however, was to court disaster at the hands of publishers, editors, critics, and readers, if not to be accused of sedition outright by one's fellow poets. This possibility was especially strong during the decades immediately preceding and following the Civil War. During those periods the fear and pain of disunion caused many poets deliberately to avoid criticizing their shaky society as "tinkering knaves" were doing.[30]

Another important reason for their failure to express dismay at ugly moments in the national experience is that in many cases poetry was used as a retreat from life rather than as a vehicle by which to criticize it. Occasionally one of these poets looked back guiltily at his innocuous volume and, like Cranch, regretted not having "given vent in a few more poems" to some of his "later and riper thoughts."[31] But usually the escape was admitted without any hint of awareness that the prophetic function was being betrayed. Thus James F. Clarke praised a landscape by Allston because its grace and peace "Belong not to our world of sin and strife"; and he himself chose to translate almost nothing but light and sentimental love lyrics, though he had before him the entire range of German literature.[32] Bayard Taylor was even more candid as he turned escapism into a credo. Although

Parrington speaks of the genteel tradition's taboos as "cushions for tired or lazy minds,"[33] there is something deliberate and energetic in Taylor's decision to:

> . . . leap
> O'er the herded swine and sheep,
> And in pastures far away
> Lose the Burden of the Day![34]

A certain saucy tone of independence gives such lines at least a semblance of character; Mrs. Sigourney, on the other hand, consciously sought to please the "herded swine and sheep" by offering them, through much of her verse, a solace and an escape from reality directly contradicting the prophetic role as she herself and her contemporaries defined it.

Nor was her eagerness to please limited to her own countrymen. Haight exposes her psychological need to escape the American taint and win a place among the British poets. Although Mrs. Sigourney crusaded for the Indian, hated war, and deplored ruffianism, one finds in her typical poems no reaction to evidences of American evil—for her eye was focused elsewhere. Nor was she exceptional in this regard. Just as she craved the approval of Joanna Baillie and Samuel Rogers, and toiled to acquire "the title of the 'American Hemans,' "[35] so did Charles F. Hoffman echo the songs of Thomas Moore and Walter Scott, while Seba Smith in his ballads plainly imitated Campbell. The tendency to keep unpleasant American realities out of their verse was encouraged by the verdicts of the idolized British reviewers. A lesson was to be gained when Dublin praised Hoffman's "dashing numbers" for their "aristocracy of soul and sentiment,"[36] or when Norwich acknowledged that Alonzo Lewis' volume contained "as mellifluous verse as ever Campbell or Rogers wrote."[37] Although Lewis, as we have seen in various chapters, did not permit himself to be blunted by this rather directive praise, nevertheless his unmellifluous outbursts of wrath were meticulously excluded from the ten editions of his collected poems.

This Europeanism carried through with undiminished force throughout the century, permeating the bulk of the verse produced by even such defiantly native voices as Bret Harte and Joaquin Miller. It is especially potent in genteel poets such as Edward R. Sill, who never freed himself from "the finely spun chains of Tennyson's verse."[38] It should be noted that, in escaping from America, our minor poets often escaped into the arms of their overseas counterparts, the least prophetic European poets then enjoying a critical vogue; or—as was the case with Howells, Emma Lazarus, and John Hay—they chose to derive from a Heine his most innocuous elements while ignoring the pages that blazed with inspired ferocity. Thus they were ripe and ready for the medievalist trend in mid-century European art, and for the aestheticism of the mauve decade. In their poetry if not in their lives, these poets had long since turned their backs on the reality of their time and place. Story transplanted himself, body and soul, to medieval Italy just as Miss Guiney—half a century later—migrated to Cavalier England. Following the taste of Lanier, Maurice Thompson turned hungrily back to the glow of Froissart's golden day, with its tournaments; and the early poems of Moody swarm with the stock characters of the Middle Ages.

There were also domestic obstructions in the lives of certain poets. Some of these difficulties caused a temporary blockage; others operated throughout a creative career. Thomas Chivers, for example, because of personal misfortune, and because he lacked adequate intellectual companionship, lost perspective, could not "come to terms with the world of reality," became totally self-involved, and "his poetry reflected this process."[39] William G. Simms' inability to respond to Osceola's death but a few miles away, may have resulted from the death, at that time, of the poet's baby, and a cluster of simultaneous misfortunes. We know regarding Higginson, on the other hand, that Helen Hunt Jackson was unable to incite him on behalf of the decimated tribes because "his wife, his child, and his work . . . filled his life."[40] A related cause of silence at crucial moments may have been the illness of the poet, such as the typhoid fever which incapacitated James F. Clarke throughout 1850, or the mental disease which overcame Charles F. Hoffman in 1849, when he was at the height of both his poetic and ethical power.

Then, too, a large group of minor poets selected and restricted their subject matter for financial reasons. Abolition-minded poets such as Mrs. Oakes-Smith and the Cary sisters, whose survival depended on their contributions to magazines, could scarcely be expected to undermine their livelihood by submitting wrathful stanzas on society or government to editors, publishers, and readers who demanded "lightness, purity, and beauty." If one wished to be a popular poet, one studied the market and found that the "simple home songs" of Morris "appealed . . . to the hearts of the people,"[41] that Mrs. Sigourney was turning verse into a spectacularly lucrative trade by milking such dependable themes as reverence for age and resignation to adversity. On the other hand, it was as clear as a warning to them that Garrison, Alcott, and Parker were the most unpopular men in Boston, that Mrs. Child was a marked woman, that even the beloved Harriet Martineau had been anathematized for identifying herself with the anti-slavery cause during her visit to Boston. Throughout the century we find that money could play a determining role in the poet's choice of subject matter. Thus, for the sake of his Southern market, Thomas D. English excluded from his ballad-book of American history the entire experience of the Civil War. And even Helen Hunt Jackson, at least according to Nevins, would not have risen to prophecy on behalf of the Indian had she remained financially dependent. What freed her from the need to satisfy genteel magazine editors was, we are told, her 1875 marriage to a wealthy banker.[42]

Closely connected with their financial concern, although the poets themselves might not think so, was the aspiration for fame—which also depended on keeping their names clean. To be identified with notorious or insignificant moral rhymers, to be linked with shrill partisan publications, was as unthinkable before the Civil War as "doing something wrong or unpolished" was considered by Lanier's weak-souled contemporaries. In both cases the "morbid fear" kept many poets from heeding their own prophetic impulses.[43] There is no shift whatever in the sixty years between Story's revulsion at a Garrison "emitting serpents from his mouth,"[44] and Sterling's shunning of the bombastic poets with whose radical cause he sympathized.[45] For every Whittier who believed that Freedom's poets were likeliest to "acquire a name that would live on the records of humanity in imperishable brightness," a cluster of Willises was ready to wager on the lasting power of "rouge and raven tresses."[46] When Griswold pointed to the innocuous stanzas of Elizabeth

Oakes-Smith as "concentrated poetical power of a very high, possibly of the very highest order,"[47] it is easy to guess what subject matter a poet would choose if he burned for a place in Griswold's next edition. Bayard Taylor's affinity for the exotic and aloof, Aldrich's concern with red and white roses, are more than a cowardly avoidance of reality: they include the deliberate aim and confident expectation of living past their time and place by omitting both time and place from their work.

One final obstructive factor needs to be considered in the apparent ethical lethargy among America's minor poets. It is evident that excessive loyalty to faction, creed, or region blinded some of them to the victimization of an opposition group, or blocked their ability to be disturbed. But here, more than in other areas, we are dealing largely in conjecture. Among the Garrisonians, for example, there seems to have been a poetic paralysis at the death of Lovejoy in 1837, the Mormons and the Irish in 1844, and John Brown in 1859; this must, at least in part, be connected with a detestation of carnal weapons even when used in self-defense. Similarly, the silence of Mrs. Sigourney during the Civil War probably reflects her increasing conviction that any kind of war is wrong. The failure, even among abolition poets, to portray the fugitive slave or to celebrate those of his deliverers who were not white, can in some cases be linked with their personal dislike for Negroes. It is not surprising, with this in mind, to discover a non-abolitionist poet such as Richard H. Stoddard presenting an idyllic picture of the South in 1851; his refusal to take note of the slave within that landscape makes even more sense when we hear Stoddard, at Lincoln's funeral, urging the Negro mourners to bow "amid the master-race" and weep:

. . . weep—I would ye might—
Your poor black faces white![48]

This factor becomes even more prominent when we turn to the Southern poets, such as Grayson and Simms, who went beyond the silence of their colleagues and defended their ethically beleaguered homeland by accusing the North of labor slavery and ruffianism. Within some of the North's most gentle and enlightened poets, the sediment of various prejudices remained embedded throughout their lives. To understand Edward E. Hale's poetic silence on the mistreatment of the Indian, for instance, we need merely turn to his letters, with their snide references to "the surliness or *mauvaise honte*" of the North American aborigine.[49]

iii

These philosophic and personal factors were responsible, in varying degrees, for the conspicuous prophetic failure of America's minor nineteenth century poets, at least with regard to the fugitive slave cases, the abuse of Indian tribes, and mob violence. It must again be noted, as in the Introduction, that the touchstones I have chosen are not the only ones—and perhaps not the best ones—by which the ethical sensitivity of our poets could have been gauged. Some who failed to function prophetically in these particular areas of shame stood alone on moral issues not encompassed by the present study.[50] Embattled labor, for instance, won the poetic support of John Hay and Thomas Dunn English, both of whom were ethically non-committal on other issues. James Whitcomb Riley, while mouthing the very phrases most comforting to the advocates of the anti-Indian and anti-Filipino campaigns, was the sole American poet of reputation who supported Eugene V. Debs in verse during the 1894 Pullman strike hysteria. Similarly, Richard Watson Gilder, who remained silent on the decimation of the aborigines and on the war with Spain, though he privately deplored both, was the poet who cried out in verse against the 1894 murder of a reform leader.

Nor should it be overlooked that, despite a formidable assortment of inhibitive factors, our touchstones *have* led us to many courageous and a few extraordinary utterances. Surely some of the poems by Jones Very, Julia Ward Howe, Lloyd Mifflin, and Louise I. Guiney achieve the level of inspired prophetic song. We have also found, amid a great mass of artistically worthless outbursts, several little-known poems or passages of poems by John Quincy Adams, Richard Realf, Trumbull Stickney, and Edwin Markham, as well as others, in which high moral fervor is matched by felicity of form.

Nevertheless, a central fact that emerges from this investigation is that—in the main—the minor poets did not, as poets, demonstrate a high degree of ethical sensitivity and courage; did not respond to the concrete instances of iniquity in their time and place; did not fulfill their own prophetic definition and vow. Dozens of them, including some who privately feared that their nation was becoming morally bankrupt, permitted scarcely a syllable of social comment to appear in their collections. Many others, in pseudo-prophetic righteousness, throve consistently on the side of power, giving aid and comfort through their stanzas to that which history calls Evil, and rebuking their few colleagues who fulfilled the unblinding, discomposing role of prophecy. The magnitude of their failure can best be measured when we consider the performance of America's major figures at the same moment, in the same cities, and operating under the same formidable inhibitions. To restate it positively, the magnitude of their failure underscores and illuminates the superb prophetic achievement of America's major nineteenth-century figures.

None, for instance, were more insistent on the principle of aloofness from the mean battles of the workaday world than were our greatest poets; yet each found ways of registering his unceasingly intense moral involvement in the events of that world—through editorials, letters, public orations, and a surprisingly large number of poems. Holmes had pledged to bring only beauty to his readers and leave controversy to the newspapers; yet his poems show an increasing tendency to wrestle with the ethical decay of his nation. Robinson and Santayana maintained their hermitic stance stubbornly, yet tore loose to challenge their country's 1898 war in major poems. In a series of incisive satires, Bierce contradicted his own strictures against propaganda; and Moody did not hold back from a great frontal assault on America's leaders despite his conviction that "imperialist-minded presidents and senators" could not be blamed "for man's alienation from the ideal."[51]

As for personal obstructions, the major figures had enough to contend with. Stephen Crane, sick unto death at the close of the century, harrowed at the same time by other griefs, nevertheless succeeded in transforming his Caribbean experiences into a large-voiced outcry against the agony of war and the moral shoddiness of its makers. Just so, although Emily Dickinson's mother was an invalid from 1875 and the burden of caring for her "left

Emily small time for little else,"[52] this poet's great spiritual war raged on unabated, in a commonwealth and a nation spiritually dormant. To the zeal of Mrs. Jackson she offered the nourishment of a devoted and exalted admiration; and against the centennial arrogance of her neighbors she shaped her modest definition of the true nation. Similarly, the paralytic stroke which Whitman suffered in 1873 did not keep him from responding with fiery lines to "the published shame"[53] of scandal in high places; nor did sickness, although it frustrated Whittier's desire for physical involvement in the fugitive slave struggle, keep the early fifties from being the peak years of his incendiary song.

No American poet spoke more insultingly of the Indian character or more blandly of the red man's inevitable doom than did Emerson; yet in a benumbed land it was Emerson alone, in his flaming reproof to Van Buren, who stirred the public conscience against the Cherokee removal. Again, no American poet but Emerson spoke of the mob as an inevitable phenomenon whose evil would be productive of good; yet it was he who rocked a sedate Boston with a spectacular tribute to the recently martyred Lovejoy.

Whittier was no more suicidal than other American poets, yet several times he faced death at the hands of mobs; and, although he too craved the tranquility necessary to gestate a poem like "Snowbound," he begrudged himself that luxury so long as a single man remained enslaved. His hatred of carnal weapons blocked his ability to respond wholeheartedly to violent campaigns; yet it did not keep him from writing poems in support of such imprisoned advocates of violence as Thomas W. Higginson and John Brown.

CASH SWEEPSTAKES AUTHORIZATION

FINANCIAL DEPARTMENT, Reader's Digest, Pleasantville, N.Y. 105

IMPORTANT NOTICE TO:

MR. ALBERT MCLEAN JR.

A personal 10¢ CHECK and a $50,000.00 Book of Sweepstakes Tickets described on the other side are being sent to you by Reader's Digest and will arrive after the time indicated.

To enter the Sweepstakes with a chance to win the Bonus Award of $1,000.00-A-Day (up to $10-000), in addition to the Grand Prize of $50,000.00 cash, you must return the Tickets within a few days after you receive them.

If you do not respond promptly, your documents will be invalidated for the Grand Prize in accordance with regulations.

RD Form P/CB-4668

MR. ALBE
2333 SO
PITTSBU

CASH SWEEPSTAKES AUTHORIZATION

J COULD BECOME A

DATE OF AUTHORIZATION June 14, 1977

T														

)¢ CHECK and Book of Sweepstakes Tickets on or about . . .
ckets within a few days to qualify for a
)O-A-Day (up to $10,OOO) in addition to
,OOO.OO cash.

In the event you are chosen as the Grand Prize winner, Reader's Digest hereby authorizes:

IK

le to:

LEAN JR.

$1,OOO.OO-A-DAY BONUS AWARD
$5O,OOO.OO CASH—OR—
$25,OOO.OO CASH NOW, PLUS
$1OO.OO A MONTH FOR LIFE
15,216 OTHER PRIZES—ALL GIVEN AWAY!

Despite Lowell's personal hatred for politics and distaste for Negroes, he wrote some of the most memorable political and anti-slavery poems in our literature. It is true that Lowell's post-war prominence and growing conservatism reduced his responsiveness to the ethical lapses of his society and its leaders, but he could still—in Jeremiah's vein—turn his countrymen pale with a series of devastating outbursts on his 1874 return from overseas.

Longfellow husbanded his reputation with as much care as did the lesser poets; yet he dared publish, at the most unpropitious moment, an indignant volume with the word "slavery" in its very title, and a number of major pro-Catholic poems in the midst of his readers' anti-Catholic hysteria. In his own most anti-Indian mood, right after the Custer massacre, he could still blame his public and its government for the tragedy.

Bryant was as fierce in his "spread-eagle" Americanism as were any of his lesser colleagues, but he did not feel it necessary to prove his loyalty by ignoring the ethical sores that covered the land he loved; on the contrary, he watched like a sentry for every sign of moral disease, and at once raised the alarm—more often in prose, but occasionally in lofty passages of verse against predatory war, against mob violence, against the idea of slavery.

Despite his alienation from America, his increasing hopelessness, and his conviction that poets should *know* evil rather than fight it, Melville offered America an urgent admonitory image of itself. In the very hour of his countrymen's centenary pride, he issued a crushing jeremiad against Anglo-Saxon crime. This he could do despite his fear that no one would listen, and despite his knowledge of the wrath that would descend upon him if, by some miracle, his grim truths *were* heard out. He remembered well the penalty imposed upon him by America for having written *Mardi* instead of an exotic entertainment, but this did not dissuade him from the herculean labor of creating *Clarel.*

Whitman, clinging persistently to the tenet that he was the poet of both evil and good, and that he would condemn nothing, was nevertheless far from the "superficial innocence of evil"[54] of which Yeats accuses him. In spite of himself, and in spite of his overriding concern for the existence of the Union, from time to time the rage within him reached the bursting point; at such moments he was impelled to execrate the monstrosities of Washington, Boston, and the slave-driving, ruffian-spawning South. His low opinion of Negroes did not exclude them from his universal embrace, as is evidenced in many kindly passages; his dislike for the fanaticism of the abolitionists did not keep him from outroaring them in his prose and in some of his early poems; in the same way, his insistence on seeing only the beauty of America did not hold back his anger at the execution of the Haymarket anarchists in 1886 while almost all other poets were silent.

Though Thoreau cherished his freedom more than any other poet, it was he who insisted on being imprisoned when the actions of his government maddened him. Though he hated crowds more than any other poet, he summoned them again and again to make the reality of their world detestable to them and recall the manliness of a Concord they had betrayed. Though he had no patience for newspapers while there were eternities to be read, Thoreau studied the daily reports mercilessly, year after year, with the expectancy of a hero awaiting his clarion call.

Here, then, is the core of our findings. The greatest

souls of the century were most desirous of rising above partisan issues, most eager to avoid contact with the contagious meanness of their place and time. They yearned for cosmic truths and eternal values, and they wished to symbolize that disinterested largeness of spirit so scarce in any age, so potent a contrast to the dominant pettiness and self-interest of nineteenth-century America. Yet those very souls were magnetized, more than others, by the reality of ugliness around them; only *they* could fully appreciate this ugliness, thanks to the keenness and relentlessness of their sight and the violent contrast afforded by their vision of the ideal. Further, those were the only souls courageous enough to challenge the status quo, egged on by the very threat of physical penalties which cowed lesser spirits.

This was the dramatic dichotomy and lifelong tension demonstrated in almost all areas of ethical concern: though they shunned the commonplace, on no other battleground could their greatness be meaningfully gauged. Thus, at almost every zero hour, when most of the minor poets were swayed or silent, these larger spirits emerged magnificently to betray their anchorite vows, surmounting personal limitations and hesitations in order to serve as the inspired instruments of truth.

Notes

Introduction

1. In the first half of this chapter, aside from those separately noted, there are quotations from the following works: Baudelaire's "At One O'Clock in the Morning"; Blake's "London"; Browning's "The Lost Leader"; Burns' "The Holy Fair," "Scots Wha Hae," "For A' That"; Byron's *Don Juan* (Dedication and Canto III) and "The Vision of Judgment"; Chaucer's "Lak of Stedfastnesse"; Coleridge's *Biographia Literaria* and "Religious Musings"; Crabbe's "The Village"; Dante's *Paradiso* (Cantos XXV and XXII); Horace's "The Art of Poetry"; Jeffers' "Night"; Jonson's "Of Judging Poets and Poetry"; Keats' "Written on the Day that Mr. Leigh Hunt Left Prison," "To My Brother George," "Isabella," "The Fall of Hyperion"; Lorca's "Ode to Walt Whitman"; Mayakovsky's "The Cloud in Trousers," "Conversation With a Tax Collector"; Milton's "On the same," "On the new forcers of Conscience under the Long Parliament," "On the Lord General Fairfax"; Morris' "The Day is Coming"; Poe's "Dream-Land," "A Dream Within a Dream," "The Poetic Principle"; Pushkin's "The Prophet"; Rilke's "The Poet"; Rimbaud's "A Season in Hell"; Shakespeare's *A Midsummer Night's Dream* (V, i) and *Richard II* (II, i); Shelley's "A Defense of Poetry," "To Wordsworth," "The Mask of Anarchy"; Sidney's An Apology for Poetry"; Stevens' "Asides

on the Oboe"; Swinburne's "A Song in Time of Order: 1852"; Tennyson's "Locksley Hall"; Williams' "Smell!"; Wordsworth's "Ode: Intimations of Immortality," "Expostulation and Reply," "London, 1802," "Written in London, September, 1802"; Yevtushenko's "Later," "The Knights."

2. "An Apology for Poetry": ". . . as if they took a medicine of cherries . . ."

3. "The Figure a Poem Makes": "It begins in delight and ends in wisdom."

4. *Volpone,* Prologue: "To mix profit with your pleasure."

5. Preface to the Second Edition of *Lyrical Ballads.*

6. "Epilogue": ". . . if the smack is sour,/The better for the embittered hour."

7. Matthew Arnold, "To a Friend."

8. Eliot, "Tradition and the Individual Talent."

9. Lawrence, "Whitman," *Studies in Classic American Literature.*

10. *New York Times,* Dec. 21, 1964; Jan. 10, 1965.

11. It must be noted, however, that few Americans chose to translate Heine's political verse.

12. Philip P. Cooke, "The Power of the Bards," *Froissart Ballads and Other Poems* (Philadelphia, 1847), p. 175.

13. Henry D. Thoreau, "Greece," *Collected Poems,* ed. C. Bode (Chicago, 1943), p. 218.

14. Richard W. Gilder, "When the True Poet Comes," *Five Books of Song* (New York, 1900), p. 128.

15. Sidney Lanier, "Psalm of the West," *Poems* (New York, 1897), pp. 116–17.

16. Edna D. Proctor, "Robert Burns," *Complete Poetical Works* (Boston, 1925), p. 359.

17. "No Earnest Work That Will Expand the Frame," *op. cit.,* p. 191.

18. "John Endicott," Prologue, *Complete Poetical Works* (Boston, 1893), p. 466.

19. "The Ghost-Seer," *Complete Poetical Works* (Boston, 1917), p. 85.

20. Lanier, "Ode to the Johns Hopkins University," *op. cit.,* p. 111.

21. "The Poet of To-Day," *Poems* (Boston, 1851), p. 177.

22. "The Freedmen of the Mississippi Valley," *Poems and Essays* (Boston, 1886), p. 445.

23. "The Rusty Man," *Works* (London, 1924), XVI, 412.

24. "The Death of Schiller," *Poetical Works* (New York, 1878), p. 264.

25. "Song of the Open Road," "The Sleepers," "By Blue Ontario's Shore," *Leaves of Grass,* ed. E. Holloway (New York, 1954), pp. 123, 355, 290.

26. Ambrose Bierce, *Letters,* ed. B. C. Pope (San Francisco, 1922), p. 52.

27. "Walt Whitman," *A Book of Verses* (Chicago, 1898), p. 129.

28. "The Elements and Functions of Poetry," *American Poetry and Poetics,* ed. D. G. Hoffman (Garden City, 1962), p. 439.
29. "An After-Dinner Poem," *Poetical Works* (Boston, 1895), p. 65.
30. "Romans in Dorset," *Happy Ending* (Boston, 1927), p. 18.
31. "Clarel," Part II, Canto XXXIV; Part IV, Canto XXII, *op. cit.,* XIV, 314; XV, 251.
32. "I Took My Power in My Hand," *Complete Poems,* ed. T. H. Johnson (Boston, 1960), p. 263.
33. "Epicedium," *Poetical Works* (Boston, 1883), p. 239.
34. "William Cullen Bryant," *Later Poems* (Boston, 1905), p. 69.
35. "These Songs Will Perish," "To William Watson," *The Man With the Hoe* (New York, 1899), pp. 134, 58.
36. "The Lyric I," *Words for the Hour* (Boston, 1857), p. 6.
37. "On the Nature of Poetry," *Prose Writings,* ed. Parke Godwin (New York, 1884), I, 12.
38. "The Phantom Leaders," *Poetical Works* (Philadelphia, 1881), I, 350.
39. "Giles Corey," *op. cit.,* p. 511.
40. "The Men of Old," *Complete Poetical Works* (Boston, 1894), p. 370.
41. "The Daguerrotype," *Poems* (Boston, 1901), p. 103.
42. "The Men of Old," *op. cit.,* p. 370.
43. "To Lamartine," *op. cit.,* p. 101.
44. "The Birthplace of Robert Burns," *Poems* (Portland, Me., 1906), p. 81.
45. "By Blue Ontario's Shore," *op. cit.,* p. 285.
46. "Zola," *Collected Poems* (New York, 1944), p. 85.
47. "The Poet," "Merlin," *Works* (Boston, [c. 1903, 1918]), III, 32; IX, 120.
48. "The New Ezekiel," *Poems* (Boston, 1889), II, 14–15.
49. "For the Meeting of the Burns Club," *op. cit.,* p. 138.
50. "By Blue Ontario's Shore," *op. cit.,* p. 285.
51. "Vorwarts, Bruder! Vorwarts!" "Tyrtaeus," *Liberator,* Nov. 14, 7, 1845.
52. "Vale! America," *Poetical Works* (New York, 1923), p. 336.
53. "Away! Away! Away! Away!" *op. cit.,* p. 54.
54. "To Benjamin Lundy," *Songs of the Free,* ed. M. W. Chapman (Boston, 1836), p. 126.
55. "War and Hell," *Swords and Ploughshares* (New York, 1902), pp. 23–24.
56. Thoreau, "Away! Away! . . ." *op. cit.,* p. 55.
57. "Merlin," early draft, *op. cit.,* IX, 441n.
58. "The Rusty Man," *op. cit.,* XVI, 412.
59. "I Seek the Present Time," *op. cit.,* pp. 165–66.
60. "Io Victis!" *Poems* (Boston, 1886), II, 178.
61. "Dante," *op. cit.,* p. 148.
62. Christopher P. Cranch, "The Poet," *Poems* (Philadelphia, 1844), p. 40.

63. "Visitation Day Hymn, 1847," quoted by Anna M. Wells, *Dear Preceptor* (Boston, 1963), p. 54.
64. "Sonnets: XV," *op. cit.,* p. 22.
65. Lazarus, "On the Proposal to Erect a Monument in England to Lord Byron," *op. cit.,* I, 154.
66. "Young Sammy's First Wild Oats," *A Hermit of Carmel* (New York, 1901), p. 209.
67. "L'Envoi," *op. cit.,* p. 108.
68. "War is Kind: XII, XXII," *Collected Poems,* ed. W. Follett (New York, 1930), pp. 91, 102.
69. "An Ode in Time of Hesitation," *op. cit.,* pp. 17–18.
70. *Spoon River Anthology* (New York, 1915), p. 78.
71. "Sonnet," "Zola," *op. cit.,* pp. 93, 85.
72. "Ezekiel," *op. cit.,* pp. 423–24.
73. [Edgar L. Masters], "Ballad of Jesus of Nazareth," *The Blood of the Prophets* (Chicago, 1905), p. 39.
74. "A Friend's Greeting," *op. cit.,* p. 207.
75. "To Abolitionists," *Anti-Slavery Poems* (Boston, 1843), p. 46.
76. "Ballad of Jesus of Nazareth," *op. cit.,* p. 24.
77. "Prometheus," *op. cit.,* p. 185.
78. "Fragments of an Unfinished Poem," *Poems* (Little Rock, 1900), p. 477.
79. "The Singer," *op. cit.,* II, 405–08.
80. "A Footnote to a Famous Lyric," "The Cherry Bough," *op. cit.,* pp. 103, 70–71.
81. "Much Madness is Divinest Sense," *op. cit.,* p. 209.
82. "Sonnet," *Liberty Bell,* 1843, p. 68.
83. "The World," *Journal of the Knights of Labor,* Oct. 25, 1894.
84. James F. Clarke, translation of Goethe's "Epilogue to Schiller's Song of the Bell," quoted by J. W. Thomas, *James Freeman Clarke* (Boston, 1949), p. 70.
85. Thomas N. Page, "The Poet on Agradina," *The Coast of Bohemia* (New York, 1906), p. 26.
86. George S. Jackson, *Early Songs of Uncle Sam* (Boston, 1933), p. 124.
87. *Life and Letters,* ed. J. T. Morse, Jr. (Boston, 1896), I, 296.
88. "Great Are the Myths," *op. cit.,* p. 466.
89. Samuel T. Pickard, *Life of John Greenleaf Whittier* (Boston, 1894), pp. 617–18.

Chapter 1: War With Mexico

1. Philip Graham, ed. *Early Texas Verse (1835–50)* (Chapel Hill, 1936), pp. xii, xiv.
2. *Poems* (New York, 1853), II, 168–70.
3. Graham, pp. 3–5.

4. William H. Wharton, "Ben Milam," *Poems of American History*, ed. B. E. Stevenson (Boston, 1908), p. 355.

5. "The Santa Fe Prisoners," "Remember the Alamo," *National Songs, Ballads, and Other Patriotic Poetry*, ed. W. M'Carty (Philadelphia, 1846), pp. 107–08.

6. Albert F. McLean, Jr. *William Cullen Bryant* (New York, 1964), p. 41.

7. "Our Country," *Poetical Works* (London, 1850), pp. 220–22.

8. "The Mississippi," *Three Hours* (Philadelphia, 1848), pp. 175, 179.

9. William H. C. Hosmer, "Song of Texas," *Poetical Works* (New York, 1854), II, 154.

10. *Liberator*, May 3, 1844.

11. "Texas," "The World's Convention," *Complete Poetical Works* (Boston, 1894), pp. 291–92, 286.

12. "To the Future," *Complete Poetical Works* (Boston, 1917), p. 65.

13. "The Arsenal at Springfield," *Complete Poetical Works* (Boston, 1893), p. 56.

14. *Liberator*, May 31, 1844.

15. "The Decay of a People," *op. cit.*, p. 168.

16. *Liberator*, April 26, 1844. The motto does not appear in his *Works*.

17. *Ibid.*, April 26, May 17, 1844.

18. "A Rhymed Lesson," *Complete Poetical Works* (Boston, 1895), p. 63.

19. "The Thriving Family," *op. cit.*, p. 195.

20. "Champions of Liberty," *Poems* (New York, [c. 1860]), p. 169.

21. George S. Jackson, ed. *Early Songs of Uncle Sam* (Boston, 1933), p. 36.

22. "Taylor on the Rio Grande," "War," "A War Song for the Texan Volunteers," "To the Battle," M'Carty, pp. 5–6, 64, 12–13, 50.

23. *Ibid.*, pp. 110, 50.

24. William H. Lytle, "The Siege of Chapultepec," Stevenson, p. 371.

25. "The Empire of the West," Jackson, p. 37.

26. "A War Song," "The Union's Call," M'Carty, pp. 12–13, 110.

27. "Arm On! Arm On! Ye Brave and Free," *op. cit.*, p. 123.

28. "Buena Vista," "When California was a Foreign Land," *Poems* (Little Rock, 1900), pp. 177–83, 357–59.

29. "Our Country," M'Carty, p. 128.

30. "To Arms," Stevenson, p. 362.

31. "The Rio Grande," M'Carty, p. 70.

32. "Fling Out That Starry Banner," *op. cit.*, p. 153.

33. "War Song," M'Carty, p. 46.

34. "The Fallen Brave of Mexico," "Champions of Liberty," "The Soldier's Welcome Home," *op. cit.*, pp. 166, 169, 184–85.

35. Stevenson, pp. 368–69.

36. "Buena Vista," *op. cit.*, pp. 182-83.

37. "Independence Ode," *op. cit.*, p. 160.
38. "The Day of the Three Fights," *Poems* (New York, 1867), II, 155–60.
39. "To the Battle," M'Carty, p. 50.
40. "Captain May," *op. cit.*, p. 136.
41. "The Volunteer in Mexico," "The Day of the Three Fights," *op. cit.*, pp. 141, 155–60.
42. *Boy's Book of Battle Lyrics* (New York, 1885), pp. 156–59.
43. "To the Battle," M'Carty, p. 50.
44. *Poems* (Philadelphia, 1873), pp. 196, 182–83, 181–82, 219–21, 184–86. Hoffman's notes reveal a close reading of the current press. He discusses the reported migration of "millions of vultures swooping southward"—which had not been connected with "news of the bloody field of Buena Vista"—as in fact "the fearful augury of a great battle or raging pest in Mexico." He incorporates in "Buena Vista" the details of an officer's letter which had appeared in the *Knickerbocker.*
45. *Views and Reviews in American Literature, History and Fiction,* ed. C. H. Holman (Cambridge, 1962), pp. 62–63.
46. *Lays of the Palmetto* (Charleston, 1848), introduction.
47. Vernon L. Parrington, *Main Currents in American Thought* (New York, 1930), II, 125–27.
48. "Churubusco," "War Song of the Palmetto Regiment," "The Gathering," "The Welcome of Carolina to the Palmetto Regiment," "The Call to Arms," "Oh! Stern was the Voice of that Anguish," "The March to Alvarado," "Our Place Within the Picture," "The Palmetto Flag in Battle," "Welcome to the Chief," "Palo Alto and Resaca de la Palma," *op. cit.*, pp. 22–23, 11–12, 10, 6–7, 9, 32, 14, 17, 27, 39, 40–41.
49. "The Battle of Contreras," "The Widow of the Warrior," "And What, When His Country," "Oh! Stern Was the Voice . . .," "The Return of the Palmettos," *ibid.*, pp. 19, 28, 29, 32, 34–35.
50. "The City of the Silent," "Ballad," *Poems,* I, 328–48; II, 183.
51. Emory Holloway, *Free and Lonesome Heart* (New York, 1960), p. 159.
52. "By Blue Ontario's Shore," *Leaves of Grass,* ed. E. Holloway (New York, 1954), p. 290.
53. *The Gathering of the Forces,* eds. C. Rodgers and J. Black (New York, 1920), I, 240–43, 245–48, 252–54, 257, 261, 263.
54. "The War for Slavery," "Plea for Peace," "A Knightly Portrait," "National Anti-Slavery Hymn," *Liberator,* Feb. 12, 1847; June 19, 1846; Nov. 12, 1847; July 17, 1846.
55. "New England," *Poems, Second Series* (Boston, 1847), p. 3.
56. "To My Country," *Poetry of Life* (Boston, 1848), pp. 154–55.
57. "Stanzas," *Liberator,* March 26, 1847. This is signed "Lynn Bard," which Allibone identifies as a pseudonym for Alonzo Lewis.
58. "Justice: an Ode," *Poems of Religion and Society* (New York, 1848), p. 97.

59. *Plays and Poems* (Philadelphia, 1883), II, 284–86. This poem was completed in July, 1848. A large group of poems sympathetic to Spain indicates no Anglo-Saxonism in Boker's thinking.
60. *Op. cit.,* p. 21. This 1850 volume includes 1846 and later poems. The poem quoted here does not appear in Mrs. Sigourney's 1844 collection.
61. *Songs of the Sea* (Boston, 1847), pp. 121–22.
62. Joseph E. Chamberlin, *The Boston Transcript* (Boston, 1930), p. 95.
63. *Op. cit.,* p. 206.
64. *Op. cit.,* p. 105.
65. *Views and Reviews,* pp. 62–63.
66. James Kennard, Jr., "Lines," *Liberator,* May 7, 1847.
67. *Poems* (Boston, 1851), pp. 109–11.
68. Tappan, "Fill Up!" *op. cit.,* p. 276.
69. "The Song of the Earth," *op. cit.,* pp. 284–86.
70. Lewis, "Anti-Slavery Ode," *Liberator,* May 7, 1847.
71. "Love and Be Kind," *Froissart Ballads and Other Poems* (Philadelphia, 1847), pp. 206–07.
72. *Poems* (Boston, 1851), pp. 69–73.
73. *Poem, delivered before the Phi Beta Kappa Society, August 27, 1846* (Boston, 1846), p. 9.
74. "Progress," *Poems* (Boston, 1875), pp. 242–43; poem dated July, 1846.
75. "Rise!" *Liberator,* Dec. 10, 1847.
76. *The Writings of Margaret Fuller,* ed. M. Wade (New York, 1941), pp. 426–27, 470.
77. "Fragments," *Liberty Bell,* 1847, p. 115. Adams' publisher admits (*op. cit.,* p. v) that his "collection . . . is . . . incomplete," but does not explain the omission of this widely circulated, major declaration. One cannot overlook the fact that the posthumous poems were issued at the height of General Taylor's election campaign.
78. Tappan, "I Am For Peace," *op. cit.,* pp. 194–96.
79. "Religion and Politics," *Liberty Bell,* 1849, pp. 286–90.
80. "Plea for Peace," *Liberator,* June 19, 1846.
81. "Justice . . . ," *op. cit.,* p. 97.
82. *Poems* (Boston, 1864), pp. 169–70.
83. P. 281; letter of October 25, 1847.
84. Homer F. Barnes, *Charles Fenno Hoffman* (New York, 1930), pp. 267–68.
85. *American Renaissance* (New York, 1941), p. 382.
86. L. S. Mansfield, "Melville's Comic Articles on Zachary Taylor," *American Literature,* IX (January, 1938), 411-18. Matthiessen turns out to be wrong on several basic points: a) The "hearty series" (which Mansfield, p. 418, more accurately calls "hastily written hack work") was written *not* "in the summer after the Mexican War" but in the very thick of it; b) Only the first and fourth letters *might* be in-

terpreted as reflecting "enthusiasm" for the General, and even they include obviously vulnerable material "given straight."

87. "Mardi," *Works* (London, 1922), IV, 245. For a brief discussion of contemporary reactions see Mentor L. Williams, "Park Benjamin on Melville's 'Mardi,'" *American Notes and Queries,* VIII (December, 1949), 132–34.

88. *Journals,* ed. O. Shepard (Boston, 1938), p. 183; dated July 4, 1846.

89. John Bigelow, *William Cullen Bryant* (Boston, 1890), pp. 151, 339.

90. McLean, p. 106.

91. *Poetical Works* (New York, 1878), pp. 309–11.

92. *Ibid.,* pp. 229–31, 292–95.

93. Russell Blankenship, *American Literature as an Expression of the National Mind* (New York, 1949), p. 338.

94. Samuel Longfellow, *The Life of Henry W. Longfellow* (Boston, 1891), II, 39, 42, 92.

95. "Tegner's Drapa," *op. cit.,* pp. 111–12.

96. "Victor Galbraith," *ibid.,* p. 193. This long period of gestation is repeated for his Civil War sonnet, "A Nameless Grave," produced in 1874, ten years after he received the newspaper clipping on which it is based.

97. Matthiessen, p. 8.

98. "The Apology," "Merlin," *Works* (Boston, [c. 1918]), IX, 119, 122.

99. Alcott, *op. cit.,* p. 183; journal entry for July 25, 1846.

100. *Journals,* eds. E. W. Emerson and W. E. Forbes (Boston, 1912), VII, 219–23.

101. "Ode: Inscribed to W. H. Channing," *op. cit.,* pp. 76–77.

102. *Op. cit.,* p. 196; entry for March, 1847: "I don't like to have merchants and politicians find refuge from their own duplicity under his broad shield. Let him send them swift, with glaring eyes, to the horns of the altar of justice . . ."

103. *Journals,* VII, 201.

104. Quoted by Philip L. Nicoloff, *Emerson on Race and History* (New York, 1961), p. 24.

105. *Journals,* VII, 206, 149; *Works,* IX, 428n, 123.

106. "Walden," *Writings* (Boston, 1893), II, 355–61, 512.

107. *Ibid.,* X, 137–38, 149, 165–66; Alcott's journal entry for Jan. 26, 1848, reports a Thoreau lecture at the Lyceum on that date which must be at least a preliminary version of "Civil Disobedience." (*op. cit.,* p. 201.)

108. "What the Voice Said," "Worship," "The Pine Tree," "To a Southern Statesman," "The Branded Hand," "Lines From a Letter to a Young Clerical Friend," *op. cit.,* pp. 424–25, 429–30, 293–98, 300.

109. *Ibid.,* pp. 302–03.

110. "The Angels of Buena Vista," *ibid.,* pp. 35–36.

111. *Ibid.,* pp. 308–10.
112. "To the Past," "To the Future," *op. cit.,* pp. 63–64.
113. *Ibid.,* pp. 80–82. Similar in theme and tone, this poem also shares with "The Biglow Papers" references to editor Buckingham, Hosea's "Buckenam" or "Buckinum."
114. "An Extract," "The Falconer," *Liberty Bell,* 1848, pp. 180–83; 1846, pp. 241–44. T. M. Smith, in *Uncollected Poems of Lowell* (Philadelphia, 1950), p. xviii, wrongly dates the composition of "An Extract" in "1848 at the close of the Mexican War." The *Liberator* had already reprinted it in early January, 1848.
115. *Op. cit.,* p. 366.
116. *Poetical Works,* p. 166; letter to T. Hughes, *Biglow's* British editor.
117. "The Biglow Papers, First Series," *ibid.,* pp. 188, 182, 186, 202, 187, 177, 196, 185, 195, 187, 189, 188, 202, 213, 209, 214.
118. Justin H. Smith, "The Biglow Papers as an Argument Against the Mexican War," *Proceedings of the Massachusetts Historical Society,* XLV (May, 1912), p. 610.
119. "Ode," "The Ghost-Seer," *Poetical Works,* pp. 12, 85.
120. Brander Matthews, "American Satires in Verse," *Harper's Monthly,* CIX (July, 1904), pp. 296, 299.
121. Justin H. Smith, pp. 611, 610, 602–03.
122. In "A Rhymed Lesson," *Poetical Works,* p. 53, delivered before a largely anti-war audience in Boston on October 14, 1846, Holmes honors the fresh graves of soldiers "dead without a name" whom history shall "proclaim/Pure as the holiest . . . " Defending this poem against Lowell's severe attack, he admits his admiration for "the beauty of heroism and self-devotion which the battlefield has witnessed" even "in so poor a quarrel as we are engaged in." But more interestingly, he expresses "a growing hatred and disgust to this mode of settling national quarrels," and claims "some credit for not lugging in Major Ringgold and General Taylor." *Life and Letters,* ed. J. T. Morse, Jr. (Boston, 1896), I, 296.

Chapter 2: The Return of Fugitive Slaves to Their Masters

1. Lorenzo Turner, *Anti-Slavery Sentiment in American Literature Prior to 1865* (Washington, 1929), pp. 70–71.
2. "Sonnet to Jesus," *Liberator,* Jan. 2, 1846; "A Sonnet for the Times," *Liberty Bell,* 1851, p. 147; "Hymn," *Liberator,* Apr. 16, 1852.
3. Quoted by Wilbur H. Siebert, *The Underground Railroad from Slavery to Freedom* (New York, 1899), p. 90. Among other significant Parker works on this issue are his 1843 "Socrates in Boston," published in the *Liberty Bell,* and his great Thanksgiving Day sermon of 1850, "The State of the Nation."

4. "The Weekly Contribution," "Fugitive Slaves Shall Be Returned," "Connecticut," *Liberator,* Dec. 27, 1839; Jan. 31, June 26, 1840; "Sonnet," *Liberty Bell,* 1841, p. 100. For her attitude on this issue see Larry Gara, *The Liberty Line* (Lexington, Ky., 1961), pp. 75–76.

5. "To Benjamin Lundy," "To the Memory of the Same," "To Isaac T. Hopper," 'Liberty and Slavery," *Sonnets and Other Poems* (Boston, 1843), pp. 48, 49, 77, 75; also see "O'Connell's Appeal to His Pro-Slavery Countrymen in America," *Liberator,* Dec. 8, 1843, and "The Triumph of Freedom," *Liberty Bell,* 1845, pp. 192–93.

6. "The Stars and Stripes," *Liberty Bell,* 1858, pp. 122–85. She does attempt a lyrical response to an actual slave escape, and "The Fugitives' Prayer," though somewhat hackneyed in tone and phrase, deserves attention for its prominence in the play, pp. 151–53.

7. *The Duty of Disobedience to the Fugitive Slave Act* (Boston, 1860), pp. 5, 12. Among the best of the narrative poems are Susan Wilson's "The Fugitives in Boston" and Martha Hempstead's "The Fugitive," *Liberty Bell,* 1844, pp. 200–08; 1845, pp. 209–14.

8. "The Fugitive Slave to the Christian," *The Garland of Freedom,* ed. W. Armistead (London, 1853), p. 53.

9. "American Union," "Fugitive Slave's Song," *Liberator,* Mar. 19, 1852; July 9, 1858.

10. "Hide the Outcasts," *Autographs for Freedom,* ed. J. Griffiths (Boston, 1853), pp. 29–31.

11. "The Fugitive," "Song of the Freed," *Liberator,* July 29, Sept. 16, 1842. Both poems are signed "E. D. H." Other regionally prominent activists who write well are Alonzo Lewis, Charles List, and Isaac H. Julian.

12. *The Branded Hand* (Pawtucket, 1845), introduction.

13. *Liberator,* Apr. 30, 1852.

14. *Thrice Through the Furnace* (Pawtucket, 1852), pp. 3–4.

15. Fugitive slave poems by this group appear in the *Liberator* on the following dates: F. M. ADLINGTON: Sept. 1, 1843; Oct. 10, 1845; Nov. 14, 1851; Aug. 11, 1854; G. W. BUNGAY: May 10, Sept. 13, 1850; Feb. 28, Apr. 4, May 30, 1851; Oct. 22, 1852; Feb. 4, Nov. 25, 1853; Feb. 17, 1854; June 4, 1858; CARRIE: June 20, 1851; July 30, 1852; May 27, 1853; June 30, July 7, 1854; July 31, 1857; Apr. 16, 1858; Mar. 11, Apr. 8, July 22, 1859; F. D. GAGE: July 12, 1850; Jan. 9, 23, 1852; Aug. 5, 1853; E. R. PLACE: Apr. 19, 1850; Mar. 7, Dec. 12, 1851; Oct. 13, 1854; G. W. PUTNAM: Nov. 1, Dec. 6, 1850; Jan. 17, Apr. 25, 1851; Jan. 2, 1852; June 23, 1854; Feb. 2, June 8, 1855; Mar. 14, 1856; Aug. 26, 1859; H. N. SPOONER ("OLD COLONY"): July 6, 13, 1849; Apr. 5, 19, May 24, June 7, 1850; Mar. 19, Dec. 17, 1852; Aug. 19, Sept. 9, 1853; June 30, July 28, 1854.

16. "George B. Cheever," *ibid.,* June 4, 1858.

17. Pennsylvania *Freeman,* June 26, 1852. A reader had asked for her feelings on the 1850 Law. Her reply, quoted above, is followed by the militant stanzas of her "Address to the Northmen."

18. Ruth E. Finley, *The Lady of Godey's* (Philadelphia, 1931), pp. 175–76.

19. "New England," *Songs of the Free,* ed. M. W. Chapman (Boston, 1836), p. 43; "Song. September, 1852," *Poetical Works* (Boston, 1859), II, 385–86.

20. "To the Morning Star," *The North Star,* ed. J. G. Whittier (Philadelphia, 1840), p. 9; "Gelon of Syracuse," "Fragments," *Liberty Bell,* 1842, pp. 142-43; 1847, p. 114.

21. "Ode," *Freeman,* Aug. 22, 1839, and editor's note.

22. "The Union," "King Cotton," *Poems* (New York, [c. 1860]), pp. 217, 230–31.

23. "Independence Ode," "Webster," *Poetical Works* (New York, 1854), II, 166, 222. Other Webster poems include H. T. Tuckerman's "On a Bust of Webster," *Poems* (Boston, 1851), p. 156, and T. W. Parsons' "On the Death of Webster," *Poems* (Portland, Me., 1906), pp. 62–64. That Whittier's "Ichabod" represents a distinctly minority reaction is demonstrated by H. D. Foster, "Webster's Seventh of March Speech and the Secession Movement, 1850," *American Historical Review,* XXXVII (July, 1932), 723–50.

24. *Songs of the Free,* pp. 49–50, 74, 138–40, 206. G. S. Haight claims, however, that abolition had "surprisingly little effect" on her: *The Sweet Singer of Hartford* (New Haven, 1930), p. 170.

25. "The Thriving Family," *Poems* (London, 1850), pp. 194–95.

26. *Poems* (New York, 1860), pp. 106–07, 119–21, 125–26.

27. "Rise!" *Liberator,* Dec. 10, 1847; "France is Free!" *Lays and Ballads* (Philadelphia, 1849), pp. 65–66.

28. *Poetical Works* (Philadelphia, 1881), I, 178; II, 239–40.

29. L. R. Harley, *Confessions of a Schoolmaster* (Philadelphia, 1914), p. 123.

30. *Songs and Poems of the South* (Mobile, 1857), pp. 41–44.

31. John H. Franklin, *From Slavery to Freedom* (New York, 1956), p. 259.

32. Henry Timrod, *Uncollected Poems,* ed. E. W. Parks (Athens, Ga., 1942), p. 85 and note.

33. Jay B. Hubbell, *The South in American Literature, 1607–1900* (Durham, 1954), pp. 293–96, 310.

34. Paul H. Hayne, "Ode," *Poems* (Boston, 1882) p. 10; delivered Feb. 10, 1856.

35. "The Hireling and the Slave," *Selected Poems* (New York, 1907), pp. 42, 46, 72.

36. V. L. Parrington, *Main Currents in American Thought* (New York, 1930), II, 106, 108.

37. "The Slave of Guadaloupe," *Liberator,* Oct. 25, 1844.

38. "The Heart of the People," "Daniel Webster," *ibid.,* Apr. 4, 1851; Mar. 29, 1850.

39. *Neighbor Jackwood* (Boston, 1857).

40. *Life and Letters,* eds. M. Hansen-Taylor and H. E. Scudder (Boston, 1885), I, 372–74.

41. [E. C. W.] "Idiot Era," *Liberty Bell,* 1848, p. 163.

42. *Poetical Writings* (New York, 1845). "The Jewish Captive," based on Psalm 137, may pertain indirectly to the fugitive slave furore.

43. *Liberty Bell,* 1848, pp. 51, 53; *Life and Letters,* I, 173; *The American Legend* (Cambridge, 1850), p. 26.

44. *Unpublished Letters,* ed. J. R. Schultz (San Marino, 1937), introduction.

45. *Autobiography, Diary and Correspondence* (Boston, 1891), p. 166.

46. "Letter from America to a Friend in Tuscany," *op. cit.,* p. 129.

47. "The Fairer Land," *Poetical Works,* II, 79–81.

48. John Bigelow, *William Cullen Bryant* (Boston, 1890), p. 102.

49. Mary A. Wyman, *Two American Pioneers* (New York, 1927), pp. 127, 142.

50. *Ibid.,* p. 216. It was Mrs. Oakes-Smith who sent the letter. Mrs. Wyman quotes Phillips' acknowledgment.

51. "Rhymes," *Complete Poetical Works* (Boston, 1916), p. 268.

52. *Poetical Works* (Philadelphia, 1836), pp. 93–94.

53. *Poems* (Boston, 1873), pp. 3–12; see especially Sections III and V.

54. "The New Ginevra," *Liberator,* June 10, 1859.

55. *Poems* (Boston, 1851), pp. 80–82.

56. *Poems* (Philadelphia, 1841), pp. 201–02, 149, 118, 95–97, 160–63.

57. William B. Tappan, *Poetry of Life* (Boston, 1848), pp. 125–26, 48–49.

58. "To Elizabeth Barrett Browning," *Liberator,* June 24, 1853.

59. "The New Year," "To the Hopeful," *Poems* (Boston, 1855), pp. 114, 152.

60. *Poems and Essays* (Boston, 1886), pp. 445, 449–50, 323; *Liberator,* March 24, 1854. The remarkable series of political poems contradicts a biographer's assertion that "his attitude never suggests the militant zeal of Whittier." Perhaps, loving peace, "he was most himself when he chose a subject less controversial than that of slavery." (William I. Bartlett, *Jones Very, Emerson's "Brave Saint,"* Durham, 1942, p. 117). In that case the strength and number of his fugitive slave poems is even more impressive.

61. *The Bird and the Bell* (Boston, 1875), pp. 322, 287.

62. *Poems* (Boston, 1847), pp. 194, 118–21, 157.

63. *Liberty Bell,* 1842, pp. 112–13; 1843, pp. 69–70.

64. *Liberator,* June 19, 1846.

65. Henry James, *William Wetmore Story and His Friends* (Edinburgh, 1903), I, 60–63.

66. *Journals,* ed. O. Shepard (Boston, 1938), pp. 190, 186, 188, 188n, and important disunion comments on p. 200.

67. Sonnets XXIV, XXVI, XXII, XIV, *Sonnets and Canzonets* (Boston, 1882).

68. George Santayana, "The Elements and Functions of Poetry," *American Poetry and Poetics,* ed. D. G. Hoffman (Garden City, 1962), p. 439. Higginson's memorable account in *Cheerful Yesterdays* (Boston, 1898), pp. 157–58, concludes: "under the circumstances, neither Plato nor Pythagoras could have done the thing better."

69. *Liberator,* May 2, Dec. 5, 19, 1851; Jan. 2, 1852.

70. "To Henry," *Near Home* (Boston, 1858), p. 6.

71. "Verses for A. S. W. (During the Fugitive Slave Agitation in Boston)," *Collected Poems,* ed. John M. Moran (Hartford, 1964), pp. 18, 107n.

72. "America," *Poems Read at the Opening of the Fraternity Lectures, 1858–1859* (Boston, 1859), pp. 19–20, 22, 25–28.

73. Maud H. Elliot and Laura E. Richards, *Julia Ward Howe* (Boston, 1915), I, 151, 168, 176–77.

74. "A Protest from Italy," *Passion Flowers* (Boston, 1854), pp. 42–43.

75. "Slave Eloquence," *Words for the Hour* (Boston, 1857), pp. 25–26.

76. "The First Martyr," "The Question," *Later Lyrics* (Boston, 1866), pp. 13–14, 22–23.

77. *Anti-Slavery Poems* (Boston, 1843), pp. 29–33, 34–38.

78. "Hymn for the First of August," *ibid.,* pp. 51–52; "The Chase," *Liberty Bell,* 1843, pp. 111–16; "Hymn," *Liberator,* August 4, 1843.

79. "The Prisoner," "Ode: The Kidnapping of Sims," *Liberator,* Oct. 25, 1850; April 16, 1852 (reprinted in above-quoted report of Sims anniversary meeting).

80. *Discourse on the Covenant with Judas* (Boston, 1842), p. 34.

81. "Slavery Intolerance," "The Fugitive Slave Law," *Liberator,* July 26, Oct. 11, 1850. A footnote to Garrison's "The Free Mind," bravely included in *The Poets of America* (New York, [c. 1835]), p. 57, illustrates Cheever's professional valor at the height of abolition's unpopularity: "Every man who can speak, every editor who can influence the public mind, should certainly be doing all in his power to hasten . . . complete emancipation."

82. *God Against Slavery* (New York, 1857), p. iv. His greatest outbursts against the 1850 Law and the Dred Scott Decision appear on pp. 140 and 142, and on pp. 8–9 of *The Fire and Hammer of God's Word Against the Sin of Slavery* (New York, 1858). Slight references occur in the poems "1857" and "A Year of Conflicts," *Memorabilia in Verse and Prose* (New York, 1890), pp. 59, 171.

83. "To George B. Cheever," *Complete Poetical Works* (Boston, 1894), p. 198.

84. J. W. Thomas, *James Freeman Clarke* (Boston, 1949), pp. 119–20.

85. "Original Poem," *Liberator,* Jan. 9, 1857. Two fine fourteen-line similes (Alpine and river) begin and end the poem.

86. *Causes and Consequences of the Affair at Harper's Ferry* (Boston, 1859), pp. 3, 8. He calls Brown "a hero, and the martyr to a principle."

87. Anna M. Wells, *Dear Preceptor* (Boston, 1963), pp. 50–52. Miss Wells' jaundiced eye misreads the prophetic element in Higginson as "an adolescent desire to shock." His "Tyrtaeus" appears in the *Liberator,* Oct. 7, 1845; "The Fugitives' Hymn" in *Liberty Bell,* 1848, pp. 94–96. Gara (*op. cit.,* p. 77) discusses Higginson's attitude toward the underground railroad.

88. *Cheerful Yesterdays,* pp. 139–46. Howe's report of the insurrectionary address is paraphrased in Henrietta Buckmaster's *Let My People Go* (New York, 1941), p. 205.

89. Buckmaster, pp. 232–33.

90. *Liberator,* June 9, 1854.

91. *Massachusetts in Mourning* (Boston, 1854), pp. 12, 14. The sermon's theme is from Jeremiah: "Shall the iron break the Northern iron and the steel?"

92. Santayana, *op. cit.,* p. 439.

93. Francis O. Ticknor, *Poems* (Philadelphia, 1879), pp. 26, 30, 35, 50–53; Paul H. Hayne, *op. cit.,* 65–67, 83; Henry Timrod, *Uncollected Poems,* p. 104; and almost every one of his major anthologized poems.

94. Allan Nevins, *The Evening Post* (New York, 1922), pp. 246, 250, 253.

95. Bigelow, p. 81. See "The Death of Lincoln" for slavery reference.

96. Albert F. McLean, Jr., *William Cullen Bryant* (New York, 1964), p. 109.

97. "A Rhymed Lesson," "A Poem," "Birthday of Daniel Webster," "Ode for Washington's Birthday," *Poetical Works* (Boston, 1895), pp. 49, 53, 133, 139–40, 138–39; "Latter-Day Warnings," "Avis," *ibid.,* pp. 168, 142–44.

98. F. O. Matthiessen, *American Renaissance* (New York, 1941), pp. 383, 508; Newton Arvin, *Melville* (New York, 1950), pp. 239-41. Arvin explains that Melville was "too tired."

99. "Misgivings," *Works* (London, 1924), XVI, 7.

100. Samuel Longfellow, *The Life of Henry Wadsworth Longfellow* (Boston, 1885), I, 426, 421.

101. *Complete Poetical Works* (Boston, 1893), pp. 20–23.

102. Barrett Wendell thinks Longfellow's fugitive the most "humorous example of the way in which philanthropic dreamers . . . constructed negroes," and Russell Blankenship quotes Wendell approvingly in *American Literature as an Expression of the National Mind* (New York, 1949), p. 338.

103. *Liberty Bell,* 1846, pp. 25–26.

104. *Life,* II, 162, 177, 180–84, 190, 192–95, 225–26, 241, 246–48, 300, 347. S. Longfellow (p. 247) tells how the poet sat for his portrait during the Burns case: ". . . conversation upon the recent capture of the fugitive slave brought to his . . . face a look of animation and indignation" which the painter caught. Spiller, however, as quoted

above, emphasizes the poet's aloofness; *Literary History of the United States* (New York, 1948), p. 566.

105. George F. Whicher, *This Was a Poet* (New York, 1939), pp. 200–01, 191–94.

106. *Letters,* ed. T. H. Johnson (Cambridge, 1958), I, 91, 212.

107. *Complete Poems,* ed. T. H. Johnson (Boston, 1960), pp. 40, 47, 59, 32–33.

108. *Collected Poems,* ed. C. Bode (Chicago, 1943), p. 85.

109. *The American Transcendentalists* (Garden City, 1957), p. 229.

110. "I Seek the Present Time," "Man's Little Acts . . . ," "The Hero," "Greece," "Away! Away! . . . ," "No Earnest Work . . . ," "At Midnight's Hour . . . ," "Our Country," "The Peal of the Bells," *op. cit.,* pp. 165–67, 57, 161–63, 218, 54–55, 191, 164, 135, 111.

111. "Slavery in Massachusetts," *Writings* (Boston, 1893), X, 171–73.

112. "Wait Not Till Slaves Pronounce the Word," *Poems,* pp. 198–99.

113. "Slavery in Massachusetts," p. 172.

114. "The Vessel of Love . . . ," *Poems,* p. 182.

115. "Slavery in Massachusetts," pp. 179–81.

116. "Wait Not . . . ," "Expectation," "The Hero," "My Friends . . . ," *op. cit.,* pp. 199, 188, 162, 190.

117. "A Plea for Captain John Brown," "The Last Days of John Brown," *Writings,* X, 197, 216–17, 237, 247–48.

118. "I Seek the Present Time," "Away! Away! . . . ," *op. cit.,* pp. 165, 54.

119. "Thoreau," "Fugitive Slave Law: II," "Emancipation in the British West Indies," "Fugitive Slave Law: I," "John Brown," *Works* (Boston, [c, 1932]), X, 455–56; XI, 217, 228–29, 129–35, 181, 192–94, 198–205, 271–73.

120. *Works* (Boston, [c. 1918]), IX, 76–77, 399, 166–67, 473–74, 428, 199–200, 468.

121. *Collected Prose* (Philadelphia, 1892), pp. 339–40.

122. Quoted by Emory Holloway, *Free and Lonely Heart* (New York, 1960), p. 70.

123. "I Sit and Look Out," "Starting from Paumanok," *Leaves of Grass,* ed. E. Holloway (New York, 1954), pp. 230, 19.

124. *Complete Poetry and Selected Prose and Letters,* ed. E. Holloway (London, 1938), pp. 503–04, 1087.

125. *Op. cit.,* p. 373. See Bliss Perry, *Walt Whitman* (Boston, 1906), p. 33. Although an 1842 poem, "No Turning Back," recently discovered by T. O. Mabbott, illustrates the liberal thinking of the young poet, its tame blank verse is a far cry from the slashing lines of "Blood Money." See "Walt Whitman Edits the *Sunday Times,* July, 1842–June, 1843," *American Literature,* XXXIX (March, 1967), 99–102.

126. *Free and Lonesome Heart,* p. 70.

127. *Collected Prose,* pp. 372–73.

128. *Liberator,* Nov. 22, 1850; reprinted from the *Tribune* as "The House of Friends."

129. *Complete Poetry and Selected Prose,* pp. 588, 599.
130. Gay W. Allen, *The Solitary Singer* (New York, 1960), p. 370.
131. James E. Miller, Jr., " 'Song of Myself' as Inverted Mystical Experience," and Carl F. Strauch, "The Structure of Walt Whitman's 'Song of Myself,' " *Whitman's "Song of Myself"—Origin, Growth, Meaning,* ed. J. E. Miller, Jr. (New York, 1964), pp. 139, 120.
132. "To the States," "A Boston Ballad (1854)," *Leaves of Grass,* pp. 234, 223–25.
133. Matthiessen, p. 569; Allen, p. 402.
134. Parrington, II, 366–67, 369; John B. Pickard, *John Greenleaf Whittier* (New York, 1961), p. 34.
135. E.g., Spiller, p. 565, and *Cambridge History of American Literature* (New York, 1917–21), III, 113.
136. Edwin Markham, ed. *The Book of American Poetry* (New York, 1934), p. 51.
137. "Lines," "The Cross," "Rantoul," "To Charles Sumner," "Massachusetts to Virginia," "The Sentence of John L. Brown," "The Branded Hand," "Moloch in State Street," "The Rendition," "Ichabod," "For Righteousness' Sake," "Derne," "A Sabbath Scene," "In the Evil Days," "Official Piety," "Ezekiel," *op. cit.,* pp. 170–71, 192, 193–94, 196, 286–91, 296–98, 314–16, 186, 312–18, 423.
138. "Class Poem," *Uncollected Poems,* ed. T. M. Smith (Philadelphia, 1950), pp. 231–32.
139. *Complete Poetical Works* (Boston, 1917), pp. 24–25, 14, 55, 67–68, 75, 84.
140. *Ibid.,* pp. 82–83.
141. *Liberator,* July 25, 1845.
142. *Works,* pp. 80–82, 104, 215–17, 102, 94–95.
143. "The Northern Sancho Panza and His Vicarious Cork Tree," "A Dream I Had," "A Rallying-Cry for New-England," *Uncollected Poems,* pp. 74–78, 42–44, 254–55. "On Receiving a Piece of Flax-Cotton," pp. 79–80, comments indirectly on the Sims kidnapping.
144. "A Fable for Critics," *Works,* pp. 144–45.
145. Hope J. Vernon, ed., *The Poems of Maria Lowell* (Providence, 1936), p. 33.
146. *Letters of James Russell Lowell,* ed. C. E. Norton (New York, 1894), I, 178, 188.
147. Vernon, pp. 17–18.
148. *Letters,* I, pp. 212, 261–62, 277, 298, 192.
149. Allen, pp. 401–02.
150. B. A. Botkin. *A Treasury of Southern Folklore* (New York, 1949), pp. 476–78. Of course, the fiction of Harriet Beecher Stowe, which deservedly gave her the name of "prophetess," is in a class by itself. " 'The Lord Himself wrote it,' she said afterwards many times. 'I was but an instrument in His hand,' " Forrest Wilson, *Crusader in Crinoline* (Philadelphia, 1941), p. 270. The point is that Mrs. Stowe, like many others considered in this chapter, excluded the fugitive from her verse.

Chapter 3: Mobbism Rampant

1. Clement Eaton, "Mob Violence in the Old South," *Mississippi Valley Historical Review,* XXIX (December, 1942), 352.
2. Heathcote W. Garrod, *Poetry and the Criticism of Life* (New York, 1963), pp. 8, 10.
3. "The Century and the Nation," *The Bird and the Bell* (Boston, 1875), p. 261.
4. *Liberator,* Nov. 2, 1855; on the twentieth anniversary of the Boston outrage.
5. "To George Thompson," *Songs of the Free,* ed. M. W. Chapman (Boston, 1836), p. 123.
6. "A Word to the South," *Poems* (Philadelphia, 1841), pp. 86-88.
7. "To Benjamin Lundy," *Songs of the Free,* pp. 125–26; "On Completing My Thirtieth Year," *Sonnets and Other Poems* (Boston, 1843), p. 78.
8. Merton L. Dillon, *Elijah P. Lovejoy, Abolitionist Editor* (Urbana, 1961), p. 98. John Quincy Adams is being quoted.
9. *Memoirs of the Rev. Elijah P. Lovejoy* (New York, 1838). The Boston *Recorder* excerpt is one of many anti-mob comments quoted on pp. 322–37.
10. Thomas T. Stone, *The Martyr of Freedom* (Boston, 1838), p. 4.
11. [S. S.,] "On the Death of Rev. E. P. Lovejoy," *National Enquirer,* Nov. 30, 1837.
12. E. Mack, "Dirge"; Unsigned, "Hymn"; Rev. W. H. T. Barnes, "Addressed to the Co-Workers of the Martyred Lovejoy," *Liberator,* Dec. 8, 1837; Feb. 2, 9, 1838.
13. [Helen,] "To Mrs. Lovejoy," *National Enquirer,* Jan. 18, 1838.
14. P. P. Morse, "Hymns," *Liberator,* Jan. 26, 12, 1838.
15. [B.,] "An Acrostic"; [J. H. K.,] "Lines to the Memory of Rev. Elijah P. Lovejoy," *National Enquirer,* Dec. 7, 21, 1837. The second poet is undoubtedly Joseph H. Kimball, editor of the *Herald of Freedom.*
16. J. Blanchard, "The Voice of Blood"; [S.,] "Alton, or the Doomed City," *Liberator,* Dec. 14, 1837; Oct. 2, 1840.
17. Unsigned, "The Witness Cloud," *ibid.,* Jan. 12, 1838.
18. [B.,] "The City of Blood"; [Mace,] "The Alton Riot," *ibid.,* Dec. 22, 8, 1837. "B." is probably J. Blanchard; their tone and imagery are alike.
19. *National Enquirer,* Nov. 30, 1837.
20. *Liberator,* Dec. 22, 1837.
21. "Sonnet—The Anniversary of Lovejoy's Martyrdom," *Liberty* Bell, 1839, pp. 69–70.
22. Burleigh's position is stated in a long, valuable letter to Garrison, *Liberator,* Feb. 9, 1838; Lewis' "Lovejoy" appears Dec. 8, 1837, *ibid.*

23. Of six sonnets originally in the *National Enquirer,* Nov. 30, 1837, signed "W. H. B.," four are included in his 1841 *Poems,* pp. 226–29. The others are omitted, I am sure, when Burleigh learns that the grown children of Lovejoy he addresses do not exist. A seventh sonnet, "Here rests, oh God! thy martyr!" appears in the 1841 and 1871 collections.

24. *Anti-Slavery Poems* (Boston, 1843), p. 16.

25. *St. Jonathan, The Lay of a Scald* (New York, 1838), pp. 20, 44n.

26. *Liberator,* Feb. 16, 1838.

27. Robert E. Spiller, *Literary History of the United States* (New York, 1948), I, 563–64.

28. *Autobiography, Diary and Correspondence* (Boston, 1891), pp. 222–23.

29. "Heroism," *Works* (Boston, 1903), II, 262–63, 425–26n. "Compensation" has a remarkable passage on mobs and martyrs, pp. 119–20.

30. *Poetical Works* (New York, 1878), pp. 260–61.

31. Allan Nevins, *The Evening Post* (New York, 1922), pp. 170–72.

32. *Works* (Boston, [c. 1918]), IX, 39.

33. Samuel Longfellow, *The Life of Henry Wadsworth Longfellow* (Boston, 1885), I, 267.

34. *Life and Letters,* ed. J. T. Morse, Jr. (Boston, 1896), I, 297.

35. "Class Poem," *Uncollected Poems,* ed. T. M. Smith (Philadelphia, 1950), p. 232.

36. "Stanzas for the Times," "To William Lloyd Garrison," "To the Memory of Charles B. Storrs," *Complete Poetical Works* (Boston, 1894), pp. 271, 262, 170.

37. "Address to Patrons," *National Enquirer,* Jan. 4, 1838.

38. Pennsylvania *Freeman,* July 12, 1838.

39. "The New Year," "The Relic," *op. cit.,* pp. 282–83.

40. "Pennsylvania Hall," *Liberator,* Apr. 17, 1840.

41. "The Lamp of Liberty," *Freeman,* July 5, 1838; see the issues of May 31, June 7, 21, 1838, for other poems on this outrage.

42. "The Tocsin," *op. cit.,* pp. 18, 20.

43. "Faneuil Hall, Jan. 28, 1842," *Liberator,* Feb. 4, 1842.

44. "To Cassius M. Clay," *Liberty Bell,* 1845, pp. 21–22.

45. "Sonnet," *ibid.,* 1843, p. 68.

46. *Our Country* (Allegheny, 1841), pp. 29–30, 41. See also "An Appeal to a Clerical Friend" and "Expostulation," *Poems* (Philadelphia, 1841), pp. 63–64, 224–25.

47. "Sonnet," *Liberty Bell,* 1843, p. 69.

48. John Bigelow, *William Cullen Bryant* (Boston, 1890), p. 150.

49. Edward C. Wagenknecht, *Longfellow* (New York, 1955), p. 195.

50. "Ode," "Sonnet VI," "Prometheus," *Complete Poetical Works* (Boston, 1917), pp. 13, 22, 42.

51. "Blood-Money," *Collected Prose* (Philadelphia, 1892), pp. 372–73.

52. Spiller, I, 564–65.

53. Alice F. Tyler, *Freedom's Ferment* (New York, 1962), pp. 361, 363. On pp. 370–71 she tells of the 1834 Beecher-instigated anti-Irish mob which burned down Boston's Ursuline convent. This is interesting here because a) it shows the city's ripeness for the 1835 mob-effort against "foreigner" Thompson, and b) it gave Edward E. Hale, at thirteen, a subject for his first poem: *Life and Letter,* ed. E. E. Hale, Jr. (Boston, 1917), I, 14–15.

54. Philadelphia *Native American,* May 16, 1844.

55. George S. Jackson, ed. *Early Songs of Uncle Sam* (Boston, 1933), pp. 56–59, 73–75; *Flying Cloud* (Virginia, Minn., 1922), pp. 113–15.

56. Philadelphia *Spirit of the Times,* May 28, 1844.

57. *Liberator,* July 12, 1844. The New York *Post,* July 10, 1844, quotes the same excuse. In neither case, however, does this represent the editor's view.

58. Boston *Pilot,* May 25, 1844; Philadelphia *Daily Chronicle,* May 31, 1844; *The Catholic Herald,* May 23, 1844.

59. *Liberator,* July 12, 1844.

60. "The Perils of the People," Philadelphia *Public Ledger,* July 12, 1844.

61. Joseph E. Chamberlin, *The Boston Transcript* (Boston, 1930), pp. 94–95.

62. *Poetry of Life* (Boston, 1848), pp. 208–23. This group, one of Tappan's major efforts, shows more passion than is usual for him. An anti-immigrant poem, equally vicious, is "Since You, O Europe! Crowd Our Shores," p. 82.

63. *Poems* (Boston, 1864), p. 46.

64. Homer F. Barnes, *Charles Fenno Hoffman* (New York, 1930), pp. 242–43. Barnes also refers to an unsigned 1837 article in which "The exalting of 'Native Americanism' strongly suggests Hoffman." *Ibid.,* p. 324.

65. *Poetical Works* (London, 1850), p. 96.

66. *The Burden of the South* (New York, [c. 1864]), p. 51.

67. *Freedom's Ferment,* pp. 97–106. Mrs. Tyler's succinct narrative, while apparently impartial, is in fact sharply slanted against Smith.

68. Brooklyn *Eagle,* June 25, 28; July 1, 2, 4; *Niles' National Register,* June 26, July 13, 20; New York *Post,* July 8; *Liberator,* July 19, 1844. As early as June 17th the Brooklyn *Eagle* had sharply rebuked the Quincy, Ill., *Herald* of May 31st for suggesting to its readers, through a hoax account, "the destruction of Nauvoo and the massacre of . . . its inhabitants."

69. Eliza R. S. Smith, "The Kidnapping of Lt. Gov. Joseph Smith," *A Treasury of American Ballads,* ed. C. O. Kennedy (New York, 1954), pp. 59–61.

70. *Liberator,* July 12, 1844.

71. "Ode on the Present Crisis," *Poetical Works,* ed. T. O. Mabbott (New York, 1938), pp. 51–52.

72. "Our Country," *op. cit.,* p. 222.

73. [Elbert H. Smith], *Black Hawk, and Scenes in the West* (New York, 1848), pp. 13–15.

74. "Anti-Slavery Verses, After Hearing the Speeches in Faneuil Hall on a Late Anniversary Occasion," "New England and New Englanders," "The Gospel of Nature," *Liberator,* May 31, 1844; June 11, 1847; Oct. 13, 1854.

75. "A Latter-day Saint," *op. cit.,* pp. 107–08. If Tuckerman is referring not to the Mormons but to one of Miller's doomsday prophets, the point remains unblunted. On October 22, 1843, "it took the whole Cincinnati police force to protect Miller's . . . believers" from a mob: Forrest Wilson, *Crusader in Crinoline* (Philadelphia, 1941), p. 218.

76. *Correspondence of Henry D. Thoreau,* eds. W. Harding and C. Bode (New York, 1958), p. 137. Canby's index labels several ambivalent incidents as examples of dislike for the Irish; the most pertinent items are on pp. 11, 183, and 361 of his *Thoreau* (Boston, 1939). The poems quoted are in *Collected Poems,* ed. C. Bode (Chicago, 1943), pp. 17, 177–78, 367.

77. *Works* (New York, 1903), IV, 270–71; III, 304, 320, 322–23.

78. "A Rhymed Lesson," *Poetical Works* (Boston, 1895), pp. 55–56.

79. *Life and Letters,* I, 300.

80. Gay W. Allen, *The Solitary Singer* (New York, 1955), pp. 370, 51, 64.

81. "L. of G.'s Purport," "A Song for Occupations," "A Song of the Rolling Earth," "With Antecedents," *Leaves of Grass,* ed. E. Holloway (New York, 1954), pp. 457, 181, 187, 204.

82. *Op. cit.,* pp. 130, 156, 200–01; 146–47, 157, 99.

83. "The Voyage to Vinland," *ibid.,* p. 314.

84. "The Death of Schiller," *op. cit.,* p. 264.

85. New York *Post,* July 13, 15, 1844.

86. "The Winds," *op. cit.,* p. 274.

87. "The Last Walk in Autumn," "Pastoral Letter," "From Perugia," "Kathleen," *op. cit.,* pp. 152, 276, 379–80, 37–39.

88. *Ibid.,* pp. 12–21, 33–35.

89. Wagenknecht, pp. 296–97, 292.

90. Walter V. Gavigan, "Longfellow and Catholicism," *The Catholic World,* CXXXVIII (Oct., 1933), 49.

91. Introduction to "The Reapers and the Flowers," *Complete Poetical Works* (Boston, 1893), p. 3.

92. Gavigan, p. 46.

93. Wagenknecht, p. 295.

94. *Op. cit.,* pp. 77, 80–81, 83, 95–96.

95. *Ibid.,* pp. 116, 235, 466.

96. "Politics," *op. cit.,* III, 212.

97. "Fable," "Hamatreya," *ibid.,* IX, 75, 37.

98. Almira Seymour, "Song of the Kansas Emigrant"; Lucy Larcom, "Call to Kansas," *Liberator,* Apr. 13, Mar. 9, 1855. Harriet B. Stowe's "Pilgrim's Song in the Desert" was written at this time.

99. "An Appeal to Northern Freemen," "Brothers, Awake!" "Free Thought and Speech," "Thoughts Suggested by the Times," "To the Liberator," "Appeal for Kansas," "The March of Freedom," "Barber and Shannon," *ibid.*, Nov. 23, May 11, Oct. 12, 1855; Apr. 18, May 2, Jan. 22, May 9, 1856.

100. Louis Filler does precisely this in *The Crusade Against Slavery, 1830–1860* (New York, 1960), pp. 240–42. 245.

101. Henry D. Sedgwick, "The Mob Spirit in Literature," *Atlantic Monthly,* XCVI (July, 1905), 10.

102. Anna M. Wells, *Dear Preceptor* (Boston, 1963), p. 100.

103. "America," *Poems Read at the Opening of the Fraternity Lectures* (Boston, 1859), p. 22.

104. *Liberator,* Sept. 14, 1855; "Scorn (To Brooks of South Carolina)," *Richard Realf's Free State Poems,* ed. R. J. Hinton (Topeka, 1900), p. 72.

105. Daniel Hitchings, "Not Carnal but Spiritual Weapons," *Liberator,* Sept., 5, 1856; the pro-Southern quotations come from unsigned verses reprinted from the Boston *Post, ibid.*, Apr. 24, 1856; Aug. 27, 1858.

106. *The Hireling and the Slave* (Charleston, 1856), pp. 163n, and 45; see also note on Giddings as inciter to riot, p. 160.

107. *Op. cit.*, pp. 253–55. Though this is a conjectural reading, I feel that the poetry of *André* loses much of its point if its 1856 context is ignored. Lord was among Jefferson Davis' "more intimate friends," according to Mabbott's introductory remarks.

108. "Wanted," *Complete Poetical Writings* (New York, 1900), pp. 472–73. This sonnet, titled "Men," first appeared anonymously in the Springfield *Republican.* Holland's verse usually avoids issues of the day.

109. "A Birthday Thought in Italy," *Poetical Works* (Philadelphia, 1881), II, 352. See "The Apostrophe," *ibid.*, III, 280, for an expanded recollection of that ominous vision written ten years later.

110. "Micah and the Levite," *Poems* (New York, 1860), pp. 92, 94.

111. *William Wetmore Story and His Friends* (Edinburgh, 1903), II, 31.

112. "A Welcome to Parker Pillsbury," "Charles Sumner," "Listen, Brothers!" "Chivalry Versus Yankees," "Modern Chivalry," *Liberator,* June 13, 27, Oct. 24, 1856; Jan. 30, 1857.

113. "The Fiery Cross," "To the Brandywine," "A Wail for Massachusetts," *Liberator,* June 20, 1856; Feb. 20, Apr. 3, 1857.

114. *The Night of Freedom* (Boston, 1857), pp. 29, 31, 33. There is a long passage on the caning of Sumner, pp. 22–23.

115. "Rallying Song for Kansas Emigrants," "The Border-Ruffian's Flag," "Don't Go Back," "We'll Not Go Back," "Peace," "The Irish Thief," *Free State Poems,* pp. 121, 123, 111, 113, 130, 116–18.

116. "The Defense of Lawrence," "Kansas," "Free-State Lyrics—Nos. IV, II, III, VII," "The Inauguration: March 4, 1857," "No. VI," "Sonnet," "Stanzas for the Times," *ibid.*, pp. 31–34, 63, 44, 36, 40, 50, 75, 48, 61, 103.

117. Clarke, *op. cit.*, p. 203; Hale, *op. cit.*, II, 283; "New England's Rally—A Song for the Times," "Prologue," "The Call of Kansas," "The Ruffian Rally," *Liberator,* Oct. 3, 1856; Feb. 19, 1858; Aug. 8, 1856.

118. *Poems and Essays* (Boston, 1886), pp. 441, 461, 255. The last appeared in the *Christian Register,* June, 1856.

119. *Words for the Hour* (Boston, 1857), pp. 23–24, 27–31, 7–22.

120. George H. Haynes, *Charles Sumner* (Philadelphia, 1909), p. 213. Haynes gives the fullest story of the Senate incident. On pp. 245–46 he tells of Sumner's second narrow escape from a violent death in April, 1861, when a Baltimore mob learned he was there. Forty Massachusetts soldiers were killed or wounded by those persons the next day. See Mrs. Howe's "Harvard Student's Song," *Later Lyrics* (Boston, 1866), p. 29, and Bayard Taylor's "Through Baltimore," *Poetical Works* (Boston, 1883), p. 137.

121. *Liberator,* Apr. 4, 1856. This is an expansion of views expressed by Holmes in a widely resented New York address.

122. Henry D. Thoreau, "Life Without Principle," *Writings* (Boston, 1893), X, 279.

123. "The Night Journey of a River," "A Rain Dream," *op. cit.*, pp. 343, 326.

124. *Letters,* ed. T. H. Johnson (Cambridge, 1958), II, 324, 411–12; *Complete Poems,* ed. T. H. Johnson (Boston, 1960), p. 707.

125. Spiller, I, 909.

126. *Life,* II, 279–81, 286–87. On p. 286 we come upon a great verse fragment, "So from the bosom of darkness," welling up from his Sumner agony.

127. *Op. cit.,* pp. 274, 482. For 1856 dating see pp. 361–62, 677.

128. *Letters,* ed. C. E. Norton (New York, 1894), I, 212.

129. *Uncollected Poems,* p. 264.

130. "Ode for Washington's Birthday," "Latter-Day Warnings," "Album Verses," *op. cit.*, pp. 139, 168, 168–69. For his attitude toward mobs and martyrs, see "St. Anthony the Reformer," p. 166.

131. "Brahma," "The Assault Upon Mr. Sumner," "Speech on Affairs in Kansas," *op. cit.,* IX, 195; XI, 248, 251, 263. Bancroft is quoted on p. 597.

132. Newton Arvin, *Whitman* (New York, 1938), pp. 65–66. In "The House-Top" Melville sees "The Town . . . taken by its rats," and warns that the Republic's basic creed—man's natural goodness—has been undermined. If Whitman could admit that "Calvin's creed" was thus corroborated, the center pole of his tent would topple: *Works* (London, 1924), XVI, 64, The only other serious verse response to the 1863 riots I have found is a long, colorful passage in Burke's *The Burden of the South.*

133. *Complete Poetry and Selected Prose and Letters,* ed. E. Holloway (London, 1938), pp. 588–89, 509–10.

134. "Starting from Paumonok," *Leaves of Grass,* p. 16.

135. "The Kansas Emigrants," "Letter," "Burial of Barber," "The Panorama," "To Pennsylvania," "What of the Day?" "Le Marais du Cygne," *op. cit.,* pp. 317–30.
136. Eugene Current-Garcia, "Newspaper Humor in the Old South, 1835–1855," *The Alabama Review,* II (April, 1949), 119.
137. Harriet B. Stowe, in a newspaper letter following the 1836 attacks on Birney's abolitionist press, wrote: "Every man is glad of a mob that happens to fall in with his views. . . . The minister and Christian must treat with as much severity a mob against gambling as a mob against ministers and churches . . ." F. Wilson, *op. cit.,* p. 185.

Chapter 4: Mistreatment of the Indian

1. Grant Foreman, "John Howard Payne and the Cherokee Indians," *American Historical Review,* XXXVII (July, 1932), 724.
2. Helen H. Jackson, *A Century of Dishonor,* ed. A. F. Rolle (New York, 1965), p. 270.
3. Grace S. Woodward, *The Cherokees* (Norman, 1963), pp. 197, 212.
4. Edwin C. McReynolds, *The Seminoles* (Norman, 1957), pp. 202, 200, 179.
5. Myer M. Cohen, *Notices of Florida,* ed. O. Z. Tyler, Jr. (Gainesville, 1964), pp. xvii, xviii.
6. Philip Graham, *The Life and Poems of Mirabeau B. Lamar* (Chapel Hill, 1938), p. 52.
7. Guy A. Cardwell, Jr., "William Henry Timrod, the Charleston Volunteers, and the Defense of St. Augustine," *North Carolina Historical Review,* XVIII (Jan., 1941), 37.
8. *Notices of Florida,* pp. 106, 211.
9. Albert B. Street, "The Camp in the Forest," *Poems* (New York, 1867), I, 197–98.
10. George S. Jackson, ed. *Early Songs of Uncle Sam* (Boston, 1933), pp. 109, 182–84.
11. Thomas H. Chivers, "Liberty," *Nacoochee* (New York, 1837), p. 110.
12. New York *Mirror,* Nov. 10, 1838.
13. "Seneca Lake," *The Dream of a Day* (New Haven, 1843), p. 30.
14. Lydia H. Sigourney, "Pocahontas," *Poetical Works* (London, 1850), p. 99.
15. William H. C. Hosmer, "Ode," "Freedom's Oak," *Poetical Works* (New York, 1854), II, 192, 119.
16. *Liberator,* Apr. 26, 1839.
17. "New England," *Poems* (Boston, 1847), p. 1; "The Concord Sexton's Story," *Poems of Sixty Five Years* (Philadelphia, 1902), p. 78.
18. "McKenney and Hall's *History of the North American Indians,*" *North American Review,* XLVII (July, 1838), 138. A crushing denunciation of Indian character and life follows.

19. Benjamin T. Spencer, "A National Literature, 1837–1855," *American Literature,* VIII (May, 1936), 131, 126.
20. "Nacoochee's Prayer," *op. cit.,* p. 15.
21. "Sassacus," "The Sachem's Death," *Poems* (Boston, 1851), pp. 44, 47.
22. Seba Smith, *Powhatan* (New York, 1841), pp. 6, 14.
23. Gordon S. Haight, *The Sweet Singer of Hartford* (New Haven, 1930), p. 26.
24. "Pocahontas," "Oriska," *op. cit.,* pp. 120–21, 1. Reference is made to Mrs. Hale's "The Empire of Woman," *Three Hours* (Philadelphia, 1848), p. 87, and Morris' "The Chieftain's Daughter," *Poems* (New York, [c. 1860]), p. 78.
25. "The Pioneer," "Onneko," "The Chieftain of the Lake," "Moranah," *op. cit.,* I, 130, 30, 178–86; II, 76–77.
26. *Songs of the Sea* (Boston, 1847), pp. 86–88.
27. Homer F. Barnes, *Charles Fenno Hoffman* (New York, 1930), p. 315.
28. *Poems* (Boston, 1864), pp. 135-47.
29. James M. Legare, "Toccoa," *Orta-Undis and Other Poems* (Boston, 1848), p. 56.
30. Philip P. Cooke, "The Murder of Cornstalk," *Froissart Ballads and Other Poems* (Philadelphia, 1847), pp. 200–02.
31. New York *Mirror,* Oct. 21, 1837; *North American Review,* July, 1838, p. 141.
32. "On the Condition of the 'Eagwehoe We' . . . in 1845," *Liberator,* Dec. 12, 1845; "Geehale, An Indian Lament," *The Poets and Poetry of America,* ed. R. Griswold (Philadelphia, 1852), p. 531.
33. "Ode to the Sea Serpent," *op. cit.,* p. 83.
34. [E. C. W.], "Idiot Era," *Liberty Bell,* 1848, p. 166.
35. *Black Hawk, and Scenes in the West* (New York, 1848), pp. 136–38.
36. *Poems and Essays* (Boston, 1886), pp. 470–71, 205.
37. "Ode on the Present Crisis," *Poems* (New York, 1845), pp. 51–52.
38. *Tecumseh: or the West Thirty Years Since* (New York, 1842), pp. 79, 68.
39. "Pocahontas," "Last Words of an Indian Chief," *Pocahontas* (New York, 1841), pp. 21, 32, 181–82.
40. *Liberator,* Dec. 15, 1837; Pennsylvania *Freeman,* Nov. 1, 1838; *National Enquirer,* Jan. 4, 1838. It would be wrong, however, to ignore Poe's satirical thrust against "the late tremendous swamp-fight, away down South, with the Bugaboo and Kickapoo Indians," in his 1839 sketch, "The Man That Was Used Up," *Works* (New York, 1903), IV, 44–57.
41. "To the Hon. Theodore Frelinghuysen," *The Poets of America,* ed. G. B. Cheever (New York, [c. 1835]), p. 202.
42. *Liberator,* Jan. 9, 1836, Sept. 19, 1838; *National Enquirer,* Jan. 14, Nov. 23, Dec. 21, 1937.

43. "Governor Everett Receiving the Indian Chiefs, November, 1937," *The Female Poets of America,* ed. R. Griswold (Philadelphia, 1854), pp. 251–52.

44. "A Dream," *Liberator,* Feb. 7, 1840.

45. "The Seminole's Reply," "Saevacola Lamentatio," *National Enquirer,* May 6, July 20, 1837.

46. Charles O. Kennedy, ed. *A Treasury of American Ballads* (New York, 1954), pp. 129–30.

47. "Powell and his Associates," *National Enquirer,* Dec. 28, 1837.

48. "Fragment of an Indian Sketch," New York *Mirror,* Dec. 30, 1837.

49. [James B. Ransom], *Osceola: or, Fact and Fiction* (New York, 1838), pp. 145–46. The *Mirror* critic writes (Aug. 11, 1838): "The 'poetry' is, if possible, worse than the prose; and the prose is such as a schoolboy should be whipped for perpetrating . . . a book . . . inconceivably and superfluously execrable . . ."

50. *Female Poets,* p. 297.

51. [Cleveland Coxe], *St. Jonathan, The Lay of a Scald* (New York, 1838), pp. 20–21, and stinging note on p. 45.

52. "The Tocsin," *Airs of Palestine* (Boston, 1840), pp. 297–98. As usual, he underscores a hackneyed verse passage with a moving footnote: "Bear witness, ghost of the great-hearted, broken-hearted Osceola!"

53. Barnes, p. 212.

54. *Tecumseh,* pp. 80, 265.

55. "Osceola," *op. cit.,* I, 50–54.

56. *Tecumseh,* p. 307.

57. "New Pastoral," *Poetical Works* (Philadelphia, 1881), II, 216, 225–26, 15, 11; *Lays and Ballads* (Philadelphia, 1849), p. 100.

58. *Writings* (Boston, 1897), I, 94.

59. "The Last Fields of the Biloxi," "The Tryst of Acayma," "The Sioux Boy," *Poems* (New York, 1853), I, 273–87, 304–06, 321–23.

60. "Chicora," "The Hireling and the Slave," *The Hireling and the Slave, Chicora, and Other Poems* (Charleston, 1856), pp. 81, 67–68, and 164–65n.

61. *Scribner's Monthly,* XIII (Dec., 1876), 288.

62. *Main Currents in American Thought* (New York, 1930), III, 53–54.

63. "Spring in New England," *op. cit.,* II, 7.

64. Andrew McLean, "An Ode for the Fourth of July, 1877," *Tom Moore and Other Verses* (Brooklyn, 1878), p. 30.

65. "Hospes Civitatis," *Scribner's Monthly,* XII (Aug., 1876), 589.

66. "The Old Cabinet," editor's column, *ibid.,* July, 1876, p. 433.

67. *Poetical Works* (Boston, 1883), p. 110.

68. "My Country," *Poems* (New York, 1903), pp. 34–36. A few years later Charles E. Norton warns Woodberry that we should "love our country . . . with keen-eyed and disciplined passion, not blindly exalting her."

69. "England and America," *Harper's New Monthly Magazine,* LIV (Dec., 1876), 111.

70. "A Sennight of the Centennial," *Atlantic Monthly,* XXXVIII (July, 1876), 103.

71. As for civilians, "the commissioners of Lawrence County were reported to have offered a reward of $250 for the body of any Indian found in the county . . ." Paul Fatout, *Ambrose Bierce and the Black Hills* (Norman, 1956), p. 11.

72. George F. Whicher, *This Was a Poet* (Ann Arbor, 1957), pp. 132–33.

73. Quoted by Marion R. Murray, "The 1870's in American Literature," *American Speech,* I (March, 1926), 324.

74. Laura S. Webb, *Custer's Immortality* (New York, 1876), pp. 9, 6, 13, 10, 11, 14, 12.

75. *Complete Poetical Works* (Boston, 1916), pp. 77–80.

76. Louis Untermeyer, *Modern British and American Poetry* (New York, 1942), p. 92. Untermeyer, however, says nothing about this ballad.

77. *Custer's Immortality,* p. 22. These verses are unidentified.

78. "Custer," *Poems of American History,* ed. B. E. Stevenson (Boston, 1922), p. 583.

79. Laura Stedman and George M. Gould, *Life and Letters of Edmund Clarence Stedman* (New York, 1910), II, 283, 536.

80. *Custer's Immortality,* p. 20. These verses are unidentified.

81. "Custer's Last Charge," Stevenson, p. 582.

82. "Custer," *Poetical Works* (New York, 1923), p. 386.

83. *Atlantic Monthly,* XXXIX (Mar., 1877), 329.

84. "Little Big Horn," *Poems* (New York, 1896), pp. 235–37.

85. *Custer, and Other Poems* (Chicago, 1896), pp. 94–134.

86. Arthur H. Quinn, *The Literature of the American People* (New York, 1951), p. 624.

87. Whicher, p. 133.

88. Sidney Lanier, "Corn," "Individuality," "The Symphony," "Psalm of the West," *Poems* (New York, 1897), pp. 58, 11, 68, 133; Richard W. Gilder, "Congress: 1878," *Five Books of Song* (New York, 1900), p. 110; Bayard Taylor, "A Statesman," "A President," *op. cit.,* p. 214.

89. "O, the Mockery of Pity," *op. cit.,* p. 350.

90. *Sidney Lanier Centennial Edition* (Baltimore, 1945), VI, 31–32.

91. Allan Nevins, "Helen Hunt Jackson, Sentimentalist vs. Realist," *American Scholar,* X (Summer, 1941), 281.

92. Roger R. Walterhouse, *Bret Harte, Joaquin Miller, and the Western Local Color Story*: part of a dissertation (Chicago, 1939), p. 56.

93. *Complete Poetical Works* (Boston, 1912), II, 253–55.

94. *Op. cit.,* pp. 169, 247–49. There are also strong passages in "The Last Taschastas" and "Resurgo San Francisco."

95. "The Old Santa Fe Trail," "The Race of the 'Boomers,'" *Collected Poems* (Indianapolis, 1931), pp. 157, 75.

96. *Complete Poetical Works* (Boston, 1925), pp. 109, 141.

97. *The Statues in the Block* (Boston, 1887), pp. 63, 98.
98. *Songs of History* (Boston, 1887), pp. 60, 112, 87.
99. "The Drum," "The Delectable Ballad of the Waller Lot," "A Battle in Yellowstone Park," *Poems* (New York, 1933), pp. 277, 284–85, 443–46.
100. James W. Riley, "George Mullen's Confession," "What the Wind Said," "A Child's Home—Long Ago," "Liberty," *Complete Poetical Works* (Garden City, 1941), pp. 69, 75, 98, 91–93; Rose T. Cooke, "After the Camanches," "Done For," *Poems* (New York, 1888), pp. 383–84, 387-88.
101. "The Mountains," "The Passing of the Buffalo," "Home from Wild Meadows," "Rushing Eagle," *Prairie Songs* (Cambridge, 1893), pp. 69, 54, 100, 105–06.
102. Rolle, *A Century of Dishonor,* p. xiv.
103. Nevins, p. 276.
104. Rolle, p. xix.
105. *CHAL,* III, 89–90.
106. Robert E. Spiller, *Literary History of the United States* (New York, 1948), p. 869.
107. Rolle, p. xii.
108. Nevins, p. 285.
109. "H. H.," *op. cit.,* p. 135.
110. "To the Memory of H. H.," quoted in Anna M. Wells' *Dear Preceptor* (Boston, 1963), pp. 262, 268. Higginson read proof for *A Century of Dishonor.*
111. "An Indian at the Burial-Place of His Fathers," "Among the Trees," *Poetical Works* (New York, 1878), pp. 84, 456.
112. A copy of his handwritten letter, dated July 26, 1876, is bound into the front cover of Mrs. Webb's book.
113. "Robinson of Leyden," "The Pilgrim's Vision," "At the Banquet to the Grand Duke Alexis," "A Family Record," "Grandmother's Story of Bunker-Hill Battle," *Poetical Works* (Boston, 1895), pp. 180, 28, 256, 316, 301.
114. John A. Pollard, *John Greenleaf Whittier* (Boston, 1949), p. 76.
115. "Haverhill," "The Panorama," "On the Big Horn," *Complete Poetical Works* (Boston, 1894), pp. 473, 330, 324, 384–85.
116. "To the Driving Cloud," "The Baron of St. Castine," "The Song of Hiawatha," "The Revenge of Rain-in-the Face," *Complete Poetical Works* (Boston, 1893), pp. 64, 261, 164, 336–37. Albert Keiser, *The Indian in American Literature* (New York, 1933), p. 189, states that the Omaha chief was "visiting the city named after his tribe," The city, however, was Boston; Omaha had not yet been founded. For a refutation of the "revenge" legend, see Donald C. Seitz, *The Dreadful Decade* (Indianapolis, 1926), pp. 257, 259.
117. "L'Envoi," "A Fable for Critics," "To Whittier," "Pessimoptimism," "An Ode for the Fourth of July, 1876," *Complete Poetical Works* (Boston, 1917), pp. 27, 135, 386, 406, 370–71; "Class Poem," *Uncollected Poems,* ed. T. M. Smith (Philadelphia, 1950), p. 236.

118. "A Broadway Pageant," "Pioneers! O Pioneers!" "Great Are the Myths," "The Beauty of the Ship," "Song of Myself," "The Sleepers," "To Those Who've Failed," "From Far Dakota's Cañons," "Osceola," *Leaves of Grass,* ed. E. Holloway (New York, 1954), pp. 207, 195, 467, 486, 62, 32, 358, 421, 402, 453.

119. " 'Tis whiter than an Indian pipe," "There came a wind like a bugle," "I've got an arrow here," "The Heart is the Capitol of the Mind," *Complete Poems,* ed. T. H. Johnson (Boston, 1960), pp. 625, 660, 701–02, 585. The dating is Johnson's.

120. "A Week on the Concord and Merrimac Rivers," "The Maine Woods," *Writings* (Boston, 1893), I, 66; III, 6.

121. "Wait Not Till Slaves Pronounce the Word," *Collected Poems,* ed. C. Bode (Chicago, 1943), p. 198.

122. Keiser, p. 209.

123. "Our Country," *Collected Poems,* p. 134. In this poem Thoreau untypically sounds the note of Anglo-Saxon supremacy. See Bode's note, p. 360.

124. Albert Keiser, "Thoreau's Manuscripts on the Indians," *Journal of English and Germanic Philology,* XXVII (Apr., 1928), p. 183.

125. Keiser, *The Indian in American Literature,* p. 210.

126. Philip L. Nicoloff, *Emerson on Race and History* (New York 1961), p. 251.

127. Keiser, *The Indian in American Literature,* p. 205.

128. *Works* (Boston, [c. 1918]), IX, 193.

129. Kenneth W. Cameron, *Index-Concordance to Emerson's Sermons* (Hartford, 1963), I, 273.

130. "Historical Discourse," "Letter to Martin Van Buren," *Works* (Boston, [c. 1932]), XI, 61–62, 571n, 93. This great letter originally appeared in the *Yeoman's Gazette,* Concord, May 19, 1838.

131. *The Letters of Ralph Waldo Emerson,* ed. Ralph L. Rusk (New York, 1939), VI, 297.

132. "Clarel," "John Marr," *Works* (London, 1924), XIV, 78; XV, 192, 250; XVI, 199–200.

Chapter 5: War With Spain

1. "Apostrophe to the Island of Cuba," "Cuba," "The Gospel of Peace," *Poems of American History,* ed. B. E. Stevenson (Boston, 1908), pp. 606–08.

2. "Letter," *Complete Poetical Works* (Boston, 1894), p. 319.

3. "Prologue," *Liberator,* Feb. 19, 1858.

4. "Cuba," Stevenson, p. 608.

5. Will Carleton, "Cuba to Columbia," *ibid.,* p. 608.

6. "Cuba Libre," *Poetical Works* (New York, 1923), pp. 444–45.

7. William H. Venable, "War," *Spanish American War Songs,* ed. S. A. Witherbee (Detroit, 1898), p. 903.

8. "Hands Across the Sea," "Why the Army Became Quiet," *Poems* (New York, 1910), pp. 196–97, 167.

9. Joseph B. Gilder, "The Parting of the Ways," Stevenson, p. 609.

10. Lloyd Mifflin, "Half-Mast"; Danske Dandridge, "On the Eve of War" *ibid.,* pp. 611–12; R. U. Johnson, "The Listening Sword," *op. cit.,* p. 221.

11. R. Hughes, "The Martyrs of the Maine"; Edith M. Thomas, "To Spain—A Last Word," Stevenson, pp. 612–13.

12. Ella Higginson, "For Honor and For God," Witherbee, p. 442.

13. William H. Hayne, "The Caged Eagle," *ibid.,* p. 479.

14. Venable, "Battle Cry," Stevenson, p. 164.

15. James McKay, "Our Anglo-American Alliance"; L. B. Freeman, "Song of the Average Man," Witherbee, pp. 588, 372–73.

16. "Cuba," *Poetical Works* (Boston, 1903), p. 344.

17. Herbert B. Swett, "The Gathering," Stevenson, p. 629.

18. Sam Foss, "Mother Asia," *Songs of War and Peace* (Boston, 1899), pp. 80–81.

19. Richard Le Gallienne, "War Poem," *War Poems, 1898* (San Francisco, 1898), pp. 31–32.

20. S. P. Butler, "The Day of Wrath," Witherbee, p. 113.

21. Venable, "Battle Cry," Stevenson, p. 614.

22. "Mene, Mene, Tekel, Upharsin," *ibid.,* pp. 620–21.

23. Tudor Jenks, "The Spirit of the Maine"; Thomas A. Janvier, "Santiago," *ibid.,* pp. 621, 633–34.

24. Frederick Almy, "To Vice-President Roosevelt," *Roosevelt as the Poets Saw Him,* ed. C. H. Towne (New York, 1923), p. 35.

25. John H. Boner, "America," *Poems* (New York, 1903), p. 59.

26. Ina D. Coolbrith, "The Blood of a Nation," *War Poems,* pp. 89–90.

27. Marion C. Smith, "Ballad of the Rough Riders," Towne, pp. 18–20.

28. Corinne Roosevelt Robinson, *ibid.,* p. xix.

29. John K. Bangs, "A Change of Ambition," *War Poems,* pp. 120–21.

30. Faith Baldwin, "Hobson's Choice," Witherbee, p. 85.

31. Lansing C. Bailey, "Eight Volunteers," Stevenson, p. 626.

32. Thomas C. DeLeon, "As One," *War Rhymes Grave and Gay* (Atlanta, 1898), p. 16.

33. Unsigned, "Chickamauga"; David Witherington, "The Sons of Former Foes"; Albert B. Paine, "The New Memorial Day," Witherbee, pp. 31, 929, 703.

34. James L. Gordon, "Wheeler at Santiago," Stevenson, pp. 631–32.

35. Wallace Rice, "Wheeler's Brigade at Santiago," *Ballads of Valor and Victory* (New York, 1903), pp. 104–05.

36. John J. Rooney, "Joined the Blues"; Frank L. Stanton, "The Warship Dixie," Witherbee, pp. 739–40, 852.

37. DeLeon, "The Colored Immune," *op. cit.,* p. 17.

38. *James Russell Lowell and His Friends* (Boston, 1899), p. 185. V. W. Brooks wrongly indicates that Hale opposed the war: *New England: Indian Summer* (New York, 1940), pp. 418–19.

39. W. R. Thayer, "John Hay's Policy of Anglo-Saxonism," *The World's Work,* XXXV (Nov., 1917), 37–40.

40. Thomas N. Page, "The Shepherd of the Seas," "The Dragon of the Seas," *The Coast of Bohemia* (New York, 1906), pp. 27, 32–35.

41. Mary B. Eddy, "The United States to Great Britain," Witherbee, p. 348.

42. John P. Bocock, "Rough Riding at El Caney"; Unsigned, "Turn Them Loose!"; Stephen F. Whitman, "The Ballad of Teddy's Terrors," Towne, pp. 14, 27, 22–26; Unsigned, "An Unhappy Patriot," Witherbee, p. 16.

43. *Lowell and His Friends,* pp. 216–17.

44. "War Poem," *War Poems,* pp. 31–32.

45. Unsigned, "The War News at Deadman," Witherbee, pp. 33–34.

46. "An Unhappy Patriot," *ibid.,* p. 16.

47. Robert Bridges, "Roosevelt in Wyoming"; Whitman, "Teddy's Terrors," Towne, pp. 36–37, 22–26.

48. Edwin L. Sabin, "Rough Riders"; Bridges, "On the Hill"; Guiterman, "The Rough Riders," *ibid.,* pp. 28, 32, 30.

49. Joseph R. Taylor, "Breath of the Oat," Stevenson, p. 641.

50. Sam Foss, "1898 and 1562," "Uncle Sam's Spring Cleaning," "Mother Asia," *op. cit.,* pp. 142–43, 87–88, 80–81.

51. "A Song of the New," Witherbee, p. 869.

52. Bridges, "On the Hill"; Roger Sterrett, "Gray is the Pall of the Sky"; George M. Moore, "San Juan"; "Turn Them Loose!" Towne, pp. 32, 142, 17, 27.

53. "In Gladstone's Day (And Now)," *Liberty Poems* (Boston, 1900), pp. 16–17.

54. "The Word of the Lord from Havana," Stevenson, p. 619; "The Battle of Manila Bay," "Day and Night," *Last Songs from Vagabondia* (Boston, 1901), pp. 16–17, 15; "Unmanifest Destiny," *An Anthology of American Poetry,* ed. A. Kreymborg (New York, 1941), pp. 231–32.

55. "In the Wreckage of the Maine," "A Song for Our Fleets," "The March of the Volunteers," "The Victory-Wreck," "Do Not Forget the Wounded," "Columbia to Cuba," *Songs of Two Centuries* (New York, 1902), pp. 117, 112, 104, 125, 105, 120–21.

56. "The Soldier," "The Home-Voyage," "The Name of Old Glory," *Complete Poetical Works* (Indianapolis, 1937), pp. 674–76, 649–50, 640–41.

57. "Deeds of Valor at Santiago," Stevenson, p. 630; "Private Blair of the Regulars," "The Deed of Lieutenant Miles," "The Signal-Man of Paco Town," "Motherland," *Ballads of Valor,* pp. 102–03, 126–27, 123–25, 9–11.

58. "The Islands of the Sea," "Essex Regiment March," "Exeter

Ode," "Ode," "Children's Hymn," "My Country," *Poems* (New York, 1903), pp. 171–73, 168–70, 188–94, 165–66, 174, 29–30.

59. Arthur H. Quinn, *The Literature of the American People* (New York, 1951), p. 625; F. H. Harrington, "Literary Aspects of American Anti-Imperialism, 1898–1902," *New England Quarterly,* X (Dec., 1937), 666.

60. "House," *Selected Poems* (New York, 1926), p. 142; *Always the Young Strangers* (New York, 1953), p. 418.

61. Ernest H. Crosby, "Woman and War," *War Echoes* (Philadelphia, 1898), p. 7.

62. "From the Graves," "Anglo-Saxon Union," *War Poems,* pp. 100–01, 91–93.

63. "One Woman's Voice Against War," "The Healing Hand," "The Vintage of Sorrow," *The Dancers* (Boston, 1903), pp. 56–57, 58, 45.

64. "In the Beginning," "Memorial Day," "The Directory," "War," *The Testimony of the Suns* (San Francisco, 1904), pp. 102–04, 18–24, 142, 108.

65. "The American Fireman," "War and April," "A Vision of Peace," *Ballads of Valor,* pp. 131–33, 134–35, 136–38.

66. "The Illusion of War," *The Cry for Justice* (Philadelphia, 1915), p. 567; "The Cry of the Little Peoples," *Liberty Poems,* pp. 51–53. Both the title-page of the 1941 reprint and Eva Le Gallienne's introduction incorrectly claim that this was "written in 1903"; significantly, three strong stanzas of the 1900 *Liberty Poems* version are left out, and three lame ones added.

67. Richard Le Gallienne, *Rudyard Kipling* (London, 1900), pp. 63, 51, 133.

68. Harrington, pp. 658–59.

69. "Put Up Thy Sword," "Light of the Southern Cross," "After the Battle," *Poetical Works,* pp. 405, 450–51, 423.

70. "Peace," *Complete Poetical Works* (Boston, 1916), p. 239; Sandburg, *Always the Young Strangers,* p. 418. A letter dated May 8, 1898, shows how comfortably Hay solved his clash of feelings: "I detest war, and had hoped I might never see another, but this was as necessary as it was righteous. I have not for two years seen any other issue." William R. Thayer, *John Hay* (Boston, 1915), II, 167.

71. *CHAL,* III, 118.

72. W. M. Gibson, "Mark Twain and Howells, Anti-Imperialists," *New England Quarterly,* XX (Dec., 1947), p. 435.

73. Harrington, p. 665.

74. Helen G. Cone, "By the Blockhouse on the Hill," *Harvest Home* (New York, 1930), pp. 125–26.

75. Louise C. Moulton, "Dead Men's Holiday," *At the Wind's Will* (Boston, 1899), pp. 26–27.

76. Lloyd Mifflin, "Oh, Not on the Field," *The Slopes of Helicon* (Boston, 1898), p. 89.

77. Charles G. D. Roberts, "A Ballad of Manila Bay," Stevenson, p. 619.

78. Rice, "The Destroyer of Destroyers," "Dewey and His Men," *Ballads of Valor,* pp. 113–15, 97–99.

79. Leigh Bierce, "Cadiz," Witherbee, pp. 174–75.

80. "The Conqueror," "The End of All," *Castalian Days* (London, 1903), pp. 24, 20.

81. "The Statue of Liberty," *Collected Poems* (Minneapolis, 1909), I, 254.

82. "Oneiropolos," "Mnemosyne," untitled sonnets, *Dramatic Verses* (Boston, 1902), pp. 10–12, 25, 71, 81.

83. "Exordium," Witherbee, pp. 276–77.

84. "In the Night," *The Quiet Singer* (New York, 1908), p. 62.

85. John V. Cheney, "My Choice," *Lyrics* (Boston, 1901), p. 12.

86. Edmund V. Cooke, "Humbler Heroes," *Impertinent Poems* (New York, 1903), p. 45.

87. "Heroes of War and Peace," *War Poems,* pp. 72–73.

88. "The Bravest Soldier of All," Witherbee, p. 954.

89. "The Rhymed Roosevelt—A Stumping Ode," *The New Flag* (Chicago, 1899), p. 41.

90. Edmund V. Cooke, "Shoot Him Down!"; Solomon Solis-Cohen, "At the Gates of God," *Liberty Poems,* pp. 4–5, 1–2.

91. Robert U. Johnson, "The White Man's Burden," *Poems,* pp. 232–33.

92. John W. Chadwick, "The New Humanity," *Later Poems* (Boston, 1905), p. 118.

93. "The Cannibal Conquest," *Medley and Palestina* (New Haven, 1902), p. 96.

94. "I Had a Dream That was Not All a Dream," *op. cit.,* pp. 19–20.

95. "Uncivilized," *The Book of American Poetry,* ed. E. Markham (New York, 1934), pp. 367–68.

96. "Shoot Him Down!" *Liberty Poems,* pp. 4–5.

97. "Two Prayers," *op. cit.,* p. 57.

98. "To the New Century," *Castalian Days,* p. 33.

99. Solis-Cohen, "To a Tyrant," *Liberty Poems,* p. 10; Fuller, "Invocation," *op. cit.,* pp. 3–4.

100. "War Notes," "The Background Group," "Cities of Eld," "The City of Laish," *Collected Poems* (Indianapolis, 1931), pp. 12–23, 164, 123–24, 162–63.

101. "The Toilers," "The Desire of Nations," "In Poppy Fields," "A Look Into the Gulf," "To the High-born Poets," *The Man With the Hoe* (New York, 1899), pp. 113, 33–34, 89, 19–20, 110–11; "The Sower," "The Witness of the Dust," "The Need of the Hour," *Lincoln and Other Poems* (New York, 1901), pp. 6, 21–22, 70–71.

102. "The Colour-Bearer," *Happy Ending* (Boston, 1927), pp. 132–33; "Because No Man Hath Hired Us," "Sanctuary," *The Martyrs' Idyl* (Boston, 1900), pp. 48–49, 58.

103. "Arboricide," *Happy Ending,* pp. 68–69; *Letters,* ed. G. Guiney (New York, 1926), I, 223–24, 232–33.
104. Van Wyck Brooks, *New England: Indian Summer,* pp. 450–51.
105. "Outdoor Litany," *Happy Ending,* p. 126.
106. *Letters,* I, 252; II, 3–4, 7–8, 15.
107. Thirteen sonnets and "Onward, Christian Soldier!" *Liberty Poems,* pp. 108–20, 36–37.
108. "Victory," "The Maine Disaster," "Arguments in Favor of War," "Glory," "Spain," "The Spanish Galleon," "Spain's Reward," "War," "Prayer Before Battle," "Kipling's Recessional Misapplied," "Day-break," "The Burden of Blood," *America and Other Poems* (Chicago, 1899), pp. 26–27, 18–19, 23, 20, 17, 12, 22, 23, 19, 78–79, 36–37.
109. *Op. cit.,* p. 656.
110. "The Regiment," "Song of the New Freedom," *Plain Talk in Psalm and Parable* (Boston, 1899), pp. 109–10, 154; "War and Hell," *Swords and Ploughshares* (New York, 1902), pp. 13, 22, 14, 18, 23–24; "The God of War," *War Echoes,* p. 9n.
111. Harrington, pp. 666–67.
112. *Op. cit.,* pp. 470, 437–39, 466.
113. *Letters,* ed. B. C. Pope (San Francisco, 1922), pp. 61, 47.
114. *Collected Works* (New York, 1911), VII, 13, 15, 70, 100, 218, 248, 295, 338; 57, 73, 347, 359, 368.
115. *Ibid.,* VI 165, 205–06, 229, 249, 273–74, 290, 292, 305, 307–08, 311–14.
116. *A Hermit of Carmel* (New York, 1901), pp. 204–15.
117. *Ibid.,* pp. 216–31; Harvard's President Eliot is quoted by Emery Neff, *Edwin Arlington Robinson* (New York, 1948), p. 98.
118. *Poems* (Boston, 1901), pp. 12–21.
119. *Ibid.,* pp. 22–25.
120. Harrington, pp. 653–54. See discussion by Martin Halpern, *William Vaughn Moody* (New York, 1964), pp. 83, 75–76.
121. Gibson, p. 436n; Neff, p. 108.
122. Halpern, pp. 191n, 79; Neff, p. 113.
123. *Collected Poems* (New York, 1944), pp. 221–25, 231–32.
124. *Ibid.,* pp. 169, 116, 125–26, 143, 166.
125. Neff, pp. 127–28.
126. *War Dispatches,* eds. R. W. Stallman and E. R. Hagemann (New York, 1964), pp. 111, 119, 130, 140, 142, 145–46, 242–43.
127. *Ibid.,* pp. 285–86, 295.
128. *Collected Poems,* ed. W. Follett (New York, 1930), pp. 130, 108–09, 94, 86, 77, 99, 91, 102, 96.
129. *The New Star Chamber* (Chicago, 1904), pp. 20, 26, 32–36, 149, 181, 179, 151, 157.
130. Louis Untermeyer, *Modern American Poetry* (New York, 1942), p. 160.
131. [Dexter Wallace, pseud.], "Jesus of Nazareth," "Ballade of Dead Republics," "America," "The World Saver," "Memorabilia," "The

Pioneer," "Banner of Men Who Were Free," "America in 1804," "America in 1904," *The Blood of the Prophets* (Chicago, 1905), pp. 27, 51, 61, 99–100, 68–71, 66, 76–77, 82–85, 101–03, 104–05.
132. "At Sagamore Hill," Towne, p. 120.

Conclusion

1. He worked this belief into rhyme: "But the God said, 'Not so; Theme not this for lyric flow . . .' " *Works* (Boston, [c. 1918]), IX, 468.
2. *Complete Poetical Works* (Boston, 1925), p. xvii.
3. Heathcote W. Garrod, *Poetry and the Criticism of Life* (New York, 1963), p. 8.
4. *CHAL,* III, 113.
5. Quoted in *Complete Poetical Works of James Russell Lowell* (Boston, 1917), p. xi.
6. Robert E. Spiller, *Literary History of the United States* (New York, 1948), p. 386.
7. "Memoir of the Author," *The Poetical Works of Nathaniel P. Willis* (London, 1888), p. 11.
8. Spiller, p. 564.
9. "Freedom," *Poems* (Boston, 1851), p. 147.
10. "To Young America," *Lincoln and Other Poems* (New York, 1901), p. 82.
11. Arthur H. Quinn, *The Literature of the American People* (New York, 1951), p. 622.
12. "Margites," *Poems* (Boston, 1864), p. 170.
13. Gordon S. Haight, *The Sweet Singer of Hartford* (New Haven, 1930), p. 99.
14. "A Life Well Lost," *Later Poems* (Boston, 1905), p. 67.
15. William W. Story, "The Mighty Makers," *Poems* (Boston, 1886), II, 273.
16. Bayard Taylor, "Shakespeare," *Poetical Works* (Boston, 1883), p. 225.
17. "The Marshes of Glynn," *Poems* (New York, 1897), p. 17.
18. "The Poet's Chart," *The Martyrs' Idyl* (Boston, 1900), p. 56.
19. *Poems* (Philadelphia, 1844), pp. 61–66.
20. J. W. Thomas, *James Freeman Clarke* (Boston, 1949), p. 97.
21. "The Bards," *Poems* (Boston, 1847), p. 124, and (Philadelphia, 1865), p. 190. This omission is one of many such manifestations that could be offered in Read's case.
22. Roger R. Walterhouse, *Bret Harte, Joaquin Miller, and the Western Local Color Story:* part of a dissertation (Univ. of Chicago, 1939), p. 56; Bret Harte, *Letters,* ed. G. B. Harte (Boston, 1926), p. 41.

23. Louise I. Guiney, *Letters,* ed. G. Guiney (New York, 1926), II, 13. She too held a library post.
24. *Sidney Lanier Centennial Edition* (Baltimore, 1945), VI, xi-xii, 31–32, 196; IX, 198.
25. Jay B. Hubbell, *The South in American Literature, 1607–1900* (Durham, 1954), p. 278.
26. "America: Greeting," *The Coast of Bohemia* (New York, 1906), p. 22.
27. Bayard Taylor, *The American Legend* (Cambridge, 1850), p. 26.
28. "Wanted.—A Theme," *Poems* (Boston, 1851), p. 65.
29. George Wurts, "The Summons," *Scribner's Monthly,* XII (July, 1876), 428.
30. T. B. Read, "The New Pastoral," *Poetical Works* (Philadelphia, 1881), II, 238.
31. *Life and Letters,* ed. L. C. Scott (Boston, 1917), p. 89.
32. Thomas, p. 87, quotes this poem on art, reprinted from *The Dial* of 1840.
33. *Main Currents in American Thought* (New York, 1930), III, 54.
34. "The Burden," *Poetical Works,* p. 179.
35. Haight, p. 81, quotes from a review by Poe.
36. Homer F. Barnes, *Charles Fenno Hoffman* (New York, 1930), p. 147.
37. *Allibone's Dictionary* (Philadelphia, 1886), I, 1090.
38. Spiller, p. 900.
39. *Virginalia* (Brooklyn, 1942), preface.
40. Anna M. Wells, *Dear Preceptor* (Boston, 1963), p. 262.
41. Mary A. Wyman, *Two American Pioneers* (New York, 1927), pp. 210, 127, 108.
42. Allan Nevins, "Helen Hunt Jackson, Sentimentalist vs. Realist," *American Scholar,* X (Summer, 1941), 275.
43. Quinn, p. 623.
44. Henry James, *William Wetmore Story and His Friends* (Edinburgh, 1903), I, 62.
45. *The Letters of Ambrose Bierce,* ed. B. C. Pope (San Francisco, 1922), pp. 49–50, 52–54.
46. Pennsylvania *Freeman,* Aug. 22, 1839; introductory note to Willis' ode on slavery.
47. Oakes-Smith, *Poetical Writings* (New York, 1845), p. 7.
48. "The South," "Abraham Lincoln," *Poems* (New York, 1880), pp. 39–41, 282.
49. *Life and Letters,* ed. E. E. Hale, Jr. (Boston, 1917), II, 315.
50. Hay, "Liberty," "Thy Will Be Done," *Complete Poetical Works* (Boston, 1916), pp. 107–08, 255–56; English, "The Coal Baron," "The Three Kings," "The Money-King's Chorus," *Select Poems* (Newark, 1894), pp. 676, 682, 686; Riley, "And there's 'Gene Debs," "Them Flowers," *Debs and the Poets,* ed. R. LePrade (Pasadena,

1920), pp. 40, 56–61; Gilder, "A Hero of Peace," *Five Books of Song* (New York, 1900), p. 206. In the case of Hay, however, we are also confronted with a strong bias against the "foreign workingmen, mostly Irish," who struck in 1877—a bias which blossomed several years later in the form of an anonymously published novel, *The Breadwinners,* "the first important polemic in American fiction in defense of Property." See William R. Thayer, *John Hay* (Boston, 1915) II, 2–16.

51. Martin Halpern, *William Vaughn Moody* (New York, 1964), pp. 111–12.

52. George F. Whicher, *This Was a Poet* (Ann Arbor, 1957), p. 141.

53. "Nay, Tell Me Not To-Day the Published Shame," *Leaves of Grass,* ed. E. Holloway (New York, 1954), p. 461.

54. Quoted by F. O. Matthiessen, *American Renaissance* (New York, 1941), p. 624.

Bibliography

Part One: The Poets

ADAMS, JOHN Q. *Poems of Religion and Society*. New York, 1848.

ALCOTT, A. BRONSON. *Sonnets and Canzonets*. Boston, 1882.

——— *Journals,* ed. Odell Shepard. Boston, 1938.

ALDRICH, THOMAS B. *Writings*. Vols. 1, 2. Boston, 1897.

ARMISTEAD, WILSON, ed. *The Garland of Freedom*. London, 1853.

BENJAMIN, PARK. *Poems*. New York, 1948.

BIERCE, AMBROSE. *Collected Works*. Vols. 6, 7. New York, 1911.

——— *Letters,* ed. B. C. Pope. San Francisco, 1922.

BOKER, GEORGE H. *Plays and Poems*. Vol. 2. Philadelphia, 1883.

BONER, JOHN H. *Poems*. New York, 1903.

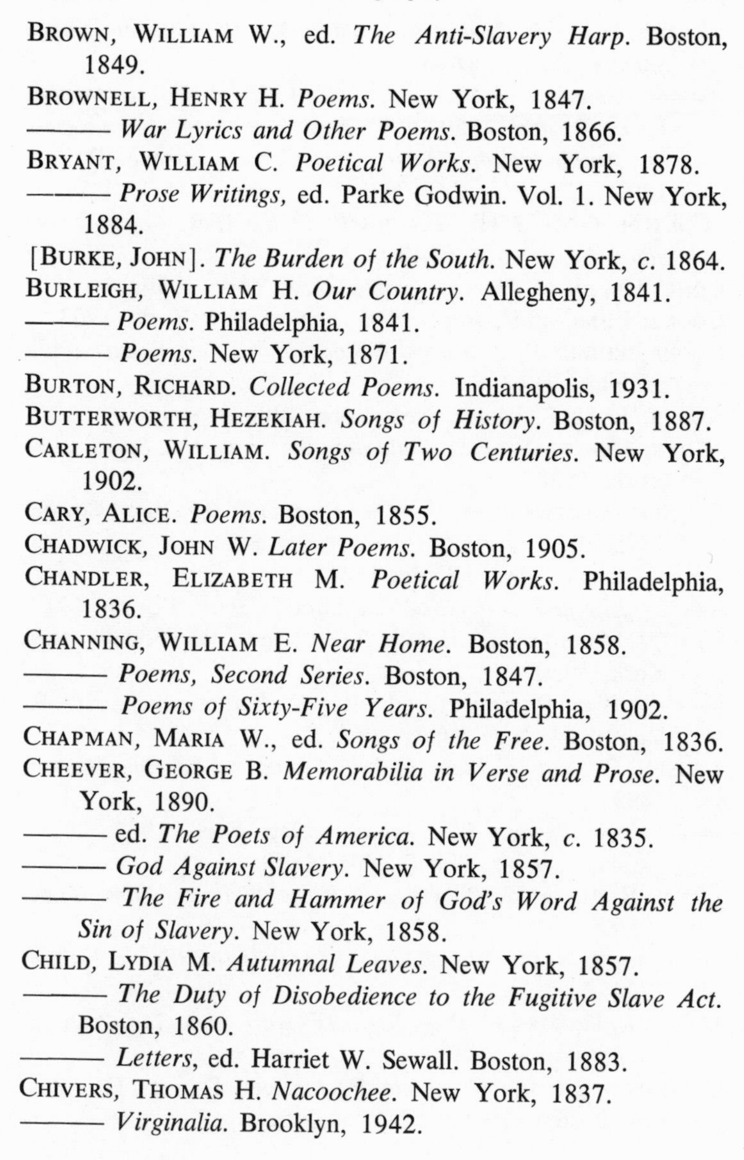

BROWN, WILLIAM W., ed. *The Anti-Slavery Harp*. Boston, 1849.

BROWNELL, HENRY H. *Poems*. New York, 1847.

——— *War Lyrics and Other Poems*. Boston, 1866.

BRYANT, WILLIAM C. *Poetical Works*. New York, 1878.

——— *Prose Writings*, ed. Parke Godwin. Vol. 1. New York, 1884.

[BURKE, JOHN]. *The Burden of the South*. New York, *c*. 1864.

BURLEIGH, WILLIAM H. *Our Country*. Allegheny, 1841.

——— *Poems*. Philadelphia, 1841.

——— *Poems*. New York, 1871.

BURTON, RICHARD. *Collected Poems*. Indianapolis, 1931.

BUTTERWORTH, HEZEKIAH. *Songs of History*. Boston, 1887.

CARLETON, WILLIAM. *Songs of Two Centuries*. New York, 1902.

CARY, ALICE. *Poems*. Boston, 1855.

CHADWICK, JOHN W. *Later Poems*. Boston, 1905.

CHANDLER, ELIZABETH M. *Poetical Works*. Philadelphia, 1836.

CHANNING, WILLIAM E. *Near Home*. Boston, 1858.

——— *Poems, Second Series*. Boston, 1847.

——— *Poems of Sixty-Five Years*. Philadelphia, 1902.

CHAPMAN, MARIA W., ed. *Songs of the Free*. Boston, 1836.

CHEEVER, GEORGE B. *Memorabilia in Verse and Prose*. New York, 1890.

——— ed. *The Poets of America*. New York, *c*. 1835.

——— *God Against Slavery*. New York, 1857.

——— *The Fire and Hammer of God's Word Against the Sin of Slavery*. New York, 1858.

CHILD, LYDIA M. *Autumnal Leaves*. New York, 1857.

——— *The Duty of Disobedience to the Fugitive Slave Act*. Boston, 1860.

——— *Letters*, ed. Harriet W. Sewall. Boston, 1883.

CHIVERS, THOMAS H. *Nacoochee*. New York, 1837.

——— *Virginalia*. Brooklyn, 1942.

CLARKE, JAMES F. *Poem Delivered Before the Phi Beta Kappa Society*. Boston, 1846.

——— *Causes and Consequences of the Affair at Harper's Ferry*. Boston, 1859.

——— *Autobiography, Diary and Correspondence*. Boston, 1891.

[COLTON, GEORGE H.] *Tecumseh: or the West Thirty Years Since*. New York, 1842.

CONE, HELEN G. *Harvest Home*. New York, 1930.

COOKE, EDMUND V. *Impertinent Poems*. New York, 1903.

COOKE, PHILIP P. *Froissart Ballads and Other Poems*. Philadelphia, 1847.

COOKE, ROSE T. *Poems*. New York, 1888.

[COXE, CLEVELAND]. *St. Jonathan, The Lay of a Scald*. New York, 1838.

CRANCH, CHRISTOPHER P. *The Bird and the Bell*. Boston, 1875.

——— *Poems*. Philadelphia, 1844.

——— *Life and Letters*, ed. Leonora C. Scott. Boston, 1917.

CRANE, STEPHEN. *Collected Poems*, ed. W. Follett. New York, 1930.

——— *War Dispatches*, ed. R. W. Stallman and E. R. Hagemann. New York, 1964.

CROSBY, ERNEST H. *Plain Talk in Psalm and Parable*. Boston, 1899.

——— *Swords and Ploughshares*. New York, 1902.

——— *War Echoes*. Philadelphia, 1898.

DANA, RICHARD H. *Poems and Prose Writings*. New York, 1850.

DE FOREST, JOHN W. *Medley and Palestina*. New Haven, 1902.

DELEON, THOMAS C. *War Rhymes Grave and Gay*. Atlanta, 1898.

DICKINSON, EMILY. *Complete Poems*, ed. Thomas H. Johnson. Boston, 1960.

——— *Letters,* ed. Thomas H. Johnson. Vols. 1, 2. Cambridge, 1958.

DUGANNE, AUGUSTINE J. H. *Poetical Works.* Philadelphia, 1865.

EMERSON, RALPH W. *Works.* Vols. 2, 3, 9–11. Boston, 1904-32.

——— *Journals,* eds. Edward W. Emerson and Waldo E. Forbes, Vol. 7. Boston, 1912.

——— *Letters,* ed. Ralph L. Rusk. Vol. 6. New York, 1939.

ENGLISH, THOMAS D. *Select Poems.* Newark, 1894.

——— ed. *Boy's Book of Battle Lyrics.* New York, 1885.

FIELD, EUGENE. *Poems.* New York, 1933.

Flying Cloud and 150 Other Songs. Virginia, Minn., 1922.

FOSS, SAM. *Songs of War and Peace.* Boston, 1899.

FULLER, HENRY B. *The New Flag.* Chicago, 1899.

GARLAND, HAMLIN. *Prairie Songs.* Cambridge, 1893.

——— *Book of the American Indian.* New York, 1923.

GARRISON, WILLIAM L. *Sonnets and Other Poems.* Boston, 1843.

GILDER, RICHARD W. *Five Books of Song.* New York, 1900.

GRAHAM, PHILIP, ed. *Early Texas Verse, 1835—50.* Chapel Hill, 1936.

GRAYSON, WILLIAM J. *The Hireling and the Slave, Chicora, and Other Poems.* Charleston, 1856.

——— *Selected Poems,* ed. Mrs. William H. Armstrong. New York, 1907.

GREENWOOD, GRACE, pseud. *Poems.* Boston, 1851.

GRISWOLD, RUFUS, ed. *The Female Poets of America.* Philadelphia, 1854.

——— ed. *The Poets and Poetry of America.* Philadelphia, 1852.

GUINEY, LOUISE I. *Happy Ending.* Boston, 1927.

——— *The Martyrs' Idyl.* Boston, 1900.

——— *Letters,* ed. Grace Guiney. 2 vols. New York, 1926.

HALE, EDWARD E. *Works.* Vol. 10. Boston, 1901.

——— *Life and Letters,* ed. Edward E. Hale, Jr. 2 vols. Boston, 1917.

HALE, SARAH J. *Three Hours*. Philadelphia, 1848.

HALLECK, FITZ-GREENE. *Poetical Writings*. New York, 1869.

HARTE, BRET. *Poetical Works*. 2 vols. Boston, 1912.

——— *Letters,* ed. Geoffrey B. Harte. Boston, 1926.

HAY, JOHN. *Complete Poetical Works*. Boston, 1916.

HAYNE, PAUL H. *Poems*. Boston, 1882.

HIGGINSON, THOMAS W. *Carlyle's Laugh and Other Surprises*. Boston, 1909.

——— *Cheerful Yesterdays*. Boston, 1898.

——— *Massachusetts in Mourning*. Boston, 1854.

HOFFMAN, CHARLES F. *Poems,* ed. E. F. Hoffman. Philadelphia, 1873.

HOLLAND, JOSIAH G. *Complete Poetical Writings*. New York, 1900.

HOLMES, OLIVER W. *Poetical Works*. Cambridge, 1895.

——— *Life and Letters,* ed. John T. Morse, Jr. Vol. 1. Boston, 1896.

HOSMER, WILLIAM H. C. *Poetical Works*. Vol. 2. New York, 1854.

HOVEY, RICHARD and CARMAN, BLISS. *Last Songs from* Vagabondia. Boston, 1901.

HOWE, JULIA W. *Passion Flowers*. Boston, 1854.

——— *Later Lyrics*. Boston, 1866.

——— *Words for the Hour*. Boston, 1857.

HOWELLS, WILLIAM D. *Poems,* Boston, 1873.

——— *Stops of Various Quills*. New York, 1895.

JACKSON, HELEN H. *Poems*. Boston, 1892.

——— *A Century of Dishonor,* ed. Andrew F. Rolle. New York, 1965.

JOHNSON, ROBERT U. *Poems*. New York, 1910.

KENNEDY, CHARLES O., ed. *A Treasury of American Ballads*. New York, 1954.

KREYMBORG, ALFRED, ed. *An Anthology of American Poetry*. New York, 1941.

LAMAR, MIRABEAU B. *Life and Poems,* ed. Philip Graham. Chapel Hill, 1938.

LANIER, SIDNEY. *Poems.* New York, 1897.

——— *Centennial Edition.* Vols. 6, 9. Baltimore, 1945.

LAZARUS, EMMA. *Poems.* 2 vols. Boston, 1889.

LE GALLIENNE, RICHARD. *The Cry of the Little Peoples,* ed. Eva Le Gallienne. Camden, 1941.

——— *Rudyard Kipling.* London, 1900.

LEGARE, JAMES M. *Orta-Undis.* Boston, 1848.

LEPRADE, RUTH, ed. *Debs and the Poets.* Pasadena, 1920.

LEWIS, ALONZO. *Poems.* Boston, 1851.

Liberty Poems. Boston, 1900.

LITTLE, SOPHIA L. *The Branded Hand.* Pawtucket, 1845.

——— *Thrice Through the Furnace.* Pawtucket, 1852.

LONGFELLOW, HENRY W. *Complete Poetical Works.* Boston, 1893.

LORD, W. W. *Poems.* New York, 1845.

——— *Poetical Works,* ed. Thomas O. Mabbott. New York, 1938.

LOWELL, JAMES R. *Complete Poetical Works.* Boston, 1917.

——— *Uncollected Poems,* ed. T. M. Smith. Philadelphia, 1950.

——— *Letters,* ed. Charles E. Norton. Vol. 1. New York, 1894.

LOWELL, MARIA W. *Poems,* ed. Hope J. Vernon. Providence, 1936.

MARKHAM, EDWIN. *Lincoln and Other Poems.* New York, 1901.

——— *The Man With the Hoe.* New York, 1899.

——— ed. *The Book of American Poetry.* New York, 1934.

[MASTERS, EDGAR L.] Dexter Wallace, pseud. *The Blood of the Prophets.* Chicago, 1905.

——— *A Book of Verses. Chicago,* 1898.

——— *The New Star Chamber.* Chicago, 1904.

MCCARTHY, WILLIAM, ed. *National Songs, Ballads, and Other Patriotic Poetry.* Philadelphia, 1846.

McGaffey, Ernest. *Poems.* New York, 1896.

McLean, Andrew. *Tom Moore and Other Verses.* Brooklyn 1878.

Meek, Alexander. *Songs and Poems of the South.* Mobile, 1857.

Melville, Herman. *Works.* Vols. 4, 14–16. London, 1922–24.

Mifflin, Lloyd. *Castalian Days.* London, 1903.

——— *The Slopes of Helicon.* Boston, 1898.

Miller, Joaquin. *Poetical Works,* ed. Stuart P. Sherman. New York, 1923.

——— *Life Among the Modocs.* London, 1873.

Moody, William V. *Poems.* Boston, 1901.

Moore, Clement. *Poems.* New York, 1844.

Morris, George P. *Poems.* New York, *c* 1860.

Moulton, Louise C. *At the Wind's Will.* Boston, 1899.

Oakes-Smith, Elizabeth. *Poetical Writings.* New York, 1845.

O'Reilly, John B. *In Bohemia.* Boston, 1886.

——— *The Statues in the Block.* Boston, 1887.

Ossoli, Margaret F. *Writings,* ed. Mason Wade. New York, 1941.

Page, Thomas N. *The Coast of Bohemia.* New York, 1906.

Palmer, John W. *For Charlie's Sake.* New York, 1901.

Parsons, Thomas W. *Poems.* Portland, Me., 1906.

Paulding, James K. *Letters,* ed. Ralph M. Aderman. Madison, 1962.

Peabody, Josephine P. *Fortune and Men's Eyes.* Boston, 1900.

Percival, James G. *The Dream of a Day.* New Haven, 1843.

——— *Poetical Works.* Vol. 2. Boston, 1859.

Pierpont, John. *Airs of Palestine.* Boston, 1840.

——— *Anti-Slavery Poems.* Boston, 1843.

——— *Discourse on the Covenant with Judas.* Boston, 1842.

Pike, Albert. *Poems.* Little Rock, 1900.

Poe, Edgar A. *Complete Tales and Poems.* New York, 1938.

——— *Works.* Vols. 3, 4. New York, 1903.

PROCTOR, EDNA D. *Complete Poetical Works.* Boston, 1925.

[RANSOM, JAMES B.] *Osceola: or, Fact and Fiction.* New York, 1838.

READ, THOMAS B. *Lays and Ballads.* Philadelphia, 1849.

——— *Poems.* Boston, 1847.

——— *Poems.* Philadelphia, 1865.

——— *Poetical Works.* 3 vols. Philadelphia, 1881.

REALF, RICHARD. *Free State Poems,* ed. Richard J. Hinton. Topeka, 1900.

——— *Poems.* New York, 1898.

RICE, WALLACE and CLINTON SCOLLARD. *Ballads of Valor and Victory.* New York, 1903.

RILEY, JAMES W. *Complete Poetical Works.* Garden City, 1941.

ROBINSON, EDWIN A. *Collected Poems.* New York, 1944.

RYAN, FATHER ABRAM J. *Poems.* Baltimore, 1888.

SANBORN, FRANKLIN B. *Collected Poems,* ed. John M. Moran. Hartford, 1964.

——— et al. *Poems Read at the Opening of the Fraternity Lectures.* Boston, 1859.

——— *Memories of John Brown.* Concord, 1878.

SANDBURG, CARL. *Selected Poems.* New York, 1926.

——— *Always the Young Strangers.* New York, 1953.

SANTAYANA, GEORGE. *A Hermit of Carmel.* New York, 1901.

SARGENT, EPES. *Songs of the Sea.* Boston, 1847.

SAXE, JOHN G. *Poems.* Boston, 1875.

SCOLLARD, CLINTON, ed. *Ballads of American Bravery.* New York, 1900.

SHADWELL, BERTRAND. *America and Other Poems.* Chicago, 1899.

SIGOURNEY, LYDIA H. *Pocahontas and Other Poems.* New York, 1841.

——— *Poems.* New York, 1860.

——— *Poetical Works.* London, 1850.

SILL, EDWARD R. *Poetical Works.* Boston, 1906.

SIMMS, WILLIAM G. *Lays of the Palmetto.* Charleston, 1848.

——— *Poems.* 2 vols. New York, 1853.

——— *Views and Reviews in American Literature, History and Fiction,* ed. C. Hugh Holman. Cambridge, 1962.

——— *Letters.* Vol. 1. Columbia, S.C., 1952.

SINCLAIR, UPTON, ed. *The Cry for Justice.* Philadelphia, 1915.

[SMITH, ELBERT H.] *Black Hawk, and Scenes in the West.* New York, 1848.

SMITH, SEBA. *Powhatan.* New York, 1841.

——— *My Thirty Years Out of the Senate.* New York, 1859.

STEDMAN, EDMUND C. *Poems.* Boston, 1908.

——— *Life and Letters.* ed. Laura Stedman and George M. Gould. Vol. 2. New York, 1910.

STERLING, GEORGE. *The Testimony of the Suns.* San Francisco, 1904.

STEVENSON, BURTON E., ed. *Poems of American History.* Boston, 1908.

STICKNEY, TRUMBULL. *Dramatic Verses.* Boston, 1902.

STODDARD, RICHARD H. *Poems.* New York, 1880.

STORY, WILLIAM W. *Poems.* Boston, 1847.

——— *Poems.* 2 vols. Boston, 1886.

STREET, ALFRED B. *Poems.* 2 vols. New York, 1867.

TAPPAN, WILLIAM B. *Poetry of Life.* Boston, 1848.

——— *Sacred and Miscellaneous Poems.* Boston, 1848.

TAYLOR, BAYARD. *The American Legend.* Cambridge, 1850.

——— *Poetical Works.* Boston, 1883.

——— *Life and Letters,* ed. Marie Hansen-Taylor and Horace E. Scudder. Vol. 1. Boston, 1885.

——— *Unpublished Letters,* ed. J. R. Schultz. San Marino, Calif., 1937.

THAXTER, CELIA. *Poems.* Boston, 1896.

THOMAS, EDITH M. *The Dancers.* Boston, 1903.

——— *Selected Poems.* New York, 1926.

THOMPSON, MAURICE. *Poems.* Boston, 1892.

THOREAU, HENRY D. *Collected Poems,* ed. Carl Bode. Chicago, 1943.

——— *Correspondence,* ed. W. Harding and C. Bode. New York, 1958.

——— *Journal.* Vols. 2, 6, 12. New York, 1962.

——— *Writings.* Vols. 1–3, 10. Boston, 1893.

TICKNOR, FRANCIS O. *Poems.* Philadelphia, 1879.

TIMROD, HENRY. *Poems.* Boston, 1899.

——— *Uncollected Poems.* ed. Edd W. Parks. Athens, Ga., 1942.

TORRENCE, RIDGLEY. *House of a Hundred Lights.* Boston, 1900.

TOWNE, CHARLES H. *The Quiet Singer.* New York, 1908.

——— ed. *Roosevelt as the Poets Saw Him.* New York, 1923.

TRAUBEL, HORACE. *Chants Communal.* Boston, 1904.

TREADWELL, AUGUSTUS. *A Volume of Verse.* New York, 1906.

TROWBRIDGE, JOHN T. *Poetical Works.* Boston, 1903.

TUCKERMAN, FREDERICK G. *Poems.* Boston, 1864.

TUCKERMAN, HENRY T. *Poems.* Boston, 1851.

UPSON, ARTHUR W. *Collected Poems.* Vol. 1. Minneapolis, 1909.

VERY, JONES. *Poems and Essays.* Boston, 1886.

VERY, LYDIA L. A. *Poems.* Andover, 1856.

War Poems, 1898. San Francisco, 1898.

WEBB, LAURA S. *Custer's Immortality.* New York, 1876.

WHITMAN, WALT. *Leaves of Grass,* ed. Emory Holloway. New York, 1954.

——— *Complete Poetry and Selected Prose and Letters,* ed. E. Holloway. London, 1938.

——— *Collected Prose.* Philadelphia, 1892.

——— *The Gathering of the Forces,* ed. C. Rodgers and J. Black. Vol. 1. New York, 1920.

WHITTIER, JOHN G. *Complete Poetical Works.* Boston, 1894.

——— ed. *The North Star: the Poetry of Freedom.* Philadelphia, 1840.

WILCOX, ELLA W. *Custer and Other Poems.* Chicago, 1896.

WILLIS, NATHANIEL P. *Poetical Works.* London, 1888.

WILSON, ROBERT B. *The Shadows of the Trees.* New York, 1898.

WINTER, WILLIAM. *Poems.* New York, 1909.

WITHERBEE, SIDNEY A., ed. *Spanish American War Songs.* Detroit, 1898.

WOODBERRY, GEORGE E. *Poems.* New York, 1903.

Part Two: The Background (Books)

ADKINS, NELSON F. *Fitz-Greene Halleck.* New Haven, 1930.

ALDRICH, LILLIAN W. *Crowding Memories.* Boston, 1920.

ALLEN, GAY W. *The Solitary Singer.* New York, 1955.

Allibone's Dictionary. Philadelphia, 1886.

ARVIN, NEWTON. *Herman Melville.* New York, 1950.

——— *Whitman.* New York, 1938.

BARNES, HOMER F. *Charles Fenno Hoffman.* New York, 1930.

BARLETT, WILLIAM I. *Jones Very, Emerson's "Brave Saint."* Durham, 1942.

BEECHER, EDWARD. *Narrative of Riots at Alton.* Alton, 1838.

BEERS, H. A. *Nathaniel Parker Willis.* Boston, 1885.

BIGELOW, JOHN. *William Cullen Bryant.* Boston, 1890.

BLANKENSHIP, RUSSELL. *American Literature as an Expression of the National Mind.* New York, 1949.

BOTKIN, B. A., ed. *A Treasury of Southern Folklore.* New York, 1949.

BROOKS, VAN WYCK. *The Flowering of New England.* New York, 1936.

——— *New England: Indian Summer.* New York, 1940.

——— *The Times of Melville and Whitman.* New York, 1947.

BUCKMASTER, HENRIETTA, pseud. *Let My People Go.* New York, 1941.

Cambridge History of American Literature. Vols. 2, 3. New York, 1917–21.

CAMERON, KENNETH W. *Index-Concordance to Emerson's Sermons.* Hartford, 1963.

FILLER, LOUIS. *The Crusade Against Slavery, 1830–1860.* New York, 1960.

FINLEY, RUTH E. *The Lady of Godey's.* Philadelphia, 1931.

GARA, LARRY. *The Liberty Line.* Lexington, Ky., 1961.

GARROD, HEATHCOTE W. *Poetry and the Criticism of Life.* New York, 1931.

GRIFFITHS, JULIA, ed. *Autographs for Freedom.* Boston, 1853.

GRISWOLD, RUFUS. *Passages from Correspondence.* Cambridge, 1898.

HAIGHT, GORDON S. *The Sweet Singer of Hartford.* New Haven, 1930.

HALE, EDWARD E. *James Russell Lowell and His Friends.* Boston, 1899.

HALPERN, MARTIN. *William Vaughn Moody.* New York, 1964.

HARLEY, L. R. *Confessions of a Schoolmaster.* Philadelphia, 1914.

HAYNES, GEORGE H. *Charles Sumner.* Philadelphia, 1909.

HOFFMAN, DANIEL G., ed. *American Poetry and Poetics.* Garden City, 1962.

——— and Samuel Hynes, eds. *Literary Criticism: Romantic and Victorian.* New York, 1963.

HUBBELL, JAY B. *The South in American Literature, 1607–1900.* Durham, 1954.

JACKSON, GEORGE S. *Early Songs of Uncle Sam.* Boston, 1933.

JAMES, HENRY. *William Wetmore Story and His Friends.* 2 vols. Edinburgh, 1903.

JOHNSON, THOMAS H. *Emily Dickinson.* Cambridge, 1955.

KEISER, ALBERT. *The Indian in American Literature.* New York, 1933.

KRUTCH, JOSEPH W. *Henry David Thoreau.* New York, 1948.

LIVERMORE, ABIEL A. *The War With Mexico Reviewed.* Boston, 1850.

LONGFELLOW, SAMUEL. *The Life of Henry Wadsworth Longfellow.* 2 vols. Boston, 1885.

CANBY, HENRY S. *Thoreau.* Boston, 1939.

CHAMBERLIN, JOSEPH E. *The Boston Transcript.* Boston, 1930.

COHEN, MYER M. *Notices of Florida,* ed. O. Z. Tyler, Jr. Gainesville, 1964.

COLERIDGE, SAMUEL T. *Biographia Literaria,* ed. J. Shawcross. Vol. 2. London, 1958.

CUNLIFFE, MARCUS. *The Literature of the United States.* Baltimore, 1954.

Dictionary of American Biography. Vol. 14.

DILLON, MERTON L. *Elijah P. Lovejoy.* Urbana, 1961.

ELLIOTT, MAUD H. and LAURA E. RICHARDS. *Julia Ward Howe.* Boston, 1915.

FATOUT, PAUL. *Ambrose Bierce and the Black Hills.* Norman, 1956.

MACY, JOHN A. *The Spirit of American Literature.* 1913.

MADISON, CHARLES A. *Critics and Crusaders.* New York, 1959.

MATTHIESSEN, F. O. *American Renaissance.* New York, 1941.

MCLEAN, ALBERT. *William Cullen Bryant.* New York, 1964.

MCREYNOLDS, EDWIN C. *The Seminoles.* Norman, 1957.

Memoirs of the Rev. Elijah P. Lovejoy. New York, 1838.

MILLER, DAVID H. *Custer's Fall: the Indian Side of the Story.* New York, 1957.

MILLER, JAMES E., Jr., ed. *Whitman's "Song of Myself"—Origin, Growth, Meaning.* New York, 1964.

MILLER, PERRY. *The American Transcendentalists.* Garden City, 1957.

NEFF, EMERY. *Edwin Arlington Robinson.* New York, 1948.

NEVINS, ALLAN. *The Evening Post.* New York, 1922.

NICHOLS, ALICE. *Bleeding Kansas.* New York, 1954.

NICOLOFF, PHILIP L. *Emerson on Race and History.* New York, 1961.

NORMAN, CHARLES. *Poets on Poetry.* New York, 1962.

PARRINGTON, VERNON L. *Main Currents in American Thought.* Vols. 2, 3. New York, 1930.

PERRY, BLISS. *Walt Whitman: His Life and Work.* Boston, 1906.

PICKARD, JOHN B. *John Greenleaf Whittier.* New York, 1961.

PICKARD, SAMUEL T. *Life of John Greenleaf Whittier.* Boston, 1894.

POLLARD, J. A. *John Greenleaf Whittier.* Boston, 1949.

QUINN, ARTHUR H. *The Literature of the American People.* New York, 1951.

RUSK, RALPH L. *The Literature of the Middle Western Frontier.* 2 vols. New York, 1925.

SCHLESINGER, ARTHUR M. *The Age of Jackson.* Boston, 1945.

SEITZ, DON CARLOS. *The Dreadful Decade.* Indianapolis, 1926.

SHAPIRO, KARL, ed. *Prose Keys to Modern Poetry.* Evanston, 1962.

SHEPARD, ODELL. *Pedlar's Progress.* Boston, 1939.

SIEBERT, WILBUR H. *The Underground Railroad from Slavery to Freedom.* New York, 1899.

SINGLETARY, OTIS A. *The Mexican War.* Chicago, 1960.

SPILLER, ROBERT E. *Literary History of the United States.* Vol. 1. New York, 1948.

STONE, THOMAS T. *The Martyr of Freedom.* Boston, 1838.

THAYER, WILLIAM R. *John Hay.* Vol. 2. Boston, 1915.

THOMAS, J. W. *James Freeman Clarke.* Boston, 1949.

TILTON, ELEANOR M. *Amiable Autocrat.* New York, 1949.

TURNER, LORENZO. *Anti-Slavery Sentiment in American Literature Prior to 1865.* Washington, 1929.

TYLER, ALICE F. *Freedom's Ferment.* New York, 1962.

UNTERMEYER, LOUIS, ed. *Modern British and American Poetry.* New York, 1942.

WAGENKNECHT, EDWARD C. *Longfellow.* New York, 1955.

WALTERHOUSE, ROGER R. *Bret Harte, Joaquin Miller, and the Western Local Color Story:* part of a dissertation. U. of Chicago, 1939.

WELLS, ANNA M. *Dear Preceptor.* Boston, 1963.

WHICHER, GEORGE F. *This Was a Poet.* Ann Arbor, 1957.

WILSON, FORREST. *Crusader in Crinoline*. Philadelphia, 1941.

WISAN, JOSEPH E. *The Cuban Crisis as Reflected in the New York Press (1895–98),* New York, 1934.

WOODWARD, GRACE S. *The Cherokees*. Norman, 1963.

WYMAN, MARY A. *Two American Pioneers*. New York, 1927.

Part Three: The Background (Articles)

ADKINS, NELSON F. "Emerson and the Bardic Tradition," *Publications of the Modern Language Association,* LXIII (June 1948), 662–77.

ALLEN, GAY W. "Biblical Echoes in Whitman's Works," *American Literature,* VI (November 1934), 302–15.

ARVIN, NEWTON. "The Failure of Edward Rowland Sill," *Bookman,* LXXII (February 1931), 581–89.

——— "Melville's *Mardi,*" American Quarterly, II (Spring 1950), 71–81.

CARDWELL, GUY A., JR. "William Henry Timrod, The Charleston Volunteers, and the Defense of St. Augustine," *North Carolina Historical Review,* XVIII (January 1941), 36–37.

CONANT, C. A. "Literature of Expansion," *International Quarterly,* III (June 1901), 719–27.

CURRENT-GARCIA, EUGENE. "Newspaper Humor in the Old South, 1835–1855," *Alabama Review,* II (April 1949), 102–21.

CURTI, M. "Walt Whitman, Critic of America," *Sewanee Review,* XXXVI (April 1928), 130–38.

DE MILLE, G. E. "Stedman, Arbiter of the Eighties," *Publications of the Modern Language Association,* XLI (September 1926), 756–66.

EATON, CLEMENT. "Mob Violence in the Old South," *Mississippi Valley Historical Review,* XXIX (December 1942), 351–70.

FERGUSSON, H. "The Cult of the Indian," *Scribner's,* LXXXVIII (August 1930), 129–33.

FORD, N. A. "Henry David Thoreau, Abolitionist," *New England Quarterly,* XIX (September 1946), 359–71.

FOREMAN, GRANT. "John Howard Payne and the Cherokee Indians," *American Historical Review,* XXXVII (July 1932), 723–50.

FOSTER, H. D. "Webster's Seventh of March Speech and the Secession Movement, 1850," *American Historical Review,* XXVII (January 1922), 245–70.

GAVIGAN, WALTER V. "Longfellow and Catholicism," *Catholic World,* CXXXVIII (October 1933), 42–50.

GIBSON, WILLIAM M. "Mark Twain and Howells, Anti-Imperialists," *New England Quarterly,* XX (December 1947), 435–70.

GLASHEEN, F. J. and A., "Moody's 'Ode in Time of Hesitation," *College English,* V (December 1943), 121—29.

HARRINGTON, F. H. "Literary Aspects of American Anti-Imperialism, 1898–1902," *New England Quarterly,* X (December 1937), 650–67.

BRET HARTE Number. *Overland Monthly,* XL (September, 1902), 201–45.

HOWE, M. A. DeW. "Bret Harte and Mark Twain in the Seventies," *Atlantic Monthly,* CXXX (September 1922), 341–48.

HOWELLS, WILLIAM D. "A Sennight of the Centennial," *Atlantic Monthly,* XXXVIII (July 1876), 92—107.

KEISER, ALBERT. "Thoreau's Manuscripts on the Indians," *Journal of English and Germanic Philology,* XXVII (April 1928), 183–99.

LONG, W. S. "The Early Verse of Robert Frost and Some of His Revisions," *American Literature,* VII (May 1935), 181–87.

"McKenney and Hall's *History of the North American Indians," North American Review,* XLVII (July, 1838), 134–48.

MABBOTT, THOMAS O. "Poe and the Philadelphia Irish Citizen," *Journal of the American Irish Historical*

Society, XXIX (1930–31), 121–31.

——— "Walt Whitman Edits the *Sunday Times,* July, 1842–June, 1843," *American Literature,* XXXIX (March, 1967), 99–102.

MANSFIELD, L. S. "Melville's Comic Articles on Zachary Taylor," *American Literature,* IX (January 1938), 411–18.

MATTHEWS, BRANDER. "American Satires in Verse," *Harper's,* CIX (July 1904), 294–99.

JOAQUIN MILLER Number. *Overland Monthly* n.s. LXXV (February 1920), 93–148.

MURRAY, MARION R. "The 1870's in American Literature," *American Speech,* I (March, 1926), 323–28.

NEVINS, ALLAN. "Helen Hunt Jackson, Sentimentalist vs. Realist," *American Scholar,* X (Summer 1941), 269–85.

RICHARDSON, L. N. "Men of Letters and the Hayes Administration," *New England Quarterly,* XV (March, 1942), 117–27.

SEDGWICK, H. D. "The Mob Spirit in Literature," *Atlantic Monthly,* XCVI (July 1905), 9–15.

SILVER, R. G. "Emerson as Abolitionist," *New England Quarterly,* VI (March, 1933), 154–58.

SMITH, JUSTIN H. "The Biglow Papers as an Argument Against the Mexican War," *Proceedings of the Massachusetts Historical Society,* XLV (May 1912), 602–11.

SPENCER, BENJAMIN T. "A National Literature, 1837–1855," *American Literature,* VIII (May 1936), 125–59.

TAMONY, P. "Writers Supported by Government Sinecures," *American Notes and Queries,* VIII (December 1949), 138–39.

THAYER, W. R. "John Hay's Policy of Anglo-Saxonism," *World's Work,* XXXV (November 1917), 33–41.

WILLIAMS, M. L. "Park Benjamin on Melville's 'Mardi,' " *American Notes and Queries,* VIII (December 1949), 132–34.

NOTE: The following periodicals were consulted both for the verse they contain and for the historical insights they offer:

Alton *Observer,* 1837.
Atlantic Monthly, 1876–77.
Boston *Pilot,* 1844.
The Catholic Herald, 1844.
Harper's New Monthly Magazine, 1876–77.
Journal of the Knights of Labor, 1894.
The Liberator, 1831–60.
The Liberty Bell, 1839–58.
Lippincott's, 1876–77.
The Living Age, 1876–77.
Long Island *Democrat,* 1876.
The Nation, 1876.
National Enquirer, 1837–38.
New York *Evening Post,* 1837–38, 1844, 1856.
Niles' National Register, 1844.
North American Review, 1838.
Pennsylvania Freeman, 1838–39.
Philadelphia *Native American,* 1844.
Philadelphia *Public Ledger,* 1844.
Philadelphia *Spirit of the Times,* 1844.
Scribner's Monthly, 1876–77.

Index